The Emergence of Civilisation Revisited

Sheffield Studies in Aegean Archaeology, 6

SHEFFIELD STUDIES IN AEGEAN ARCHAEOLOGY

ADVISORY EDITORIAL PANEL

SHEFFIELD STUDIES IN
AEGEAN ARCHAEOLOGY

The Emergence
—— of ——
Civilisation Revisited

Edited by
John C. Barrett and Paul Halstead

Oxbow Books

Published by
Oxbow Books, Park End Place, Oxford OX1 1HN

© Oxbow Books, John C. Barrett and Paul Halstead
and the contributors 2004

ISBN 1 84217 166 6

A CIP record for this book is available from the British Library

Cover: Mediterranean polyculture and the palace at Knossos
(photograph: John Bennet)

This book is available direct from
Oxbow Books, Park End Place, Oxford, OX1 1HN
(Phone: 01865-241249; Fax: 01865-794449)

and

The David Brown Book Company
PO Box 511, Oakville, CT 06779, USA
(Phone: 860-945-9329; Fax: 860-945-9468)

and

via our website
www.oxbowbooks.com

Printed in Great Britain by
Alden Press
Oxford

Contents

Abbreviations

AAA	*Athens Annals of Archaeology*
ADelt	*Arkhaiologiko Deltio*
AE	*Arkhaiologiki Efimeris*
AEMTh	*To Arkhaiologiko Ergo sti Makedonia kai Thraki*
AJA	*American Journal of Archaeology*
AM	*Mitteilungen des Deutschen Archäologischen Instituts, Athenische Abteilung*
AR	*Archaeological Reports*
ASA	*Annuario della Scuola Archeologica di Atene*
BAM	Beiträge zur Ur- und Frühgeschichtlichen Archäologie des Mittelmeer-Kulturraumes
BAR	*British Archaeological Reports*
BCH	*Bulletin de Correspondance Hellénique*
BICS	*Bulletin of the Institute of Classical Studies of the University of London*
BSA	*Annual of the British School at Athens*
CAJ	*Cambridge Archaeological Journal*
CMS	Corpus der minoischen und mykenischen Siegeln
CP	*Classical Philology*
CQ	*Classical Quarterly*
Ergon	*To Ergon tis Arkhaiologikis Etairias*
G&R	*Greece and Rome*
JAS	*Journal of Archaeological Science*
JHS	*Journal of Hellenic Studies*
JMA	*Journal of Mediterranean Archaeology*
Kr Chron	*Kritika Chronika*
OJA	*Oxford Journal of Archaeology*
PAE	*Praktika tis en Athinais Arkhaiologikis Etairias*
PBA	*Proceedings of the British Academy*
PCPS	*Proceedings of the Cambridge Philological Society*
SIMA	Studies in Mediterranean Archaeology
SMEA	*Studi Micenei ed Egeo-Anatolici*

Preface

John C. Barrett and Paul Halstead

Archaeologists share three expectations about the past: that it was different from the world of today, that it changed through time, and that we can understand it. It follows that in some important aspects, however different the past must have been, and however much it may have changed through time, it must also share some common elements with our own world and thus with our own experiences. And it is upon these common uniformities that our understanding of the significance of our evidence is based.

The history of archaeology is a history of great discoveries and a history of the debate about the uniformities that determine the human condition. It is a history of how we understand the things that we discover, of what links us with our past. It should come as no real surprise that archaeology itself changes, not simply because we find more things but because the debate concerning the generalities upon which our interpretations are based remains one of active engagement.

The seventh Round Table of the Sheffield Centre for Aegean Archaeology marked the 30th anniversary of the publication of Colin Renfrew's *The Emergence of Civilisation* (1972). The proceedings of that Round Table are published here. All the contributors make some comment upon the impact *The Emergence* had on Aegean archaeology at the time it was published, and many reflect upon its place in the wider history of archaeological thought. Cherry explores this point in his contribution to this volume and Renfrew also offers a retrospective on *The Emergence*. To review a work that is thirty years old in a rapidly developing field of study may seem to invite little more than testimonies to how much more we know today, and to demonstrate how much more refined our understandings have become. If this had indeed been the outcome we would have achieved little, other than to reassert that the growth of knowledge is cumulative and that our interpretive schemes progress sequentially. For more than forty years Anglo-American archaeology in particular has clung to the view that Archaeology moves through a series of paradigmatic shifts, each rendering its predecessor redundant, so that what was once *New* is only to be by-passed by what has become *Post-*. *The Emergence* itself certainly laid out a different agenda for thinking about social and cultural change in the Aegean, and this was part of a larger programme in which Renfrew sought to re-think the ways cultural change was explained in European prehistory. Paradigmatic models have therefore been used with good effect to mark out the intellectual history of archaeology, where each intellectual advance can claim a break with its own past. The problem for such intellectual postures is that they tend to be structured by the very things they reject. Diffusionism as employed in traditional archaeology was certainly a lazy form of explanation, but surely that does not mean we need slavishly adhere to the view that all social change is autonomously derived. And if we question the functional reasoning inherent to the systems thinking employed by processual archaeology, this need not blind us to the fact that historical forces do exist that operate beyond the understanding of human agency. Paradigms exist as the principles that organize our understanding of experience and through which we hope to solve the problems which confront us. But the idea that the history of science can be written in terms of the clear-cut sequences of paradigmatic change contrasts with the experience of most practitioners. They are likely to regard scientific advance to be won from a more pragmatic negotiation, a kind of intellectual bricolage that is the reworking of available ideas, new and old, to make better sense of the problems that confront the investigator.

The studies published in this volume engage with *The Emergence* in ways that set out neither to test the redundancy nor to attest to the continuing viability of Renfrew's argument for the endogenous development of the Aegean Bronze Age. Rather they draw upon the idea that, by writing *The Emergence of Civilisation*, Colin Renfrew explored themes that remain basic to our discipline. First is the way we characterize the conditions of the past and the nature of change. The terms *complexity* and *civilization* evoke conditions of organizational heterarchy and cultural achievement where the latter is normally linked with elite practices and developed forms of ideological representation. Are these two conditions directly linked? This question is addressed here by Schoep and Knappett, while Georgousopoulou critically considers the use of *complexity* as a measure of social variability.

One reason why we might find organizational complexity so difficult to apply as a measure of variability is that we need to establish the unit of analysis to which it is to be applied. Only when we are secure regarding this point will we know that we are comparing like with like. One solution has been to take the unit of analysis as society itself, although this poses two further problems: the extent to which societies are analytically closed units and therefore directly comparable in terms of their internal structures; and the means by which archaeologists are able to observe these units. The suggestion that the social unit is indeed the object of analysis, and that such units existed in relative autonomy, is basic to models of autonomous social development. In practice this autonomy finds expression in the concept of the *polity* whose archaeological representation is sought in the pattern of settlement residues, their scale, and the variability of the activities to which those residues bear witness. Other solutions to the analytical problem of tracing change in organizational complexity have been applied.

Regional studies for example have been employed to map changes in the density and organization of activity represented by residue patterns. This work enables us to display a diachronic image of change as the snapshot sequences of period-based maps, and it facilitates comparative studies between different regional systems. Whitelaw returns to these issues of regional comparison with a critical review of the ways comparative studies operate while Relaki questions the basis upon which we might accept the region to be a useful analytical unit. As Cherry emphasizes, the patterns of regional activity as known from field survey have changed enormously in the last thirty years. Whitelaw and Relaki then force us to rethink the bases upon which we use a regional frame of analysis.

A third approach towards the mapping of complexity is through the analysis of production and exchange. Here the focus for analysis moves more towards artefact assemblages, the evidence for production itself, and patterns of artefact distribution. In such studies the assumption is that organizational change is witnessed in the ways stages of production, the allocation of resources, and the supply of finished materials are networked, with increasing levels of complexity being marked by increasing degrees of specialized production fed by larger exchange networks. Tomkins demonstrates how the analysis of production can help expose organizational change in the Neolithic while Bevan employs the distribution, use and imitation of Egyptian stone vases around the eastern Mediterranean to evaluate the degree to which local processes of organizational change were contingent upon wider regional contacts.

The second theme, found throughout Renfrew's work and shared by all the studies so far mentioned, concerns the methodological procedures that are capable of linking the available data to the historical issues that interest us. At one level this appears to be a matter of measurement and description, as if heterarchy in organizational terms might be mapped directly by heterarchy in the structure of the archaeological record; to measure the latter is to recover the former. But this in itself offers no feel for explanation, no real understanding of dynamics and the motivation for change. It is these forces that must ultimately interest us and in our attempt to engage with them we confront the third theme that is central to all Renfrew's work, that of explanation in terms of social processes. If the patterns recovered in the archaeological record characterize the organization of past activities then that same material must presumably unlock access to the process that brought about change in those organizations, and how this might be done is a very complex issue indeed.

An initial attempt to move towards an understanding of dynamics is to examine the link between diversity in organization (which as we have seen, is normally taken to mean social organization) and social structure, in particular structures of hierarchy. One obvious problem, as Schoep and Knappett point out, is the relationship between heterarchy and hierarchy: is one the cause of the other? The presumption is often that the development of hierarchy draws into view competitive processes that are directed towards the accumulation of wealth and status and which seek access to increasingly restricted resources. Consequently, exchange processes can be regarded as having a social dynamic in these terms, and they obviously operate in every cycle of production and consumption, from the ubiquity of agricultural production and food consumption, that Renfrew characterized as a subsistence subsystem and the archaeology of which is reconsidered here by Halstead, to the control of restricted and sacred goods. As Wolpert, Barrett and Damilati note, the movement from one cycle of exchange to another is to move between different regimes of value, where value pertains both to people and to objects. This must mean, as Wright argues, that the creation of elites is a matter of cultural production as well as a matter of power, themes that lie at the heart of our commonplace definitions for civilization itself. Human identities and values are therefore entangled with the places and the objects around which they move, including the architecture, images and artifacts discussed by Peperaki and Bennet. It is these things that anchor those identities and give their spoken narratives substance.

In re-reading *The Emergence of Civilisation* and in working with the themes it explored, the participants in the Round Table, and the authors of the papers collected here, continue to engage with themes that animate all archaeological research: to understand how historical conditions may be characterized; to understand the nature of the variability in those conditions; and to attempt to recognize the historical forces that brought such variability into existence. The application of these issues to the particular study of the Neolithic and Bronze Age sequences of the Aegean reminds us of the remarkable challenge presented by archaeology to bring a critical perspective to bear upon our own understandings of the world through our encounter with another period whose complexity and achievements we struggle to grasp by means of such terms as civilization.

As ever, in the course of holding the Round Table and bringing this volume to fruition, we have incurred many obligations. In addition to Colin Renfrew himself and the authors of the papers that follow, Cyprian Broodbank, Despina Catapoti, Yannis Hamilakis and Vance Watrous presented stimulating papers to the Round Table, but were unable to contribute to this volume. For help with organizing the Round Table, we are indebted to Eleni Nodarou, Ulrich Thaler, Giorgos Vavouranakis and Andrea Vianello, while assistance in the production of this volume was provided by John Bennet, Rob Craigie, Rocky Hyacinth and Valasia Isaakidou. Hospitality was masterminded by Nancy Krahtopoulou, with assistance from Valasia Isaakidou, Vangelio Kiriatzi and Sevi Triantaphyllou and motivation from John Bennet. The Round Table was made possible by generous financial assistance from INSTAP.

Contributors

JOHN C. BARRETT
Department of Archaeology, University of Sheffield, Northgate House, West St., Sheffield S1 4ET, UK.

JOHN BENNET
Department of Archaeology, University of Sheffield, Northgate House, West St., Sheffield S1 4ET, UK.

ANDREW BEVAN
Institute of Archaeology, University College London, 31-34 Gordon Sq., London WC1H 0PY, UK.

JOHN CHERRY
Department of Classical Studies, University of Michigan, 2160 Angell Hall, 435 South State St., Ann Arbor, MI 48109-1003, USA.

KRYSTALLI DAMILATI
Department of Archaeology, University of Sheffield, Northgate House, West St., Sheffield S1 4ET, UK.

THEODORA GEORGOUSOPOULOU
Ptolemeon 37, Thrakomakedones, Athina 13676, Greece.

PAUL HALSTEAD
Department of Archaeology, University of Sheffield, Northgate House, West St., Sheffield S1 4ET, UK.

CARL KNAPPETT
Department of Archaeology, University of Exeter, North Park Rd., Exeter EX4 4QE, UK.

OLYMPIA PEPERAKI
Department of Archaeology, University of Sheffield, Northgate House, West St., Sheffield S1 4ET, UK.

MARIA RELAKI
Department of Archaeology, University of Sheffield, Northgate House, West St., Sheffield S1 4ET, UK.

COLIN RENFREW
Department of Archaeology, Cambridge University, Downing St., Cambridge CB2 3DZ, UK.

ILSE SCHOEP
Department of Archaeology, University of Leuven, PB33 3000 Leuven, Belgium.

PETER TOMKINS
Départment d'Archéologie et d'Histoire de l'Art, Place B. Pascal 1, B-1348 Louvain-la-Neuve, Belgium.

TODD WHITELAW
Institute of Archaeology, University College London, 31-34 Gordon Sq., London WC1H 0PY, UK.

AARON WOLPERT
Department of Classics, University of Cincinnati, Cincinnati, Ohio 45221-0226, USA.

JAMES C. WRIGHT
Department of Classical and Near Eastern Archaeology, Bryn Mawr College, Bryn Mawr, PA 19010-2899, USA.

1

Chapter 14 Revisited: Sites, Settlement and population in the Prehistoric Aegean since *The Emergence of Civilisation*

John Cherry

The Context of *Emergence*

The Emergence of Civilisation (Renfrew 1972a) is now more than 30 years old. At this remove of time, it is difficult to convey the immense gratitude with which those of my generation fell upon the volume when it arrived in our libraries in 1972. *The Emergence*, a great brick of a book, not only felt and looked good, but seemingly provided all the wider context for which we budding Aegean prehistorians had been looking. For this was a volume that not only deployed concepts and terminology radical in an Aegean setting – systems theory, cybernetics, locational analysis, statistics and quantification, and so on – but one that displayed a refreshing awareness of the wider world of archaeology, especially in Mesopotamia, Mesoamerica and Europe, as well as a warm sympathy for at least some of the tenets of the New Archaeology.

The impact of *Emergence* was quite overwhelming, at least for those predisposed to be open to such notions. Its synthesis of Cycladic and Aegean prehistory, of course, was on a scale and at a level of detail not previously attempted. But that is not what made it so very *different* from any previous book in Aegean prehistory (just how different may be readily gauged by consulting the monthly bibliographic newsletter *Nestor* (n.d.) to see what sorts of other publications in this field also appeared during 1972). Unlike then-recently published textbooks, such as Emily Vermeule's *Greece in the Bronze Age* (1964), organized in terms of lively description and a pseudo-historical, narrative structure, *Emergence* placed culture process and the explanation of culture change unabashedly front and centre. By proposing causal, systems-based models, it seemed to provide, for the first time, a coherent, over-arching framework for trying to understand how and why palace-based state polities emerged where and when they did in the Aegean Bronze Age. *Emergence* placed Aegean prehistory squarely in face-to-face interaction with archaeologies well outside the Classical tradition, to a degree seen earlier perhaps only in the writings of V. Gordon Childe (to whose memory, indeed, *Emergence* was dedicated). In fact, *Emergence*, and the work it subsequently stimulated, could be said to constitute a major crossing of that divide separating anthropological archaeologies from those in the 'Great Tradition', about which Renfrew (1980) was to write a few years later.

So much water has flowed under the bridge since then – in archaeology as a discipline and in Aegean prehistory more specifically – that it is all too easy to be uncharitably dismissive or scornful of both the factual foundations and the theoretical discourse that underpins much of *Emergence*. Yet it is important to grasp just what an exciting time in archaeology that was – especially for a Skeptical Graduate Student such as myself, trained in Classics and Classical Archaeology, but coming under the influence of anthropological archaeology, the teaching of Lewis Binford, and what was later to be dubbed 'the processual school'. It is not simply the rose-tinted spectacles of retrospect that suggest to me that 1972 was indeed an *annus mirabilis* for archaeological publication. Aside from *Emergence*, that same year saw the publication of Binford's *An Archaeological Perspective*, David Clarke's *Models in Archaeology* (and his influential 'loss of innocence' paper a few months later in 1973), Kent Flannery's famous article on 'the cultural evolution of civilizations', Michael Schiffer's first paper on 'archaeological context and systemic context', widely influential books such as Marshall Sahlins' *Stone Age Economics*, some important edited collections of papers and conference proceedings – for example, Eric Higgs' *Papers in Economic Prehistory*, Mark Leone's *Contemporary Archaeology*, Ed Wilmsen's *Social Exchange and Interaction*, Peter Ucko *et al.*'s *Man, Settlement and Urbanism* (with the publication of Colin Renfrew's own similar mega-conference *The Explanation of Culture Change: Models in Prehistory* following hot on its heels the next year)… The 1972 list is long and very impressive.

But besides *Emergence*, this list also included *The Minnesota Messenia Expedition: Reconstructing a Bronze Age Regional Environment* (McDonald and Rapp 1972). The timing here is rather significant. Because the New Archaeology accorded considerable importance to 'regional systems' and quantification, there already existed considerable interest among archaeologists in the work of quantitative and spatial geographers such as Peter Haggett (1965), Richard Chorley (e.g. Chorley and Haggett 1967; Haggett and Chorley 1969), and Edward Soja (1971). Equally, this was the era of the first wide availability, to students at least, of mainframe computing, with powerful (if cumbersome) statistical and graphical capabilities. Into this mix was thrown *Emergence*, which not only advanced variant models with testable consequences, but which was replete with tables of comparative numerical data bearing on all manner of subjects – site sizes, mortuary assemblages, subsistence items, mensuration systems, and so on. And then, just at this very moment, came the detailed publication of the Messenia survey, providing what was (for Greece) the first large-scale set of semi-quantified regional data. Many of us who were postgraduate students in Aegean prehistory at that time rushed off to enter the mass of information (conveniently tabulated in Appendix A of *The Minnesota Messenia Expedition*) onto IBM punch-cards for SPSS computer analysis, hoping to apply locational and statistical techniques to gain insights into the structure and organization of a Mycenaean palatial polity (a.k.a. Nestor's kingdom), and perhaps actually to evaluate some of the models Renfrew had developed in the *Emergence*. Even McDonald himself tried his hand at this a little later, teaming up with one of his own students (Carothers and McDonald 1979).

This, then, was the rather heady atmosphere surrounding the appearance of *Emergence*. The book's emphasis on framing concepts such as regional-level synthesis and comparison, quantification, sociopolitical structures, networks of exchange and interaction, the natural and humanly constructed environment, and so on, pointed inexorably towards one of the big sea-changes that was to occur in Aegean prehistory in the years to come – namely, the huge growth of interest and activity in field survey, landscape archaeology and regional analysis, to which I turn below. In my own case, as a doctoral student working under Colin Renfrew in the mid-70s, it led to an invitation to organize an island-wide survey of Melos, in conjunction with his ongoing excavations (1974–77) at Phylakopi. Whatever the flaws of that project, published as part of *An Island Polity* (Renfrew and Wagstaff 1982), it does seem to have served as one catalyst for the flood of new fieldwork in many parts of Greece, aimed at a fuller understanding of changes in regional settlement patterns throughout the Aegean.

Regional Survey in the Aegean since 1972

Part II of *Emergence* ('Culture Process') opens with Chapter 14, entitled 'Patterns of settlement and population in the prehistoric Aegean'. Its prominent placement reflected Renfrew's assertion that, within the overall systems framework of his analysis, the human population of the Aegean 'does not constitute a subsystem in itself', but rather 'it is a parameter, a relevant statistic of all the subsystems' (Renfrew 1972a: 225). As he went on to explain:

> Precisely because population is a fundamental parameter of all the subsystems which constitute a society, and settlement pattern an obvious record and symptom of so many activities, their study must form the starting point for any investigation of a prehistoric culture or society. They are considered here as a preliminary to the discussion of the various subsystems, undertaken in succeeding chapters (Renfrew 1972a: 225).

Chapter 14 proceeded to summarize the data then available from the whole of Greece on a series of related topics: settlement density in the different regions of the Aegean; patterns of settlement increase; settlement size; settlement continuity; population density and population size; and settlement location and hierarchy, concluding with a discussion of factors underlying two seemingly quite distinct patterns of growth in different regions of the Aegean.

This chapter, along with a shorter summary of some of its main arguments in the *Man, Settlement and Urbanism* volume (Renfrew 1972b), was something many of us read and consulted repeatedly in the 1970s, and I had supposed I knew it very well. Returning to it after so many years, however, generated something of a shock – shock occasioned by realization of the very limited size and low quality of the database with which Renfrew then (i.e. the late 1960s) had to work. Once again, timing is critical: for *Emergence* was researched and written just too early to take advantage of several foundational works. *The Minnesota Messenia Expedition*, as already mentioned, appeared in the self-same year, and thus finds no mention in *Emergence* (although the basic results of many years of topographic exploration in the southwestern Peloponnese, available in a series of papers by McDonald and Hope Simpson [1961; 1964; 1969], were heavily utilized). *Neolithic Greece* (Theocharis 1973), with its publication of substantial settlement pattern data for Neolithic Thessaly, came out a few months later. The standard work of reference on Bronze Age settlement in the Aegean (excluding Crete) – the *Gazetteer of Aegean Civilisation in the Bronze Age* – was not published until seven years later (Hope Simpson and Dickinson 1979), and so Renfrew could consult only Hope Simpson's more limited and far less thorough proto-version, his *Gazetteer and Atlas of Mycenaean Sites* (1965).

Quite possibly works of this kind, had they been available in time for *Emergence*, would not have made much difference to the overall picture of settlement and population sketched out in Chapter 14. In their very different ways, after all, they represent the late flowering of a venerable, and relatively unchanged, tradition of topographic prospection and personal autopsy reaching back to the earliest decades of prehistoric research in Greece during the later 19th century. What is much more significant is the fact that the appearance of *Emergence* in 1972 shortly preceded the start of what subsequently turned out to be a deluge of survey-based regional studies undertaken in most parts of the Aegean, an area where only a handful of surveys had taken place in the three decades after World War II. Indeed, this is a development that has changed the face of Mediterranean archaeology as a whole in recent times; although only a tiny proportion of the total has yet been covered, we now know in rich detail, from organized pedestrian reconnaissance, about the long-term history of settlement and land use within huge tracts of these landscapes.

Accurate quantification is impossible, but I offer here some proxy measures of the distance that separates the late 1960s world of the *Emergence* from where we stand today.[1] Figure 1.1 shows data drawn from a literature review of 15 journals, which together provide reasonably good coverage of archaeological research in the majority of the countries bordering the Mediterranean, over the period 1967–1999 (for more details of this study, see Cherry 2003). Of the 8,467 articles published in these journals during those three decades, 978 have been devoted either to the primary publication of survey data, or to studies which in one way or another draw importantly on evidence derived from surveys. The categorization of individual papers is inevitably rough and subjective, and it has also to be conceded that survey-based papers only comprise a little over 10% of the total. But the trend of the graph is undeniably and inexorably upwards:

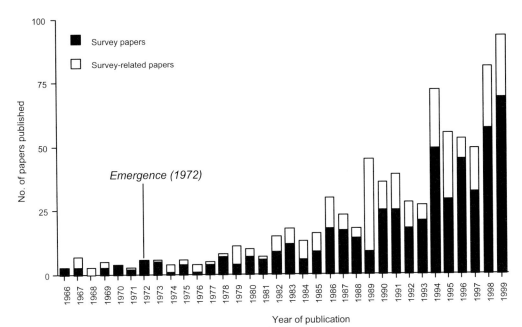

Figure 1.1. Numbers of articles devoted to the primary publication of survey data, or to studies drawing on survey evidence, as published during the period 1967–1999 in 15 archaeological journals providing coverage of archaeological research in the majority of circum-Mediterranean countries. (For details, see Cherry 2003.)

indeed, there was a ten-fold increase in the quantity of survey publications over the period in question.

A similar picture emerges for Greece alone. Figure 1.2 presents data culled from a reading of all 2,255 pages of the thorough annual summary 'Archaeology in Greece', published in the journal *Archaeological Reports* since 1954. This graph simply tabulates the number of survey projects for which a report was published in each year's issue; once again, the picture is one of sustained and quite marked long-term growth, with the 'take-off' point coming four or five years after the *Emergence*. A third potentially useful index is the number of annual start-ups of *new* survey projects in Greece over the past 30 years (Alcock and Cherry 2003: fig. 1.3), where we see substantially more activity in the 1980s and 1990s; and the citation of survey publications over the years in *Nestor* offers yet another useful means of measuring this growth. These are trends that could be replicated in a number of other parts of the Mediterranean.

Graphs of this kind, of course, express only changes in the amount of work going on under the rubric of 'survey', and they do not take account of what that term encompasses. We should remember that the search for sites, especially those that can be equated with known toponyms, has been going on in Greece, and in the Classical lands more generally, since antiquity itself. Several Mediterranean

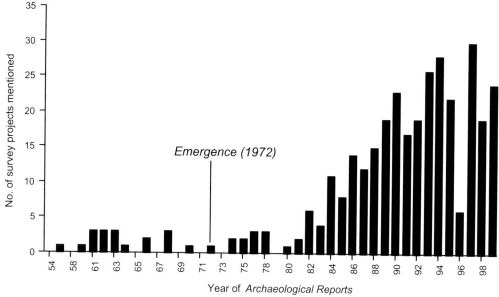

Figure 1.2. Numbers of archaeological survey projects in Greece reported annually in the journal Archaeological Reports, *1954–1999.*

countries, in fact, can boast long traditions of topographic prospection, more often than not conducted by enthusiastic local amateurs (see, e.g., Barker 1996). This, parenthetically, tends to be a point overlooked by New World archaeologists, who remain convinced that it was primarily they who first developed survey and settlement pattern studies, and that Mediterranean archaeology only '[came] around rather late to the idea of a regional approach' (Blanton 2001: 627). Gordon Willey's famous Virú Valley survey in the 1940s (Willey 1953) did not in fact lead on directly to much of anything: Andean archaeologists only turned to survey a generation later, and – with certain notable exceptions, such as the Valley of Mexico – it was mainly the boom in salvage archaeology, beginning in the early 1970s, that got things rolling. Figure 1.3, showing a ten-fold increase over the past four decades in the proportion of lead articles in *American Antiquity* dealing with settlement pattern themes (data from Fish 1999: table 14.1), documents this rather nicely, and incidentally demonstrates a close parallelism between archaeological developments in the Old and the New Worlds.

My main point, however, is the vast gulf that separates the regional settlement data in Greece available three decades ago from those of today. Renfrew (1972a: 226) back then wrote enthusiastically: 'Recent systematic and intensive site surveys... have made the Aegean one of the most comprehensively surveyed areas in the world'. But, whether or not this comparative claim was accurate, we should recall that the information actually available to him consisted of a crude lumping together of all data about sites – including even those sites classed as

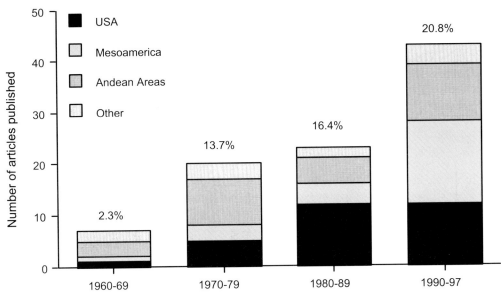

Figure 1.3. Lead articles with settlement pattern themes published in American Antiquity, *1960–1997, showing a ten-fold increase between the 1960s and the 1990s. (Data from Fish 1999: table 14.1.)*

'doubtful' by their discoverers (Renfrew 1972b: 385) – in each of six regions (Renfrew 1972a: 231–32):

- for Euboia, the gazetteer of Sackett *et al.* (1966);
- for Laconia, a single article by Waterhouse and Hope Simpson (1961);
- for Messenia, preliminary papers by McDonald and Hope Simpson (1961; 1964; 1969);
- for central Macedonia, Heurtley's pre-war *Prehistoric Macedonia* (1939) and David French's privately published *Index of Prehistoric Sites in Central Macedonia* (1967);
- for Crete, Pendlebury's gazetteer in *The Archaeology of Crete* (1939), along with the reports of travels by Hood (1965; 1967) and Hood *et al.* (1964);
- for the Cyclades, personal autopsy and the gazetteer published in the *Emergence* itself (Renfrew 1972a: 507–25).

In short, some of these data were already 30 years old, none of them had been collected in the context of organized fieldwalking by survey teams, and by no stretch of the imagination would any of them today be described as either 'systematic' or 'intensive'. No criticism is implied or intended here: Renfrew had to rely on what then existed – but it was simply not a great deal, nor in certain respects very reliable. It serves no useful purpose to be dismissive about fieldwork conducted in another age; yet the truth is that these data on which Renfrew's analyses ultimately depended were generated for the most part by lone wolves

Table 1.1. Some features of 'New Wave' surveys conducted in Greece and elsewhere in the Mediterranean in recent years (Alcock and Cherry 2003)

(a) A clearly demarcated territory as the target of fieldwork.
(b) The region itself as the focus of research design.
(c) The use of labour-intensive pedestrian survey by teams of surveyors.
(d) A more systematic approach to the coverage of terrain, often involving explicit sampling designs.
(e) Carefully thought-out procedures for standardizing the collection and recording of data.
(f) An interest in recovering information about the full range of archaeological phenomena surviving on the surface, including very small-scale sites and (often, but by no means always) 'non-site' or 'off-site' artifact distributions as well.
(g) The full integration within project design of studies of erosion, alluviation, soil formation, coastal change, vegetation history, etc., since landscape settings are not static and are themselves impacted by human occupation.
(h) The expansion of regional projects to become progressively more multi- or inter-disciplinary (*e.g.* through the incorporation of parallel studies in such fields as cultural anthropology, ethnohistory, ethnoarchaeology, historical geography, archival research, analysis of travel literature, geophysical prospection, etc.).
(i) A growing interest in the material culture and regional archaeology of the Mediterranean in periods (*e.g.* Arab, Frankish, Crusader, Venetian, Ottoman, Early Modern) hitherto undervalued or poorly studied by earlier surveys.
(j) Greatly increased use of relational databases, Geographical Information Systems, and the Internet for storing, analyzing and serving data.

Table 1.2. Aspects of prehistoric settlement in the Aegean considered in Chapter 14 of Emergence *(after Renfrew 1972a: 226)*

(a) Settlement density in the different regions of the Aegean.
(b) Patterns of settlement increase in selected regions.
(c) Development of settlement size from the Neolithic to the Late Bronze Age.
(d) Continuity and discontinuity of settlement occupation.
(e) Population density and size in the various regions.
(f) Settlement location and settlement hierarchy.

following their noses, their hunches, and the guidance of native informants: John Pendlebury striding across the Cretan countryside, Sinclair Hood quizzing the locals about antiquities through the wound-down window of the Land Rover, Roger Howell surveying all of eastern Arcadia on a bicycle, and so on.

What emerged on the scene very shortly after *Emergence* was published was what have been dubbed the 'New Wave' surveys (Cherry 1994), whose primary characteristics, as I see them, are set out in Table 1.1. Among their key features are a massive increase in labour investment and survey intensity (i.e. teamwork); interdisciplinarity; a diachronic focus; enormously more sophisticated understanding of taphonomic, geomorphological, and environmental parameters; and the use of the region as the conceptual basis for addressing historical or anthropological questions. As we enter the 21st century, consequently, we are awash with data: to my knowledge, nearly 100 formal survey projects have taken place since *Emergence*, with many more smaller-scale enterprises by individual scholars, so that hardly any part of Greece now remains unexplored, if only to some extent (further details will appear in Cherry, in prep.). So far as the primary database is concerned, then, we really have moved into another era, compared with that of *Emergence*.

Reassessment

So have all these developments made any difference? What of the principal topics of interest proposed in Chapter 14 three decades ago (Renfrew 1972a: 226)? They were: regional settlement densities, patterns of growth, settlement size, continuity and discontinuity, regional population density, and locational and hierarchical aspects of settlement (Table 1.2).

Some of these issues perhaps now seem rather less central than they once did. For example, the estimation, in both absolute and relative density terms, of the populations of sites or regions has not proven to be a major pre-occupation for archaeologists in recent times, even though in general terms one may readily agree with Renfrew (1972a: 225) that 'the human population... obviously reflects the absolute size of the culture system in terms of individuals, and population density influences all subsystems of the culture'. Certainly, the subject-matter of once-influential books such as Brian Spooner's *Population Growth: Anthropological Implications* (yet another publication of 1972) or Fekri Hassan's *Demographic Archaeology* (1981) no longer seems to be at the forefront of most archaeologists' interests. Of course, it may be that the recent European-wide collaboration of the POPULUS project, with its declared goal of advancing 'the study of the ancient demography of the [Mediterranean] region on a broad comparative front' (Barker and Mattingly 1999–2000: iv; cf. Bintliff and Sbonias 1999), will breathe some fresh life into such matters.

More specifically, large-scale comparative studies of the relationship of people to settlement space (e.g. Fletcher 1981; 1995; Whitelaw 1989) have demonstrated some of the limits to growth, the great variability in residential behaviour even within a single culture, and thus the necessity of locally contextual archaeological analysis, rather than the application of cross-cultural formulae. One aspect of Chapter 14 that has not stood up well over time is the use of estimates of urban population densities in Mesopotamia as a means of converting site sizes to population figures in the Aegean (Renfrew 1972a: 250–55). The numbers proposed (as much as 300–400 persons per ha.) would be very high by any standard, and in any case no longer command support from most Near Eastern specialists, so that

– as many have pointed out since the publication of *Emergence* – the estimated approximate population figures suggested therein are certainly much too high. Even if the error factor on such 'guesstimates' will always be large, this provides no justification for abandoning attempts to refine our understanding of prehistoric demography: population, as Renfrew emphasized forcefully at the outset of the chapter, is too fundamental an aspect of all societies to be ignored. Happily, Whitelaw (2001), in a brilliant paper presented at the 5th Sheffield Round Table on Aegean Archaeology, has shown some ways forward, with his convincing demonstration that 'there is considerably more relevant data, both for Neopalatial house size and for community organization, than has previously been considered in attempts to estimate Neopalatial site populations' (2001: 31).

Some of Renfrew's topics of interest (Table 1.2), on the other hand, could be claimed to have become susceptible of more sophisticated answers – at least in some regions – not because of the advent of high-intensity survey or the development of more appropriate analytical methods, but simply through the accumulation of data over many years. Thessaly perhaps serves as a good case in point. As is well known, the exceptional density of long-term Neolithic settlements there was recognized from the beginning of the last century, and successive casual or extensive-mode surveys in the following decades increased the number of sites recognized to more than 300. This allowed Halstead in his doctoral dissertation (1984), and later Gallis in his *Atlas Proïstorikon Oikismnon tis Anatolikis Thessalikis Pediadias* (1992), to propose quite diverse ideas about Neolithic expansion, its relationship to environmental factors, the extent of site clustering, and so on. Now, in Catherine Perlès' recent book *The Early Neolithic of Greece*, we can find not only a chronologically fine-grained analysis of EN settlement, but some elements of the sorts of locational analysis I suspect Renfrew, had he had at his disposal suitable data to do so, would have liked to try out in the *Emergence* – first-order nearest neighbour analysis, territorial analyses, Thiessen polygons, etc., all as applied to Thessalian EN 2 settlements (Perlès 2001: 121–51, figs. 7.7–7.9). The moral here is that high-tech, intensive 'New Wave' surveys need not be the only path to a better understanding.

This leads into a related point of some importance. Renfrew's analysis of Aegean settlement patterns was undertaken at a truly regional level – comparing Messenia, Crete, central Macedonia, and so on. But the whole thrust of subsequent work has actually been in a different direction, driven by the belief that increased intensification of survey method, in ever smaller areas, represents an improvement over the more primitive extensive-mode surveys and grab sampling of earlier decades. Thus, John Bintliff and Anthony Snodgrass's Boeotia survey, after two decades of fieldwork in the 80s and 90s, has still managed to cover only a few dozen square kilometers. As a co-director of the Northern Keos survey, I cannot except myself in this respect: this was a project dealing with only about 20 sq. km, yet it generated a monograph (Cherry *et al.* 1991) over 500 pages long! These examples, however, come from fieldwork initiated not so many years after

Renfrew (1972b: 384) had written, in all innocence, that 'complete survey of the terrain is so time-consuming… as to be scarcely practical for areas greater than a few hundred square kilometres'!

There exist sound reasons for this trend towards intensification, primary among them the realization that sites are interpretative, not given, constructs, which find adequate definition only against the background of off-site artefact densities that can be most informative in their own right, despite being very labour-intensive to record. But as Richard Blanton (2001) noted recently in 'Mediterranean myopia' (his thoroughly dyspeptic review of the POPULUS volumes), such methodological progress militates against regional analysis itself – or, to put it another way, Mediterranean survey archaeology as a whole seems to have lost interest in the kinds of large-scale social and demographic processes that engaged earlier researchers. Blanton's own preference would be for the 'full-coverage survey' favoured by many in the New World (Fish and Kowalewski 1990). But this does not provide a complete sample (as the name misleadingly implies), only coverage of a spatially contiguous block of land examined with relatively broad-brush survey methods; it regards 'sites' as self-defining, wholly unproblematized entities, whose functions and roles can be read directly from site size; and it takes no interest at all in those 'carpets' of artefacts/off-site scatters which are so characteristic and potentially informative a feature of the archaeological landscapes we claim to be trying to understand (cf. Tartaron 2003: 23–24). This is particularly so, if we subscribe to the radical and highly controversial view recently proposed by Bintliff *et al.* (1999; cf. Bintliff *et al.* 2002; Davis 2003) that, in the Aegean and perhaps more widely, prehistoric sites are largely obscured or have suffered severe attrition, so that original patterns and densities can be glimpsed only partially through the windows provided by very detailed tract surveying and hyper-intensive on-site collection.

In fact, the dominant trend in Aegean survey work since *Emergence* has been towards the detailed quantification of surface artefact densities, entailing a very significant penalty in limiting landscape coverage, and placing such methods to some extent at odds with the very sort of regional research orientation Renfrew advocated so powerfully. Paradoxically, therefore, if we try to use the more recent survey data to reassess some of the larger conclusions of his Chapter 14 – to cite just one example, the claim that it is possible to discern two regionally distinct patterns of long-term settlement growth (Pattern A 'exponential' and Pattern B 'retarded exponential': Renfrew 1972a: 230–36, 255–62; 1972b: 385–8) – it is surprisingly hard to do so. The ready equation of 'sites' with 'settlements' has broken down; much of the information does not come from sites at all; and all the various subsequent regional projects have collected information in remarkably diverse ways that make direct comparison tricky and the use of data in any simple additive manner ill-advised.

This seems to me to be the current crisis point for regional studies of settlement and population in the Aegean: a vast body of data has been built up, willy-nilly, containing information of variable quality, patchily distributed, and published in ways that often actually impede the direct comparison of one survey with another. On a more positive note, however, there seems now to be a growing interest and willingness to attempt intra- and inter-regional studies encompassing multiple sets of survey data, setting side-by-side information from projects in adjacent areas. In the past several years, survey data from Greece have been used, for example, to investigate:

- the apparent north-south divide in Greek prehistory (Halstead 1994);
- the development of states on the southern Greek mainland in the later Bronze Age (Cavanagh 1995);
- the seeming northwestward shift in the centre of gravity of political power in mainland Greece throughout the first millennium B.C. (Bintliff 1997);
- long-term patterns in the prehistory of the Peloponnese (Mee 1999);
- the role of pastoralism in the Greek Neolithic (Cavanagh 1999);
- the regional context for the emergence of the palatial centre of Mycenae and the polity it controlled (Cherry and Davis 2001);
- divergent political hierarchies in different areas of Crete in the Old and New Palace periods (Driessen 2001; Cunningham 2001).

Similar efforts are underway in other areas too: for instance, the use of survey evidence from six areas in the ambitious comparative study by Ikeguchi (1999–2000) of settlement patterns and agricultural structures in ancient Italy.

I hope that a recent international workshop 'Side-by-Side Survey: Comparative Regional Studies in the Mediterranean World' (Alcock and Cherry 2003) has made some contribution here, by providing a forum both for discussion of some of the practical and methodological problems to be faced when dealing with more than one set of survey data, and for illustrating some of the insights that can emerge from such analysis. This volume contains a study (Wright 2003) of comparative settlement patterns in the northeastern Peloponnese during the Bronze Age, which provides a nice contrast with *Emergence* in terms of the scale and style of its analytical comparisons; Wright's work suggests the need for subtle and sophisticated handling of the data, while also making clear the considerable variability in settlement that existed at quite local levels.

Site Sizes, and Other Related Issues

I turn lastly to some briefer comments on other themes treated in Ch. 14. One of the more significant of these was the issue of site size, or rather 'the development of settlement size from the Neolithic to the Late Bronze Age'. That there was marked growth both in site diversity and in the absolute extent of highest-order settlements, as Renfrew (1972a: 236–44) maintained, remains true. What has drawn some criticism is, firstly, whether these estimates of site size were soundly based, and, secondly, whether the comparison of Bronze Age Aegean with Near Eastern settlements, including the suggestion of an order-of-magnitude difference between the two (Renfrew 1972a: figs. 14.6–14.8), is a fair one.

On the first point, the paper by Whitelaw (2001), already mentioned, has set matters on an altogether new footing, at least for Minoan Crete in the Neopalatial period – and the methodology could doubtless be extended, with profit, to other periods and regions in the Aegean. His approach is to begin at the level of the individual house or structure, compiling a substantial database of examples, and working up to the community and site level, taking due notice of factors affecting residential patterns and the internal organization of communities. It is also an approach that is essentially comparative in nature: the size distributions of the houses at different Neopalatial Minoan sites (2001: figs. 2.4), as well as between Egyptian, Old Babylonian, Neo-Assyrian, Levantine and Minoan cultures (2001: fig. 2.3); the sizes of individual 'urban' houses, 'villas' and isolated 'farms' (2001: fig. 2.5); the extent of better-documented Neopalatial sites, all drawn to the same scale, the better to underscore the substantial variability in size (2001: fig. 2.9); and, finally, a comparative diagram of estimated site sizes for Minoan, 'Minoanized' and Mycenaean sites, together (importantly) with evaluations of the data quality in each case (2001: fig. 2.10). This last figure – although it covers only the Late Bronze Age – should effectively replace that of Renfrew (1972a: fig. 14.5); indeed, no one ought now to read Chapter 14 without also consulting Whitelaw's new study.

On the second point, too, some useful progress has been made. Without question, one of the more striking illustrations in *Emergence* is the figure displaying the plans of several of the more important Minoan and Mycenaean sites, alongside that of the (much larger) Early Dynastic Uruk (Renfrew 1972a: fig. 14.8). It has led to repeated assertions that the centres of Aegean civilization look relatively small-scale, when compared with their Near Eastern counterparts (e.g., most recently, Manning 2000; Cherry and Davis 2001: 141). But as Whitelaw (2001: 32 n. 5) and others before him have pointed out, we need to be sure not only that our spatial estimates are sound (What about 'lower towns'? Populated sectors beyond the walled area? Zones within the walls given over to horticulture?), but also that we are not inappropriately comparing apples with oranges (the central places of small centralized polities, with capitals of large states or even empires). Branigan (2001) has addressed these issues well, providing a most illuminating chart (his table 3.2) comparing the estimated sizes of Minoan towns with those of towns in the contemporary civilizations of Turkey, the Levant and Mesopotamia during the second millennium BC. It shows that Uruk (450 ha), Nippur (135 ha) and Boghazkoy (120–160 ha) are indeed in a class of their own, 'but thereafter, Minoan large towns are a match for those of the Near Eastern states' (2001: 41). Ugarit and Byblos, certainly two of the most important trading centres in the ancient Near East, were both much smaller than the four or five largest Minoan towns (for the size of Knossos, e.g., see, most recently, Whitelaw 2000: figs. 1–2, table 1; 2001: fig. 2.8). And smaller towns like those in Crete are to be found

Table 1.3. *Limitations of survey data discussed by Renfrew (1972a; 1972b: 383–85)*

(a) Site loss/invisibility, because of geological agency or human activity.
(b) Unknown relationship between total and sample site populations.
(c) Site numbers may merely reflect differential intensity of archaeological activity.
(d) Easily recognizable types of site may be over-represented (and *vice versa*).
(e) Certain types of site may be favoured by particular research goals.
(f) Periods lacking characteristic artefact types will be under-represented.

throughout the Bronze Age civilizations of Turkey, Syria and Lebanon, Palestine, and Mesopotamia. Branigan's conclusion (2001: 42) is that '...although Minoan Crete might be said to stand comparison alongside the imperial states of the contemporary Near East, the closest comparisons in terms of urban hierarchy still lie with the towns of second millennium Palestine'. Renfrew's stark order-of-magnitude contrast in scale now seems much less compelling – at least when contemporary and comparable polities are set side-by-side.

All such discussion, though, presupposes that original site sizes are in fact accurately knowable. Here, then, it is important to recognize a valuable contribution of the post-*Emergence* years – namely, the growing use of gridding and total surface collection of large sites, or what is sometimes (rather mis-leadingly, perhaps) referred to as 'urban survey'. Recent examples from Boeotia (Snodgrass and Bintliff 1988; 1991) and the Corinthia (Alcock 1991) show how detailed an impression we can gain, by such techniques, of settlement shifts, expansions and contractions over long time-periods. A more recent example, from the work of John Bennet for the Pylos Regional Archaeological Project, is the gridding of the Ano Englianos ridge around the Palace of Nestor. Renfrew (1972a: table 14.V) had estimated the size of the Pylos settlement – as distinct from the palace proper – at 12.6 ha, based on Blegen's published plans. The Messenia survey offered a much more conservative estimate of 6.5 ha (McDonald and Rapp 1972: 1). Tract-walking by PRAP in 1992, on the other hand, had revealed remains extending up and down the ridge for as much as 20 or 30 ha. Yet it was only by throwing in a large team of fieldwalkers, collecting some 35,700 artefacts from 468 20-meter squares, that there was revealed a far more precise diachronic picture of Pylos's growth: from almost nothing prior to MH, to a late MH settlement extending for 5.5 ha around the later palatial structures, to 7 ha in LH I-II, and an eventual peak of 12.4 in LH IIIA-B (Bennet 1999: 11–13, fig. 2.3; cf. Davis *et al.* 1997: 427–30, fig. 12) – ironically, very close to Renfrew's initial surmise, but now more credible, because precisely quantified.

Even despite such careful fieldwork (backed up, too, by geophysical investigations), there still remain uncertainties related to geomorphological and taphonomic factors: to what extent material of earlier periods finds representative expression on the surface, how far finds have been obscured or destroyed by the erosion of the marl, what impact deep-ploughing may have had, and so on.

These are, in fact, among the several limitations of survey data that Renfrew touched upon in Ch. 14, and spelled out more explicitly in his companion conference paper (Renfrew 1972b: 383–85), as summarized here in Table 1.3. On the whole, I incline to the view that, while they cannot altogether *control* for such factors, Aegean prehistorians in recent times have nevertheless become much more sensitive to their impact.

A major development that has taken place almost entirely since *Emergence*, of course, has been the routine involvement of geologists, geomorphologists, palynologists and soil scientists in regional projects. Donald Davidson, Rip Rapp, John Kraft, Tjeerd van Andel, John Gifford, Kevin Pope, Ann Demitrack, Peter James, Michael Timpson, Charles Frederick, Eberhard Zangger, Sergei Yzvenko, Zhichun Jing, and a good number of others (see, e.g., papers in Halstead and Frederick 2000) have made major advances in helping us understand site data in the context of the dynamic and reflexive co-evolution of changing landscape, landuse and settlement. Here, too, new technologies undreamed of in the days of *Emergence* come into play – GIS, most prominently, but also the classification of multispectral digital satellite imagery (e.g. Wiseman and Zachos 2003: 13–17), or the new-found powers of ground-penetrating radar (for a Mediterranean-based review, see Sarris and Jones 2000: 32–37).

Of the other limitations on Renfrew's list, some (e.g. Table 1.3: c, e) now seem less pressing than they once did, in light of greatly enhanced survey intensity, the aspiration of many regional projects to be fully diachronic in scope, and the much wider coverage of different parts of the Aegean. Others (e.g. Table 1.3: d, f), however, still need more attention. It is regrettable, for instance, that no one has yet systematically pursued the implications of Jeremy Rutter's brief, but provocative, 1983 paper, in which he noted major differences throughout the various cultural phases of Aegean prehistory in terms of the relative visibility and diagnosticity of pottery types, especially when recovered in the highly fragmented or eroded state so typical of survey finds. Yet other limitations (e.g. Table 1.3: b) remain largely intractable: David Clarke# (1973) was quite correct in pointing out that archaeologists deal with samples of samples of samples, with unknown relationships governing every stage.

Conclusion

There is, of course, much else in Chapter 14 on which one could usefully comment, given the benefit of 30 years' hindsight and so much basic research undertaken in the interim. I conclude, however, with a verdict sufficiently uncontroversial that the author himself might perhaps agree with it. The data on settlement and population in the prehistoric Aegean discussed by Renfrew in *Emergence* are now hopelessly out of date (indeed, as I have tried to show, they are essentially from an altogether different era of archaeological practice). Likewise, some of the conceptual apparatus brought to bear on them no longer seems as helpful as once it did. Nonetheless, the issues and questions Renfrew raised, and his insistence on human population and its distribution as fundamental to an understanding of the emergence of civilization, remain as fresh and challenging as in 1972 – although we have, I would maintain, made some progress with them since then.

Endnote

1.   I make no apology for presenting here illustrations that have already appeared, or will appear, elsewhere (Cherry 2003; in prep.; Alcock and Cherry 2003). The scale of these changes in archaeological practice is huge, but I suspect that they are under-appreciated even by some of the practitioners themselves.

Bibliography

Alcock, S.E.
    1991   Urban survey and the polis of Phlius. *Hesperia* 60: 421–63.
Alcock, S.E., and J.F. Cherry (eds.)
    2003   *Side-by-Side Survey: Comparative Regional Studies in the Mediterranean World.* Oxford: Oxbow Books.
Barker, G.
    1996   Regional archaeological projects: trends and traditions in Mediterranean Europe. *Archaeological Dialogues* 3(2): 160–75.
Barker, G., and D. Mattingly, (series eds.)
    2000   *The Archaeology of Mediterranean Landscapes* (5 vols.). Oxford: Oxbow Books.
Bennet, J.
    1999   Pylos: the expansion of a Mycenaean palatial center. In M.L. Galaty and W.A. Parkinson (eds.), *Rethinking Mycenaean Palaces: New Interpretations of an Old Idea* (Cotsen Institute of Archaeology Monograph 41): 9–18. Los Angeles: The Cotsen Institute of Archaeology, UCLA.
Binford, L.R.
    1972   *An Archaeological Perspective.* New York: Academic Press.
Bintliff, J.L.
    1997   Regional survey, demography, and the rise of complex societies in the ancient Aegean: core-periphery, neo-Malthusian, and other interpretive models. *Journal of Field Archaeology* 24: 1–38.
Bintliff, J., E. Farinetti, P. Howard, K. Sarri and K. Sbonias
    2002   Classical farms, hidden prehistoric landscapes and Greek rural survey: a response and an update. *JMA* 15: 259–65.
Bintliff, J., P. Howard and A. Snodgrass
    1999   The hidden landscape of prehistoric Greece. *JMA* 12: 139–68.
Bintliff, J., and K. Sbonias (eds.)
    1999   *Reconstructing Past Population Trends in Mediterranean Europe* (The Archaeology of Mediterranean Landscapes 1). Oxford: Oxbow Books.
Blanton, R.E.

2001   Mediterranean myopia. *Antiquity* 75: 627–9.

Branigan, K.
   2001   Aspects of Minoan urbanism. In K. Branigan (ed.), *Urbanism in the Aegean Bronze Age* (SSAA 4): 38–50. Sheffield: Sheffield Academic Press.

Carothers, J., and W.A. McDonald
   1979   Size and distribution of the population in Late Bronze Age Messenia: some statistical approaches. *Journal of Field Archaeology* 6: 433–54.

Cavanagh, W.G.
   1995   Development of the Mycenaean state in Laconia: evidence from the Laconia survey. In R. Laffineur and W.-D. Niemeier (eds.), *POLITEIA: Society and State in the Aegean Bronze Age* (*Aegaeum* 12): 81–87. Liège: Université de Liège.
   1999   Revenons à nos moutons: surface survey and the Peloponnese in the Late and Final Neolithic. In J. Renard (ed.), *Le Peloponnèse: archéologie et histoire*: 31–65. Rennes: Les Presses Universitaires.

Cherry, J.F.
   1994   Regional survey in the Aegean: the 'New Wave' (and after). In P.N. Kardulias (ed.), *Beyond the Site: Regional Studies in the Aegean Area*: 91–112. Lanham, MD: University Press of America.
   2003   Archaeology beyond the site: regional survey and its future. In R. Leventhal and J. Papadopoulos (eds.), *Theory and Practice in Mediterranean Archaeology: Old World and New World Perspectives*: 137–60. Los Angeles: Cotsen Institute of Archaeology, UCLA.
   In prep The impact of regional survey on Aegean prehistory, ca. 1970–2000. To be submitted to *Hesperia*.

Cherry, J.F., and J.L. Davis
   2001   'Under the sceptre of Agamemnon': the view from the hinterlands of Mycenae. In K. Branigan (ed.), *Urbanism in the Aegean Bronze Age* (SSAA 4): 141–59. Sheffield: Sheffield Academic Press.

Cherry, J.F., J.L. Davis and E. Mantzourani
   1991   *Landscape Archaeology as Long-Term History: Northern Keos in the Cycladic Islands from Earliest Settlement until Modern Times* (Monumenta Archaeologica 16). Los Angeles: Institute of Archaeology, UCLA.

Chorley, R.J., and P. Haggett (eds.)
   1967   *Models in Geography*. London: Methuen.

Clarke, D.
   1972   (ed.) *Models in Archaeology*. London: Methuen.
   1973   Archaeology: the loss of innocence. *Antiquity* 47: 6–18.

Cunningham, T.
   2001   Variations on a theme: divergence in settlement patterns and spatial organization in the far east of Crete during the Proto- and Neopalatial periods. In K. Branigan (ed.), *Urbanism in the Aegean Bronze Age* (SSAA 4): 72–86. Sheffield: Sheffield Academic Press.

Davis, J.L.
   2003   Are the landscapes of Greek prehistory hidden? A comparative approach. In S.E. Alcock and J.F. Cherry (eds.), *Side-by-Side Survey: Comparative Regional Studies in the Mediterranean World*. Oxford: Oxbow Books.

Davis, J.L., S.E. Alcock, J. Bennet, Y.G. Lolos and C.W. Shelmerdine
   1997   The Pylos Regional Archaeological Project, part I: Overview and the archaeological survey. *Hesperia* 66: 391–494.

Driessen, J.

2001   History and hierarchy: preliminary observations on the settlement pattern in Minoan Crete. In K. Branigan (ed.), *Urbanism in the Aegean Bronze Age* (SSAA 4): 51–71. Sheffield: Sheffield Academic Press.

Fish, S.K.
1999   Conclusions: the settlement pattern concept from an Americanist perspective. In B.R. Billman and G.M. Feinman (eds.), *Settlement Pattern Studies in th Americas: Fifty Years since Virú*: 203–08. Washington D.C.: Smithsonian Institution Press.

Fish, S.K., and S.A. Kowalewski (eds.)
1990   *The Archaeology of Regions: A Case for Full-Coverage Survey.* Washington, D.C.: Smithsonian Institution Press.

Flannery, K.V.
1972   The cultural evolution of civilizations. *Annual Review of Ecology and Systematics* 3: 399–426.

Fletcher, R.
1981   People and space: a case study in material behaviour. In I. Hodder, G. Isaac and N. Hammond (eds.), *Pattern of the Past: Studies in Honour of David Clarke*: 97–128. Cambridge: Cambridge University Press.
1995   *The Limits to Settlement Growth.* Cambridge: Cambridge University Press.

French, D.H.
1967   *Index of Prehistoric Sites in Central Macedonia.* Privately circulated manuscript.

Gallis, K.
1992   *Atlas Proïstorikon Oikismnon tis Anatolikis Thessalikis Pediadias.* Larisa: Ephoria of Antiquities.

Haggett, P.
1965   *Locational Analysis in Human Geography.* London: Edward Arnold.

Haggett, P., and R.J. Chorley
1969   *Network Analysis in Geography.* New York: St. Martin's Press.

Halstead, P.
1984   *Strategies for Survival: An Ecological Approach to Social and Economic Change in the Early Farming Communities of Thessaly, N. Greece.* PhD dissertation, Cambridge University.
1994   The north-south divide: regional paths to complexity in prehistoric Greece. In C. Mathers and S. Stoddart (eds.), *Development and Decline in the Mediterranean Bronze Age*: 195–219. Sheffield: J.R. Collis Publications.

Halstead, P., and C. Frederick (eds.)
2000   *Landscape and Land Use in Postglacial Greece* (SSAA 3). Sheffield: Sheffield Academic Press.

Hassan, F.A.
1981   *Demographic Archaeology.* New York: Academic Press.

Heurtley, W.A.
1939   *Prehistoric Macedonia: An Archaeological Reconnaissance of Greek Macedonia (East of the Struma) in the Neolithic, Bronze, and Early Iron Ages.* Cambridge: Cambridge University Press.

Higgs, E.S. (ed.)
1972   *Papers in Economic Prehistory.* London: Cambridge University Press.

Hood, M.S.F.
1965   Minoan sites in the far west of Crete. *BSA* 60: 99–113.
1967   Some ancient sites in south-west Crete. *BSA* 62: 47–56.

Hood, M.S.F., P.M. Warren and G. Cadogan
1964   Travels in Crete, 1962. *BSA* 59: 50–99.

Hope Simpson, R.
   1965   *A Gazetteer and Atlas of Mycenaean Sites* (BICS Supplement 161). London: Institute of
         Classical Studies.
Hope Simpson, R., and O.T.P.K. Dickinson
   1979   *A Gazetteer of Aegean Civilization in the Bronze Age, Vol. 1: The Mainland and the Islands.*
         (*SIMA* 52). Göteborg: Paul Åströms Förlag.
Ikeguchi, M.
   2000   A comparative study of settlement patterns and agricultural structures in ancient
         Italy: a methodology for interpreting field survey evidence. *Kodai, Journal of Ancient
         History* 10: 1–59.
Leone, M.P. (ed.)
   1972   *Contemporary Archaeology.* Carbondale: Southern Illinois Press.
McDonald, W.A., and R. Hope Simpson
   1961   Prehistoric habitation in the south-western Peloponnese. *AJA* 65: 221–60.
   1964   Further exploration in the south-western Peloponnese. *AJA* 68: 229–45.
   1969   Further exploration in the south-western Peloponnese: 1964–68. *AJA* 73: 123–77.
McDonald, W.A., and G.R. Rapp Jr (eds.)
   1972   *The Minnesota Messenia Expedition: Reconstructing a Bronze Age Regional Environment.*
         Minneapolis: University of Minnesota Press.
Manning, S.
   2000   Knossos and the limits of settlement growth. In P. Betancourt, V. Karageorghis, R.
         Laffineur, W.-D. Niemeier (eds.), *MELETEMATA: Studies in Aegean Archaeology
         Presented to Malcolm H. Wiener* (*Aegaeum* 20), Vol. II: 469–80. Liège: Université de
         Liège.
Mee, C.B.
   1999   Regional survey projects and the prehistory of the Peloponnese. In J. Renard (ed.), *Le
         Peloponnèse: archéologie et histoire*: 67–79. Rennes: Les Presses Universitaires.
Nestor
   n.d.   *http://classics.uc.edu/nestor/index.html*
Pendlebury, J.D.S.
   1939   *The Archaeology of Crete.* London: Methuen.
Perlès, C.
   2001   *The Early Neolithic of Greece.* Cambridge: Cambridge University Press.
Renfrew, C.
   1972a *The Emergence of Civilisation.* London: Methuen.
   1972b Patterns of population growth in the prehistoric Aegean. In P.J. Ucko, R. Tringham
         and G.W. Dimbleby (eds.), *Man, Settlement and Urbanism*: 383–99. London: Duckworth.
   1973   (ed.) *The Explanation of Culture Change: Models in Prehistory.* London: Duckworth.
   1980   The Great Tradition versus the Great Divide: archaeology as anthropology? *AJA* 84:
         287–98.
Renfrew, C., and M. Wagstaff (eds.)
   1982   *An Island Polity: the Archaeology of Exploitation in Melos.* Cambridge: Cambridge
         University Press.
Rutter, J.B.
   1983   Some thoughts on the analysis of ceramic data generated by site surveys. In D.R.
         Keller and D.W. Rupp (eds.), *Archaeological Survey in the Mediterranean Area* (BAR
         International Series 155): 137–42. Oxford: British Archaeological Reports.
Sackett, L.H., V. Hankey, R.J. Howell, T.W. Jacobsen and M. Popham
   1966   Prehistoric Euboia: contributions towards a survey. *BSA* 61: 33–112.

Sahlins, M.D.
    1972   *Stone Age Economics*. Chicago: Aldine.
Sarris, A., and R E. Jones
    2000   Geophysical and related techniques applied to archaeological survey in the Medi-
            terranean: a review. *JMA* 13: 3–75.
Schiffer, M.B.
    1972   Archaeological context and systemic context. *American Antiquity* 37: 156–65.
Snodgrass, A.M., and J.L. Bintliff
    1988   Mediterranean survey and the city. *Antiquity* 62: 57–71.
    1991   Surveying ancient cities. *Scientific American* 264.3: 88–93
Soja, E.W.
    1971   *The Political Organization of Space*. Washington, D.C.: Association of American
            Geographers.
Spooner, B. (ed.)
    1972   *Population Growth: Anthropological Implications*. Cambridge, Mass.: MIT Press.
Tartaron, T.F.
    2003   The archaeological survey: sampling strategies and field methods. In J. Wiseman and
            K. Zachos (eds.), *Landscape Archaeology in Southern Epirus, Greece I* (Hesperia
            Supplement 32): 23–45. Princeton: American School of Classical Studies at Athens.
Theocharis, D.R. (ed.)
    1973   *Neolithic Greece* (trans. D. Hardy and A.-M. Lefkaditi). Athens: National Bank of
            Greece.
Ucko, P.J., R. Tringham and G.W. Dimbleby (eds.)
    1972   *Man, Settlement and Urbanism*. London: Duckworth.
Vermeule, E.
    1964   *Greece in the Bronze Age*. Chicago: University of Chicago Press.
Waterhouse, H., and R. Hope Simpson
    1961   Prehistoric Laconia, part II. *BSA* 56: 114–75.
Whitelaw, T.M.
    1989   *The Social Organisation of Space in Hunter-Gatherer Communities: Implications for Social
            Inference in Archaeology*. PhD dissertation, University of Cambridge.
    2000   Beyond the palace: a century of investigation in Europe's oldest city. *BICS* 44: 223–6
            [abstract].
    2001   From sites to communities: defining the human dimensions of Minoan urbanism. In
            K. Branigan (ed.), *Urbanism in the Aegean Bronze Age* (SSAA 4): 15–37. Sheffield:
            Sheffield Academic Press.
Willey, G.R.
    1953   *Prehistoric Settlement Patterns in the Virú Valley, Peru*. Washington D.C.: U.S.
            Government Printing Office.
Wilmsen, E.N. (ed.)
    1972   *Social Exchange and Interaction* (Anthropological Papers 46). Ann Arbor: University of
            Michigan Museum of Anthropology.
Wiseman, J., and K. Zachos (eds.)
    2003   *Landscape Archaeology in Southern Epirus, Greece I* (Hesperia Supplement 32). Princeton:
            American School of Classical Studies at Athens.
Wright, J.C.
    2003   Comparative settlement patterns during the Bronze Age in the Northeastern
            Peloponnesos, Greece. In S.E. Alcock and J.F. Cherry (eds.), *Side-by-Side Survey:
            Comparative Regional Studies in the Mediterranean World*. Oxford: Oxbow Books.

2

Dual Emergence: Evolving Heterarchy, Exploding Hierarchy

Ilse Schoep and Carl Knappett

'Emergence'

Of the two nouns in the title of Renfrew's magisterial 1972 work *The Emergence of Civilisation*, it is the latter – *civilisation* – that tends to attract the most vigorous discussion and criticism (not least for its neo-evolutionist implications). The term *emergence*, on the other hand, although given implicit consideration insofar as it refers to temporal change, is barely discussed as a theme in and of itself. In this paper, therefore, we aim to thematize emergence, driven in no small part by two recent developments. The first relates to the burgeoning field of 'complexity theory', which concerns itself with complex adaptive systems and the self-organizing, *emergent* properties that such systems show. So central is the theme of emergence to this new field that at least two recently published volumes have simply been entitled *Emergence* (Holland 1998; Johnson 2001). The second development is the promising use of these kinds of ideas by a handful of archaeologists to try and explain early complex societies (McGlade and van der Leeuw 1997; Doran 2000; Lehner 2000). Lehner, for example, uses the concepts of emergent order and self-organization to tackle social complexity in ancient Egypt. Drawing on these twin strands, we aim to consider in a simple way some of the implications of complexity theory for the question of the *emergence* of palatial society on Crete in the late Prepalatial and Protopalatial periods. This was, of course, one of the central questions Renfrew tackled in *The Emergence of Civilization*.

Although in *The Emergence* Renfrew devotes relatively little attention to emergence as a theme, on the occasions when it does arise it is in the context of cybernetics.[1] He draws on cybernetics to construct a theoretical framework capable of treating cultures as systems. In cybernetics a system is composed of subsystems, with each subsystem operating homeostatically to counter perturbations and maintain overall systemic equilibrium. This notion of homeostasis, or negative feedback, is drawn from the work of the British cybernetician W. Ross Ashby (1952; 1956). But Renfrew envisaged the possibility of positive as well as negative feedback operating in the interaction between subsystems, an idea he derives from Maruyama (1963). That is to say, there may also be some processes at work that act to amplify deviation rather than diminish it – what Maruyama called 'deviation-amplifying mutual causal processes'. It is in this way that a large system may have *emergent* properties (Renfrew 1972: 17), as systemic change arises unpredictably from the interactions among its subsystems.

Cybernetics served to thematize emergence as a process of open-ended becoming (Pickering 2002). But by the time Renfrew was writing, cybernetics was already in decline; indeed, Renfrew is only able to cite a handful of cyberneticians, such as Ashby, Wiener, von Bertalanffy, Tustin and Maruyama. As an approach to mental phenomena, which is certainly how Ashby at least had envisaged cybernetics, with his 1952 book *Design for a Brain*, it was surpassed in the late 1950s and 1960s by the artificial intelligence approach (e.g., Newell and Simon 1956). It only returned, in spirit if not in name, and in the physical rather than the cognitive sciences, with Ilya Prigogine's groundbreaking work on dissipative structures in the 1970s (Prigogine and Stengers 1984; Capra 1996). In a similar vein one might also note Manfred Eigen's work on self-organizing chemical reaction cycles (Eigen 1971). Biological systems too have been studied for their self-organizing properties at a range of levels, from the cell to the organism to entire ecosystems. Indeed, the principle of self-organization seems to be applicable to all kinds of systems, be they physical, biological, economic or social, and at a range of different scales. Phenomena as diverse as neural networks, the Internet, ant colonies, urban dynamics and the stock market have all been tackled from this perspective (Buchanan 2002; Barabási 2002). This resurgence of interest in self-organizing systems, embodied in 'complexity theory', is a truly interdisciplinary endeavour, perhaps best exemplified by the activities of the Santa Fe Institute.

One of the unifying principles of the now vast and diverse body of work known as 'complexity theory' is that order in an adaptive system need not be linear, hierarchical and externally imposed – order can also result from non-linear, non-hierarchical processes that are entirely self-regulating. This is perhaps not so very far away from the first cybernetics and Renfrew's project to apply a systemic understanding to culture. One wonders how the *Emergence* might have turned out if written within a more mature and interdisciplinary theoretical environment. This is precisely what has now emerged with complexity theory, and Renfrew's much-maligned concepts of homeostasis, positive feedback and the multiplier effect suddenly seem peculiarly prescient.

Self-Organization, Hierarchy and Heterarchy

Let us take one of the above examples as a means of explaining a little further what is actually implied by self-organization. One of the most fascinating cases is that of the ant colony, particularly well documented in the work of Hölldobler and Wilson (1994) and Gordon (1999). The complex organization within an ant colony arises without a centralized command structure. Order emerges not from the top down but from the bottom up. The higher-level order of the colony as an entity *emerges* out of the low-level rules followed by each individual ant. Micro-rules (such as emit pheromone trail, recognize pheromone trails of others, adjust behaviour according to neighbours' actions) create macro-behaviour, in such a way that the whole far exceeds the sum of its parts. Thus, in the case of the ant colony, integrated, low-level, bottom-up interaction patterns lead to a complex form of order that is not hierarchical, but 'heterarchical'. It is important that we are clear about this differentiation between hierarchy and heterarchy: they are not mutually exclusive structures, but tend to co-occur in most real-world complex (social) systems. We shall explore this point further below.

In the case of the ant colony, it appears that 'bottom-up' self-organization leads to heterarchy. Yet we should be careful not to create a simple equation between bottom-up processes and heterarchical structure. In other cases, self-organization creates a hierarchical structure – recent research on the World Wide Web, for example, has shown how the structure has self-organized into a hierarchical form, with a disproportionate amount of the overall traffic flowing through certain key hubs (Barabási 2002). Nonetheless, the World Wide Web could also be described as democratic or egalitarian, which suggests, among other things, that egalitarianism need not go together with heterarchy.

It is also interesting to examine ways in which hierarchy and heterarchy can work for each other and against each other within a single complex system. One example of this is the city: an urban agglomeration may be described as a *superorganism* in much the same way as an ant colony (although one wouldn't want to push too far the analogy between ants and humans). It has been argued (Jacobs 1961) that the success of a city as superorganism owes much to sidewalk interactions, what Jacobs calls 'intimacy of sidewalk use'. These interactions, whereby people on the street pay attention to their neighbours' actions and adjust their own accordingly, are the means by which neighbourhoods self-organize through a kind of 'tacit consensus' (Johnson 2001).[2] Bottom-up processes of this kind may well contribute to continuing order within the city, and they may form the basis for heterarchical structures too. Nevertheless, cities do also tend to have city authorities, planning commissions, and a mayor – in other words, hierarchical structures of centralized authority. Thus it seems we need to distinguish between bottom-up and top-down *processes*, and between heterarchical and hierarchical *structures*. Bottom-up processes can encourage, according to circumstance, both heterarchical and hierarchical structures, as indeed can top-down processes. Exactly how these processes and structures come together in urban organization is a major question. Although sometimes heterarchical and hierarchical structures, and bottom-up and top-down processes, may be at loggerheads (cf. Jacobs 1961), more often than not they do successfully interact and work off each other.

This perspective on self-organizing systems demonstrates that bottom-up processes can lead to complexity. It also serves to counter the common assumption that complexity implies the existence of central authority.

Hierarchy and Heterarchy: Archaeological Perspectives

The emergence of urban order and the emergence of 'civilization' can be treated as comparable phenomena. What we are dealing with in both cases is essentially the emergence of *complexity*. In archaeological theory, complexity has been defined in various ways, but is generally thought to consist of both vertical and horizontal differentiation (e.g., Blanton *et al.* 1993: 17). Rothman (1994: 4) employs a similar kind of definition, although the terms used are 'centralization' for vertical differentiation, and 'integration' for horizontal differentiation. Despite the varying terminology, in each case what we are dealing with is essentially a combination of both *hierarchy* and *heterarchy*. However, in archaeological approaches to emergent complexity the emphasis has fallen far more heavily on the former than the latter (Lehner 2000). By alluding to some of the tenets of 'complexity theory', our aim here is simply to redress the balance – to show that hierarchical structures are not the only means through which organized complexity is achieved. We need to pay much more attention to heterarchical structures in our archaeological analyses (Crumley 1995; Schoep 2002), and in particular to the relationship *between* heterarchy and hierarchy. Whilst hierarchy is a concept familiar to most archaeologists, *heterarchy* is a more recent addition to the vocabulary of archaeological theory.[3] In this context, heterarchy has been defined as 'the relation of elements to one another when they are unranked or when they possess the potential for being ranked in a number of different ways' (Crumley 1995: 3). A further key point, underlined by Crumley, is that heterarchy and hierarchy are by no means mutually exclusive. It is not as if one is present while the other is absent, or that one replaces the other (Zagarell 1995). Both are always present, although their relative strength may fluctuate over time. Thus heterarchy is a crucial concept if we are to recognize 'patterns of relations that are complex but not hierarchical' (Crumley 1995: 3; see also Potter and King 1995).

Thus in trying to characterize and explain *the* emergence of civilization/complexity, we should really be looking for two different (yet often interrelated) phenomena – hierarchy and heterarchy. We have normally assumed that once one sees vertical differentiation then horizontal differentiation must also be in place; that hierarchy predicts heterarchy. Yet the two need not go quite so neatly hand in hand – they may, for example, develop differentially over time. If this is the case then we may be mistaken in seeking a singular emergence, which is what is implied in the term *The Emergence*. Might it in fact be the case that the emergence of complexity is a DUAL process? If we pull apart complexity, and argue that significant heterarchical developments may have emerged separately from significant hierarchical ones, then we are no longer tied to the idea of a single watershed of major societal change. We may go further still and argue that, in Minoan Crete at least, changes in heterarchical structures *prefigured* any major hierarchical developments. Indeed, we shall argue here that the MMIB watershed, seen to be the defining moment when Minoan palatial society emerged, can be dismantled, torn apart from two directions at once:

1. First, many complex developments, notably heterarchical/integrative ones, occurred before MMIB, as far back as EMI-II. Heterarchical structures do of course continue into MMII, but we argue that they were already substantially developed during the Prepalatial.
2. Secondly, many complex developments of the hierarchical kind occur not in MMIB but a little later, in MMII. There were of course hierarchical structures existent during the EM period, but our argument here is that they did not become significant and explicit until much later, in MMII indeed, when they prepared the ground for more centralized authority.

So now let us look at the local and regional evidence for these processes, in Minoan administration, craft production, architecture, settlement pattern and burial customs.

Administration

Weingarten, Godart, Olivier (Weingarten 1990: 105–6; 1994: 177; Olivier 1989) and others have argued that administration and writing are directly connected with the emergence of the palaces. The first point to make here is that the application of Linear A and Cretan Hieroglyphic for administrative purposes, and the concomitant development of a range of document types for each of these scripts, does not seem to have gone hand in hand with the first occurrence of the earliest palaces, particularly if these predate the MMIB period. In fact the administrative documents with writing date to a later phase of the Protopalatial period, as is attested by the MMIIB deposits from the palaces of Phaistos and Petras and from Quartier Mu at Malia. The date of the 'Hieroglyphic Deposit' from Knossos seems to be no earlier than MMIIB and is perhaps later (Schoep 2001). The earliest document at present is a tablet fragment from the South-West House at Knossos that was found together with a basket sealing and a nodulus and is dated to MMIIA (Macdonald and Knappett forthcoming). At any rate, the written documents from the palaces all date to the final destruction of these buildings in MMIIB. Related to this is of course the issue of whether they are indicative of top-down or bottom-up processes. Although there is a degree of regionalism, with Linear A confined to (south) central Crete and Cretan Hieroglyphic predominant in the east, the two are in fact both found at Knossos. The distribution does not look like a controlled top-down bureaucratic imposition from a single centre and does not seem to reflect a top-down process.

The second point concerns the argument that before the emergence of the palaces there would have been no need for an administrative system (Weingarten 1990; 1994; Olivier 1989). The direct object sealing from Fournou Korifi (Warren 1972) and the EMIIA sealings from the West Court House (Wilson 1994) were long isolated instances and were therefore considered as accidental, rejected as evidence for a 'Prepalatial' administrative system (Weingarten 1990). Although no deposit comparable in size to the mainland deposits of Lerna and Geraki has as yet been found on Crete, new evidence has come to light in the last couple of years. The discovery of sealings at Khania (EMII or EMIII), Khamalevri (EMIII/MMIA), Trypiti (EMII or EMIII), Malia (EMIIB) (Vlasaki and Hallager 1995; Pelon 1993), Psathi (EMIIB or EMIII/MMIA) and Mochlos (Soles and Davaras 1992: 436) suggests that some kind of accounting system, making use of perhaps two document types (direct object sealings and noduli), existed on Crete from EMII onwards. With these new finds the prior tendency to dismiss Prepalatial documents out of hand as one-offs has been replaced by more serious considerations of their socio-economic and political context (Vlasaki and Hallager 1995; Schoep 1999; Perna 1999; Hallager 2000). It is especially interesting to note that Prepalatial seal-use was geographically widespread and not confined to central buildings, but found in what seem to qualify as private houses (Schoep forthcoming). Does such a pattern point to the presence of complex 'integrative' structures rather than the existence of a central authority (*contra* Schoep 1999)? In other words, could it be that the first administrative practices on Crete emerged within socio-economic structures that were heterarchical in character?

Craft Production

As Day and Wilson (2002) and others (Whitelaw *et al.* 1997; Day *et al.* 1997; Kiriatzi *et al.* 2000) have demonstrated, specialized pottery production existed from EMI onwards. Moreover, provenance studies of EM pottery have made clear that a complex economy existed in which pottery was moving interregionally as early as EMI (Wilson and Day 1994; 1999; 2000). In some cases the distribution patterns are similar to patterns attested in the Protopalatial period (Kiriatzi *et al.* 2000). Specialized production may also be inferred for other crafts such as sealstones (Pini 1990; Sbonias 2000), bronze artifacts (Branigan 1968), and stone vases (Warren 1969). The existence of specialized craft production can therefore no longer be regarded as directly connected to the emergence of the palaces. These patterns of horizontal differentiation have nonetheless been interpreted as indicative of the emergence of central authority, well before the creation of the palaces proper (Day and Wilson 2002: 155). This is an example of the close association between craft specialization and vertical hierarchy that is commonly proposed in the literature. It also illustrates how vertical hierarchy is equated with central authority (as for example in Schoep 1999). We argue here, in contrast, that the craft specialization seen in EMI-II could very easily be the result of bottom-up dynamics, and need not imply any kind of hierarchical top-down processes or centralized authority.

One might argue that it is only significantly later that there is reasonable evidence for hierarchical intervention in craft production, as witnessed by the apparent presence of *attached* specialists occupying the MMIIB ateliers at Quartier Mu, Malia (Poursat 1996). However, such on the ground evidence for craft production is so rare that its absence earlier in the archaeological record cannot reliably be taken as evidence for absence (thus one dare not rule it out for earlier periods such as MMI). Equally, it is widely accepted that the potter's wheel, an important attribute of specialized craft production, was introduced in MMIB in the context of the emergence of the palaces. Nevertheless, it only saw application on a wider scale at a later stage of the Protopalatial period (Knappett 1999b). Taken together, these observations demonstrate two points. First, craft specialization, rather than occurring at a single watershed in MMIB, developed as a drawn out process stretching from EMI to MMII. Secondly, specialized production may have emerged initially as a bottom-up process, only later becoming implicated in top-down hierarchical processes.

Architecture

We normally consider the development of monumental palatial architecture to have been a MMIB phenomenon (e.g., Cherry 1983; 1986). However, the mobilization of resources and labour on a large scale is seen prior to this date: not only are there several well-known examples of monumental architecture already in EMII and EMIII at Palaikastro, Tylissos, Knossos (Branigan 1970) and perhaps Mochlos (Soles and Davaras 1996), but the Malia palace itself was built in EMIII/MMI (Pelon 1992).[4] At Knossos, the EMIII North-West Platform also seems to form part of a large-sized structure preceding the MMIA and MMIB structures and for which space had been cleared on top of the Kephala hill (Wilson 1994). Although the plan and precise function of the earlier erased buildings is not clear, as pointed out by Cherry (1983; 1986), it is generally accepted that these buildings were not domestic in character. At Knossos, Day and Wilson (1998; 2002) have argued for a ceremonial function on the basis of the high quality of the pottery, the range of shapes and the quantity of imports.

The early date of the palace at Malia and the existence at Knossos of consecutive earlier structures of monumental character beneath the MMIB palace suggests that the development of monumental palatial architecture can no longer be considered to have been an exclusively MMIB phenomenon. Instead it suggests that this was a more drawn out process than previously suggested. Although this paper seeks to sketch an overall picture for Crete, it must be stressed that there are important regional developments, the discussion of which, however, falls outside the scope of this paper.

Another aspect that needs to be considered is the misconception that exists concerning the nature of palatial architecture in the Protopalatial period. 'Palatial' architectural features such as light-wells, lustral basins and pier-and-door partitions are not actually found within the first palaces. For example, the lustral basins in the Phaistos and Knossos palaces cannot be dated to the Protopalatial period, but to MMIII (La Rosa 2002; Catling 1988: 68). Other hallmarks of the monumentality of the palaces, such as the ashlar west façades at Knossos and Malia, date not to MMIB but actually to MMIII (Momigliano 1991; Pelon 1980).[5] Instead, the earliest evidence in the Protopalatial period for so-called 'palatial' architecture, such as light-wells, lustral basins and pier-and-door partitions, is in fact attested *outside* the palaces. This is the case at Malia where such features occur in buildings that distinguish themselves from domestic architecture by their size, layout, architectural features and finds, and have been labeled 'semi-official' buildings. Although no ashlar masonry was used in the west façade of the Protopalatial palace this technique was employed in Quartier Mu and in the Crypte Hypostyle. Ashlar limestone is furthermore attested in Chryssolakkos and in a building discovered during the Malia survey (Müller 1991: 743). Furthermore, Quartier Mu features a Minoan Hall with light-well and the largest lustral basin on Crete, and pier-and-door partitions are also attested in the Crypte Hypostyle (Allegrette and Schmid 1997).

Interestingly, at Malia the appearance of these 'palatial' architectural features in Quartier Mu dates not to MMIB but to MMII. Whereas the plan of the palace remains basically the same throughout, marked changes take place in the town. These are reflected in the use of a new elite architectural vocabulary and in the construction of new buildings and modification of earlier MMIB ones (cf. Poursat 1988: 72). Elite architectural features can be seen as part of conspicuous consumption, an important strategy in the building of alliances and promoting group cohesion. This points towards a climate of competition. It would seem, therefore, that only in MMII does hierarchy enter into a dynamic interface with heterarchy within the settlement at Malia. This could be explained by the increased wealth of certain groups and their decision to invest in monumental architecture.

Settlement Patterns

The question we must first ask ourselves again comes down to the issue of a MMIB watershed – is such a watershed visible in settlement patterns? It seems not, as we are informed that the real crunch period is EMIII/MMIA, a time when the landscape is 'filling up' (Haggis 1999; 2002). The general picture provided by the regional data is that of a wide dispersal in EMIII/MMIA and an enormous growth in MMIA at sites such as Knossos, Archanes-Phourni and Malia. Dispersal has also been noted for MMI-II, but mainly in the immediate area of the palaces of Malia and Phaistos.

But when does settlement *hierarchy* make itself felt? This is difficult to specify as far as site size is concerned (as it is hard to date fluctuations in site size with much precision). One means, however, may be to look at the regional level, and the extent to which 'central' sites seem to be having a regional impact. Material culture patterning at the regional level gives us some clues, and fineware pottery styles are a relatively easy form of material culture to date (seals may be another – see Sbonias 1999). And indeed, if we look at the area of east-central Crete, where such evidence happens to be particularly clear, we can say that it is in MMII rather than MMI that central sites start to have a pronounced regional impact. Myrtos Pyrgos, having had fine wares in MMI that shared similarities with Knossos, Malia and other regions, begins in MMII to look almost exclusively towards Malia. The fine wares at the two sites in MMIIB really are strikingly similar, but this is a rather short-lived affair restricted to MMII (Knappett 1999a). It is also only in MMII(A) that the palace at Petras is built (Tsipopoulou 1999); moreover, it is at this time that finewares at the site stop looking Knossian and start to become distinctly Maliote.

Once again, this time with settlement patterns, we are able to apply pressure on the MMIB watershed from both sides, identifying significant changes both before (in EMIII-MMIA) and after (in MMII) the MMIB watershed.

Burial

The incomplete study and publication of some cemeteries, coupled with problems of dating, mean that a clear overall picture of the burial evidence is far from forthcoming. The picture for Crete as a whole is further complicated by what seems to be a considerable degree of regionalism in burial customs. What is clear, however, is that there is little evidence for a watershed in MMIB.

It seems that not MMIB but the late prepalatial EMIII and MMIA periods were of great importance. At sites such as Malia and Phourni Archanes one can note an important growth in the size of the cemeteries in EMIII-MMIA, with a wide variety of tomb types being constructed (Baurain 1987; Soles 1992; Maggidis 1998). Other changes occurring in the late Prepalatial period include an overall tendency for the objects in tombs to decrease in quantity from EMIII onwards, and the increasing popularity of pithoi and larnakes burials in separate cemeteries or associated with or inside built structures (Branigan 1970; 1993; Petit 1987).

There seems to be a reasonable distribution of wealth throughout the tombs in EMII, EMIII and MMI, which could be interpreted as indicative of a heterarchical structure. At the same time, however, the presence of luxury grave goods, diversification of tomb types and elaboration of their architectural form could all suggest hierarchical structures; both Branigan (1984) and Soles (1988) have indeed argued for some kind of differentiation or social ranking. Although existent from EMII onwards, elaboration and diversification become more pronounced in EMIII and MMIA with, for example, the construction of paved areas and altars in association with some house and tholos tombs (e.g., at Mochlos, Apesokari,

Kamilari). This seems to make certain tombs the focus of attention, a move which has been connected with the emergence of an elite, seemingly in EMIII and MMIA (Soles 1988; Branigan 1970: 93–4). At Malia, the first phase (EMIII or MMIA) of Chrysolakkos, with the benched rooms below the later East portico, may be an expression of the same phenomenon.[6] In terms of diversification, the evidence from Archanes Phourni of a wide variety of tomb types (Maggidis 1998) may point towards intensifying competition between local elite groups. If so, this too precedes the MMIB watershed.

As for MMII, when we noted that hierarchy becomes more visible and pronounced in the realm of the living (domestic architecture), developments at some sites may suggest that a similar tendency can be noted in the realm of the dead. At some of the larger sites, special efforts seem to have been directed towards the construction of grander burial structures. At Archanes Phourni, five annexes were added to Tholos B in the Protopalatial period (Watrous 2001: 188), making it into a large rectangular two-storey structure. The construction of the monumental enclosure of Chrysolakkos at Malia, with its cut limestone blocks and orthostats, may perhaps also illustrate this (difficult to date with precision but perhaps MMII like other large buildings at Malia, cf. Poursat 1988: 72–3). The MMII period may also see the use of a new tomb type, the rock-cut tomb, as for example at Knossos and Poros, in areas previously not used for burial.

At other (smaller) sites, Prepalatial tombs continue in use into MMI-II and the only change that can be noted in their long time-span is a decrease in the quantity of grave goods (Sphoungaras, Pachyammos, Phourni, Vorou B) and the appearance of larnax burials. The absence of evidence for a stronger and more visible hierarchical structure is perhaps connected with the relative size and importance of such sites in the MMI-II periods.

Conclusions

In this paper we have criticised the idea of a MMIB watershed, and suggested instead a *dual* emergence spread over a much longer timespan. The idea of dual emergence stresses that searching for THE emergence of complexity, as a single horizon, may be a wild goose chase. By acknowledging the existence of different dimensions of complexity, namely heterarchical and hierarchical dimensions, we have shown how some aspects of complexity are more important before the MMIB watershed while others come to the fore afterwards. Both hierarchical and heterarchical structures are present throughout, but their relative strength fluctuates over time.

We need to *explode* the orthodox use of the concept of hierarchy and subject it to critical scrutiny instead of simply assuming it to be the all-important dimension of social organization. At the same time, we need to develop substantially the concept of heterarchy, to give it the chance to *evolve* to analytical maturity. This will not be easy, as archaeological theory has consistently tended toward a top-down, 'highly aggregate perspective' (Lehner 2000: 282; citing Epstein and Axtell 1996).

There is of course another, rather more tenuous sense in which the exploding/evolving metaphor takes on meaning. We have suggested in relation to Minoan Crete that whereas heterarchy might have been a slow-boiling, *evolving* process, hierarchy *exploded* onto the scene, perhaps as a direct, albeit non-linear result of heterarchical developments. Might it be the case that certain changes in heterarchical structures were in some way a precondition for new hierarchical structures?

Complexity theory holds implicit within itself the idea that change may emerge unpredictably from homeostasis.[7] The idea of self-organization comes from this very notion that it is through solely internal processes – through the constant interaction of subsystems – that new properties may arise in the system as a whole. That adequate data on large complex systems are only now being collated means that study of the actual *mechanisms* of self-organization and emergence has only recently become realistic. Thanks to this we have begun to understand some of the self-organizing and emergent properties of adaptive systems such as ant colonies and cities, to come back to two examples used earlier in this paper. The theme of *emergence* is certainly a hot topic, and looks set to grow apace as the study of all kinds of complex systems, be they physical, biological, economic or social, continues to reveal very similar topologies and dynamics. This serves to put in perspective the heavy criticism of Renfrew's explicitly systemic approach in the *Emergence*. Indeed, with this new kind of science, spread across very diverse fields (economic theory, cell biology, artificial intelligence, etc.), there is considerable scope for looking in a new light upon Renfrew's conceptualization of systems, subsystems and the multiplier effect. He was, after all, concerned with how long-term systemic changes emerged from small adjustments in local conditions. Moreover, a new and updated concern with systems need not be anti-agency or anti-history, as many forms of systemic modelling are now firmly 'agent-based'.

Criticism has been part and parcel of the life of the *Emergence* over the last 30 years; but it may yet be one of its most maligned features, the use of a systems approach derived from cybernetics, that proves to be its most enduring contribution.

Acknowledgements

We would like to thank the organizers of the Round Table, John Barrett and Paul Halstead, for inviting us to make this contribution. CK is grateful to Karen Godden and Mike Parker Pearson for their hospitality during the Round Table.

Endnotes

1   Note that Doran (2000: 90-91) cites Flannery's (1972) early work as an example of a cybernetic approach, and suggests that the nature of the relationship between such work (and one might include that of Renfrew alongside Flannery) and current agent-based approaches is an important yet largely unexplored question.
2   Note also the computer simulation game 'SimCity' to which Johnson refers - this too runs on the basis of neighbourly interactions.
3   Some other works with an archaeological theory component and dealing with heterarchy are: Crumley (1987); Brumfiel (1995); Keswani (1996); and Stein (1998).
4   There is increasing evidence that a predecessor stood at this place in EMIIB.
5   At Knossos, soundings in the southwestern corner of the palace (DVII 14) revealed an earlier wall in limestone and gypsum blocks (Catling 1988: 69) associated with a floor of MMIB date (MacGillivray 1998: 35). At Malia, there is no evidence to suggest that the west façade was built in anything other than large irregular blocks (as is the case for the north stretch of the west façade wall and the east wall of the palace which are dated to the Protopalatial period).
6   The influence of Egyptian elements, pointed out by Watrous (2001), may perhaps also be interpreted in this way.
7   This gives us a framework for overcoming the unnecessary polarization between Renfrew's evolution and Cherry's revolution. Although Renfrew saw EMII as linked to MMIB through a gradual stepped set of changes, and Cherry implied that the two need not actually have been connected, we can instead imagine EMII as being causally related to MMIB, albeit in a non-linear fashion.

Bibliography

Allegrette, A. and M. Schmid
    1997   Travaux de l'école française en Grèce en 1996. Malia, Crypte hypostyle (Bâtiment KB). *BCH* 121, 2: 790–91.
Ashby, W. Ross
    1952   *Design for a Brain.* London: Chapman and Hall.
    1956   *An Introduction to Cybernetics.* London: Chapman and Hall.
Barabási, A.-L.
    2002   *Linked: The New Science of Networks.* Cambridge, MA: Perseus Publishing.
Baurain, C.
    1987   Les nécropoles de Malia. In R. Laffineur (ed.), *Thanatos. Les coutumes funéraires en Egée à l'âge du bronze* (Aegaeum 1): 62–73. Liège: Université de Liège.
Blanton, R.E., S.A. Kowalewski, G.M. Feinman and L.M. Finsten
    1993   *Ancient Mesoamerica. A Comparison of Change in Three Regions.* 2nd ed. Cambridge: Cambridge University Press.
Branigan, K.
    1968   *Copper and Bronze Working in Early Bronze Age Crete* (SIMA 19). Lund: P. Åström.
    1970   *The Foundations of Palatial Crete. A Survey of Crete in the Early Bronze Age.* London: Routledge and Kegan Paul.
    1984   Early Minoan society: the evidence of the Mesara tholoi reviewed. In C. Nicolet (ed.), *Aux origines de l'Hellénisme: la Crète et la Grèce. Hommage à Henri van Effenterre*: 29–37. Paris: Centre Gustav Glotz.

1993   *Dances with Death. Life and Death in Southern Crete, c. 3000–2000 B.C.* Amsterdam: Hakkert.

Brumfiel, E.M.
1995   Heterarchy and the analysis of complex societies: comments. In R.M. Ehrenreich, C.L. Crumley and J.E. Levy, *Heterarchy and the Analysis of Complex Societies*: 125–31. Arlington: American Anthropological Association.

Buchanan, M.
2002   *Small World: Uncovering Nature's Hidden Networks.* London: Weidenfeld and Nicolson.

Capra, F.
1996   *The Web of Life: A New Scientific Understanding of Living Systems.* New York: Doubleday.

Catling, H.
1988   Archaeology in Greece. *Archaeological Reports* 1987–88.

Cherry, J.F.
1983   Evolution, revolution and the origins of complex society in Minoan Crete. In O. Krzyszkowska and L. Nixon (eds.), *Minoan Society*: 33–45. Bristol: Bristol Classical Press.
1986   Polities and palaces: some problems in Minoan state formation. In C. Renfrew and J.F. Cherry (eds.), *Peer Polity Interaction and Socio-Political Change*: 19–45. Cambridge: Cambridge University Press.

Crumley, C.L.
1987   A dialectical critique of hierarchy. In T.C. Patterson and C.W. Gailey (eds.), *Power Relations and State Formation*: 155–69. Washington DC: American Anthropological Association.
1995   Heterarchy and the analysis of complex societies. In R.M. Ehrenreich, C.L. Crumley and J.E. Levy, *Heterarchy and the Analysis of Complex Societies*: 1–5. Arlington: American Anthropological Association.

Day, P.M. and D.E. Wilson
1998   Consuming power: Kamares ware in Protopalatial Knossos. *Antiquity* 72: 350–58.
2002   Landscapes of memory, craft and power in Prepalatial and Protopalatial Knossos. In Y. Hamilakis (ed.), *Labyrinth Revisited: Rethinking Minoan Archaeology*: 143–66. Oxford: Oxbow Books.

Day, P.M., D.E. Wilson and E. Kiriatzi
1997   Reassessing specialization in Prepalatial ceramic production. In R. Laffineur and P.P. Betancourt (eds.), *TEXNH: Craftsmen, Craftswomen and Craftsmanship in the Aegean Bronze Age* (Aegaeum 16): 275–89. Liège: Université de Liège.

Doran, J.E.
2000   Trajectories to complexity in artificial societies: rationality, belief and emotions. In T.A. Kohler and G.J. Gumerman (eds.), *Dynamics in Human and Primate Societies: Agent-Based Modeling of Social and Spatial Processes*: 89–105. Oxford: Oxford University Press.

Eigen, M.
1971   Self-organization of matter and the evolution of biological macro-molecules. *Naturwissenschaften* 58: 465–523.

Epstein, J.M. and R. Axtell
1996   *Growing Artificial Societies: Social Science from the Bottom Up.* Cambridge, MA: MIT Press.

Flannery, K.V.
1972   The cultural evolution of civilizations. *Annual Review of Ecology and Systematics* 3: 399–426.

Gordon, D.
   1999   *Ants at Work: How an Insect Society is Organised.* New York: Free Press.
Haggis, D.C.
   1999   Staple finance, peak sanctuaries, and economic complexity in late prepalatial Crete.
           In A. Chaniotis (ed.), *From Minoan Farmers to Roman Traders. Sidelights on the Economy
           of Ancient Crete*: 17–23. Stuttgart: Franz Steiner.
   2002   Integration and complexity in the late Prepalatial period: a view from the countryside
           in eastern Crete. In Y. Hamilakis (ed.), *Labyrinth Revisited: Rethinking Minoan
           Archaeology*: 120–42. Oxford: Oxbow Books.
Hallager, E.
   2000   New evidence for seal use in the Pre-and Protopalatial periods. In I. Pini (ed.),
           Minoisch-Mykenische Glyptik, Stil, Ikonographie, Funktion (Corpus der Minoischen und
           Mykenischen Siegel 6): 97–105. Berlin: Mann.
Holland, J.H.
   1998   *Emergence: from Chaos to Order.* Oxford: Oxford University Press.
Hölldobler, B. and E.O. Wilson
   1994   *Journey to the Ants: a Story of Scientific Exploration.* Cambridge, MA: Harvard University
           Press.
Jacobs, J.
   1961   *The Death and Life of Great American Cities.* New York: Vintage Books.
Johnson, S.
   2001   *Emergence: The Connected Lives of Ants, Brains, Cities and Software.* London: Penguin.
Keswani, P.S.
   1996   Hierarchies, heterarchies, and urbanisation processes; the view from Bronze Age
           Cyprus. *OJA* 9: 211–50.
Kiriatzi, E., P.M. Day and D.E. Wilson
   2000   Diakinisi tis keramikis kai koinonopolitiki organosi: i grapti keramiki tis PMII kai I
           periodou stin anatoliki Kriti. In *Proceedings of the Eighth International Cretological
           Congress*: 99–115. Heraklion: Historical Society of Crete.
Knappett, C.
   1999a   Assessing a polity in Protopalatial Crete: the Malia-Lasithi state. *AJA* 103: 619–45.
   1999b   Tradition and innovation in pottery forming technology: wheel-throwing at Middle
           Minoan Knossos. *BSA* 94: 91–119.
La Rosa, V.
   2002   Révision préliminaire du second palais de Phaistos. In J. Driessen, I. Schoep and R.
           Laffineur (eds.), *Monuments of Minos: Rethinking the Minoan Palaces* (Aegaeum 23): 71–
           96. Liège: Université de Liège.
Lehner, M.
   2000   Fractal house of Pharaoh: ancient Egypt as a complex adaptive system. In T.A. Kohler
           and G.J. Gumerman (eds.), *Dynamics in Human and Primate Societies: Agent-Based
           Modeling of Social and Spatial Processes*: 275–353. Oxford: Oxford University Press.
Macdonald, C.F. and C.J. Knappett
forthcoming *Knossos: MM IB and MM IIA Pottery from the South-West Area.* London: British
           School at Athens.
MacGillivray, J.A.
   1988   *Knossos: Pottery Groups of the Old Palace Period* (BSA Studies 5). London: British School
           at Athens.
Maggidis, C.
   1998   From polis to necropolis: social ranking from architectural and mortuary evidence in

the Minoan cemetery at Phourni, Archanes. In K. Branigan (ed.), *Cemetery and Society in the Aegean Bronze Age* (SSAA 1): 87–102. Sheffield: Sheffield Academic Press.

Maruyama, M.
   1963   The second cybernetics: deviation amplifying mutual causal processes. *American Scientist* 51: 164.

McGlade, J. and S.E. van der Leeuw
   1997   Introduction: archaeology and non-linear dynamics – new approaches to long-term change. In S.E. van der Leeuw and J. McGlade (eds.), *Time, Process and Structured Transformation in Archaeology*: 1–31. London: Routledge.

Momigliano, N.
   1991   MM IA pottery from Evans' excavations at Knossos: a reassessment. *BSA* 86: 149–269.

Müller, S.
   1991   Prospection de la plaine de Malia. *BCH* 115: 741–49.

Newell, A. and H. Simon
   1956   The logic theory machine. *IRE Transactions on Information Theory* 3: 61–79.

Olivier, J.-P.
   1989   Les écritures Crétoises. In R. Treuil, P. Darcque, J.-C. Poursat and G. Touchais, *Les civilisations Égéennes du néolithique et de l'âge du bronze*: 237–52. Paris: Presses Universitaires de France.

Pelon, O.
   1980   *Le Palais de Malia, V* (Études Crétoises 25). Paris: Geuthner.
   1992   *Guide de Malia. Le palais et la nécropole de Chrysolakkos*. Paris: Boccard.
   1993   La salle à piliers de Malia (II). *BCH* 117: 523–46.

Perna, M.
   1999   Il sistema amministrativo minoico nella Creta prepalaziale. In V. La Rosa, D. Palermo and L. Vagnetti (eds.), *Epi Ponton Plazomenoi. Simposio Italiano di Studi Egei*: 63–68. Rome: Italian Archaeological School Athens.

Petit, Th.
   1987   Les tombes circulaires de la Messara: problèmes d'interprétation des pièces annexes. In R. Laffineur (ed.), *Thanatos: les coûtumes funéraires en Égée à l'âge du bronze* (Aegaeum 1): 35–42. Liège: Université de Liège.

Pickering, A.
   2002   Cybernetics and the mangle: Ashby, Beer and Pask. *Social Studies of Science* 32(3): 413–37.

Pini, I.
   1990   Eine frühkretische Siegelwerkstatt? In *Proceedings of the 6th International Cretological Congress*: 115–23.

Potter, D.R. and E.M. King
   1995   A heterarchical approach to Lowland Maya socioeconomies. In R.M. Ehrenreich, C.L. Crumley and J.E. Levy (eds.), *Heterarchy and the Analysis of Complex Societies*: 17–32. Arlington: American Anthropological Association.

Poursat, J-C.
   1988   La ville minoenne de Malia: recherches et publications récentes. *Revue Archéologique*: 61–82.
   1996   *Artisans Minoens: les maisons-ateliers du Quartier Mu. Fouilles executées à Malia: le Quartier Mu III* (Études Crétoises 32). Paris : École Française d'Athènes.

Prigogine, I. and I. Stengers
   1984   *Order out of Chaos: Man's New Dialogue with Nature*. New York: Bantam.

Renfrew, C.

1972   *The Emergence of Civilisation: the Cyclades and the Aegean in the Third Millennium BC.* London: Methuen.

Rothman, M.S.
1994   Evolutionary typologies and cultural complexity. In G. Stein and M.S. Rothman (eds.), *Chiefdoms and Early States in the Near East: the Organizational Dynamics of Complexity* (Monographs in World Archaeology 18): 1–10. Madison: Prehistory Press.

Sbonias, K.
1999   Social development, management of production, and symbolic representation in Prepalatial Crete. In A. Chaniotis (ed.), *From Minoan Farmers to Roman Traders. Sidelights on the Economy of Ancient Crete*: 25–51. Stuttgart: Franz Steiner.
2000   Specialisation in the Early Minoan seal manufacture. In I. Pini (ed.), *Minoisch-Mykenische Glyptik, Stil, Ikonographie, Funktion* (Corpus der Minoischen und Mykenischen Siegel 6): 277–93. Berlin: Mann.

Schoep, I.
1999   The origins of writing and administration on Crete. *OJA* 18: 265–76.
2001   Some notes on the 'Hieroglyphic' Deposit from Knossos. *SMEA* 43, 1: 143–58.
2002   Social and political organisation on Crete in the Proto-palatial period: the case of Middle Minoan II Malia. *JMA* 15: 101–32.
forthcoming The socio-economic and political context of seal-use at Knossos. In G. Cadogan and E. Hatzaki (eds.), *Knossos: Palace, City, State*. London: British School at Athens.

Soles, J.S.
1988 Social ranking in Prepalatial cemeteries. In E. French and K. Wardle (eds.), *Problems in Greek Prehistory*: 49–62. Bristol: Bristol Classical Press.
1992   *The Prepalatial Cemeteries at Mochlos and Gournia and the House Tombs of Bronze Age Crete* (Hesperia Supplement 24). Princeton, N.J.: American School of Classical Studies at Athens.

Soles, J.S. and C. Davaras
1992   Excavations at Mochlos. *Hesperia* 61: 413–45.
1996   Excavations at Mochlos. *Hesperia* 65: 178–80.

Stein, G.J.
1998   Heterogeneity, power, and political economy: some current research issues in the archaeology of Old World complex societies. *Journal of Archaeological Research* 6: 1–44.

Tsipopoulou, M.
1999   Before, during, after: the architectural phases of the palatial building at Petras, Siteia. In P.P. Betancourt, V. Karageorghis, R. Laffineur and W.-D. Niemeier (eds.), *Meletemata: Studies in Aegean Archaeology Presented to Malcolm H. Wiener as he Enters his 65th Year* (Aegaeum 20): 847–56. Liège: Université de Liège.

Vlasaki, M. and E. Hallager
1995   Evidence for seal-use in Prepalatial western Crete. In J.-C. Poursat and W. Müller (eds.), *Sceaux Minoens et Mycéniens: chronologie, fonction et interprétation* (Corpus der Minoischen und Mykenischen Siegel 5): 251–70. Berlin: Mann.

Warren, P.M.
1969   *Minoan Stone Vases*. Cambridge: Cambridge Classical Studies.
1972   *Myrtos. An Early Bronze Age Settlement in Crete*. London: British School at Athens.

Watrous, V.L.
2001   Crete from earliest prehistory through the Protopalatial period. In T. Cullen (ed.), *Aegean Prehistory: a Review*: 157–216. Boston: Archaeological Institute of America.

Weingarten, J.

1990   Three upheavals in Minoan sealing administration. In T. Palaima (ed.), *Aegean Seals and Sealings* (Aegaeum 5): 105–20. Liège: Université de Liège.

1994   Sealings and sealed documents at Bronze Age Knossos. In D. Evely, H. Hughes-Brock and N. Momigliano (eds.), *Knossos, a Labyrinth of History. Papers Presented in Honour of Sinclair Hood*: 171–88. Oxford: Oxbow Books.

Whitelaw, T.M., P.M. Day, E. Kiriatzi, V. Kilikoglou and D.E. Wilson

1997   Ceramic traditions at EM IIB Myrtos Fournou Korifi. In R. Laffineur and P.P. Betancourt (eds.), *TEXNH: Craftsmen, Craftswomen and Craftsmanship in the Aegean Bronze Age* (Aegaeum 16): 265–74. Liège: Université de Liège.

Wilson, D.E.

1994   Knossos before the palaces: an overview of the Early Bronze Age (EM I-EM III). In D. Evely, H. Hughes-Brock and N. Momigliano (eds.), *Knossos, a Labyrinth of History. Papers Presented in Honour of Sinclair Hood*: 23–44. Oxford: Oxbow Books.

Wilson, D.E. and P.M. Day

1994   Ceramic regionalism in Prepalatial central Crete: the Mesara imports at EM I to EM IIA Knossos. *BSA* 89: 1–87.

1999   EM IIB ware groups at Knossos: the 1907–08 South Front tests. *BSA* 94: 1–62.

2000   EM I chronology and social practice: pottery from the early palace tests at Knossos. *BSA* 95: 21–63.

Zagarell, A.

1995   Hierarchy and heterarchy: the unity of opposites. In R.M. Ehrenreich, C.L. Crumley and J.E. Levy (eds.), *Heterarchy and the Analysis of Complex Societies*. Arlington: American Anthropological Association: 87–100.

3

Filling in the 'Neolithic Background': Social Life and Social Transformation in the Aegean before the Bronze Age

Peter Tomkins

All stories must begin somewhere and for Colin Renfrew's great narrative of the *Emergence of Civilisation in the Aegean*, that point begins chronologically with the Neolithic and intellectually with the work of V. Gordon Childe. In *Emergence* an essentially Childean view of simple earlier Neolithic village life is contrasted with complex Bronze Age urban living in order to sharpen our awareness of 'civilization' and to underline its long history of development. Thus while civilization is 'the complex artificial environment' that 'insulates' us from nature, the earlier Neolithic emerges as a period when people were closely bound up with nature and the quest for subsistence self-sufficiency with, apart from obsidian, little sign of interest or need for exchange (Renfrew 1972: xxvi, 3–8, 13, 52, 365–66). Renfrew hints at the possibility of socio-economic development during the later Neolithic and argues for an increasing diversification in the subsistence economy and an increase in exchange between groups with access to different resources (Renfrew 1972: 49, 52, 274–80; Halstead 1981a: 320–27; 1994: 200–02). Unfortunately, 'dim comprehension' of this period restricted further exploration of these ideas and in this respect the later Neolithic constitutes perhaps the most significant gap in Renfrew's otherwise all-encompassing study of growth in socio-economic complexity. The Neolithic thus ends very much as it began as 'the home of rather isolated communities without the effective use of metal and without evidence for a developed economic or social structure' (Renfrew 1972: 52–53).

This picture of the Neolithic serves as a useful point of departure for a consideration of the ways in which our understanding of the Neolithic has developed over the last three decades. What was the intellectual legacy of *Emergence* for Neolithic studies? How have other approaches deepened our understanding and what prospects are there for further insight? Undoubtedly, since *Emergence*, great progress has been made, but the broad questions remain the same. How did early Neolithic societies constitute themselves? How might this have changed during the later Neolithic and how might any such changes relate to subsequent developments in social complexity? These questions will be re-addressed and current concepts and frameworks critically assessed in the light of published data drawn from various regions of the Aegean, together with new results from a doctoral research project that studied ceramic production, circulation and consumption at EN-LNII Knossos through a combination of macroscopic and microscopic analytical techniques (petrology; Scanning Electron Microscopy) (Tomkins 2001).

Paradigm Shifts in the Understanding of Aegean Neolithic Communities

The Childean view of Neolithic societies, as isolated, self-sufficient entities, lacking social stratification and craft specialization and preoccupied with the production of their own subsistence (e.g., Childe 1981: 78–79) hugely influenced the standard view of three and even two decades ago (e.g., Weinberg 1970: 587; Renfrew 1972; Cherry 1983: 33). The one aspect of this view understandably not taken up by *Emergence* is the use of diffusion as an explanatory mechanism for cultural change. In this respect an indirect legacy of *Emergence* has been the development of developmental models that *avoid* diffusion as an explanatory mechanism. Models of demic diffusion for the initial Neolithization of Greece and the Aegean or the later development of ceramic technology (e.g., Weinberg 1965: 286–87; 1970: 571–72, 585) have subsequently been joined by models stressing independent local development (e.g., Broodbank 1992: 49; Vitelli 1993: xx, 39; 1995: 60–61) or a mixture of diffusion and adoption (Whittle 1996: 39–44; Halstead 1996: 299–301; Tomkins 2001: 23). Unfortunately, *Emergence*'s emphasis on indigenous processes has also, albeit unintentionally, reinforced a Childean minimalist view of exchange and diffusion in the spread of ideas, innovations and individuals between different regions of the Neolithic Aegean.

One major problem with the Neolithic of Childe and *Emergence* is that society is understood not so much in its own terms but in terms of its relationship to complex societies of the Bronze Age. Features of Neolithic society are defined *in opposition* to what were considered hall-marks of 'civilization' (e.g., social stratification, craft specialization; Renfrew 1972: 4, 7, 340) and thus the Neolithic itself remains characterized negatively in terms of what it lacked rather than positively in terms of what it comprised (see Table 3.1). This sort of top-down, polythetic approach to social organization assumes that it *is* possible and useful to make generalizations about a particular type of organization and moreover that that type is identifiable through the presence or absence of defined traits. However, by looking for particular common features within the material record, rather than approaching the data in terms of what it can tell us (bottom-up), diversity and complexity are reduced to a limited number of stereotypes and the role of individuals and groups is minimized (see Barrett 1994: 2–5, 157–64). Short

Table 3.1. Defining the Neolithic in opposition to the Bronze Age

Neolithic Society	Bronze Age Society
Simple	Complex
Domestic production	Craft specialization
Village	City
Rural	Urban
Self-sufficient	Re-distributive
Isolated	Integrated
Conservative	Dynamic
Close to nature	Insulated from nature

of identifying social organization as egalitarian, this approach allows little insight into the dynamics of pre-state societies, where inequalities in social relationships are usually less obviously represented in the archaeological record.

One answer to this impasse has been to use well-developed anthropological concepts (e.g., household) as a framework within which to situate the Neolithic data. In this way ethnographic/anthropological analogy provides an indication of some of the potential constraints and possibilities of life in a Neolithic community (Barrett and Fewster 1998). This approach, exemplified by Halstead's application of Sahlins' Domestic Mode of Production (DMP) model to early agriculture (Halstead 1981a; 1989; 1995; 1996; 1999), has revealed the basic inviability of the individual household. Households, if truly isolated, risk extinction due to their own varying productivity, itself a function of fluctuations in available labour and/or environmental failure (see Sahlins 1974: 41–99 for more detailed discussion). Halstead (1989: 70–71; 1996: 301–03) has shown that such a model could explain the nature of early agriculture, which involved labour-intensive year-round cultivation of small plots of land and an underproductive exploitation of domesticated animals. In order to offset their inviability, individual households must have relied on periodic, external assistance that was ensured by the cultivation of social relationships beyond the household, which probably took the form of networks of exchanges, alliances and obligations that included food and probably exotic materials, such as obsidian or ceramic vessels (Halstead 1989: 73–75; 1996: 304–05; 1999: 89; Renfrew 1972: 365–66). Significantly, this necessitates a subtle, but important shift in emphasis: despite the relatively small quantities of goods in circulation, exchange was not the epiphenomenon predicted by Childe, but was likely to have been a key factor ensuring the long-term survival of such communities. This paradigm shift can be most clearly seen in more recent discussions of the Neolithic economy, which emphasize the importance of exchange (e.g., van Andel and Runnels 1988: 234–38; Perlès 1992: 149; Demoule and Perlès 1993: 382, 384; Andreou *et al.* 1996: 559; Gallis 1996: 34).

This approach illustrates more generally how the detailed characterization of acts of production, when situated within ethnographically-informed interpretational frameworks, allows insight into Neolithic social reproduction. In the last two decades, other technological studies have appeared (e.g., Perlès 1992; Vitelli 1993; Perlès and Vitelli 1999). However, these studies have generally not engaged in great detail with the ideas introduced by Halstead nor in some cases have they fully escaped from Childean notions of Neolithic isolation and self-sufficiency (e.g., Vitelli 1993: 207–10). Arguably more should be done to question how well our borrowed anthropological concepts (e.g. household) and models (e.g., DMP) fit the data and whether other models are possible or preferable. In addition while the sophistication of our studies and analyses of material artefacts has increased, our theoretical frameworks have not kept equal pace. Several material culture studies, all concerned in some way with the relationship between material culture and society, have independently argued that the interactive nature of this relationship can be best understood within a framework derived from Bourdieu's theory of practice (Miller 1985: 11–12; Dobres and Hoffman 1994: 214; Dietler and Herbich 1998: 244–48; see Bourdieu 1977). Practice theory is particularly useful in a Neolithic context because it offers a means of viewing continuity and change as occurring through the actions of individuals and groups and thus provides a more sensitive and appropriate framework for understanding change in small-scale Neolithic societies than culture history or systems theory. Some of this potential has been demonstrated by recent work on the British Neolithic (e.g., Thomas 1990; Barrett 1994; Edmonds 1999), which has broken beneath the egalitarian surface of Neolithic society to reveal conflicts of interest, competition and inequality in human social relations.[1] Similar arguments have been advanced for Aegean Neolithic society (Kotsakis 1983: esp. 213–14, 264–300; 1999; Halstead 1993).

Reconfiguring the Household in the Study of Neolithic Social Organization

The DMP model, as originally formulated, was only ever intended as a generalized outline of the internal dynamics of such societies (Sahlins 1974: 74–78). Different ethnographic cases demonstrate that production often requires different degrees of cooperation resulting in it being organized 'in diverse social forms and sometimes at levels higher than the household' (Sahlins 1974: 78). However, despite this intended fluidity, application of the DMP model to the Aegean Neolithic has been more rigid: social and production organization have been conceived largely or entirely in terms of the household, with little attention paid to the possible existence of other forms of organization (e.g., Halstead 1994: 206–07; 1999; Vitelli 1993).

The reason for this focus on the household goes back to a basic assumption that the physical architectural space of the house always delimits it as the primary social and economic unit. This assumption is central to the widely-held view that earlier Neolithic communities, architecturally divided into household groups as even the earliest Old and New World farming settlements appear to have been, reflect the complete and immediate replacement of the sorts of communal social structures, associated with hunter-gatherer groups, by household units that enjoy a significant degree of social and economic independence (Flannery 1972; Halstead 1995: 12–13, 16–17; 1999). However, while the size and organization of Neolithic houses favours an individual family as the occupying group (Renfrew 1972: 365; Halstead 1999: 79–81), this does not automatically mean that such a group formed a primary and independent unit of socio-economic organization. Moreover, there are certain indications that during the earlier Neolithic (EN-MN) such units may not have acted wholly independently, but rather were largely submerged within larger social groupings.

The Submerged Household (EN-MN)

These indications are provided by a consideration of general changes in the organization of storage, space and production together with more specific changes in the production, exchange and consumption of ceramic vessels at EN-LNII Knossos. In the following discussion the chronological phases used are always those for the Greek mainland (e.g., Gallis 1996: 30).[2] More detailed discussions of research methodology and interpretation have been presented elsewhere (Tomkins and Day 2001; Tomkins *et al.* forthcoming).

Storage

Studies of Neolithic agriculture consistently assume that even the earliest Neolithic households enjoyed economic independence in the form of direct storage and thus direct ownership of normal agricultural surplus (see Halstead 1989: 71; 1994: 206; 1996: 304–05). This view is not without its problems. Firstly, it assumes that producers *necessarily* had a 'natural' right to their own produce. However, this view of the connection between production and property is not culturally universal but rather a core assumption of Western philosophy: for example, in Melanesia products are understood as having a natural relation not to their producer but to their intended exchange destination (Strathern 1988; Thomas 1991: 16).

A more serious problem concerns the evidence for independent, bulk storage of subsistence within individual household structures, which is 'sparse' and generally LN or later (see below; Halstead 1999: 82; Demoule and Perlès 1993: 362). However, the key issue is not whether storage was taking place within EN-MN households – households could not have functioned otherwise – but rather whether households individually stored all that they required for the year, including their normal surplus, and thus enjoyed economic independence.

Unfortunately, the certain use of non-ceramic containers, such as the clay or dung-lined baskets which may have been used at Tsangli (Halstead 1989: 71), means that this question can never be conclusively answered. But what does seem clear is that storage at the scale required to provision a single household for a year could *not* have taken place using ceramic containers: two independent studies of EN-MN ceramic vessels have both concluded that during this period vessels were neither large enough nor numerous enough to have been able to store all that a household would have required in a year (Vitelli 1989: 26–27; Yiouni 1996: 191–92); and this conclusion also holds true for EN-MN Knossos (Tomkins 2001: 250–66). That is not to say that EN-MN households did not store some produce in ceramic vessels, rather what appears to be absent or at least currently unsupported by the data is independent bulk storage of a household's annual subsistence requirements.

If individual EN-MN family groups did not store all that they required for the year, this not only undermines much of their supposed economic independence, but also raises the possibility that agricultural surplus was pooled and its storage organized at a higher, perhaps communal level. Evidence for such a communal form of storage remains sparse, but edge-of-site activity areas have in general been poorly tested by excavation. A possible example of communal storage might be the large cache of carbonized grain at Aceramic Knossos (stratum X; Evans 1964: 140–42) found in close association with a burnt timber structure, located just outside the settlement and thus beyond the spatial realm of any single household.

Spatial Organization

During the EN-MN period in Thessaly houses often crowd together with cooking facilities located both in and between different houses (Halstead 1995: 16–19; Andreou *et al.* 1996: 559). At Knossos during this period, houses are characterized by irregular and insubstantial walls, usually exhibiting several phases of use; private space is not always clearly marked, but rather inside space flows into outside space and different structures may crowd together (see Figure 3.1). All houses have small ash-pits cut into their occupation floors and there is also an MN example of what might be a larger cooking installation located in an open cobbled area to the north of house C (stratum VII) (see Figure 3.1; Evans 1964: 153). This and other examples suggest a distinction between small-scale, private (household) preparation and consumption and larger-scale, public preparation and consumption. Possibly private consumption of food was the regular practice with more communal consumption perhaps restricted spatially to areas adjacent to different households and temporally to specific occasions.

This sort of pattern has been interpreted as indicating the communal sharing of food, at least on certain occasions, as a mechanism to overcome household isolation (Halstead 1995: 16–17; 1996: 305). Although highly plausible, in focusing

Early Neolithic
(Area AC, Stratum IX)

Early Neolithic
(Area AC, Stratum VIII)

MiddleNeolithic
(Area AC, Stratum VII)

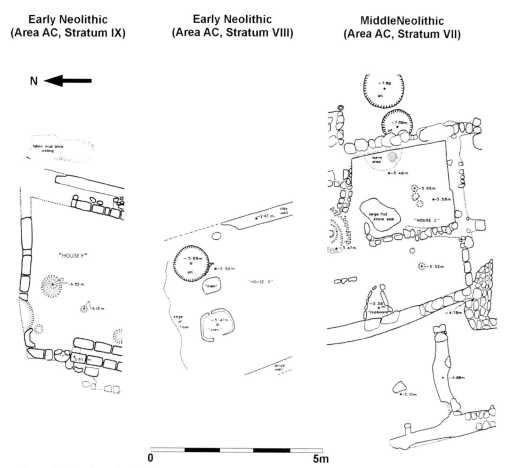

Figure 3.1. Early and Middle Neolithic house architecture at Knossos (after Evans 1964: figs. 9–11)

on household isolation as the main factor, this explanation may place too much emphasis on overcoming a theoretical situation of isolation and economic self-interest, as predicted by the general DMP model, rather than a real situation of household isolation. Households may to an extent have constituted themselves privately, as architectural units and internal food preparation installations suggest. If their economic independence was communally curtailed or controlled by social restrictions on storage, property and ownership, however, then this organization of space might be better seen to reflect the greater strength at this time of powerful, structuring ideals of communality.

Other spatial indications of an early emphasis on communality are less clear. One possible example of a communal building – what Renfrew has called a 'tribal meeting house' (1972: 365) – might be the unusually large, non-domestic[3] structure in a central location at EN Nea Nikomedeia (Rodden 1964: 114; Demoule and

Perlès 1993: 386). Similar non-domestic[4] buildings occur near the centre of early Neolithic villages in the Near East and have been interpreted as regulatory mechanisms for the *integration* of the community as whole (Byrd 1994: 639–61).

Ceramic Technology and Production at EN–MN Knossos (Strata IX–VI)

It has been argued that EN–MN ceramic production at Franchthi was restricted and specialized (Vitelli 1993: 216–17; 1995; Perlès and Vitelli 1999: 98, 102). Although this identification of early ceramic specialization has achieved a wide acceptance (e.g., Demoule and Perlès 1993: 377–82; Kalogirou 1997: 12–13), more recently its validity has been challenged (Perlès and Vitelli 1999: 101). In addition, its methodology for identification is generally open to dispute (Whitelaw *et al.* 1997: 266; Costin 1991) and there are also issues of data interpretation, such as provenance, that make its specific reading of technological variation difficult to support (Tomkins forthcoming). Further discussion of the important and complex issue of specialization remains beyond the scope of the current paper; nor is it possible to enter into a detailed discussion of ceramic production organization at Knossos. Instead the following section will merely summarize the main features of EN–MN ceramic production.

Detailed petrographic study combined with macroscopic observation of form, finish and fabric have allowed the products of a number of producing groups to be identified. The sources of these products vary from those that are local (<5–7km) to Knossos, those that are non-local but within Crete (e.g., a granodiorite fabric with a provenance in the Mirabello Bay, East Crete) and more rarely those that are likely to have a source beyond the island (see Tomkins *et al.* forthcoming). The EN–MN assemblage at Knossos thus testifies to the exploitation of a wide variety of raw materials by a variety of groups probably located in different settlements.

In general, local ceramic production during this period may be characterized as under-productive (small-scale, inefficient, labour-intensive). As at EN–MN Franchthi (Vitelli 1993: 210), the level of ceramic consumption at Knossos appears to be extremely low, suggesting that production was small-scale with a low output and low intensity (part-time or seasonal). Functional efficiency was not a factor in paste preparation: there is no evidence to suggest that the form, size, finish or function of a vessel influenced the choice or combination of raw materials; rather a full range of forms and finishes is found in each fabric. Likewise, although each producing group makes a range of similar forms, this does not represent any sort of gain in efficiency via standardization, since the forming and finishing procedure for each vessel, especially fine polished vessels, was extremely time-consuming. Production is thus very inefficient because it produces small quantities in a labour-intensive production sequence.

This situation may be directly contrasted with Early Minoan I-II ceramic production where choice of raw materials *is* made according to the form, size and decorative technique of the vessel to be produced (Wilson and Day 1999: 38; 2000: 57; Whitelaw *et al.* 1997). Here independent specialist producers seem to have consciously differentiated themselves by the adoption of complicated techniques of production and by the visual differentiation of their products through the use of distinctive forms and finishes. In contrast, during EN-MN the products of different spatially discrete producing groups (e.g., Knossos, Central Crete and Mirabello Bay, East Crete; Tomkins and Day 2001; Tomkins *et al.* forthcoming: plates 2g–h) frequently have such similar forms and finishes as to be visually indistinguishable.

The shared characteristics of different producing groups extend also to technology. Although individual fabrics vary in the choice and combination of their raw material components, the type of fabric produced (coarse-tempered) is always the same; likewise different producing groups appear to have formed certain shapes and attached handles in broadly the same way. Experimental replication work suggests that fabric recipes, forming techniques and forming sequences were relatively simple to operationalize. In this way EN-MN ceramic production could not be described as a closed technology of exclusion, but rather an open or shared one of incorporation. Production at this sort of scale, intensity and efficiency fails to satisfy conventional definitions of specialization, including ethnographic examples of household specialization (e.g., Costin 1991: 8; Arnold 1991).

One way of gaining insight into the nature of this non-specialized production is to consider the great time depth involved. One of its most striking features is the consistency with which a single way of producing (e.g., raw material selection and combination; forming and finishing techniques) is reproduced during EN-MN (or c.1000–1200 years). This stability and continuity indicates that there was an effective mechanism that ensured the transfer of the knowledge and techniques of ceramic production to the next generation. In view of the long-term inviability of individual households (Sahlins 1974: 4; Halstead 1999: 89), the generally small size of the Knossos community, especially during the EN period (ca 0.3 ha, Tomkins 2001: 529–36) and the small-scale, part-time nature of EN-MN ceramic production, this mechanism could only be the community or a large group within it. In this way EN-MN ceramic production may be best understood as a communal activity, where potters were assisted by other individuals, who participated in those parts of the production sequence that lent themselves to group activity (e.g., procuring and processing clay, decorating finished vessels, collecting fuel) (Childe 1981: 87–88; Wright 1991: 198–99; Miller 1985: 77, 110; Barley 1994: 61–66). A similar picture of collective production is provided by Miller's study of shell bead manufacture at Franchthi (Miller 1996). Detailed re-analysis demonstrated that during EN it required an enormous labour investment to produce a single necklace, implying that EN production of bead necklaces was 'a collective undertaking by some portion of the Franchthi community' (Perlès and Vitelli 1999: 104–05).

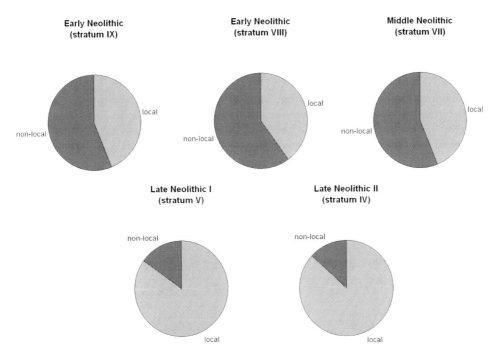

Figure 3.2. The changing proportion of local and non-local ceramics at Knossos (Trench C, Area AC)

Stability of knowledge and absence of innovation may also be understood in a more active sense. Previously, this ceramic stability has been glossed as a 'conservative' feature (e.g., Evans 1971: 114; Manteli 1996: 132). If one seeks to reconstruct past behaviour as arising from the deliberate actions of knowledgeable actors, however, then the successive recreation of the same vessel types using the same series of techniques over many centuries might be re-cast as a *deliberate* and *dynamic* attempt to maintain continuity between the past and the present (Bourdieu 1977; van der Leeuw and Torrence 1989). Collective acts of ceramic production may have *deliberately* chosen to emphasize continuity between past and present, within an essentially cyclical notion of time. By recreating past material actions and categories, producers effectively situated themselves in a timeless state between past, present and future, where the community of the present joins communities of the past. Such communal acts reinforce group cohesion and promote a particular authorized view of group identity, solidarity and cosmology, which in being reproduced publicly is likely to have been considered *doxic* or beyond dispute (Bourdieu 1977: 159–171). Within such a public context, opportunities for innovation were probably restricted and possibly actively discouraged. It was therefore the practical reproduction of this knowledge at a communal level, through shared acts of production that provided the stable mechanism for its continued maintenance.

The Exchange and Consumption of Ceramic Vessels at EN-MN Knossos (strata IX–VI)

During EN-MN, approximately half of all ceramic vessels at Knossos are non-local products (see Figure 3.2). While a very large proportion of these are broadly compatible with sources within a 7–30 km radius of Knossos, there are also vessels, comprising approximately 10% of the assemblage, which in mineralogy, form or finish seem to have either a distant source in Crete, such as the Mirabello fabric (ca 70 km) (Tomkins and Day 2001) or an even more distant origin in regions beyond the island (Tomkins *et al.* forthcoming). This evidence for long-distance acquisition indicates that ceramic vessels could potentially circulate over very long distances (*contra* Perlès 1992). Leaving aside the specific mechanisms that lie behind this circulation, it seems clear that there was a demand for objects from distant sources. The high degree of morphological and functional similarity/redundancy between local and non-local vessels suggests that the reasons for the acquisition of distant objects were qualitative and social, rather than out of economic necessity. It seems reasonable to argue that special value and special prestige accompanied objects whose source lay at a great distance. Comparative ethnographic, historical and archaeological study well illustrates the political and ideological symbolism associated with the procurement of valuable resources from distant or outside locales and their role in the negotiation of power, status and identity (Helms 1993: 210–17). In this respect it is worth noting that, in order to exploit this power, an object must be identifiably exotic. In most cases, however, non-local vessels are visually indistinguishable from local vessels and therefore this power can only have been made clear if the owner or consumer of the vessel narrated its vessel biography or told stories about its acquisition.

In this way the exchange and consumption of certain ceramic vessels may have taken place within what have been termed 'tournaments of value' (Appadurai 1986: 21ff.). Such 'tournaments of value' are not driven by economic necessity but rather by the desire to negotiate status and establish reputation. A likely context for such 'tournaments' is the more public occasions of commensality noted above. Thus it seems plausible to explain the demand for distant ceramic vessels at Knossos in terms of competition, albeit strictly limited, between different social groups within the community. By acquiring more powerful versions of local and presumably legitimate material categories, such groups could hi-jack existing registers of value without threatening the overall system of values by introducing new commodity forms. Thus the stability of the overall social system is maintained.

Summary: Community, Household and Social Competition (EN-MN)

To a large extent, the ways in which the production of ceramic vessels or shell beads was organized may be compared to agriculture, which similarly requires group co-operation at certain stages in the production process (e.g., sowing, threshing, weeding) (Wright 1991: 198–99). Although it has hitherto been the household that has been viewed as the principal productive unit in early agriculture, we should perhaps give more emphasis to those seasonal aspects of its production that necessitate cooperation. Similarly, while there is evidence for private preparation and consumption of food, there also appear to have been more public or communal occasions of commensality.

In this way, while people lived as households, the most significant moments in the year may have been those seasonal activities of production (craft, subsistence) and consumption (commensality) that brought households together as a community. In general within small-scale pre-modern societies, collective action of any sort (but especially feasts) contributes powerfully towards group cohesion and group stability (Bourdieu 1977: 167). And so through a regular rhythm of communal activities people constructed a particularly strong vision of their own shared origins, values and identity. Such collective acts provided opportunities to reproduce an idealized vision of equality and communality that reinforced the primacy of the community over any individual group within it.

Here one might think of such values of sharing and communality during the earlier Neolithic as *doxa* (Bourdieu 1977), that is as values, reproduced through practice, which appeared somehow natural and beyond dispute. In this way the striking social stability shown by EN-MN communities (Halstead 1989: 70; 1995: 14, 17; Perlès 1992: 121) – a stability which contrasts notably with modern household-based egalitarian societies where internecine strife is common (e.g., Halstead 1994: 207) – could be seen as relating to the success with which they reproduced communal ideals which effectively restricted the extent to which individual households could pursue their own self-interest. Support for the link between communality and stability is provided by modern ethnographic studies of households, which note that households that pool production and consumption tend to be stable and have generational continuity, while households that only cooperate in scheduling labour *or* in pooling consumption tend to be less stable and fragment often (Netting *et al.* 1984: 10).

However, consumption and exchange also operate at another level. It would appear that the deliberate acquisition and consumption of exotic vessels was fundamentally social in origin relating to the universal human desire to establish reputation and status. Leaders emerge in all types of community, the strategic pursuit of reputation being 'the overriding preoccupation of human life' through all periods of history and prehistory (Miller 1985: 184–85; Bourdieu 1977: 171). Halstead has suggested that, during the Neolithic, individual households competed with each other firstly to 'bank' their agricultural surplus and secondly to establish marriage alliances or exchange relationships with particularly successful households outside the immediate community (Halstead 1999: 90). However, if during EN-MN agricultural surplus was pooled and thus the exchange value of food reduced, then the opportunities and incentive for the first form of competition disappears and the second area of competition becomes more important. This may help to explain why it is during this period that status seems to have been derived from the possession of distant objects and, more importantly, the distant social relationships which those objects, as gifts, symbolized. Through their regular consumption, perhaps at more communal occasions of commensality, such objects provided the cue for the continued display of their owners' prowess through the narrating of object biographies and tales of travel and acquisition. In this way, even within an 'egalitarian' society, it is still possible to see different groups involved in a highly restricted form of competition for status.

The Emergence of a More Independent Household (LN)

During the LN period, a series of general changes in the organization of space, storage, production, exchange and consumption take place that suggest a major transformation in the ways in which Neolithic society was constituted.

Storage

On the Greek mainland the LN period in general sees an increased use of deep pits suitable for the long-term storage of agricultural surplus which has been taken to indicate an increase in the hoarding or storage capacity of households (Halstead 1989: 75–76; 1995: 17; 1996: 305–06; Renfrew 1972: 288). This same period also sees the first introduction of dedicated ceramic storage vessels (pithoi) at sites on the Greek mainland (Renfrew 1972: 276; Cullen and Keller 1990; Perlès 1992: 144). This suggests a diversification and intensification in the technologies by which individual households undertook the long-term storage of agricultural produce. The implications of this are profound because, if individual households are now storing agricultural produce in bulk, then this implies a new sense of ownership and property where households enjoyed greater control over what they produced and to what purposes it was put.

Spatial Organization

It has been observed for LN Thessaly that previously open villages become organized into courtyard groups, which would have hindered sharing between households and that, during FN-EBA, cooking facilities are now placed in internal extensions or in closed yards (Halstead 1995: 14–18; Hourmouziadis 1979). A similar phenomenon is also seen at Knossos, where during LNI-II (strata V–IV) the settlement approximately doubles in size to ca 2.5–3.0 ha (Evans 1971; Tomkins 2001: 529–36) and where in LNII (stratum IV) there is a qualitative change in house design and construction (see Figure 3.3). Houses now stand more apart

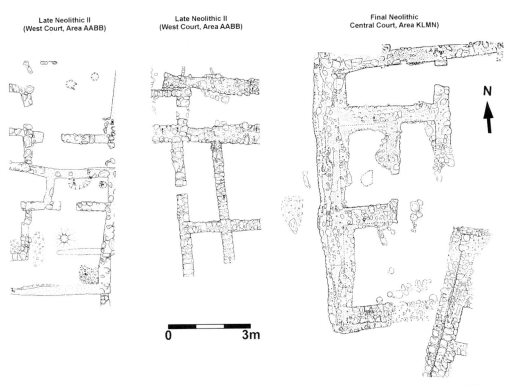

Figure 3.3. Late and Final Neolithic house architecture at Knossos (after Evans 1994: figs 5–6; 1971: fig. 7)

Figure 3.4. House model from a Late Neolithic II context at Knossos (Area AABB)

and are much more substantially constructed with thicker walls, clear inner and outer faces and more substantial foundations (Evans 1994: 11). There also seems to be a marked distinction between inside and outside space, emphasized by straight, well-built external walls, narrow entrances and a more complex internal arrangement of rooms. In addition, some of these structures are reported to have had small enclosed yards attached to them (Evans 1994: 14).

It is within the context of this new architectural isolation and elaboration of the house that one might understand the appearance for the first time at Knossos during LNII of what appear to be house models, always in local fabrics (see Figure 3.4). The timing of the appearance of these models at Knossos seems to suggest that the architectural isolation of the household also had an ideological dimension. In northern Greece house models appear as early as MN and continue into LN (Gallis 1985) and this suggests the possibility that there the ideological isolation of the household unit began earlier.

Ceramic Technology and Production at LNI-II Knossos (Strata V–IV)

During LNI-II at Knossos these quantitative and qualitative changes in space occur at the same time as a series of major changes in the technology of local ceramic production. In general there is a change in paste preparation from a coarse limestone-tempered fabric to one where the limestone is more finely crushed and more closely packed. In addition, new methods of handle attachment (plug-attached) and coil joining (pinched) are adopted that have been shown by experimental replication to improve considerably the success and strength of the join. There is a marked increase in the range of finishing methods used, with EN-MN finishes (burnished, polished, incised, plastic decoration) being joined by red scribble-burnished, brushed, dribble painted, ripple burnished and white slipped/burnished decoration. There is also a significant increase in the occurrence of incision and in the range of motifs rendered (Washburn 1983) and the more labour-intensive method of incised/pointillé decoration declines (Whitelaw 1992: 230). Finally, an increase in 'symmetry structures' means that incised designs can be reproduced across a vessel more quickly (Washburn 1983: 146 fig. 9.5; Broodbank 1992: 55). In general, these new techniques of finishing seem to represent more time- and labour-efficient ways of giving a vessel a distinctive finish.

There are also changes in the scale and intensity of local ceramic production. In LNI the estimated total quantity of ceramics in circulation goes through a significant (perhaps as much as ten-fold) increase and the proportion of local pottery present in any given assemblage increases to ca 85%. These striking increases in consumption imply a significant increase in the scale and intensity of local production and make it likely that it was no longer a part-time activity. An increase in intensity is suggested by the adoption of less labour-intensive finishing methods at this time and changes in paste preparation and forming could also be interpreted in terms of improvements in efficiency. Specialist producers are usually heavily influenced by profit or efficiency motives and depend for their existence on a wide demand for their products (Costin 1991: 11–12, 15–16). A rise in the number of consumers, an extension to the roles performed by ceramics, and increases in the scale, intensity and efficiency of ceramic production could certainly be seen in this way and it remains possible that ceramic production at this time took on a new restricted and perhaps specialized character (Tomkins 2001: 334–48).

A similar shift in the context of production from communal to private is also indicated by changes in the technology and organization of shell bead manufacture at LN Franchthi (Miller 1996). As with ceramic production at Knossos the technology changes from being highly labour-intensive in EN, with low output and requiring the collaborative effort of many, to being more efficient in labour and time in LN, with a far higher potential output and requiring the collaborative effort of a limited number of individuals, perhaps even a specialized household group (Perlès and Vitelli 1999: 104–05).

The Exchange and Consumption of Ceramic Vessels at LNI-II Knossos (Strata V–IV)

The LN period also sees a significant decrease in non-local ceramic vessels (from ca 50% to ca 15%; see Figure 3.2). At the same time ceramic vessels in general appear to have been used more frequently and in greater quantities. Furthermore, the development of new types of finish may signify the creation of new vessel categories and a widening in vessel function. These changes suggest that the role of ceramic vessels in consumption had changed, with less importance attached to qualities, such as distant origins, and more importance assigned to quantity and availability. In this same period, the enclosing of space adjacent to houses may indicate that the context of commensality altered to become more private.

Summary: Community, Household and Social Competition (LN)

It has been argued, largely for Thessaly, that the LN period saw an ideological shift amongst Neolithic households from sharing to hoarding (Halstead 1995). This ideological shift, however, seems to reflect more profound socio-economic changes. It would appear that individual households may for the first time have begun directly to control the bulk storage of agricultural produce and thus enjoyed greater freedom in how they managed their own subsistence. At the same time the architectural and ideological elaboration of the house, seen most clearly at LNII Knossos, seems to reflect an increased self-consciousness on the part of individual households and a desire to advertise their new economic and social power.

These changes seem to imply a restructuring of previously sacrosanct communal values and practices and this may help to explain why so many changes in local ceramic production occur during LN after such a long period of stability. If the context of production, whether of subsistence or craft, moved from the public or communal to the private or household, then the influence of com-munally-held values, particularly the sorts of social controls that promoted stability and restricted innovation during EN-MN, is likely to be weakened and thrown open to negotiation precisely because they were no longer being reproduced in a communal environment. A similar shift may have taken place in consumption, where the enclosing of space adjacent to households may reflect a desire to control not just the external space of production, but also the space of consumption. Thus this period may see an increase in occasions of commensality, where an individual household, rather than the community is the host. If com-mensality did shrink in scale from the communal to the private but multiplied in the locations and frequency with which it took place, then this may help to explain the increase seen in the variety of ceramic forms and the quantities of vessels consumed. An additional factor may have been the new self-consciousness of the household and more acquisitive strategies in the accumulation of material culture.

However, greater economic freedom also means that individual households were more exposed to risk (Halstead 1989). With the erosion of ideals of community and sharing, individual households became more responsible for the production of subsistence livelihood and less able to count on automatic support from the wider community. This not only made communities less stable, but also made the cultivation of relationships with other households within the same community even more important than hitherto. This factor may lie behind the significant decrease in the presence of non-local ceramic vessels seen at Knossos during this period, which seems to mark a shift in the nexus of social competition away from the procurement and display of long-distance social relationships. In view of increased household socio-economic independence, especially in relation to control of agricultural surplus, social competition from LN onwards is more likely to have focused on the forging of links with successful local households through more private acts of conspicuous consumption, gift giving and com-mensality, involving both agricultural surplus (Halstead 1999: 90) and local craft goods, such as *Spondylus* shell ornaments at Dimini (Halstead 1995: 18) or ceramic vessels at Knossos.

It should be stressed that this shift marks a renegotiation and not a rejection of communal values and practices. Households continued to live in aggregations, some of them large like LN-FN Knossos (at least 3.0 ha, Hood and Smyth 1981: 6). Certain communal values must therefore have been a maintained, perhaps through institutions and beliefs of which we currently remain unaware. A good example of this is provided by LN-EMII burial customs, which continue to emphasize the primacy of the communal over the individual (Triantaphyllou 1999: 128, 131–32; Branigan 1984; 1993). In this way pre-Neolithic ideas and ideals of communality were subject to repeated renegotiation throughout the Neolithic and Early Bronze Age.

With greater household socio-economic independence and competition, came new incentives to intensify, diversify and specialize in order to increase individual household wealth and status. During the later Neolithic in general there are hints of diversification in subsistence production (Halstead 1981a: 320–27), many of which were already picked up in *Emergence* (see Renfrew 1972: 274–80). Renfrew notes a greater diversity in the exploitation of cereals and other foodstuff crops, the introduction of new species and a trend towards increasing crop purity, which together are taken to suggest an increase in technological knowledge and specialization. There is also speculation regarding the possible first use of draft-oxen and the plough at this time (1972: 276, 280). At Knossos there is evidence in LNII for the development of a full weaving technology, while during FN there are indirect indications, in the form of the appearance of pouring vessels and individual drinking cups, for new drinking practices possibly involving wine consumption (Evans 1964: 233; Renfrew 1972: 280–81, 352–53; Halstead 1994: 201). The impetus for these innovations might plausibly be located in the realm of household competition.

It is possible that this process of household competition had already produced real inequalities in wealth and status between households before the beginning of the Bronze Age (Halstead 1995: 17–18). Halstead has argued for the development in LN-EBA Thessaly of a 'megaron elite' (1995: 14–15), although his study of spatial patterns of animal exploitation at LN Dimini did not yield evidence for any significant spatial differences in consumption (1992). More striking are the differences in the consumption of ceramic vessels that are apparent at FN sites in Crete. While 50% of any ceramic assemblage at large, lowland open settlements, such as Knossos and Phaistos, consists of finewares, this proportion drops dramatically for smaller sites located in agriculturally more marginal landscapes, such as Magasa in the Siteia uplands (Manteli 1993: 89). In addition the restriction of pouring and single-draught drinking vessels to large lowland sites, such as Knossos and Phaistos (e.g., A. Evans 1921: 39 fig. 6. 2, 9; 1928: 11 fig. 3.x.1, 2), would seem to indicate that these new drinking practices were spatially restricted. Similar differences may also be seen in access to obsidian, whose procurement, reduction and distribution seems to have been already controlled by communities located on or near the north coast (Carter 1998). Comparable differences in the diversity of material culture at small and large sites have also been noted for FN-EBA southern Greece (van Andel and Runnels 1988: 238). Such examples hint at the existence already by FN of socio-economic differences between these two main site-types.

Conclusions

Cutting-edge in its shifting of the basic explanatory paradigm and with its extraordinary grasp on data of a very broad chronological and spatial range,

Emergence represents a landmark in the quest to explain the development of Aegean Bronze Age societies. Thirty years ago, its treatment of the Neolithic, especially chronology, set new standards. However, since then our understanding of Neolithic society and economy has deepened considerably. Amongst many things that have become clearer, we can now see that the Neolithic can no longer be understood *in opposition* to Bronze Age society. Social competition, impermanent achieved hierarchies, craft specialization, agricultural intensification, long-distance exchange and conspicuous consumption can now all be found in the Neolithic. It is, therefore, becoming increasingly apparent that the key to understanding social development in the prehistoric Aegean lies in seeing how these phenomena develop and change in context, articulation, meaning and intention throughout the Neolithic and Bronze Age.

The Neolithic is thus not simple, rather its complexity is more difficult to access. The key to understanding this complexity has been provided by the critical application of well-developed anthropological concepts, such as community and household, to increasingly detailed, well-defined data-sets. Thus detailed studies of artefacts provide a window, not just on the relationships between communities (as Renfrew predicted; 1972: 366), but also on how such communities constituted themselves. In this respect understanding of these data-sets is enriched by theoretical frameworks, such as Bourdieu's theory of practice (Bourdieu 1977), that make the crucial link between the material acts of the archaeological record and the dynamic reproduction of social values, strategies and relations.

In this way the Neolithic emerges as a period of both continuity and change with at its heart an ongoing tension between the public (communal) and the private (household). Over its course, notions of community and ideals of communality were re-worked. During the earlier Neolithic people lived separately but constituted themselves communally and perhaps as a consequence such communities exhibit great stability. The emergence of a socio-economically more independent household during LN marks a major shift in emphasis, but ideals of communality certainly persisted, perhaps in the form of communal institutions and more certainly in beliefs in the 'community of the dead' that persisted well into the Bronze Age.

Finally, the role of the Neolithic in 'the emergence of civilization' requires some comment. At a very basic level, the emergence of a socio-economically more independent household is a pre-requisite for the development of greater socio-economic complexity. During the later Neolithic, communities became composed of semi-autonomous components with interests potentially divergent from those of the wider community: households were now much more free to pursue strategies more in line with their own self-interest. This opened up the possibility for the development of alternative value systems, social relations and economic practices. This facilitated the construction of different notions of community, subsistence and landscape that allowed the settlement of types of landscape (e.g., Central Cyclades; uplands) that had hitherto been unattractive to settlement. This social transformation may thus be seen as undermining the stability[5] of earlier Neolithic society and marking the beginnings of a process of socio-economic differentiation, which in LN-FN is manifest in the development of craft specialization, agricultural diversification and the colonization of more marginal landscapes.

And so in seeking to trace the development of greater socio-economic complexity in the Aegean from the Early Neolithic down to the Middle and Late Bronze Age, one must recognize the significance of the changes that took place in the later Neolithic. The more we understand later Neolithic socio-economic complexity, the better we will be able to comprehend how this was transformed in the Early Bronze Age. Renfrew was surely right, however, to view the Neolithic as background and to consider specific developments in the Early Bronze Age (e.g., the appearance of metal and its transformative potential as a long-term, storable form of wealth) as more crucial to the emergence of urban centres, monumental ceremonial centres and writing (1972: 362–403). While later Neolithic socio-economic transformation opened up the possibility of later growth in complexity, it did not make such developments inevitable. Even at the very end of the Neolithic there was little if anything that made the emergence or non-emergence of 'civilization' in different regions inevitable: greater complexity was only one of several possible developmental trajectories.

Nevertheless, in a more general sense, the models with which we try to understand later Neolithic societies, also offer the possibility of insight into Bronze Age societies. The interplay between different households and the changing ways in which community is constructed continue to lie at the heart of social development throughout the Bronze Age, not only in small rural communities (e.g., Whitelaw 1983), but also in the larger urban centres (e.g., Halstead 1995: 15; Whitelaw 2001: 17–21). In addition, it has recently become more likely that the predominantly heterarchical nature of later Neolithic society, where different households competed with each other over material, social and symbolic resources, may actually offer a useful way of understanding the nature, basis and articulation of power in the Bronze Age. Most models to explain the emergence of civilization have sought to account for the emergence of a *single,* centralized, elite authority (e.g., irrigation model – Wittfogel 1957; subsistence/redistribution model – Renfrew 1972; social storage – Halstead 1981b). More recent work on Protopalatial and Neopalatial social and political organization, however, has questioned the existence of centralized authorities, single palatial elites and rigid social hierarchies on Crete and has argued instead that power lay in the hands of competing elite groups or households (Hamilakis 2002; Schoep 2002a; 2002b). Such work marks the beginning of a serious reappraisal of the context within which monumental ceremonial centres developed and in this respect, future work focusing more specifically on the development of the household after the Neolithic, particularly the nature, growth and interaction of wealthy elite households, may offer powerful new ways of exploring changes in wealth, power and legitimation in the communities of the Bronze Age.

Acknowledgements

I would like to thank John Barrett and Paul Halstead for the invitation to speak and Eddie Faber, Eleni Nodarou and Maria Relaki for their hospitality. This article is based on doctoral research supervised by Dr. Peter Day and funded by a N.E.R.C. studentship at the University of Sheffield, England together with post-doctoral research, funded by an E.C. Marie Curie Fellowship (Contract No. HPMF-CT-2001-01385) at the Université Catholique de Louvain, Belgium. For permission to study and sample Neolithic ceramic material from Knossos, I would like to thank Prof. J.D. Evans, the Council of the British School at Athens, Herakleion Ephoreia and the Conservation Directorate of the Hellenic Ministry of Culture. Aspects of analytical work were funded by a grant from the GEOPRO TMR Research Network funded by DGXII of the European Commission (Contract No. ERBFMRX-CT980165).

Endnotes

1   For example, in the context of the Neolithic of NW Europe, Thomas (1991) has argued for the existence of more subtle forms of domination or hegemony, through the control of knowledge, ritual and belief.

2   It should be stressed that the traditional Cretan (Knossos) EN phase does not simply correspond to Greek EN, but rather spans the equivalent of EN, MN and LN on the Greek mainland. Recent re-study has allowed the construction of a new chronology equivalent to that of the Greek mainland which will be published elsewhere. In the interests of clarity and comparability, in this paper the old Cretan phasing is eschewed in favour of mainland Neolithic periods.

3   A non-domestic function is suggested by its large size, central location and unusual finds, which included two very large caches of 'exotic' flint blades, five female figurines, two 'outsize' greenstone axes, two unusual 'gourd-shaped' pottery vessels and several hundred clay 'roundels' of unknown function (Rodden 1964: 114; Demoule and Perlès 1993: 386; Halstead 1995: n.19).

4   These non-domestic buildings were distinguished on the basis of their lack of evidence for domestic activities along with a series of attributes which set them apart from other dwellings, such as greater structural complexity, greater labour investment, raised stone-slab platforms. Byrd interprets these buildings as corporate or integrative buildings, which perhaps acted as 'a venue for conducting supra-household meeting and decision-making activities, and possibly related ceremonial or ritual activities' (Byrd 1994: 657).

Bibliography

van Andel, T.H. and C.N. Runnels
   1988   An essay on the emergence of civilisation in the Aegean. *Antiquity* 62: 234–47.
Andreou, S., M. Fotiadis and K. Kotsakis
   1996   Review of Aegean prehistory V: the Neolithic and Bronze Age of northern Greece. *AJA* 100: 537–97.

Appadurai, A.
 1986 *The Social Life of Things*. Cambridge: Cambridge University Press.
Arnold, P.J.
 1991 *Domestic Ceramic Production and Spatial Organization*. Cambridge: Cambridge University Press.
Barley, N.
 1994 *Smashing Pots. Feats of Clay*. London: British Museum Press.
Barrett, J.C.
 1994 *Fragments from Antiquity. An Archaeology of Social Life in Britain, 2900–1200 BC*. Oxford: Blackwell Publishers.
Barrett, J. and K. Fewster
 1998 Stonehenge: *is* the medium the message? *Antiquity* 72: 847–52.
Bourdieu, P.
 1977 *Outline of a Theory of Practice*. Cambridge: Cambridge University Press.
Branigan, K.
 1984 Early Minoan society: the evidence of the Mesara tholoi reviewed. In C. Nicolet (ed.), *Aux origines de l'Hellénisme: la Crète et la Grèce. Hommage à Henri van Effenterre*: 29–37. Paris: Centre Gustav Glotz.
 1993 *Dances with Death. Life and Death in Southern Crete, c. 3000–2000 B.C.* Amsterdam: Hakkert.
Broodbank, C.
 1992 The Neolithic labyrinth: social change at Knossos before the Bronze Age. *JMA* 5: 39–75.
Byrd, B.F.
 1994 Public and private, domestic and corporate: the emergence of the southwest Asian village. *American Antiquity* 59: 639–66.
Carter, T.
 1998 The chipped stone. *BSA* 93: 47–50.
Cherry, J.F.
 1983 Evolution, revolution, and the origins of complex society in Minoan Crete. In O. Krzyszkowska and L. Nixon (eds.), *Minoan Society*: 33–45. Bristol: Bristol Classical Press.
Childe, V.G.
 1981 *Man Makes Himself*. Bradford-on-Avon: Moonraker Press.
Costin, C.L.
 1991 Craft specialization: issues in defining, documenting, and explaining the organization of production. In M.B. Schiffer (ed.), *Archaeological Method and Theory*, 3: 1–56. Tucson: University of Arizona Press.
Cullen, T. and D. Keller
 1990 The Greek pithos through time: multiple functions and diverse imagery. In W.D. Kingery (ed.), *The Changing Roles of Ceramics in Society: 26,000 B.P. to the Present*: 183–207. Westerville: The American Ceramics Society.
Demoule, J-P. and C. Perlès
 1993 The Greek Neolithic: a new review. *Journal of World Prehistory* 7: 355–416.
Dietler, M. and I. Herbich
 1998 *Habitus*, techniques, style: an integrated approach to the social understanding of material culture and boundaries. In M.T. Stark (ed.), *The Archaeology of Social Boundaries*: 232–63. Washington: Smithsonian Institution Press.
Dobres, M-A. and C.R. Hoffman

1994   Social agency and the dynamics of prehistoric technology. *Journal of Archaeological Method and Theory* 1: 211–57.

Edmonds, M.
1999   *Ancestral Geographies of the Neolithic.* London: Routledge.

Evans, A.J.
1921   *The Palace of Minos, I.* London: Macmillan.
1928   *The Palace of Minos, II.* London: Macmillan.

Evans, J.D.
1964   Excavations in the Neolithic settlement at Knossos, 1957–60. *BSA* 59: 132–240.
1971   Neolithic Knossos: the growth of a settlement. *Proceedings of the Prehistoric Society* 37: 95–117.
1994   The early millennia: continuity and change in a farming settlement. In D. Evely, H. Hughes-Brock and N. Momigliano (eds.), *Knossos, a Labyrinth of History: Papers Presented in Honour of Sinclair Hood*: 1–20. London: British School at Athens.

Flannery, K.V.
1972   The origins of the village as a settlement type in Mesoamerica and the Near East. In P.J. Ucko, R. Tringham and G.W. Dimbleby (eds.), *Man, Settlement and Urbanism*: 23–53. London: Duckworth.

Gallis, K. J.
1985   A Late Neolithic foundation offering from Thessaly. *Antiquity* 59: 20–24.
1996   The Neolithic World. In G.A. Papathanassopoulos (ed.), *Neolithic Culture in Greece*: 23–37. Athens: Nicholas P. Goulandris Foundation Museum of Cycladic Art.

Halstead, P.
1981a   Counting sheep in Neolithic and Bronze Age Greece. In I. Hodder, G. Isaac and N. Hammond (eds.), *Pattern of the Past*: 307–39. Cambridge: Cambridge University Press.
1981b   From determinism to uncertainty: social storage and the rise of the Minoan palace. In A. Sheridan and G. Bailey (eds.), *Economic Archaeology* (BAR International Series 96): 187–213. Oxford: British Archaeological Reports.
1989   The economy has a normal surplus: economic stability and social change among early farming communities of Thessaly, Greece. In P. Halstead and J. O'Shea (eds.), *Bad Year Economics*: 68–80. Cambridge: Cambridge University Press.
1992   Dimini and the 'DMP': faunal remains and animal exploitation in Late Neolithic Thessaly. *BSA* 87: 29–59.
1993   *Spondylus* shell ornaments from Late Neolithic Thessaly, Greece: specialised manufacture or unequal accumulation? *Antiquity* 67: 603–09.
1994   The north-south divide: regional paths to complexity in prehistoric Greece. In C. Mathers and S. Stoddart (eds.), *Development and Decline in the Mediterranean Bronze Age*: 195–219. Sheffield: J.R. Collis.
1995   From sharing to hoarding: the Neolithic foundations of Aegean Bronze Age society. In R. Laffineur and W.-D. Niemeier (eds.), *Politeia. Society and State in the Aegean Bronze Age* (Aegaeum 12): 11–21. Liège: Université de Liège.
1996   The development of agriculture and pastoralism in Greece: when, how, who, what? In D.R. Harris (ed.), *The Origins and Spread of Agriculture and Pastoralism in Eurasia*: 296–309. London: UCL Press.
1999   Neighbours from hell? The household in Neolithic Greece. In P. Halstead (ed.), *Neolithic Society in Greece* (SSAA 2): 77–95. Sheffield: Sheffield Academic Press.

Hamilakis, Y.
2002   Too many chiefs? Factional competition in Neopalatial Crete. In J. Driessen, I. Schoep

and R. Laffineur (eds.), *Monuments of Minos. Rethinking the Minoan Palaces* (Aegaeum 23): 179–99. Liège: Université de Liège.

Helms, M.
  1993   *Craft and the Kingly Ideal: Art, Trade and Power.* Austin: University of Texas Press.
Hood, M.S.F. and D. Smyth
  1981   *Archaeological Survey of the Knossos Area* (BSA Supplement 14). London: British School at Athens.
Hourmouziadis, G.
  1979   *To Neolithiko Dimini.* Volos: Society for Thessalian Studies.
Kalogirou, A.
  1997   Pottery production and craft specialization in Neolithic Greece. In P.P. Betancourt and R. Laffineur (eds.), *TEXNH. Craftsmen, Craftswomen and Craftsmanship in the Aegean Bronze Age* (Aegaeum 16): 11–16. Liège: Université de Liège.
Kotsakis, K.
  1983   *Keramiki Tekhnologia kai Keramiki Diaforopoiisi: Provlimata tis Graptis Keramikis tis Mesis Neolithikis Epokhis tou Sesklou.* PhD thesis, University of Thessaloniki.
  1999   What tells can tell: social space and settlement in the Greek Neolithic. In P. Halstead (ed.), *Neolithic Society in Greece* (SSAA 2): 66–76. Sheffield: Sheffield Academic Press.
van der Leeuw, S.E. and R. Torrence (eds.)
  1989   *What's New? A Closer Look at the Process of Innovation.* London: Unwin Hyman.
Manteli, K.
  1993   *The Transition from the Neolithic to the Early Bronze Age in Crete, with Special Reference to Pottery.* PhD thesis, University of London.
  1996   Crete (pottery). In G.A. Papathanassopoulos (ed.), *Neolithic Culture in Greece*: 132–34. Athens: Nicholas P. Goulandris Foundation Museum of Cycladic Art.
Miller, D.
  1985   *Artefacts as Categories: a Study of Ceramic Variability in Central India.* Cambridge: Cambridge University Press.
Miller, M.A.
  1996   The manufacture of cockle shell beads at Early Neolithic Franchthi Cave, Greece: a case of craft specialization? *JMA* 9: 7–37.
Netting, R.McC., R.R. Wilk and E.J. Arnould (eds.)
  1984   *Households. Comparative and Historical Studies of the Domestic Group.* Berkeley: University of California Press.
Perlès, C.
  1992   Systems of exchange and organization of production in Neolithic Greece. *JMA* 5: 115–64.
Perlès, C. and K.D. Vitelli
  1999   Craft specialization in the Greek Neolithic. In P. Halstead (ed.), *Neolithic Society in Greece* (SSAA 2): 96–107. Sheffield: Sheffield Academic Press.
Renfrew, C.
  1972   *The Emergence of Civilisation. The Cyclades and the Aegean in the Third Millennium B.C..* London: Methuen.
Rodden, R.J.
  1964   Recent discoveries from prehistoric Macedonia. An interim report. *Balkan Studies* 5: 109–24.
Sahlins, M.
  1974   *Stone Age Economics.* London: Tavistock Publications.

Schoep, I.
   2002a Social and political organisation on Crete in the Proto-Palatial period: the case of Middle Minoan II Malia. *JMA* 15: 101–32.
   2002b The state of the Minoan palaces or the Minoan palace-state? In J. Driessen, I. Schoep and R. Laffineur (eds.), *Monuments of Minos. Rethinking the Minoan Palaces* (Aegaeum 23): 15–33. Liège: Université de Liège.

Strathern, M.
   1988 *The Gender of the Gift: Problems with Women and Problems with Society in Melanesia.* Berkeley: University of California Press.

Thomas, J.
   1990 *Rethinking the Neolithic.* Cambridge: Cambridge University Press.

Thomas, N.
   1991 *Entangled Objects: Exchange, Material Culture and Colonialism in the Pacific.* London: Harvard University Press.

Tomkins, P.D.
   2001 *The Production, Circulation and Consumption of Ceramic Vessels at Early Neolithic Knossos, Crete.* PhD thesis, University of Sheffield.
   forthcoming Analyse that! Past pitfalls and future prospects for the combination of macroscopic and microscopic forms of ceramic analysis in the study of Greek Neolithic ceramics. In P.M. Day (ed.), *Analytical Approaches to Prehistoric Ceramics: Technologies and Exchange in the Aegean* (SSAA 8).

Tomkins, P. and P.M. Day
   2001 Production and exchange of the earliest ceramic vessels in the Aegean: a view from Early Neolithic Knossos, Crete. *Antiquity* 75: 259–60.

Tomkins, P.D., P.M. Day and V. Kilikoglou
   forthcoming Knossos and the Early Neolithic landscape of the Herakleion Basin. In G. Cadogan and E. Hatzaki (eds), *Knossos: Palace, City, State.* London: British School at Athens.

Triantaphyllou, S.
   1999 Prehistoric Makriyalos: a story from the fragments. In P. Halstead (ed.), *Neolithic Society in Greece* (SSAA 2): 128–35. Sheffield: Sheffield Academic Press.

Vitelli, K.D.
   1989 Were pots first invented for food? Doubts from Franchthi. *World Archaeology* 21:17–29.
   1993 *Franchthi Neolithic Pottery: Classification and Ceramic Phases 1 and 2* (Excavations at Franchthi Cave, Greece, 8). Bloomington and Indianapolis: Indiana University Press.
   1995 Pots, potters and the shaping of the Greek Neolithic. In W.K. Barnett and J.W. Hoopes (eds.), *The Emergence of Pottery: Technology and Innovation in Ancient Societies*: 55–64. Washington DC: Smithsonian Institution Press.

Washburn, D.K.
   1983 Symmetry analysis of ceramic design: two tests of the method on Neolithic material from Greece and the Aegean. In D.K. Washburn (ed.), *Structure and Cognition in Art*: 138–64. Cambridge: Cambridge University Press.

Weinberg, S.S.
   1965 The relative chronology of the Aegean in the Stone and Early Bronze Ages. In R.W. Ehrich (ed.), *Chronologies in Old World Archaeology*: 285–320. Chicago: University of Chicago Press.
   1970 The Stone Age in the Aegean. In I.E.S. Edwards. C.J. Gadd and N.G.L. Hammond (eds.), *Cambridge Ancient History, 1, 1: Prolegomena and Prehistory*: 557–618. Third Edition. Cambridge: Cambridge University Press.

Whitelaw, T.M.

1983 The settlement at Fournou Korifi, Myrtos and aspects of Early Minoan social organization. In O. Krzyszkowska and L. Nixon (eds.), *Minoan Society*: 323–40. Bristol: Bristol Classical Press.

1992 Lost in the labyrinth? Comments on Broodbank's 'Social change at Knossos before the Bronze Age'. *JMA* 5: 225–38.

2001 From sites to communities: defining the human dimensions of Minoan urbanism. In K Branigan (ed.), *Urbanism in the Aegean Bronze Age* (SSAA 4): 15–37. Sheffield: Sheffield Academic Press.

Whitelaw, T.M., P.M. Day, E. Kiriatzi, V. Kilikoglou and D.E. Wilson

1997 Ceramic traditions at EMIIB Myrtos, Fournou Korifi. In P.P. Betancourt and R. Laffineur (eds.), *TEXNH. Craftsmen, Craftswomen and Craftsmanship in the Aegean Bronze Age* (Aegaeum 16): 265–74. Liège: Université de Liège.

Whittle, A.

1996 *Europe in the Neolithic*. Cambridge: Cambridge University Press.

Wilson, D.E. and P.M. Day

1999 EMIIB ware groups at Knossos: the 1907–1908 South Front tests. *BSA* 94: 1–62.

2000 EMI chronology and social practice: pottery from the Early Palace tests at Knossos. *BSA* 95: 21–63.

Wittfogel, K.A.

1957 *Oriental Despotism, a Comparative Study of Total Power*. New Haven: Yale University Press.

Wright, R.P.

1991 Women's labour and pottery production in prehistory. In J.M. Gero and M.W. Conkey (eds.), *Engendering Archaeology: Women and Prehistory*: 194–223. Oxford: Basil Blackwell.

Yiouni, P.

1996 The Early Neolithic pottery: functional analysis. In G. Pyke and P. Yiouni (eds.), *Nea Nikomedeia I: the Excavation of an Early Neolithic Village in Northern Greece 1961–4. The Excavation and Ceramic Assemblage* (BSA Supplementary Volume 25): 181–93. London: British School at Athens.

4

The Emergence of Leadership and the Rise of Civilization in the Aegean

James C. Wright

I only started to think clearly about Aegean pre- and protohistory after I read the *Emergence*. Taken as I was by processual archaeology, but trained as a Classical archaeologist, I was struggling to understand how we could make sense of the Aegean in the Bronze Age. Renfrew offered a veritable mansion full of many ideas, and as I wandered through the corridors of the *Emergence,* I was eager to explore what lay behind its many doors. Thirty years later its ability to inspire remains; there is nothing else so comprehensive in its attention to the data and the many ways in which models can be applied to understand them. The *Emergence* remains fundamental and I require my students to study and learn from it.

Civilization

An issue that early on caught my attention was Renfrew's thoughtful and extended consideration of the definition of 'civilization' (1972: 3–14) and its application within the Aegean (1972: 38–49). If the premise of the study was the emergence of civilization, there could be no question of the importance of a characterization of its salient features. Renfrew views civilization as a stage of cultural development. Each civilization is distinct in time and place but also commingled, as 'Mesoamerican', 'Minoan-Mycenaean', or 'Western' (1972: 4–5). He does not think we can characterise civilization by any particular trait, rather that we need a polythetic set of some key features, minimally including 'written records, ceremonial centres, cities of at least 5,000 inhabitants' (1972: 7, 13; Kluckhohn 1960; Kroeber and Kluckhohn 1952). He explicitly wants his definition to be operational and returns to this point in his consideration of the multiplier effect by claiming that, for civilization to come into being, 'there should exist the possibility for sustained growth (and for positive feedback) in *at least two* of the subsystems of the culture' (1972: 39). Despite this polythetic approach, Renfrew takes seriously the identification of cities as a critical component. He notes Redfield's insights on this matter (1953: 54–64; Yoffee 1995: 284), which I summarize as the recognition that the emergence of urbanism transformed all landscapes: prior to this, the dichotomy between rural and urban did not exist, and this is why traditional discussions identify the city as the salient feature of civilization.

Nonetheless, the city is an artefact not a process. In considering this problem I turn to the approach of Baines and Yoffee (1998: 233–40), who view civilization in terms of the production of 'high culture' through the creation and maintenance of 'symbolic resources' (see also Baines and Yoffee 2000; Van Buren and Richards 2000). For them, civilization is not the interaction of different aspects of a larger system but a much more social and ideological process of harnessing the political economy to the promotion and continuation of a cosmic order without which there is no legitimacy and basis for the civilization. They identify the essential component of civilization as high culture, which they term 'a communicative complex [that] enacts, celebrates, and transmits meaning and experience' (1998: 236). They argue that knowledge and style are two fundamental elements of high culture; the former for 'control of cultural resources', the latter for 'a civilization's definition and . . . its demarcation against what lies outside' (1998: 237). Of particular importance is their claim that style (and in a sense also knowledge) 'is produced within the broader elite and consumed principally by the inner elite' (1998: 237). In this view, the process of production and maintenance of the traditions of a civilization is paradigmatic and can be continued long after the political economy that supported and sustained it has disappeared (see Wallace 1972a; 1972b). As examples Baines and Yoffee cite the persistence of the high cultures of Egypt and Mesopotamia during the later first millennium BC (1998: 240), the renascences that characterize the process of European appropriation of Antiquity, and the creation and maintenance of Western Civilization (Panofsky 1960; Choay 2001: 17–62). What is central in their view of the formation of a civilization is the role of individuals and small groups of inner elite, who through the manipulation of cultural resources are able to monopolize, promote and maintain a cosmic order and its legitimization of the civilization.

The difference between these definitions of civilization entails different approaches to its study. Our area of interest is the Aegean and, for Renfrew, the evidence for civilization in the *Emergence* was the consecutive appearance of first the palace-centred societies on Crete and then those on the mainland of Greece, while the Cyclades during the Early Bronze Age represented its emergence. On first glance this seems unproblematic, yet I have always felt that there is nonetheless at this point a problem with the argument, for by presupposing the existence of 'Minoan' and 'Mycenaean' civilizations, Renfrew conjoins process and product without specifying the necessary component or conditions for civilization to come into being, notwithstanding his focus on the cultures of the Early Bronze Age. Even though he finds in the Neolithic and Early Bronze Ages evidence for his primary models of subsistence/redistribution and craft special-ization/wealth, they are in fact derived from an analysis of the Middle and Late Bronze Age phenomena of the palaces; and that rests on problematic assumptions about the political economy of the palaces (Halstead 1988). Thus I argue that the product of the palaces has been used to explain the process of their formation.

Renfrew focused our attention on causality and derived much of his insight from biology. I agree with his observation that the ability to project symbolically differentiates humans fundamentally from other forms of life (1972: 12). In human social terms I think it is clear that the ability of humans to communicate with each other and to construct a material and symbolically projected world of culture is the primary process that leads to civilization. I think that this emphasis is different from Renfrew's argument that various subsystems act upon each other and create a multiplier effect (1972: 27–49, 489–96) that leads to civilization. In so doing, he conjoins the primary process – social and material communicative expression, with its results – population, economy, trade, etc. (see also Renfrew 1977: 107–09). In other words he follows Kroeber's early insistence that culture is the object of analysis (Kroeber 1917), but this is tantamount to reifying culture. Sapir argued against this perspective and pointed out that culture does not exist independently of individual humans acting in their socio-communicative capacities (Sapir 1917; Darnell and Irvine 1999: 27–33; Ingold 1986: 233–34), a point on which Giddens insists (1984: 163, 207–26). Thus an understanding of the emergence of civilization is not achieved through the study of culture *per se*, or of any of its components; rather it is understood through the study of the process of individuals acting through social and material communication and thereby producing mechanisms that sometimes result in civilization (see also Godelier 1977a; 1977b).

If Baines and Yoffee are correct in arguing that civilization is largely produced and maintained by the activities of elite groups composed of individuals who focus especially on the manufacture and dissemination of symbolic resources, then we may be able potentially to reconstruct the processes of that production by recovering the material expressions of the product, especially as it is developed over time through the repetition and refinement of key symbolic elements. This involves a hermeneutic reading of the past and is based on the rather obvious hypothesis that the formation of elites and of societies involves the manipulation of symbols, which are often visible archaeologically (Turner 1967; Bourdieu 1979; Hodder 1982; 1986; 1989). The success of cultural production is preserved archaeologically as the material remains of emerging societies. Symbolic expressions of this process are especially evident in the built environment: in the places and forms of residential, administrative, public, mortuary and religious architecture (Blanton 1995; Hillier and Hanson 1984: 1–24; Tuan 1977: 101–17). They also show up as the material expressions of display – in clothing, jewelry, weapons, and implements and vessels for eating and drinking and in their placement with the dead (Parker Pearson 1999; Barthes 1983; Tuan 1977: 34–50) –

and from these in language, gesture and representation (Barthes 1982; Elias 1978: 100–13; Cohen 1974).

It follows then that the study of the emergence of civilization is one of recognizing how leaders emerge within societies, how they form groups that have an elite leadership, and how the activities of these groups demarcate a geography of social, economic, political, and ideological spaces. Through competitive iteration these spaces are marked as places that give an historic, memorial structure to societies, and in turn the articulated relations of these places provide a cognitive and spiritual map that, through legend and myth, is correlated to a perceived cosmic structure that embraces and legitimizes the society (Tilley 1994; Connerton 1989). In this manner social processes forge individual social and group identities and successfully deploy the elements of a political economy throughout an emerging society. This argument attempts to explain how, through this process, a generalizing world-view emerges that permits variation in its application in symbolic and stylistic terms. This problem concerns O'Connor (2000) in his recent study of an elite 6th Dynasty Egyptian tomb. He notes that there is a difference between the generalizing style of Old Kingdom art and architecture and deviations from it in the specific elite tomb he is considering. Any successful application of Baines and Yoffee's model of order, legitimacy and wealth, must take this problem into account. Therefore the formation of the style of a high culture that identifies a civilization is a process that, in order to be successful, must incorporate variation and be mutable without losing its formal structure and agency as a mechanism of control. This is matter clarified by Wallace in his studies of the evolution of religion and culture, in his insights into the process of paradigm shift as a part of the process of culture change (1966; 1972a; 1972b).

I believe that emergence so defined has to be studied in particular in terms of the transformation of social, economic and political relations that takes place between egalitarian and stratified societies. Brumfiel observes that advocates of cultural ecology have not been overly concerned with this transformation because they view stratified societies as efficient adaptive mechanisms that are already manifest 'in simpler societies, ready to be pressed into service when they are favoured by demographic and environmental conditions' (Brumfiel 1994: 6; Price 1982: 716–20). She, along with Hayden and others, argues for a more social process that takes place in situations where the production of surplus is dependable (Brumfiel 1994: 6–7; Hayden 1995: 28–30). Blanton specifically advocates attention to the discursive social relations within households (1995). This is profoundly important since the household is the locus of education in pre-industrial societies. Within the household social rules and notions of equality and inequality, and degrees of centralization are inculcated. Members of households carry into the wider world the experiences, rules, and boundaries of their household and in interaction with each other produce the discourse of communities that Bourdieu characterizes as *habitus*. Little wonder then that the processes that drive the transformations within transegalitarian societies are local, highly variable, not yet governed by widely shared social rules, and not headed anywhere in particular. Thus I emphasize that the central question is not about resources and economy and the emergence of entities such as tribes or chiefdoms, but rather about the social practices that foster the emergence of elites and elite groups.

The Emergence of Elites in the Prehistoric Aegean

In the Aegean this transformation not only took place during the Neolithic but also recurred after the collapse of such cultural formations as those of the Early Bronze Age and the Mycenaean peer polities, and these instances offer good opportunities to study the process archaeologically. After the emergence of societies during the EBA there was an unravelling, as the socio-political formations and networks proved unable to sustain development, and the resulting turmoil affected different areas in different ways (Gamble 1979; 1982; Wagstaff and Cherry 1982: 139; Forsén 1992; Maran 1998; Broodbank 2000).

How did different areas manage in the aftermath of the EBA collapse? In large part the problem must be stated as follows: How, after the apparent failure of centralization of production, technology, and social formation, did individuals and their communities restructure themselves in a manner that led some of them to emerge again? And, conversely, why were some others not able initially to participate strongly or at all in any restructuring that occurred? I think it not an overstatement to maintain that, since at least the Late Neolithic (and in most cases before), there ceased to be egalitarian societies throughout the Aegean (compare Price 1995; van Andel and Runnels 1988). The perturbations that mark the latter part of the third millennium left many communities in a state of dissolution with diminished population, diminished access to resources and diminished access to social networks. On the Greek mainland the evidence of the material culture fairly uniformly suggests a disintegration or decomposition that left families and extended kin groups in scattered small hamlets in a few inland areas and a very few active settlements along the coasts, who maintained contact with the Aegean (Broodbank 2000). At best these were transegalitarian societies as termed by Clark and Blake (in an unpublished paper cited by Hayden 1995: 18) and operated as multi-centric economies as defined by Dietler (1999: 143; Dietler and Herbich 2001: 251–52). We are challenged to study the dynamics of these communities because, I believe, only by doing so will we be in a position to begin to explain how the larger and more complex organizations of the palaces came about (cf. Dietler 1999). In this way we can begin to have an informed understanding of the structure, function, and social outlines of the proto-historic polities of the Aegean during the second millennium BC.

There is not space here to provide a case study. I am of the opinion that the mainland during the Middle Bronze Age (and likewise the Iron Age) is ripe for such work (Wright 2001), but also that the approach I am advocating could be usefully applied in Crete and throughout the islands. Further work will have to bear this out. What follows here is an argument for a development of societies that is particularly relevant to archaeologists and the record of the production of culture in the Aegean.

If we express an interest in understanding the processes of the rise of socio-political complexity, we must admit how necessary it is to understand the role played by the structure and dynamics of individuals, especially in households and communities (Gillespie 2000b; Blanton 1995; Spencer 1994; Clark and Blake 1994). Archaeology today is concerned in many ways with identifying the individual, through study of agency and intention and through attention to bioarchaeological analysis (Triantaphyllou 2001). The notion of household archaeology is already well developed and put into practice by many archaeologists in many parts of the world and, as discussed elsewhere in this volume, must include intra-site spatial analysis and bioarchaeological analyses (Blanton 1994; 1995; Kent 1990). Indispensable to both of these is mortuary analysis including the systematic scientific study of human skeletal remains with a view to identifying kin groups, additions to the gene pool, health, diet, work and the relationship between individual humans and markers of status and wealth (Parker Pearson 1999; Triantaphyllou 2001). Last, the study of transegalitarian societies (Hayden 1995; 2001a) and the operation of their economies (Dietler 1999; 2001) is necessary, since they represent a form of organization that is essential to the emergence of leadership. It is in the nature of transegalitarian societies for there to be individuals who try to differentiate themselves from each other and from other social groups. How these individuals effect this and how they emerge as leaders is, as Hayden has elegantly demonstrated (1995), at the core of the transition to the more complex levels of organization that may result in civilizations.

In an insightful analysis of social relations among the !Kung Bushmen, Australian Aborigines of Northeastern Arnhem land, and the Ilongots of Luzon in the Philippines, Jane Collier and Michelle Rosaldo provide insight into the problem of the origins of leadership (1981). They observe that, in these hunter-gatherer and horticulturalist societies, the women produce most of a family's food by gathering it in the wild and by tending gardens – activities that keep them close to home. Men in contrast hunt, and when they kill game they distribute it, mostly among the senior generation. Because of this, Collier and Rosaldo argue that the men are the 'forgers of social relationships'. When a man marries he attains the highest status possible in this society, that of equality with other married and senior men. The focus of his relations and the source of his status are found in his relations with his in-laws. By taking their daughter in marriage the man received bride-service, which Collier and Rosaldo describe as providing 'the analytical link between productive obligations and political prowess' (1981: 289). They point out that in taking care of productive obligations, as in this example of a hunter-gatherer and horticulturalist society, there is little impetus for leadership, since nothing is to be gained by it (see also Hayden 1995: 22, 24). There is, however, every reason to celebrate the status of 'hunter', since in this manner men are able to 'assert and defend their claims to wives' (Collier and Rosaldo 1981: 294). Through distributing the kill to their in-laws and other kin they consolidate their renown and their family position. Such a system might continue to function long after contact with outside forces that are differently organized; however, in most settings, egalitarian bands did not endure long, although the fiction of an egalitarian structure does. As Hayden puts it: 'While transegalitarian communities almost universally give lip-service to an ideology of equality, this rhetoric generally masks very powerful forces working to establish inequalities of wealth, resources, influence and power' (2001a: 501; see also 1995: 20). In these instances political prowess comes into play, and individuals begin to manipulate culture to achieve personal and political goals and thereby transform the structure of relations throughout their societies.

Since I have already suggested that truly egalitarian societies in the Aegean probably disappeared during if not before the Neolithic, I think it necessary to ask what social conventions may have been like in the transegalitarian hamlets and villages that emerged during the early second millennium. What were the processes that led to differentiation in these communities and how did they lead to further transformations? Transegalitarian societies are well known ethnographically and they have been a source of archaeological theorizing in the past, especially by Friedman and Rowlands (1977) in their Marxist evolutionary model of social evolution. For them these societies were 'tribal systems', whose economy was based on small groups of lineages economically tied into a 'household' system of redistribution (Earle 1987: 215). Their importance for archaeological investigation has been re-emphasized through ethnographic and archaeological studies by Michael Dietler, Brian Hayden, Michael Clarke and Ken Ames among others in SE Asia, Africa and the American Northwest (Dietler 1999; 2001; Dietler and Herbich 2001; Hayden 1995; 2001a; 2001b; Clarke 2001; Ames 1995; 2001). These scholars focus again on the importance of the accumulation and distribution of wealth but are more concerned with the social processes than in outlining a theory of economy. Thus they discuss how wealth is accumulated through hunting, agriculture, domestic animals, regional exchange, and feasting. Here political prowess is operational in a complex social and geographic competitive landscape. Often at the core of these societies are factions operating within and among communities, with each faction headed by an emerging leader.

The Role of Factions

The importance of studying factions as a way of understanding the emergence of leadership lies in the fact that factions operate outside the traditional structures of tribal organization. Thus, they offer a social mechanism that permits the formation of semi-permanent forms of vertically integrated, leader-led, socio-political organization. In her application of factions for archaeological purposes, Brumfiel defines them as 'structurally and functionally similar groups which, by virtue of their similarity, compete for resources and positions of power and prestige' (Brumfiel 1994: 4). Because, she continues, they are 'neither classes nor functionally differentiated interest groups', they differ from corporate groups. That is to say they are neither lineal descent groups, nor segments of a tribe, nor are they non-residential groups or pan-tribal sodalities, such as clans, 'secret societies, age grades, and special-purpose groups like curing or warfare societies' (Wason 1994: 43). All these are social forms that exist in rank societies of hunter-gatherer/horticulturalists (Service 1971: 102–04, 131–32). In contrast factions result from leadership, whereby a leader recruits and maintains a group based on the members' self-interest (Bailey 1969: 52, cited in Brumfiel 1994: 4). Thus the ties that bind a faction are primarily between the leader and each member rather than by virtue of any basis of corporate similarity among the followers. As Brumfiel emphasizes, 'the individuals forming a faction lack an identity of interests that would engender common political goals beyond winning advantages for their own faction' (1994: 5). And she goes on to point out that between factions there are no differences between their members that reflect any social or political aims other than advancing the competitive claims of the faction.

Factional leadership is a dynamic and mutable status that is negotiated and manipulated through the course of quotidian social interactions and through more permanent bonds, such as kinship, marriage and alliance. Leadership is also a result of prowess, for example as a skilled mariner, hunter or warrior. Above all it is constructed through the exercise of ideology and display of symbolic resources; these establish rules, rights and obligations, and control mythmaking and cosmology, as well as access to information and the right to speak (Clark and Blake 1994: 19). Leadership is consolidated not merely by force of personality but also through the establishment of acknowledged social bonds, which are both socially performed and physically constructed and represented, especially in feasting, which accompanies most important rituals from birth through death. For the leader of a faction, building up and maintaining membership is *the* primary task. Because the bonds of membership are weak, the factional leader is always at the risk of losing members to other factions. Therefore coalition building is a critical function and it takes place within the community and outside it. The internal and external aspects of leadership are of fundamental importance to the operation of factions. As Brumfiel puts it: 'The net effect of [the] process [of coalition building] is to turn an entire region into a single political "arena", a community within which competing coalitions of faction leaders vie for resources' (Brumfiel 1994: 5). As already indicated, archaeologically one of the most visible signs of this process is in assemblages of feasting, although there are other correlates – especially in mortuary practices.

In his study of factions in South America, Spencer adopts Sahlins' model of

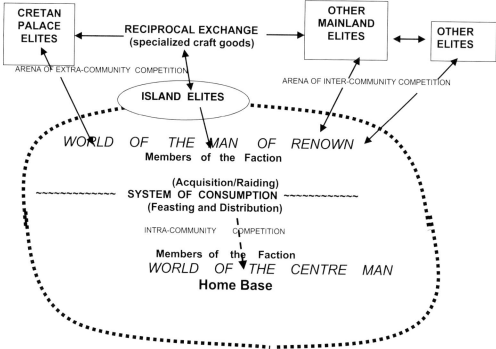

Figure 4.1. Diagram of Centre-Man/Man-of-Renown model

the Centre Man/Man of Renown in Melanesian societies to explore how factional leaders operate (Spencer 1994; Sahlins 1963). Even if it is based upon the overly dichotomous categorization of Melanesian tribal societies as opposed to Polynesian chiefdoms (Terrell *et al.* 1997), this is a powerful model, as it explains the different sources utilized by leaders and clarifies the problems of maintaining leadership in transegalitarian societies with multi-centric economies. It conforms to the evidence from comparative ethnographic studies of leadership interpreted by Helms (1984; 1988; 1993). It is flexible enough to apply to different kinship systems and community structures, whether tending towards executive or corporate forms, as explored by Blanton (1998). Hayden (1995: 25–62), however, prefers to limit the Big Man to an entrepreneurial type distinct from other categories, which he ranges on a scale of increasing socio-economic complexity (see discussion below).

The Centre Man is that persona of the leader that is concerned with the in-community definition of a faction, and thus the centre man is bound up with the social networks within a community. The Man of Renown is that persona which sets the leader apart by virtue of activities, experiences and knowledge about the world beyond the community (Figure 4.1). Whereas the former fosters intra-group relations and is limited and bounded, the latter traverses the portal to the unknown, whether it be the risk of hunting or the venture of sailing the open seas. Equally, as Feinman has clarified (1998: 107), these two aspects of factional leadership combine the horizontal and group reinforcing elements of social relations with the vertical and stress inducing ones. Those social and economic activities that are classed as horizontal promote group solidarity, mutual support (including the mobilization of labour) and social differentiation, while those classed as vertical encourage extraction of resources and production for external exchange and exploitation of labour for external purposes. How the factional leader balances them affects his (or her) ability to succeed as a leader, in particular to enlarge the group led, and ultimately to pass on leadership to a designated successor.

Factions serve intra-community needs without attaining permanent form. They are laboratories within which different experiments in supra-household and supra-kin organizations are tested. In short, they are an evolutionary mechanism out of which more permanent group formations and forms of leadership may arrive and contend with a social, physical and spiritual world larger than both the family or kin group and the community. Inherent in the activities of factions are the dual issues of group and community definition and solidarity, and how one contends with all that lies beyond them. The success of factional leaders in coping with these determines the manner by which and extent to which factions enlarge their social, spatial and physical frames of operation. Out of such processes may emerge more complex and socio-political integrations, such as chiefdoms, states and civilizations. On the other hand successful factions may also be understood as stabilizing, namely developed governing mechanisms, which maintain a dynamic balance among internal and external pressures and which lead neither to consolidation nor to collapse, as Sahlins argues for Melanesian society (1963). This underscores the fundamental community orientation of factions.

In order to secure their position, factional leaders have to be able to mobilize labour. Initially this can be accomplished through polygyny, since both through bride-service and childbirth, a leader enlarges his workforce (Friedman and Rowlands 1977). This workforce, however, has limitations, and so the challenge is to secure a larger one (Blanton 1995: 106–07). Perhaps the most successful and expedient way to accomplish this is through feasting (Dietler 1990: 365–70; Dietler and Herbich 2001). Feasting takes advantage of many of the resources a leader has at his disposal: an extensive network of social relations, access to land and other natural resources, reputation and renown, and the large workforce of his family. Feasting is one way that such leaders can increase their standing within their own faction, show off to and attract members of other factions (thereby diminishing competitors), forge alliances with other factions or extra-community families or groups, extend trading networks, increase land under cultivation, claim new land (which may be also disputed), and mobilize labour to carry out large projects that cannot be accomplished without a large workforce.

Feasting and the Importance of Animal Husbandry

Closely related to feasting is animal husbandry. As Hayden puts it in writing about hill tribes in northern Thailand (2001a: 579): 'Domestic animals serve as the primary vehicle for transforming agricultural surpluses and labour via feasting into other useful currencies such as social, economic and political mutual help or debt relationships and wealth in the form of silver or other prestige goods acquired through exchange'. The central importance of animal husbandry is twofold. Firstly, it provides a reliable source of meat that supplements and to some degree supplants that from hunting. Secondly, like hunting, it requires extensive land use.

Grazing and foraging are activities that define boundaries and inhabit different zones of the landscape. Land use and the variety of exploited land forms are related to the location and size of settlements and to the location of fields and gardens for agriculture – in other words to the definition of territory. Land-use has a socio-economic component, for it is instrumental in the relations among groups in different ecological regions, for instance between lowlanders and highlanders. Animals, of course, are particularly important for feasting, and even though grazing and foraging provide for their sustenance, Hayden points out that they thrive better when their diet is supplemented – for which the production of surplus food is necessary. So animal husbandry requires extra labour inputs (Wagstaff and Augustson 1982: 123; Gamble 1982; Halstead 1987; 1992; Cherry 1988: 22–26). Merely because of their economic value, animals are highly desirable and subject to theft. Their desirability is amplified because they also embody social and ideological meanings. For example they have social value insofar at they represent the competence and social relations of a breeder and herder, while they have ideological value by virtue of their position within the shared cosmology of different but interrelated social groups (Comaroff and Comaroff 1992; Campbell 1964). Theft through rustling is common and a source of conflict that has economic, political and symbolic meaning. Animals out on the range often define or transgress borders through their peregrinations. In this way they define land rights and may be used to extend them. Through their transgressions they may commit damage to other crops and range beyond negotiated boundaries. Conflict over animals and land may lead to warfare with all the attendant opportunities and risks for increasing or losing landholdings, land-rights and labour resources (through capture and enslavement). It is little wonder that in addition to their economic value, grazing animals, especially cattle, assume so much symbolic importance in so many societies – something eloquently emphasized by Comaroff and Comaroff in their study of Tshidi political economy in pre-colonial South Africa (1992: 108–11).

Thus animal herding may be understood as defining the outer geography of transegalitarian and chiefly societies, while agriculture defines the inner one, and in this manner is marked out a physical, political, economic, social, and cosmic geography within which the community operates. The production and con-

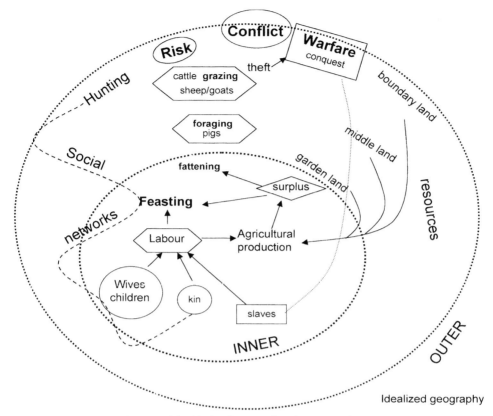

Figure 4.2. Diagram of the idealized geography of a transegalitarian community

sumption of animals is an activity that binds animal husbandry and agriculture together and engages the energies of the labour force for community purposes, which come to a head in scheduled celebrations of consumption (Halstead 1987: 80–83; 1992: 53–6; 1993; 1996: 21, 33–36). These rituals advance the aims of leaders and also create opportunities for competition among them and their factions. These are well represented through a diagram that illustrates the geographic, economic and social activities that take place within such a landscape (Figure 4.2). When coupled with the diagram of the sphere of the Centre Man/Man of Renown (Figure 4.1), it is easy to understand the dynamic structure of this model and its applicability to archaeological situations.

Time, Landscape and Leadership

There is more to this model than the socio-economic, socio-political, and socio-ideological behaviours outlined here. These diagrams illustrate a spatial domain that is marked as a series of perceptual and existential spaces that map the history of individuals, groups, the community, and extra-community relations over a span of generations (Tilley 1994). Thus a physical geography is structured in time through events marked in spaces, and the resulting cognitive map of relationships and memories importantly acts as a unifying web of identity. The behaviours that are acted out within the three above-mentioned realms also create an historic landscape of meaning that is shared, contested, interpreted, trans-formed, and memorialized by its inhabitants. Through the iterations of movement throughout this space – for example through animal husbandry and agriculture, hunting and warfare, celebration, burying, and worship – places are imbued with common realities, often marked with monuments and translated into abstract cognitive equivalents that form the basis for communication about and repre-sentation of the real world through legends, myths and cosmogonies.[1]

Archaeology is currently challenged to try to explore the material expressions of such behaviour. This is why feasting has become a topic of interest, for, along with death and burial, it is an elemental activity that is intensely social in nature, rich in symbolism, highly evocative of the many levels of relationship (from the most intimate to the most distant), culturally distinctive, and therefore inextricably bound up with identity (Hayden 1995: 24–25, 76–78). Like death and burial, feasting is an activity that makes places out of spaces and thereby marks the lived world with spatial and temporal referents. It memorializes relationships across time and space and instructs through practice the boundaries of the group. In rituals of food production and consumption and in rituals of death, societies reinforce themselves and their social structures, even as they remake them. Thus, from an archaeological perspective, the question of transformation from one level of organization to the other, and the matter of aggrandizement by individuals who seek to promote themselves and their group, are especially played out in these arenas.

The activities of leaders in such landscapes are expressly those that emphasize their special roles, as centres of both social action and achievement. The extent to which an aspiring leader and his retinue populate and circumnavigate a landscape is directly related to his ability to consolidate economic, social, political and ideological power (Kertzer 1988). The centralizing and aggrandizing activities that occur in feasts and through other ritual practices in the community enhance the leader's reputation and imbue him, his family, kin, retinue, and his place of residence with special meaning that differentiates all of them from the rest of the society. The extent to which this can be consolidated and passed on to successive generations creates an historical reality that provides legitimacy and a sense of order to the leader and his group. At the same time the repetition of ritual and the intergenerational claims to legitimacy and power authenticate claims made through story, legend and myth to special relations with the ancestors, heroes, and divinities.

Symbols, Civilization and Archaeology

These are not things that archaeologists can always easily establish but they indicate directions for the focus of archaeological fieldwork and interpretation. Let us return to Baines' and Yoffee's claims about the nature of civilizations (1998), to see how these activities produce culture that leaves an archaeological footprint. Leaders and their groups create the symbolic resources of a society. Just as they tell specific stories, sing special songs, perform selected dances, and carry out particular rituals, they also select objects for display that represent to their group meanings of status and belonging. This process of cultural production is often played out in competitive arenas where different leaders and groups contend for power and prestige. Such competition encourages a certain amount of variability, governed only by its comprehensibility within the symbolic vocabulary of the intended audience (Clarke and Blake 1994). Archaeologically this kind of activity leaves traces in burial assemblages as well as in domestic ones, where status objects are identifiable and where initially heterogeneity is more common than homogeneity. Again, many of these items are those used in the feast.

With the advance of one group over another, and with the ability of paramount factions to extend control beyond the community, there is a corresponding spread of symbolic products and an increase in potential symbolic resources. This results in both a narrowing and a widening of symbolic meaning. It is narrower because a set of common powerful and unifying symbols emerges from the competitive process among various aggrandizers; those who succeed are also those who set standards for others to follow. As the elite increase their power and build coalitions both within and beyond their communities, they create the beginnings of a stratified political economy and command the services of specialized craftspersons. The latter they use to forge and replicate symbols that they disseminate throughout the emerging society. But to be effective as a communicative device in a growing society that incorporates others, a wider set of symbols has to be deployed. This is accomplished by a widening of the elite group.[2]

In his analysis of courtly customs in early modern Europe, Elias argues for a complex system of elite behaviour around the production of style. On the one hand, he states that competitive emulation leads to a devaluation of the trend-setting style of the upper class (or inner elite), and this provokes continuous redefinition of what constitutes high style, a behaviour archaeologically studied by Miller and Cannon (Elias 1978: 100–01; Miller 1985: 184–205; Cannon 1989). On the other, Elias observes the important role of a clerical order in the dissemination of manners, because by extending them into the realm of the deity, they make it appear that these right ways are received from above (1978: 101–02). This can be restated in terms of the emergence of a functionary order (or outer elite), which can also be clerical, that standardizes and disseminates style as it manages the affairs of the society and which itself consumes products, just as it orders them to be produced (compare Redfield 1953: 64–65). Through this process, Elias claims that the nobility (inner elite) are 'bourgeoisified', as they have to respond to the trend-setting that is carried out by the functionary order (1978: 108–13). Burns has elegantly demonstrated the archaeological evidence for such a group in Mycenaean society through an examination of the distribution and sources of 'prestige' artefacts (Burns 1999). In this model the outer elite play a central role, as they are often in contact with those who inhabit the peripheries and who live beyond, especially those who provide exotic forms of social and material wealth and knowledge (Burns 1999; Helms 1988; 1993). This analysis modifies the claim by Baines and Yoffee that 'style is produced within the broader elite and consumed principally by the inner elite' (1998: 237), since it maintains that the outer elite also have a powerful role in the acquisition of symbolic resources, if not also their selection. So viewed, these two are engaged in a discursive relationship that creates and maintains civilization by standardizing the process of cultural production while also transforming it by modifying the repertory of symbols and elaborating the style of high culture.

By the time that the society has become this complex it is no longer transegalitarian, and the archaeological indicators of complexity are apparent in virtually every category of behaviour, as Cherry has observed in his analysis of Minoan palatial society (1986: 42–45). In his study of the origins of inequality, Hayden provides an evolutionary framework for studying this process by focussing on the changing dimensions of control by leaders over 'material resources and labor', for which he is criticized by Blanton because he ignores 'the many nonmaterial dimensions of behaviour underlying inequality' (Blanton 1995: 106). This criticism notwithstanding, it is in the material products of these actions that the evidence for an archaeological assessment resides. For the purposes of archaeological analysis, it is heuristically useful to subdivide the analytical categories and extend them across the spectrum of differently organized types of societies in order to have a method for comparing changes in different categories. Thus, on the basis of his ethnographic and archaeological examples, Hayden systematically breaks apart the general notion of big man into three different forms of leadership: despots, reciprocators, and entrepreneurs (1995: 23–28, fig. 3b). He attaches to each of these a variety of forms of feasting, also divided into three primary types: alliance and cooperation feasts, economic feasts, and diacritical feasts (1995: fig. 3a). These he arranges along an evolutionary scale that extends from despots to entrepreneurs.

Despot communities he describes as small, not necessarily sedentary, frequently engaged in warfare, with limited prestige goods, with grave goods mostly restricted to males, and practising feasting only minimally (1995: 41). Mostly these are 'complex hunter gatherers and simple horticulturalists'. Reciprocator communities are transegalitarian and engage in hunting and gathering and horticulture or are sedentary agriculturalists. They feast frequently, especially for ceremony and exchange. Here independent households begin to emerge concomitant with evidence of specialized architecture and built spaces, often associated with feasting. Prestige goods circulate, partly an indication of increasing contact with other communities. Burial goods may be placed with children as a sign of ascribed status (1995: 49–51). Entrepreneur communities continue to be hunters and gatherers and horticulturalists, but Hayden emphasizes that they intensively extract resources, especially agricultural ones, and they may be sedentary. A key to their economic operation is the creation of debt relations between members and leaders. Leaders mark themselves out in many ways, especially recognizable in grave goods for children, women and men. The elaboration of specialized architecture and the marking out of places is pronounced, now evident in products of mobilized labour, e.g. large-scale constructions like fortifications or irrigation networks (although see Lansing 1987 and Lansing and Kremer 1993 for a counter example). Feasting is frequent and elaborate and accompanied by vessels for production and consumption. Regional exchange extends through networks that provide prestige goods, and craft specialization is evident (1995: 60–63).

Hayden constructs archaeological correlates for the different kinds of strategies these leaders pursue (1995: 76, table 1). For example 'provoked warfare' would be visible in fortifications, armour, violent death, and trauma. These correlates also have important stylistic dimensions, which can be manipulated by leaders through their control of craft production to display messages and signs that are part of a coherent and self-conscious strategy of visual propaganda.[3] The social processes that create and sustain style are thus important to an understanding of the communicative aspects of the emergence of complex levels of socio-political organization.

Importantly Hayden also illustrates the changing and increasing levels of material expressions of complexity among the different kinds of transegalitarian communities (Hayden 1995: 80, fig 6). He shows the different forms and degrees of activities that would exhibit material remains at different levels of organization among transegalitarian communities. For example, whereas communities led by despots engage in a limited range of material and cultural activities (warfare, some rich burials, some regional exchange, and some non-corporate cult facilities), those led by entrepreneurs are highly active at almost all levels (warfare, rich burials of adult males and females and children, regional exchange, craft specialization, corporate and non-corporate feasting, corporate and non-corporate cult facilities, production of female cult figurines, raising of domesticates, production of prestige food vessels, wealth-based corporate groups (lineages and high-status households), and community hierarchies (Hayden 1995: 80, fig. 6)). Again the increasing production of cultural and material expressions directly affects the complexity, redundancy, and distribution of style and notably the centralization of style in the terms laid out by Baines and Yoffee in their definition of civilization (see above).

The transformative processes that change transegalitarian communities, chiefdoms and states are, for the purposes of this analysis, recognizable in the increase and intensification of the redundancy and distribution of the expressive vocabulary of the overall emerging society and the elites who control it. The processes that centralize power and authority also centralize and refine the style of this expression until, in the case of civilization, it has a momentum that continues its replication long after the social form and political economy that created it have ceased to operate.

Conclusions

A defining characteristic of post-modern archaeology is its return to an insistent relativistic individualism. Post-modern theory offers a powerful critique of both the positivist approach embraced by archaeologists during the 1960s and 1970s and the functionalist and structuralist approaches favoured throughout the 20th century. An emphasis on the individual and on the subjectivism that is inherent in such an approach to epistemology by definition cannot insist that these other ways of interpreting the world are false and that it is correct. Rather it observes that all are necessarily incomplete and that they err in idealizing constructs. Post-modernists argue that the original goal of the New Archaeology – the recovery and valuation of process – is achieved not through analysis of the reified mechanics of a Newtonian world view but through an analysis of how individuals are fundamental actors on a world stage (Giddens 1984). No *deus ex machina* manipulates their hands and feet and hearts and minds. Instead, individuals use their senses and through them construct the multi-sensory discourse that we call culture. How individuals act as agents, however, is not so clear, and has been at the centre of the debate between 'methodological individualism' and 'structural sociology', a point made by Giddens, who offers as an antidote his theory of structuration (1984: 1–40, 220). At the core of his argument is an attempt to negotiate between the enabling of individualistic approaches and the constraints of structuralist ones, which he resolves in his definition of history as 'the temporality of human practices, fashioning and fashioned by structural properties, within which diverse forms of power are incorporated' (1984: 220).

It is a paradox of the Western world view that it identifies the individual as the locus of humanity while also naming and idealizing the institutions forged by human social interaction. These are products of the Renaissance discovery that we can stand aside a little and examine ourselves as a collective in the phenomenon we call history. Archaeology has played a central role in that process both in its humanistic and antiquarian forms (Momigliano 1950; 1990; Choay 2001; Trigger 1989) because fundamental to the revolution of the Renaissance is the recognition of the externality of the material world and the understanding that the material products of human endeavour are enduring links to the human past. The view gained of human history has recognized as a special human achievement the creation of Civilization as a form (Kroeber and Kluckhohn 1952; Elias 1978) and civilizations as historical objects. How we define Civilization has consumed much intellectual passion and been central to the philosophy of history (Nietzsche 1995; White 1978). Archaeologists and anthropologists who have speculated on the utility of archaeology for studying human history have equally exercised themselves in pursuit of a definition of civilization (Redfield 1953; Flannery 1972; Renfrew 1972; Service 1975; Baines and Yoffee 1998).

Advocates of post-modern theory may choose to avoid the study of Civilization, preferring instead to celebrate the individual and local in historically contingent narratives of human existence, and there is much of value in such an approach – not least its valuation of context over construct (Brumfiel 2000: 131–32). These commentators ground this preference in a rejection of evolution as an historical and social process and a denial of the agency of the collective. Theirs is a repudiation of the interpretation of history and civilization that privileges various groups and ideologies over others. Yet a danger attendant on this view is a kind of reductionism that paradoxically loses the social-historical context of the individual, and this risks returning to Tyler's 'psychic unity of mankind' in a manner that is neither comparative nor historical (Orme 1981: 284; Comaroff and Comaroff 1992: xi; Brumfiel 2000: 131–32). What kind of history do we have if we abandon comparative study of the collectivities that we recognize across time and space? Post-modern theorists who insist that agency can only be located in the actions of individuals because only they have corporeal form misunderstand how humans interact in organizations. Obviously collectivities are not actors in the sense of individuals, but as Giddens points out, they represent a 'significant degree of reflexive monitoring of the conditions of social reproduction' (1984: 221). As he puts it, in corporate forums the 'participants "decide" (individually) "to decide" (corporately) upon a given course of action' (1984: 221). The focus of this article is to explore how civilizations emerge from the actions of a variety of individual agents operating in different corporate settings that themselves are in interaction with each other and different others across a broad temporal and spatial landscape.

Some may object that the pursuit of an archaeological definition of civilization and of a model of how it comes into being is merely an extension of an elitist project for controlling how we view the past. Admittedly at some fundamental spiritual level it may not make any difference to how a life is lived whether civilization exists or not or whether anyone understands what is meant by this concept. Yet an agent-oriented approach to history must admit, as I have just indicated, that agents act through corporate bodies that both enable and constrain individual action and therefore are dynamic and mutable. When we stand aside and view this process, we see the richly changing colours and shapes of a past that is materially represented in a myriad of symbolic forms. Sometimes they seem to coalesce into a large and enduring form that takes a distinct yet comparable shape to other forms perceived in other times and places of the past. These patterns assume a monumental form that we commonly term Civilization, much in the sense of monumental history as defined by Nietzsche (1995), who admonished us not to view them as moralizing object lessons but merely as artefacts of the past. They are nothing more than the material expressions of a consistent kind of human behaviour. That they dominate the material landscape is evidence that the activities of those who produced their elements had the resources, power and legitimacy to reproduce, again and again, the styles of culture.

Acknowledgements

I wish to thank the organizers, John Barrett and Paul Halstead, for the invitation to participate and for especially helpful comments on drafts of this paper. Dimitris Nakassis and Mary Dabney provided useful criticism of structure, content and meaning. I am responsible for all errors.

Notes

1   The extent to which the loss of these is culturally and individually dislocating is well evidenced in such traumatic episodes as the Highland Clearances of the early 19th century in Scotland (Mackenzie 1979), a matter only being redressed some 200 years later.

2   The relationship between inner and outer elites raises another important issue that must be noted in passing. Kinship and household structure and various rules of inclusion and exclusion play a critical role in defining how open or closed the emerging society will be (Gillespie 2000a: 6–11). The importance of this observation lies in recognizing the constraints on growth of a society as it competes with others. The more open it is to enlarging and enriching its population of elites through contact with others, the more likely it is to be able to mobilize labour and skills for the many activities needed for a growing society, not least defence. Closed societies restrict the extension of enfranchisement outside a closely defined group. A good example is the closed societies of the Etruscan polities (Torelli 2000: 197), which were unable to maintain control over enlarged territories because of the limitations on enfranchisement. In contrast the Latins and Romans were much more successful because their elites practised an open form of enfranchisement that increased and diversified the elite group (Cornell 2000: 219–24) and were therefore much more successful in incorporating others into their growing society.

3   The abundance of resources is one determinative factor in the formation and development of symbolic expression, e.g. the prevalence of wood over pottery or stone. Warfare has a strongly symbolic component, both in the manner of engagement, which has social rules, and in the form of weapons and the decoration and symbolic meaning of them and of other military accoutrements. Symbolic expression in burials is well understood; the increased redundancy, on the one hand, and the formation of specific types and styles of material expression for different age grades and sexes, on the other, is important to observe and correlate. Regional exchange involves preferences in acquisition, some of which are conditioned by the availability of local resources. Craft specialization is also individualistic

in that craftspersons either choose by themselves or are commanded to produce objects in specific forms and styles, which in different ways conform to socially determined styles. Feasting and cult facilities are expressions of social behaviour, and are governed by rules of assembly and movement, conditioned by local resources, and manipulated to create moods and feeling appropriate to particular societies (Geertz 1973: 97–125). The paraphernalia of cult are strongly conditioned by the symbolic expression of a society's beliefs and are characteristically rich in meaning and often highly redundant in application. The built environment, including pathways, routes, gathering areas, is also shaped by social processes that are communicative through their shaping of space and their mapping of place. Similarly houses and households express stylistic and formal properties that are complex – in some instances formalized expressions of social and household structure, in others mirrors of monumentally expressed styles that are projected from the top down. By tracing the continuities of stylistic expression among these categories, we are able, as archaeologists, to map the evolution of identity from its simplest forms of elite expression to very complex forms that, while still elite expression, are also emblematic of the society at large. The promulgation and maintenance of these throughout a society and among different societies over many generations is the process of the emergence of civilization.

Bibliography

Ames, K.M.
   1995   Chiefly power and household production on the Northwest Coast. In T.D. Price and G.M. Feinman (eds.), *Foundations of Social Inequality*: 155–87. New York: Plenum Press.
   2001   Slaves, chiefs and labour on the northern Northwest Coast. *World Archaeology* 33: 1–17.
van Andel, T. and C. Runnels
   1988   An essay on the 'emergence of civilization' in the Aegean world. *Antiquity* 62: 234–47.
Bailey, F.
   1969   *Strategems and Spoils*. Oxford: Blackwell.
Baines, J. and N. Yoffee
   1998   Order, legitimacy, and wealth in ancient Egypt and Mesopotamia. In G.M. Feinman and J. Marcus (eds.), *Archaic States*: 199–260. Santa Fe: School of American Research Press.
   2000   Order, legitimacy, and wealth: setting the terms. In M. Van Buren and J. Richards (eds.), *Order, Legitimacy and Wealth in Ancient States*: 13–17. New York: Cambridge.
Barthes, R.
   1982   *Empire of Signs*. New York: Hill and Wang.
   1983   *The Fashion System*. New York: Hill and Wang.
Blanton, R.E.
   1994   *Houses and Households: a Comparative Study*. New York: Plenum Press.
   1995   The cultural foundations of inequality in households. In T. Douglas Price and G. Feinman (eds.), *Foundations of Social Inequality*: 105–27. New York: Plenum Press.
   1998   Beyond centralization: steps toward a theory of egalitarian behavior in Archaic states. In G.M. Feinman and J. Marcus (eds.), *Archaic States*: 135–72. Santa Fe: School of American Research Press.
Bourdieu, P.
   1979   Symbolic power. *Critique of Anthropology* 38: 77–85.

Broodbank, C.
    2000   *An Island Archaeology of the Early Cyclades.* New York: Cambridge University Press.
Brumfiel, E.
    1994   Factional competition and political development in the New World: an introduction. In E. Brumfiel and J. Fox (eds.), *Factional Competition and Political Development in the New World*: 3–13. New York: Cambridge University Press.
    2000   The politics of high culture: issues of worth and rank. In M. Van Buren and J. Richards (eds.), *Order, Legitimacy and Wealth in Ancient States*: 131–39. New York: Cambridge University Press.
Burns, B.
    1999   *Import Consumption in the Bronze Age Argolid: Effects of Mediterranean Trade on Mycenaean Society.* PhD dissertation, University of Michigan.
Campbell, J.
    1964   *Honour, Family and Patronage: a Study of Institutions and Moral Values in a Greek Mountain Community.* Oxford: Clarendon.
Cannon, A.
    1989   The historical dimensions in mortuary status and sentiment. *Current Anthropology* 30: 437–58.
Cherry, J.F.
    1986   Polities and palaces: some problems in Minoan state formation. In C. Renfrew and J. Cherry (eds.), *Peer Polity Interaction and Socio-Political Change*: 19–45. New York: Cambridge University Press.
    1988   Pastoralism and the role of animals in the pre- and protohistoric economies of the Aegean. In C.R. Whittaker (ed.), *Pastoral Economies in Classical Antiquity* (Cambridge Philological Society Supplementary Volume 14): 6–34.
Choay, F.
    2001   *The Invention of the Historic Monument.* New York: Cambridge University Press.
Clark, J. and M. Blake
    1994   The power of prestige: competitive generosity and the emergence of rank societies in lowland Mesoamerica. In E. Brumfiel and J. Fox (eds.), *Factional Competition and Political Development in the New World*: 17–30. New York: Cambridge University Press.
Clarke, M.
    2001   Akha feasting: an ethnoarchaeological perspective. In M. Dietler and B. Hayden (eds.), *Feasts. Archaeological and Ethnographic Perspectives on Food, Politics, and Power*: 144–67. Washington: Smithsonian Institution Press.
Cohen, A.
    1974   *Two-Dimensional Man.* Berkeley: University of California Press.
Collier, J.F. and M.Z. Rosaldo
    1981   Politics and gender in simple societies. In S. Ortner and H. Whitehead (eds.), *Sexual Meanings: the Cultural Construction of Gender and Sexuality*: 275–329. Cambridge: Cambridge University Press.
Comaroff, J. and J. Comaroff
    1992   *Ethnography and the Historical Imagination.* Boulder: Westview Press.
Connerton, P.
    1989   *How Societies Remember.* New York: Cambridge University Press.
Cornell, T.
    2000   The city-states in Latium. In M.H. Hansen (ed.), *A Comparative Study of Thirty City-State Cultures*: 209–28. Copenhagen: C.A. Reitzels.
Darnell, R. and J.T. Irvine (eds.)

1999   *The Collected Works of Edward Sapir III. Culture.* New York: Mouton de Gruyter.

Dietler, M.

1990   Driven by drink: the role of drinking in the political economy and the case for Early Iron Age France. *Journal of Anthropological Archaeology* 9: 358–72.

1999   Rituals of commensality and the politics of state formation in the 'princely' societies of early Iron Age Europe. In P. Ruby (ed.), *Les princes de la protohistoire et l'emergence de l'état* (Collection de l'École Française de Rome R252): 135–52. Naples.

2001   Theorizing the feast: rituals of consumption, commensal politics, and power in African contexts. In M. Dietler and B. Hayden (eds.), *Feasts. Archaeological and Ethnographic Perspectives on Food, Politics, and Power*: 65–114. Washington: Smithsonian Institution Press.

Dietler, M. and I. Herbich

2001   Feasting and labor mobilization: dissecting a fundamental labor practice. In M. Dietler and B. Hayden (eds.), *Feasts. Archaeological and Ethnographic Perspectives on Food, Politics, and Power*: 240–64. Washington: Smithsonian Institution Press.

Earle T.

1987   Chiefdoms in archaeological and ethnohistorical perspectives. *Annual Review of Anthropology* 16: 279–308.

Elias, N.

1978   *The History of Manners.* New York: Urizen Books.

Feinman, G.

1998   Scale and social organization: perspectives on the Archaic state. In G. Feinman and J. Marcus (eds.), *Archaic States*: 95–133. Santa Fe: School of American Research.

Flannery, K.

1972   The cultural evolution of civilizations. *Annual Review of Ecology and Systematics* 3: 399–426.

Forsén, J.

1992   *The Twilight of the Early Helladics: a Study of the Disturbances in East-Central and Southern Greece toward the end of the Early Bronze Age.* Jonsered: Åström.

Friedman, J. and M.J. Rowlands

1977   Notes towards an epigenetic model of the evolution of 'civilisation'. In J. Friedman and M.J. Rowlands (eds.), *The Evolution of Social Systems*: 201–76. London: Duckworth.

Gamble, C.

1979   Surplus and self-sufficiency in the Cycladic subsistence economy. In J.L. Davis and J.F. Cherry (eds.), *Papers in Cycladic Prehistory* (Monograph 14): 122–34. Los Angeles: Institute of Archaeology, UCLA.

1982   Animal husbandry, population and urbanisation. In C. Renfrew and M. Wagstaff (eds.), *An Island Polity*: 161–71. Cambridge: Cambridge University Press.

Geertz, C.

1973   *The Interpretation of Cultures.* New York: Basic Books.

Giddens, A.

1984   *The Constitution of Society.* Berkeley: University of California Press.

Gillespie, S.D.

2000a   Beyond kinship, an introduction. In R.A. Joyce and S.D. Gillespie (eds.), *Beyond Kinship. Social and Material Reproduction in House Societies*: 1–21. Philadelphia: University of Pennsylvania.

2000b   Lévi-Strauss. *Maison* and *Sociétè Maisons.* In R.A. Joyce and S.D. Gillespie (eds.), *Beyond Kinship. Social and Material Reproduction in House Societies*: 22–52. Philadelphia: University of Pennsylvania.

Godelier, M.
  1977a Economy and religion: an evolutionary optical illusion. In J. Friedman and M.J. Rowlands (eds.), *The Evolution of Social Systems*: 3–11 London: Duckworth.
  1977b Politics as 'infrastructure': an anthropologist's thoughts on the example of classical Greece and the notions of the relations of production and economic determinism. In J. Friedman and M.J. Rowlands (eds.), *The Evolution of Social Systems*: 14–28. London: Duckworth.
Halstead, P.
  1987 Man and other animals in later Greek prehistory. *BSA* 87: 71–83.
  1988 On redistribution and the origin of Minoan-Mycenaean palatial economies. In E.B. French and K.A. Wardle (eds.), *Problems in Greek Prehistory*: 519–30. Bristol: Bristol Classical Press.
  1992 Dimini and the 'DMP': faunal remains and animal exploitation in Late Neolithic Thessaly. *BSA* 87: 29–59.
  1993 Banking on livestock: indirect storage in Greek agriculture. *Bulletin of Sumerian Agriculture* 7: 63–7.
  1996 Pastoralism or household herding? Problems of scale and specialization in early Greek animal husbandry. *World Archaeology* 38: 20–42.
Hayden, B.
  1995 Pathways to power. Principles for creating socioeconomic inequalities. In T.D. Price and G.M. Feinman (eds.), *Foundations of Social Inequality:* 15–86. New York: Plenum Press.
  2001a Dynamics of wealth and poverty in the transegalitarian societies of Southeast Asia. *Antiquity* 289: 571–81.
  2001b Richman, poorman, beggarman, chief: the dynamics of social inequality. In B. Hayden, *Archaeology at the Millennium: a Sourcebook:* 231–72. New York: Kluwer Academic/Plenum.
Helms, M.
  1984 Chiefdom rivalries, control and external contacts in lower Central America. In E. Brumfiel and J. Fox (eds.), *Factional Competition and Political Development in the New World:* 55–60. New York: Cambridge University Press.
  1988 *Ulysses' Sail: an Ethnographic Odyssey of Power, Knowledge, and Geographical Distance.* Princeton: Princeton University Press.
  1993 *Craft and the Kingly Ideal: Art, Trade, and Power.* Austin: University of Texas Press.
Hillier, B. and J. Hanson
  1984 *The Social Logic of Space.* Cambridge: Cambridge University Press.
Hodder, I.
  1982 *Symbolic and Structural Archaeology.* Cambridge and New York: Cambridge University Press.
  1986 *Reading the Past: Current Approaches to Interpretation in Archaeology.* New York: Cambridge University Press.
Hodder, I. (ed.)
  1989 *The Meanings of Things: Material Culture and Symbolic Expression.* Boston: Unwin Hyman.
Ingold, T.
  1986 *Evolution and Social Life.* New York: Cambridge.
Kent, S. (ed.)
  1990 *Domestic Architecture and the Use of Space: an Interdisciplinary Cross-Cultural Study.* New York: Cambridge University Press.

Kertzer, D.
  1988   *Ritual, Politics, and Power*. New Haven: Yale.
Kluckhohn, C.
  1960   The moral order in the expanding society. In C.H. Kraeling and R.M. Adams (eds.), *City Invincible*: 391–404. Chicago: University of Chicago.
Kroeber, A.
  1917   The superorganic. *American Anthropologist* 19: 163–213.
Kroeber, A. and C. Kluckhohn
  1952   *Culture: a Critical Review of Concepts and Definitions* (Papers of the Peabody Museum of American Archaeology and Ethnology 47). Cambridge, Mass.: Peabody Museum.
Lansing, J.
  1987   Balinese 'water temples' and the management of irrigation. *American Anthropologist* 89: 326–41.
Lansing, J. and J. Kremer
  1993   Emergent properties of Balinese water temple networks: coadaptation on a rugged fitness landscape. *American Anthropologist* 95: 97–114.
Mackenzie, A.
  1979   *History of the Highland Clearances*. Perth: Melven Press.
Maran, J.
  1998   *Kulturwandel auf dem Griechischen Festland und den Kykladen im Späten 3. Jahrtausend v. Chr.: Studien zu den Kulturellen Verhältnissen in Südosteuropa und dem Zentralen sowie Östlichen Mittelmeerraum in der Späten Kupfer-und Frühen Bronzezeit*. Bonn: R. Habelt.
Miller, D.
  1985   *Artefacts as Categories: a Study of Ceramic Variability in Central India*. New York: Cambridge University Press.
Momigliano, A.
  1950   Ancient history and the antiquarian. *Journal of the Warburg and Courtauld Institute* 13: 285–315.
  1990   *The Classical Foundations of Modern Historiography*. Berkeley: University of California Press.
Nietzsche, F.
  1995   On the utility and liability of history for life. In E. Behler (ed.), *The Complete Works of Friedrich Nietzsche, 2: Unfashionable Observations*: 85–167. Stanford: Stanford University Press.
O'Connor, D.
  2000   Society and individual in early Egypt. In M. Van Buren and J. Richards (eds.), *Order, Legitimacy and Wealth in Ancient States*: 21–35. New York: Cambridge University Press.
Orme, B.
  1981   *Anthropology for Archaeologists: an Introduction*. Ithaca, N.Y.: Cornell University Press.
Panofsky, E.
  1960   *Renaissance and Renascences in Western Art*. Stockholm: Almqvist and Wiksell.
Parker Pearson, M.
  1999   *The Archaeology of Death and Burial*. College Station: Texas A and M.
Price, B.
  1982   Cultural materialism: a theoretical review. *American Antiquity* 47: 709–41.
Price, T.D.
  1995   Social inequality at the origins of agriculture. In T.D. Price and G.M. Feinman (eds.), *Foundations of Social Inequality*: 129–51. New York: Plenum Press.
Redfield, R.

1953   *The Primitive World and its Transformations.* Ithaca, NY: Cornell University Press.
Renfrew, C.
1972   *The Emergence of Civilisation. The Cyclades and the Aegean in the Third Millennium B.C.* London: Methuen.
1977   Space, time and polity. In J. Friedman and M.J. Rowlands (eds.), *The Evolution of Social Systems*: 89–112. London: Duckworth.
Sahlins, M.
1963   Poor man, rich man, big man, chief: political types in Melanesia and Polynesia. *Comparative Studies in Society and History* 5: 285–303.
Sapir, E.
1917   Do we need a 'superorganic?' *American Anthropologist* 19: 441–47.
Service, E.
1971   *Primitive Social Organization; an Evolutionary Perspective.* New York: Random House.
1975   *Origins of the State and Civilization.* New York: W.W. Norton.
Spencer, C.
1994   Factional ascendance, dimensions of leadership, and the development of centralized authority. In E. Brumfiel and J. Fox (eds.), *Factional Competition and Political Development in the New World*: 31–43. New York: Cambridge.
Terrell, J.E., T.L. Hung and C. Gosden
1997   The dimensions of social life in the Pacific. *Current Anthropology* 38: 155–95.
Tilley, C.
1994   *A Phenomenology of Landscape.* Providence, R.I.: Berg.
Torrelli, M.
2000   The Etruscan city-state. In M.H. Hansen (ed.), *A Comparative Study of Thirty City-State Cultures*: 189–208. Copenhagen: C.A. Reitzels.
Triantaphyllou, S.
2001   *A Bioarchaeological Approach to Prehistoric Cemetery Populations from Central and Western Greek Macedonia* (BAR International Series 976). Oxford: British Archaeological Reports.
Trigger, B.
1989   *A History of Archaeological Thought.* New York: Cambridge University Press.
Tuan, Y.-F.
1977   *Space and Place. The Perspective of Experience.* Minneapolis: University of Minnesota Press.
Turner, V.
1967   *The Forest of Symbols.* Ithaca: Cornell.
Van Buren, M. and J. Richards
2000   Introduction: ideology, wealth and the comparative study of 'civilizations'. In M. Van Buren and J. Richards (eds.), *Order, Legitimacy and Wealth in Ancient States*: 3–12. New York: Cambridge University Press.
Wagstaff, M. and S. Augustson
1982   Traditional landuse. In C. Renfrew and M. Wagstaff (eds.), *An Island Polity*: 106–33. Cambridge: Cambridge University Press.
Wagstaff, M. and J.F. Cherry
1982   Settlement and population change. In C. Renfrew and M. Wagstaff (eds.), *An Island Polity*: 136–55. Cambridge: Cambridge University Press.
Wallace, A.F.C.
1966   *Religion: an Anthropological View.* New York: Random House.
1972a   Paradigmatic processes in cultural change. *American Anthropologist* 74: 467–78.

1972b *Rockdale*. New York: W.W. Norton.

Wason P.K.

1994   *The Archaeology of Rank*. New York: Cambridge University Press.

White, H.

1978   *Tropics of Discourse*. Baltimore: Johns Hopkins University Press.

Wright, J.C.

2001   Factions and the origins of leadership and identity in Mycenaean society. *BICS* 45: 182.

Yoffee, N.

1995   Political economy in early Mesopotamian states. *Annual Review of Anthropology* 24: 281–311.

5

Iconographies of Value: Words, People and Things in the Late Bronze Age Aegean

John Bennet

Teaching a course called 'Homeric Archaeology' can do funny things to you, but one beneficial effect is to make you think more deeply about the relationship between the Homeric texts and material culture in the Aegean Late Bronze Age. Archaeologists have presented radically different views of the 'reality' of Homeric society. Two years after the publication of *Emergence*, Anthony Snodgrass published an article questioning whether the society depicted in the Homeric epic had ever existed (Snodgrass 1974), essentially following Moses Finley. Oliver Dickinson (1986) claimed him as a 'poet of the Dark Age', in explicit rejection of the position taken by scholars like Emily Vermeule who had written in her *Greece in the Bronze Age* (1964):

> We say in justification [of the dominance of Homer in reconstructions of Mycenaean Age] that large parts of the poems incorporate Mycenaean traditions, that the five hundred years separating the fall of Troy VIIA from the Homeric version of its fall have wrought only minor innovations, a few misunderstandings of the past and adaptations to a more modern experience. We hope that the core of those great poems has not been terribly changed by successive improvisations of oral poets – surely poets will guard for us the heritage of the past. (Vermeule 1964: x)

Despite Dickinson's protestations, in fact few Aegean archaeologists at the time would have disagreed with Finley's verdict, originally delivered in 1957, on Homer in relation to the picture suggested by the (then recently deciphered) Linear B documents:

> Homer is not only not a reliable guide to the Mycenaean tablets; he is no guide at all. (Finley 1982: 232)

It is no surprise that Homer, although not absent, is rarely mentioned in the *Emergence*. The most extensive reference is in relation to socio-political organization (Renfrew 1972: 368–69), cautiously preceded with the statement that

Homer 'must not, of course, be taken unquestioningly as a guide to Mycenaean social structure' (Renfrew 1972: 368).

One aspect of the 'distancing' of Homer from study of the Aegean Late Bronze Age was the development of our understanding of Homeric poetry as oral. This we know through the work of scholars such as Milman Parry and Albert Lord, who carried out fieldwork in the 1930s among the *guslar* of Bosnia (e.g., Lord 2000; Parry 1987). Since we had known, at least since Evans, that the Aegean Late Bronze Age world was literate, there could be little point of contact. Even after the decipherment of Linear B, the value of Homer was more in providing linguistic parallels for the early forms of Greek attested in the Linear B tablets than in social or administrative reconstruction. In the same year as the *Emergence*, the late John Chadwick (1972) published an article entitled 'Was Homer a liar?' while a chapter of his influential and widely read book *The Mycenaean World* (published in 1976) was entitled 'Homer the pseudo-historian' (Chadwick 1976: 180–87).

I should like to argue that in fact it is the oral nature of Homeric poetry that holds the key and that the medium in which he composed can suggest one way of understanding words, people and things in the Aegean Late Bronze Age. In this respect, therefore, the interest of Homeric poetry is central not to inter-pretations of socio-political organization in the Late Bronze Age Aegean, but to those areas treated in chapter 19 of the *Emergence*, the 'Symbolic and projective systems' (Renfrew 1972: 404–39). Scholars have rightly rejected the value of Homer as a historical source. Such interpretations depend on a particular view of the epic tradition that I would term 'event primary' (Figure 5.1, upper half), and embodied in remarks like those of Vermeule just quoted. In this scheme what we have in Homer's *Iliad*, for example, is an inferior, dim reflection of a set of events in the distant past. This is, of course, a flawed view of any oral tradition, since such traditions depend above all on the continuity of practice constantly reinforced by new events and adjusted to shifting social situations in time and space (Figure 5.1, lower half).

Because Homer's poetry was oral, but came to us through written texts, we only have access to its form when it came to be written down – perhaps in the 8th c. BC. This is why, as Ian Morris argued 15 years ago, the epic reflects 8th-c. BC Greek life in so far as it presents any consistent view within the epic imperative to create 'distance' between its world and that of contemporary life (I. Morris 1986). However, linguistic evidence drawn from comparison between the language of Homer and that of the Late Bronze Age palatial elite as reflected in the Linear B documents suggests that the practice of oral poetry goes back at least to a stage prior to that of the Linear B documents – prior to the 13th c. BC (e.g., Horrocks 1980; Ruijgh 1995). Equally, it has long been recognized that some of the material culture references in the epic are to objects known archaeologically in the early Mycenaean period (e.g. Shelmerdine 1996; E.S. Sherratt 1990; *cf.* Lorimer 1950). Sue Sherratt has, of course, explored the way in which these

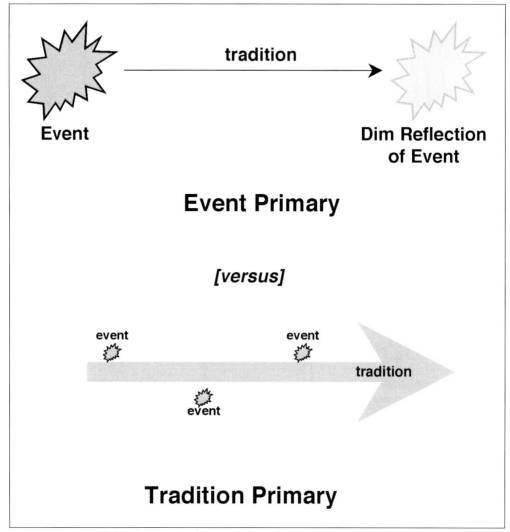

Figure 5.1. Diagram, showing two different interpretations of the epic tradition.

elements are overlain throughout the tradition, using the patterns to suggest key periods (punctuated equilibria?) in the formation of the epic, namely: the early Mycenaean period, the post-palatial of the 12th c. BC and beyond, and the 8th c. BC (E.S. Sherratt 1990: 815–21, fig. 4).

Given the notion of epic as a continuity of practice, I suggest that the Homeric texts might offer ways in which we can 'read' Late Bronze Age material culture and, further, that these 'ways of reading' – since they are embedded in epic practice – are likely to be more subtle and pervasive than the obvious and infinitely malleable phenomena such as direct reference to elements of material culture (like the use of iron) or references to social or ethnic groups (like the Phoenicians), and so forth. I propose two elements of practice that function in this way:

(i) the developed notions of objects with 'cultural biographies' (by virtue of prior ownership, or age, or exotic origins: Gosden and Marshall 1999) and 'biographical' objects (objects that combine to create the biography of an individual: *cf.* Hoskins 1998).

(ii) the idea that images on objects act as a prompt to oral narrative.

The Homeric texts frequently offer attestations of objects with a 'cultural biography'. These take the form either of a distinguished genealogy through 'vertical' transmission (Figure 5.2) within an elite lineage, such as Agamemnon's sceptre in *Iliad* 2:

> King Agamemnon
> rose to his feet, raising high in hand the sceptre
> Hephaestus made with all his strength and skill.
> Hephaestus gave it to Cronus' son, Father Zeus,
> and Zeus gave it to Hermes, the giant-killing Guide
> and Hermes gave it to Pelops, that fine charioteer,
> Pelops gave it to Atreus, marshal of fighting men,
> who died and passed it on to Thyestes rich in flocks
> and he in turn bestowed it on Agamemnon, to bear on high
> as he ruled his many islands and lorded mainland Argos.
> (Homer 1991: 102–03 = *Iliad* 2.100–108)

Alternatively, objects have an exotic origin and are transmitted through space ('horizontally') and time between various elite owners, as is the case with Achilles's Sidonian bowls in *Iliad* 23:

> Achilles quickly set out prizes for the footrace.
> A silver bowl, gorgeous, just six measures deep
> but the finest mixing bowl in all the world.
> Nothing could match its beauty – a masterpiece
> that skilled Sidonian craftsmen wrought to perfection,
> Phoenician traders shipped across the misty seas
> and mooring in Thoas' roads, presented to the king.
> Eneus son of Jason gave it to Prince Patroclus,
> the ransom paid to release Lycaon, Priam's son.
> This was the bowl Achilles offered up at games
> to commemorate his great friend...
> (Homer 1991: 582 = *Iliad* 23.740–748)

Objects act as a prompt to oral narrative, for example, in the *Odyssey* (Book 19) where Odysseus, posing as a beggar and therefore in disguise, describes

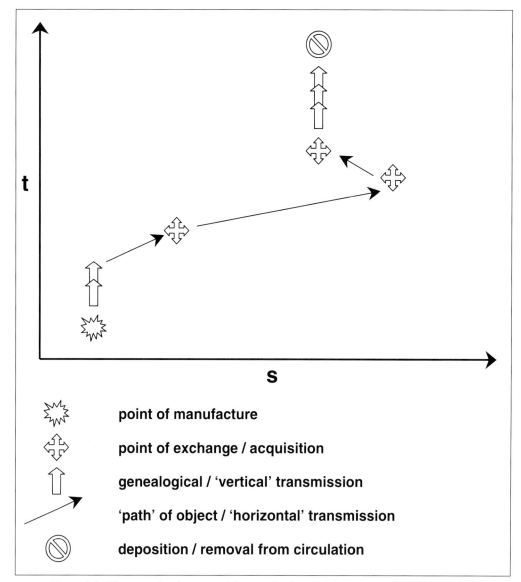

Figure 5.2. Diagram, showing potential stages in the acquisition of a 'cultural biography'.

'Odysseus' to Penelope, his own wife. In that passage, he refers to a golden pin worn by 'Odysseus' that has a representation of a deer and hound that 'comes to life' in the description:

> King Odysseus...
> he was wearing a heavy woolen cape, sea-purple

in doublefolds, with a gold brooch to clasp it,
twin sheaths for the pins, on the face a work of art:
a hound clenching a dappled fawn in its front paws
slashing it as it writhed. All marvelled to see it,
solid gold as it was, the hound slashing, throttling
the fawn in its death-throes, hoofs failing to break free.
(Homer 1996: 325–26 = *Odyssey* 19.225–231)

There are, of course, other more extended examples, notably the description of the 'Shield of Achilles' which extends over about 130 lines of text in *Iliad* 18 (Homer 1991: 483–87 = *Iliad* 18.478–608).

These phenomena are present in Early Iron Age 'practice' too as James Whitley has recently reminded us (Whitley 2002: 223–26). To take a perhaps untypical example (also discussed by Whitley [2002: 224–25, with illustrations]), the mid-10th c. BC burial and cremation in the so-called 'Heroön' at Lefkandi each contain objects that had cultural biographies: the male cremation was deposited in a late-13th or 12th c. BC bronze amphoroid krater (a shape normally used for mixing water and wine), probably manufactured in Cyprus (Catling 1993), while the female inhumation had a 1000-year old pendant perhaps of Babylonian origin around her neck (Popham 1994: 15). Not only do these objects have a cultural biography (although the specifics are obviously inaccessible to us), but they are also used by those creating the mortuary context to construct a 'biography' of the individuals interred there. The fact that the burials are within, although in a somewhat ambiguous stratigraphical relation (Popham 1993b; I. Morris 2000: 219) to a large, apparently domestic structure (the 'Heroön') might further emphasize this 'biographical' aspect of the complex, and we might also note the interment of four horses in a pit adjacent to the human burials (Popham 1993a: 21).

Objects like those included in mortuary contexts within the Toumba site at Lefkandi – even if undecorated – could no doubt have acted as prompts to narratives of their cultural biographies (i.e. their 'authenticity' in Appadurai's terminology: Appadurai 1986: 46). So, also, could objects with images and these become increasingly well attested in the later 8th c. BC and beyond, such as the bronze fibula catch plate with a duel (Snodgrass 1998: 32, fig. 12) or representations of sea battles on Attic Late Geometric (c. 750–700 BC) pottery (Snodgrass 1998: 35, fig. 14). These objects too were often deposited in tombs or were used as part of symposiastic rituals. They have been problematic to modern scholars because they suggest themes attested in contemporary and later literary works (including Homer's; see, especially, Snodgrass 1998 for problems with this view), but cannot definitively be tied to such narratives because they lack an explicit link. A problem here is that modern preconceptions demand that a representation like this is a picture 'of' something, rather than a representation that might act as a prompt 'for' a verbal rendition – the images are 'potential', not 'fixed'.

As an aside, this attitude to the use of images fits well with suggestions by Sarah Morris and Barry Powell, for example, that images from the eastern Mediterranean world acted as prompts to the generation of stories, such as those of the Herakles cycle in early Greek story-telling (S. Morris 1995: 208–09, pl. La; Powell 1997: 174–86).

Such narrative 'potential' is well exemplified by the case of the famous Eleusis Polyphemos amphora (perhaps a generation or two later, c. 675 BC) which depicts the blinding of Polyphemos, but conflates two different times: Polyphemos's drinking of Odysseus's wine (offered in accordance with Greek rituals of hospitality, as a *xenia*) and his later blinding by Odysseus and his men (Snodgrass 1998: 90, fig. 35). Anthony Snodgrass termed this style of narrative 'synoptic' (Snodgrass 1982), but the key is that, as a story, the image needs to be rendered as a verbal narrative to be 'complete'. In a slightly different direction, John Papadopoulos (1999: 638) makes the interesting observation that the small number of texts incised (not painted) on 8th-c. pots are complementary to visual images, never combined, seeing the two practices as essentially similar, because the Greek verb *'graphein'* can have either meaning. I would argue that it is the almost complete avoidance of combining text and image that is crucial and is, again, a practice that goes well back into the Aegean Bronze Age.

This practice ends with the attachment to images of text that 'anchors' (Barthes 1977: 38; *cf*. Winter 1981: esp. 25) them to a specific context. This is well exemplified in a single fragmentary Attic Black Figure potsherd on which is preserved a scene of a chariot group racing from left to right, watched by an animated crowd in a grandstand (Snodgrass 1998: 117, fig. 45), where the addition of the words 'games of Patroklos' is sufficient to tie the scene to a specific episode in the Homeric corpus. (The other inscription claims the work as that of a particular individual, Sophilos, whose work is dated c. 580–570 BC [Boardman 1974: 18–19].)

An image like that on the 'Sophilos fragment', rather than representing the beginnings of 'modern art' – as some ancient art historians might claim – in fact represents the closure of what I should like to argue is a long tradition of practice that can be traced back (at least) to the period of the Shaft Graves (17th–16th c. BC) in mainland Greece. Just as we can suggest strongly on the basis of linguistic analysis that the 'medium' of epic poetry has a history that goes back to early Mycenaean times, so, perhaps, we can imagine a continuity of 'practice' in the reading and appreciation of objects that goes back an equally long way.

In the assemblages of the two 'Grave circles' at Mycenae, but especially Circle 'A', we see numerous objects that – by virtue either of their exotic material and/or manufacture or by virtue of their modification by craftspeople, or both – can be understood as objects with cultural biographies (Figure 5.3). I have in mind particularly objects like the Egyptian baggy alabastron, inverted and transformed, by having its old mouth sealed and a new one created in its old base, into a Minoan bridge-spouted jar ultimately deposited in Grave Circle 'A'

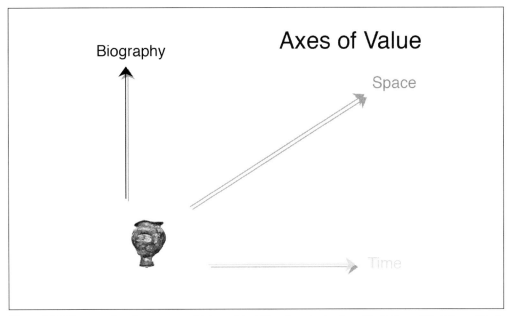

Figure 5.3. Diagram, showing axes on which an object (the silver krater from Shaft Grave IV of Grave Circle 'A' at Mycenae) might be valued.

shaft V (Karo 1930–33: pl. CXXXVII; Warren 1997: 212, pl. LXIXb), or the ostrich-egg rhyta, one transformed by the addition of faience dolphins (Karo 1930–33: pl. XXXX; Foster 1979: 132–34, pl. 42).

Most striking, perhaps, in terms of its exotic origins is the amber found in both grave circles, but in restricted contexts (Grave Circle 'A', shaft I [2 beads]; III [24 complete beads, plus pieces of 6–8 more]; IV [2 groups, one of 1290 beads]; V [c. 100 beads]; Grave Circle 'B' *iota* [1 bead]; *omicron* [119 beads] [Mylonas 1972: pl. 186B; Demakopoulou 1988: 256, no. 280]). Here is a material that, in one limited sense, acts as an indicator of exchange relations and a pointer to the central Mediterranean. But a material presumably acquired in the ambit of coastal southern Italy (to judge from the early Mycenaean pottery found there: Vagnetti 1999; Graziadio 1998) must have prompted narratives about its ultimate origin (see discussion in Hughes-Brock 1985: 260–61; 1993: 223–24; *cf.* Shennan 1993). I wonder if we should link it to later Greek tradition surrounding the golden apples of the Hesperides, since the early Greek name for the material is *electron*, reflecting its relationship in what we would term a 'folk taxonomy' with gold (*cf.* A. Sherratt 1995: 201). This link to 'mythical' time and space, if we accept it, offers an additional explanation of amber's value in the Mycenaean world.

A similar link between image and mythical time and space might be seen in the case of the griffin, which, in later representations at least, is given a life cycle

(Rehak 1995) that, for us moderns, seems unusual for what we regard as a composite, fictional animal. However, the life cycle is ambiguous, reflecting the dual nature of the animal – mammalian (feline), on a Late Helladic IIA cushion seal found in a tholos tomb at Myrsinohori *Routsi* (Demakopoulou 1988: 214, no. 194) or avian (bird) on a Late Helladic IIIC light-on-dark alabastron found in the settlement of Xeropolis at Lefkandi (Popham and Milburn 1971: 340, pl. 54,2). If the avian life cycle were current in certain times and places within the Mycenaean world, then perhaps ostrich eggs might have been interpreted as griffins' eggs (an idea aired by Paul Rehak some years ago on the AegeaNet discussion group [Rehak 1995]). As an aside, while discussing exotic objects, we might also entertain the possibility of 'exotic' people, as the bone chemistry suggests for the – probably female – outlying individual from among a group from Grave Circle 'A' sampled by Mike Richards and Robert Hedges (Tzedakis and Martlew 1999: 226).

In addition to objects whose material or manufacture required the construction of cultural biographies, a number of objects within the Shaft Grave assemblages fall nicely into the category of objects prompting oral narrative. These appear at different scales such as the miniature scale of the gold signet ring. A telling example is that often referred to as the 'Battle in the Glen' (3.5 x 2.1 cm) – again, in modern terms it has to be a picture 'of' something – found in shaft grave IV of Grave Circle 'A' (Karo 1930–33: pl. XXIV, no. 241; Hampe and Simon 1981: 176, no. 265; *cf.* Cain 1997: 135–37). On this appears a complex scene involving four combatants, each differently equipped and dressed, the whole framed by a stylised representation of rocks. The slightly larger scale of the famous silver krater (from the same shaft grave in Grave Circle 'A': Sakellariou 1974) perhaps reflects its use (in life) as the centrepiece in feasting and/or drinking events, during which – no doubt – stories would have been elaborated. On this object, two lines of distinctively dressed warriors come together, while another silver vessel from the same tomb (a rhyton, or ritual pouring vessel, frequently simply referred to as the 'siege rhyton') displays an elaborate coastal siege scene (Hampe and Simon 1981: 88, nos. 130–31; Sakellariou 1975; *cf.* Cain 1997: 131–35)

Perhaps the most striking variation in scale while preserving unity of theme is the example of another gold signet, again from shaft grave IV in Grave Circle 'A', showing two men in a chariot hunting a deer (Karo 1930–33: pl. XXIV, no. 240; Hampe and Simon 1981: 176, no. 266) and scenes of chariot hunting/warfare on a number of the large stone stelai that appear to have marked each interment in the complex (Younger 1997: 235–36, nos. I, IV, V, IX, and 13). These narratives could, of course, have been tied to individuals as part of the creation of biography through the assembly, display and deposition of objects at burial, but the stelai also acted as a more permanently available 'distributed' or 'serial' narrative within the cemetery. If reconstructions of the life span of Grave Circle 'A' are correct (Graziadio 1988; Dickinson 1977: 48), then the complex was in use only for quite a short period, perhaps two to three generations. The implication of this chronology is that the images presented on the stelai would relate to individuals well within living memory of Mycenae's inhabitants and, indeed, they would have been remembered through the media of the stelai themselves.

Narratives like these were apparently repeatedly 'retold' in the case of Grave Circle 'A', which was remodelled and contained within the extension of the LH IIIB fortification walls of Mycenae (French 2002: 79–80), unlike its predecessor, Circle 'B', which was allegedly 'forgotten' (or deliberately ignored?) (French 2002: 31–35). This is a good example of the potential for such images to be reinterpreted over a long period of time. We might also think of this as operating on a larger scale in the distribution of tholos tombs around the approaches to the central citadel at Mycenae (French 2002: 41–44, fig. 10; 69–71; Wright 1987) – they too might have acted as a 'distributed' narrative of dynastic power by the mature Mycenaean period of the 13th c. BC. Jim Wright has noted the increasing homologies between the latest tholos tomb architecture, both in terms of material (the distinctive local conglomerate rock) and form (a trilithon doorway with relieving triangle above, approached along a corridor ['dromos']), and the architecture of the citadel wall at Mycenae (Wright 1987: 177–80; *cf.* also Santillo Frizell 1998).

In the late Mycenaean phase, it seems that the types of display exemplified in the Shaft Graves have 'moved' out of the mortuary sphere and their association with particular individuals to the sphere of the built environment – the palace complex – and the office of the ruler (*wanax*), rather than the person of the individual holder of the office. We can see that memory and time scales are relevant in exploring these themes in relation to the site of Bronze Age Pylos. Study of this site in its regional context suggests an expansion of the polity at the beginning of the LH IIIB phase, which may have been commemorated in the construction of the final set of palatial buildings (Bennet and Shelmerdine 2001: 135–36; Davis and Bennet 1999: 106, with references). However, just as the form of the palace structures did not remain static in the three to four generations of the final palace (Wright 1984; Shelmerdine 2001: 337–39, 378), so perhaps areas of the polity were still negotiating their relationship with the Pylian elite (Bennet 1999: 148–49; 2002: 23–25; Bennet and Shelmerdine 2001: 138–39).

Jack Davis and I have suggested (1999: 114–18) how the imagery within the palace at its destruction reflected both the 'benign' aspects of palatial rule – through the association of the *wanax* in the main 'megaron' (McCallum 1987) with feasting and, it now seems, with sacrifice (Isaakidou *et al.* 2002; Stocker and Davis 2004) – and the coercive message in the representations in room 64 (Davis and Bennet 1999: pls. XIII–XIV). It is well worth stressing the human time scale on which these images are being created and re-created. This is quite vividly brought home to us by the evidence of re-plastering episodes within the palatial structures: in the main 'megaron' hearth five layers were laid down over a period of about a century, while up to eight episodes of floor re-plastering are attested in the central column base of Room 64 (Blegen and Rawson 1966: 85–87, 251). These re-plastering events suggest frequent renewal of the decorative programme.

Further evidence is offered by the presence of painted wall plaster dumps (Lang 1969: 5–6) around the main building, notably that on the northwest slope of the citadel. In some cases, fragments within these dumps show similar border decoration to that of decorated plaster that was on walls in the palatial complex at the destruction, suggesting they represent earlier phases of decoration in those rooms. Notable among them are the chequered border resembling the wall paintings present at the destruction in hall 64 attested in the northwest slope dump (Lang 1969: 74–75, no. 31 H nws) and outside the northeast wall of the palace (Lang 1969: 186, no. 19 M ne). The existence of these special dumps implies a special disposal regime for such (symbolically charged?) materials and also a continuity of overall style of wall decoration, but the possibility for shifts of detail.

The combination of the static, framing representations with the physical presence of an individual in the 'first person' completing the composition within the main 'megaron' effectively 'narrates' the power of the *wanax* and is perhaps the true analogy to the developed ruler iconography with both a 'third person' representation of the ruler and textual labels to 'fix' or 'anchor' the image attested, for example, in contemporary Egypt, or in later Assyria.

Narration of a different quality may have taken place in association with the representations in hall 64, where, it is plausible to argue, the static images were 'brought to life' by a parallel oral poetic performance, as suggested by the image of the lyre-player associated with the feasting scene in the main megaron (McCallum 1987: 199, pl. X; *cf.* Younger 1995: pl. LXXVI). The prevalence of oral performance – both poetic and in terms of bodily placement and movement – in the various contexts within the palace complex at Pylos provides a contrast with the existence of writing in the Mycenaean world. But perhaps the apparent contrast ought to remind us that technologies do not always function in identical manner in different social contexts; in the Mycenaean world, at any rate, writing seems neither to have replaced performance nor to have augmented it in the public sphere.

The prevalence of oral performance in late Mycenaean Pylos, I would argue, in fact sits quite comfortably alongside the apparent absence of non-'administrative' texts. Equally, even qualities of some of the Linear texts we have arguably reflect oral practice, rather than administrative practices taking place entirely within the written sphere. On Pylos tablet Ep 704.5 a dispute over the status of a particular land-holding agreement between the priestess named *e-ri-ta* (Eritha?) and a group called the *da-mo* (*damos*) is recorded in terms that suggest an oral dispute. We also have 'third-person' description of actions by officials that I have suggested might perhaps have been written by the officials themselves (Bennet 2001: 29–31; *cf.* Kyriakidis 1996–97), in one case at least, after a 'tour of inspection' (Pylos Eq 213). Similarly, Tom Palaima has suggested that the lists of equipment in the Pylos Ta series (now linked to feasting and sacrifice: Killen 1998) reflect oral dictation (Palaima 2000: 237, although I would disagree that there was a distinct scribe involved in addition to the official: see Bennet 2001: 31). It is perhaps pushing the evidence somewhat, but I wonder if even the layout of Linear B texts with their extensive range of highly representational 'commodity signs' or 'logograms' (notable, for example, in the area of vessels and chariots: Ventris and Chadwick 1973: 51, fig. 10, 324, fig. 16) is suggestive of a pre-dominately oral environment linked to images. A further point one might make in relation to administrative activities relates to the importance of sealing – a 'performative' act that demands the physical presence of two parties. The seals used to make impressions – that, we might note, only 'appear' in the correct orientation when impressed on clay and are often extremely difficult to 'read' on the original stone – often bear images that echo the iconographic world of the palace (Bennet 2001: 34–35; Pini 1997; Lang 1969).

This series of ideas was prompted partly at least by my own encounter with 'Homeric archaeology', to which I return, appropriately enough, in ring composition. I hope that some of the above can suggest a more satisfying appreciation of the use of material culture ('things'), its relation to text, primarily oral ('words') and how they are both used by and shape the lives of 'people'. In emphasizing orality and performance, I think we can more effectively detect continuities from the worlds of the palaces to those of the Early Iron Age communities of the Aegean (see, for example, E.S. Sherratt 2004). Although I propose here a continuity of 'practice' suggested by elements of the Homeric texts, I would also stress the need to bear historical contingency in mind and be aware of the time scales within which people work. The contexts in which this practice is performed can shift, as seems to have happened within the Late Bronze Age from the funerary to the architectural. Equally, it can act as the medium for a rejection of the past in the post-Mycenaean world – as Ian Morris (2000: 195–218) has reminded us – or for its rehabilitation as we see it in the poems of Homer.

Acknowledgements

For copies of material in advance of publication, I thank Jack Davis, Paul Halstead, Val Isaakidou, Sue Sherratt, Shari Stocker, Ken Wardle and James Whitley. I am also grateful to the above as well as Laura Preston and audiences in Sheffield, Glasgow, Birmingham and Heidelberg for comments on this and related oral versions. Needless to say, all errors of fact or interpretation are my own responsibility. Thanks, as ever, to Nong and Keith Branigan for their impeccable hospitality during the round table. Finally, I am particularly grateful to the 'committee' for honours received.

Bibliography

Appadurai, A. (ed.)
   1986   *The Social Life of Things: Commodities in Cultural Perspective*. Cambridge: Cambridge
          University Press.
Barthes, R.
   1977   Rhetoric of the image. In R. Barthes, *Image, Music, Text*: 32–51. New York: Hill and
          Wang.
Bennet, J.
   1999   The Mycenaean conceptualization of space or Pylian geography...yet again. In S.
          Deger-Jalkotzy, S. Hiller and O. Panagl (eds.), *Floreant Studia Mycenaea*: 131–57. Vienna:
          Austrian Academy of Sciences.
   2001   Agency and bureaucracy: thoughts on the nature and extent of administration in
          Bronze Age Pylos. In S. Voutsaki and J.T. Killen (eds.), *Economy and Politics in the
          Mycenaean Palace States* (Cambridge Philological Society Supplementary Volume 27):
          25–37.
   2002   *Re-u-ko-to-ro za-we-te*: Leuktron as a secondary capital in the Pylos kingdom? In J.
          Bennet and J. Driessen (eds.), A-NA-QO-TA: Studies Presented to J.T. Killen. *Minos*
          33–34: 11–30.
Bennet, J., and C.W. Shelmerdine
   2001   Not the palace of Nestor: the development of the 'Lower Town' and other non-
          palatial settlements in LBA Messenia. In K. Branigan (ed.), *Urbanism in the Aegean
          Bronze Age* (SSAA 4): 135–40. Sheffield: Continuum.
Blegen, C.W., and M. Rawson
   1966   *The Palace of Nestor at Pylos in Western Messenia, Volume I: the Buildings and their
          Contents*. Princeton: Princeton University Press.
Boardman, J.
   1974   *Athenian Black Figure Vases*. London: Thames and Hudson.
Cain, C.D.
   1997   *The Question of Narrative in Aegean Bronze Age Art*. PhD dissertation, University of
          Toronto.
Catling, H.W.
   1993   The bronze amphora and burial urn. In M.R. Popham, P.G. Calligas and L.H. Sackett
          (eds.), *Lefkandi II: the Protogeometric Building at Toumba, Part 2: the Excavation,
          Architecture and Finds*: 81–96. London: British School at Athens.
Chadwick, J.
   1972   Was Homer a liar? *Diogenes* 77: 1–13.
   1976   *The Mycenaean World*. Cambridge: Cambridge University Press.
Davis, J.L, and J. Bennet
   1999   Making Mycenaeans: warfare, territorial expansion, and representations of the Other
          in the Pylian kingdom. In R. Laffineur (ed.), *POLEMOS. Le contexte guerrier en Egée à
          l'âge du Bronze* (Aegaeum 19): 105–20. Liège: Université de Liège.
Demakopoulou, K.
   1988   *The Mycenaean World: Five Centuries of Early Greek Culture*. Athens: Ministry of Culture.
Dickinson, O.T.P.K.
   1977   *The Origins of Mycenaean Civilisation* (SIMA 49). Göteborg: Paul Åströms Förlag.
   1986   Homer, the poet of the Dark Age. *Greece and Rome* 33: 20–37.
Finley, M.I.

1982 Homer and Mycenae: property and tenure. In M.I. Finley, *Economy and Society in Ancient Greece*: 213–32. Harmondsworth: Penguin.

Foster, K.P.
1979 *Aegean Faience of the Bronze Age*. New Haven: Yale University Press.

French, E.B.
2002 *Mycenae: Agamemnon's Capital*. Stroud: Tempus.

Gosden, C. and Y. Marshall
1999 The cultural biography of objects. *World Archaeology* 31: 169–78.

Graziadio, G.
1988 The chronology of the graves of circle B at Mycenae: a new hypothesis. *AJA* 92: 343–72.
1998 Trade circuits and trade-routes in the Shaft Grave period. *SMEA* 40: 29–76.

Hampe, R., and E. Simon
1981 *The Birth of Greek Art: from the Mycenaean to the Archaic Period*. New York: Oxford University Press.

Homer
1991 *Iliad*. Transl. R. Fagles. New York: Penguin.
1996 *Odyssey*. Transl. R. Fagles. London: Penguin.

Horrocks, G.C.
1980 The antiquity of the Greek epic tradition: some new evidence. *PCPS* 206: 1–11.

Hoskins, J.
1998 *Biographical Objects: How Things Tell the Stories of People's Lives*. London: Routledge.

Hughes-Brock, H.
1985 Amber and the Mycenaeans. *Journal of Baltic Studies* 16: 257–67.
1993 Amber in the Aegean in the Late Bronze Age: some problems and perspectives. In K.W. Beck and J. Bouzek (eds.), *Amber in Archaeology*: 219–29. Prague: Institute of Archaeology.

Isaakidou, V., P. Halstead, J. Davis and S. Stocker
2002 Burnt animal sacrifice at the Mycenaean 'Palace of Nestor', Pylos. *Antiquity* 76: 86–92.

Karo, G.H.
1933 *Die Schachtgräber von Mykenai*. Munich: F. Bruckmann

Killen, J.T.
1998 The Pylos Ta tablets revisited. *BCH* 122: 421–22.

Kyriakidis, E.
1997 Some aspects of the rôle of scribes in Pylian administration. *Minos* 31–32: 201–29.

Lang, M.
1969 *The Palace of Nestor at Pylos in Western Messenia. Volume II: the Frescoes*. Princeton: Princeton University Press.

Lord, A.B.
2000 *The Singer of Tales*. Second edition, edited by S. Mitchell and G. Nagy. Cambridge, MA: Harvard University Press.

Lorimer, H.L.
1950 *Homer and the Monuments*. London: Macmillan.

McCallum, L.R.
1987 *Decorative Program in the Mycenaean Palace of Pylos: The Megaron Frescoes*. PhD dissertation, University of Pennsylvania.

Morris, I.
1986 The use and abuse of Homer. *Classical Antiquity* 5: 81–138.

2000   *Archaeology as Cultural History: Words and Things in Iron Age Greece.* Oxford: Blackwell.
Morris, S.P.
  1995   Prehistoric iconography and historical sources. In R. Laffineur and J.L. Crowley (eds.), *EIKΩN: Aegean Bronze Age Iconography: Shaping a Methodology* (Aegaeum 8): 205–12. Liège: Université de Liège.
Mylonas, G.E.
  1972   *O Tafikos Kyklos B ton Mykinon,* vol. 2: plates (Vivliothiki tis en Athinais Arkhaiologikis Etairias 73). Athens: Archaeological Society.
Palaima, T.G.
  2000   The Pylos Ta series: from Michael Ventris to the new millennium [Mycenaean Seminar abstract]. *BICS* 44: 236–37.
Papadopoulos, J.
  1999   Tricks and twins: Nestor, Aktorione-Molione, the Agora oinochoe and the potter who made them. In P. Betancourt, V. Karageorghis, R. Laffineur and W.-D. Niemeier (eds.), *MELETHMATA: Studies in Aegean Archaeology Presented to Malcolm H. Wiener as he Enters his 65th Year* (Aegaeum 20): 633–9. Liège: Université de Liège.
Parry, M.
  1987   *The Making of Homeric Verse: the Collected Papers of Milman Parry.* New York: Oxford University Press.
Pini, I.
  1997   *Die Tonplomben aus dem Nestorpalast von Pylos.* Mainz: Philipp von Zabern.
Popham, M.R.
  1993a   The main excavation of the building (1981–3). In M.R. Popham, P.G. Calligas and L.H. Sackett (eds.), *Lefkandi II: the Protogeometric Building at Toumba, Part 2: the Excavation, Architecture and Finds:* 7–31. London: British School at Athens.
  1993b   The sequence of events, interpretation and date. In M.R. Popham, P.G. Calligas and L.H. Sackett (eds.), *Lefkandi II: the Protogeometric Building at Toumba, Part 2: the Excavation, Architecture and Finds:* 97–101. London: British School at Athens.
  1994   Precolonisation: early Greek contact with the East. In G.R. Tsetskhladze and F. de Angelis (eds.), *The Archaeology of Greek Colonisation: Essays Dedicated to Sir John Boardman* (OUCA Monograph 40): 11–34. Oxford: Oxford University Committee for Archaeology.
Popham, M.R. and E. Milburn
  1971   The Late Helladic IIIC pottery of Xeropolis (Lefkandi): a summary. *ABSA* 66: 333–52.
Powell, B.B.
  1997   From picture to myth, from myth to picture. Prolegomena to the invention of mythic representation in Greek art. In S. Langdon (ed.), *New Light on a Dark Age: Exploring the Culture of Geometric Greece:* 154–93. Columbia, MO: University of Missouri Press.
Rehak, P.
  1995   Aegean griffins and papyrus. AegeaNet discussion list, 18 February.
Renfrew, C.
  1972   *The Emergence of Civilisation: the Cyclades and the Aegean in the Third Millennium B.C.* London: Methuen.
Ruijgh, C.J.
  1995   D'Homère aux origines proto-mycéniennes de la tradition épique. In J.P. Crielaard (ed.), *Homeric Questions: Essays in Philology, Ancient History and Archaeology):* 1–96. Amsterdam: J.C. Gieben.

Sakellariou, A.
  1974   Une cratère d'argent avec scène de bataille provenant de la IVe tombe de l'acropole de Mycènes. *Antike Kunst* 17: 3–20.
  1975   La scène du 'siège' sur le rhyton d'argent de Mycènes d'après une nouvelle reconstitution. *Revue Archéologique* 1975: 195–208.
Santillo Frizell, B.
  1998   Giants or geniuses? Monumental building at Mycenae. *Current Swedish Archaeology* 6: 167–84.
Shelmerdine, C.W.
  1996   From Mycenae to Homer: the next generation. In E. de Miro, L. Godart and A. Sacconi (eds.), *Atti e memorie del secondo congresso internazionale di micenologia, Roma-Napoli, 14–20 ottobre 1991* (Incunabula Graeca 98): 467–92. Rome: Gruppo editoriale internazionale.
  2001   Review of Aegean Prehistory VI: the palatial Bronze Age of the southern and central Greek mainland. In T. Cullen (ed.) *Aegean Prehistory: a Review* (AJA Supplement 1): 329–81. Boston: Archaeological Institute of America.
Shennan, S.J.
  1993   Amber and its value in the British Bronze Age. In K.W. Beck and J. Bouzek (eds.), *Amber in Archaeology* 59–66. Prague: Institute of Archaeology.
Sherratt, A.G.
  1995   Review of C.W. Beck and J. Bouzek (eds.), Amber in Archaeology. *Antiquity* 69: 200–03.
Sherratt, E.S.
  1990   'Reading the texts': archaeology and the Homeric question. *Antiquity* 64: 807–24.
  2004   Feasting in Homeric epic. In J.C. Wright (ed.), The Mycenaean Feast, *Hesperia*, 73, 2.
Snodgrass, A.M.
  1974   An historical Homeric society? *JHS* 94: 114–25.
  1982   *Narration and Allusion in Archaic Greek Art.* London: Leopard's Head Press.
  1998   *Homer and the Artists. Text and Picture in Early Greek Art.* Cambridge: Cambridge University Press.
Stocker, S. and J.L. Davis
  2004   Animal sacrifice, archives, and feasting at the Palace of Nestor. In J. Wright (ed.), The Mycenaean Feast. *Hesperia*, 73, 2.
Tzedakis, Y. and Martlew, H. (eds.)
  1999   *Minoans and Mycenaeans: Flavours of their Time.* Athens: Greek Ministry of Culture
Vagnetti, L.
  1999   Mycenaean pottery in the central Mediterranean: imports and local production in their context. In J.P. Crielaard, V. Stissi, G.J. van Wijngaarden (eds.), *The Complex Past of Pottery: Production, Circulation and Consumption of Mycenaean and Greek pottery (Sixteenth to Early Fifth Centuries BC)*: 137–61. Amsterdam: J.C. Gieben.
Ventris, M.G.F., and J. Chadwick
  1973   *Documents in Mycenaean Greek.* 2nd edition. Cambridge: Cambridge University Press.
Vermeule, E.
  1964   *Greece in the Bronze Age.* Chicago: Chicago University Press.
Warren, P.M.
  1997   The lapidary art – Minoan adaptations of Egyptian stone vessels. In R. Laffineur and P.P. Betancourt (eds.) *TEXNH. Craftsmen, Craftswomen and Craftsmanship in the Aegean Bronze Age* (Aegaeum 16): 209–23. Liège: Université de Liège.

Whitley, J.
  2002   Objects with attitude: biographical facts and fallacies in the study of Late Bronze Age and Early Iron Age warrior graves. *Cambridge Archaeological Journal* 12: 217–32.
Winter, I.J.
  1981   Royal rhetoric and the development of historical narrative in New-Assyrian reliefs. *Studies in Visual Communication* 7: 2–38.
Wright, J.C.
  1984   Changes in form and function of the palace at Pylos. In C.W. Shelmerdine and T.G. Palaima (eds.), *Pylos Comes Alive: Industry and Administration in a Mycenaean Palace*: 19–29. New York: Archaeological Institute of America/Fordham University.
  1987   Death and power at Mycenae. In R. Laffineur (ed.), *THANATOS: les coutumes funéraires en Égée à l'âge du bronze* (Aegaeum 1): 171–84. Liège: Université de Liège.
Younger, J.G.
  1995   The iconography of rulership in the Aegean: a conspectus. In P. Rehak (ed.), *The Role of the Ruler in the Prehistoric Aegean* (Aegaeum 11): 151–211. Liège: Université de Liège.
  1997   The stelai of Mycenae grave circles A and B. In R. Laffineur and P.P. Betancourt (eds.), *TEXNH. Craftsmen, Craftswomen and Craftsmanship in the Aegean Bronze Age* (Aegaeum 16): 229–39. Liège: Université de Liège.

6

Emerging Civilized Values?
The Consumption and Imitation of Egyptian Stone Vessels in EMII-MMI Crete and its Wider Eastern Mediterranean Context

Andrew Bevan

Introduction

The title of this paper, 'Emerging civilized values?,' picks out the rather awkward role of Egyptian stone vessels as an important piece of evidence of early cultural contact in the Aegean. In the *Emergence of Civilisation* (1972), these objects fitted into Renfrew's trade subsystem and could be seen as indicative of increasingly complex social systems and elite consumption. However, they remained awkward to interpret, not least because they might also be seen as material signatures for the diffusion of a wider civilized package (e.g., palaces, writing, some religious beliefs) to the Aegean from a Near Eastern core (Childe 1957; Evans 1921; 1928; 1930; 1935), an agenda that the *Emergence* was seeking to pull apart.

Indeed, it is no accident that stone vessels are still at the heart of debate on early contacts. Stone is a highly durable material which is well-preserved in archaeological contexts. But this durability is both a boon and a curse, ensuring a highly recognizable and often more complete dataset (e.g. than metals or organic materials), but also encouraging various forms of ancient curation and re-use that wreak havoc with our attempts at chronological control. As a result, the relatively uninformative or worse, confusing, findspots of these potentially early trade objects often leaves us little to play with in terms of their exact social context. Given these problems, if we are to control for and exploit the informational potential of these artifacts, then a comparative perspective is required that not only pays attention to contextual details where these are available, but also situates them within a wider geographical context in Crete and in the eastern Mediterranean.

This paper begins by exploring the theoretical and practical parameters of eastern Mediterranean trade. It then assesses the evidence for early stone vessel imports, starting with those sometimes assigned to Late Neolithic-EMIIA trade before moving on to consider the later Prepalatial evidence for imports and local imitations. Finally, it addresses the thorny issue of Predynastic-Old Kingdom vessels found in unstratified or much later Bronze Age Aegean contexts.

The Movement of Goods and Analytical Scales

Before looking at the stone vessels themselves, it is worth addressing briefly three issues underpinning how we might approach these objects as trade items: i) the different ways in which goods move about; ii) voyaging parameters, trade routes and their implications in the eastern Mediterranean; and iii) the analytical scales at which we describe the causes and effects of trade.

   Firstly, we can clarify the nature of how goods move about by considering a simple matrix (Figure 6.1). Goods can be exchanged either voluntarily or under compulsion and they travel either with their original owners or without them. Most analyses assume that the majority of trade between the Aegean and the Near East in the third millennium is likely to have fallen into the bottom right category in Figure 6.1. It is worth emphasizing, however, that as we move from the third to the second millennium BC and, generally-speaking, from less to more complex societies in the Aegean, particularly on Crete, the range of mechanisms involved is likely to include some or all of the other three quadrants, even if we will often find them difficult to identify archaeologically. Likewise, as the scale of trade and contact increases during the third and early second millennia, so too does the range of explanations we might plausibly assign to it.

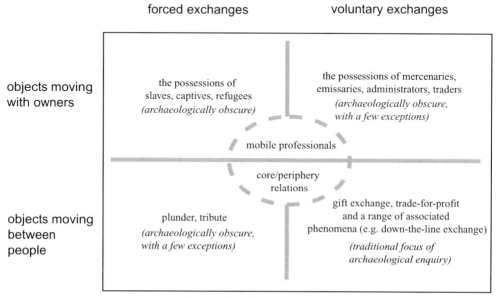

Figure 6. 1. Diagram describing the movement of goods

Secondly, we must understand the changing nature of maritime travel, more precisely the appearance of sailing ships, arguably the crucial trading dynamic in the third millennium. The first evidence for experimentation with sails is found in late fourth millennium Egyptian iconography (Bowen 1960: 117, fig.1; Casson 1995: fig.6), though a parallel, roughly contemporary invention in Mesopotamia may also have occurred. By the third millennium, large ship burials, imported artifacts and textual or pictorial references to seagoing ships (Breasted 1906: passages 324, 360; Casson 1995: 17 n.32; Faulkner 1940: 3; Marcus 1998: 112; O'Connor 1991; Wachsmann 1997: 12–18) all attest to Egyptian use of sailing ships to forge maritime links with the Levantine coast. Maritime activity appears to increase in scale, intensity and reach over the course of the millennium, gradually impacting on other regions. In the Aegean, however, maritime travel is still canoe-borne until late in the period (Broodbank 2000: 96–102). Cycladic longboat images point to one high-risk, limited range and low carrying capacity method by which extra-local maritime travel was probably conducted (e.g., Renfrew 1972: esp. 225ff), but we can identify a crucial change, sometime towards the end of the millennium, when the first sail-driven vessels appear in EB3-MB1 Aegean iconography (Basch 1991: 48–49; McGeehan-Liritzis 1996: 256, figs. 7.5.3a–b; Rutter 1993: 777–79, figs. 13–14; Yule 1980: 165–66, 28–29.52). The impact – technological, organizational and ideological – of the full-sized counterparts to these sailing images will have been profound, at least for certain communities and social groups, revolutionizing not just the speed, but also the scale of potential regional communication and exchange (Broodbank 2000: 341ff).

Nevertheless, sailing was still a form of travel and interaction which followed preferred routes reflecting the fact that eastern Mediterranean winds and currents strongly encourage *anti-clockwise* shipping (Lambrou-Phillipson 1991). Prior to the appearance of brailed sails sometime at the end of the Bronze Age – which permit more effective control of sail shape and hence allow navigators to chart a much wider range of courses in relation to wind direction (Casson 1995: 21, 273; Marcus 1998: 101; Roberts 1991: 55–56; 1995: 308–10) – this directionality is likely to have been even more pronounced and therefore we must constantly consider the Levant as a likely intermediary in trade from Egypt *to* Crete.[1] In particular, the site of Byblos, with its large numbers of early imports (see below) and association with maritime trade and travel in the early Egyptian written sources (e.g. Breasted 1906: passages 432–433; Simpson 1960), was probably a major filter.

Third and finally, the role and impact of imported items can be viewed at various analytical scales. Renfrew's *Emergence* reacted against large-scale diffusionism which linked Europe and the Near East in a pattern of inspirational dependence. However, world-systems perspectives (e.g. Sherratt 1993) have to some extent returned to this large scale, by emphasizing the search for certain commodities such as metals and the effect of Near Eastern core values on the Aegean and then later in the second millennium on a fairly extensive European margin. Certainly, at this scale, the third millennium is a period in which previously separate regions in the eastern Mediterranean gradually become incorporated into larger networks. More direct and intensive interactions are established between Egypt and the Levant, but the degree to which this growing trade impacts on other areas such as Cyprus, western Anatolia and the Aegean is difficult to assess. As Sherratt and Sherratt (1991) point out, inter-regional trade between the Aegean and the rest of the Near East in the third millennium may have been limited in terms of the quantities exchanged, but disproportionately significant in social and political terms. This argument risks overburdening the limited evidence available but nonetheless highlights the way exotic artifacts carry disproportionate prestige value as markers of liminal knowledge and power (Helms 1988).

By contrast, the *Emergence* concentrated on the pan-Aegean scale, occasionally addressing the peculiarities of behaviour at the level of individual regions, but often synthesizing a single discursive point of view. Even so, as Renfrew recognized (1972: 446), early imports have to be explained at a smaller scale than this. For example, early imported Egyptian stone vessels and imitations, both definite and disputed, all come from Crete. Therefore, they tell a particular story about Crete's path towards greater social complexity and it would be inappropriate to build these observations into an explanation of cultural change in the wider Aegean at this time. As will become clear, we can sometimes also glimpse patterns within Crete at regional or even site-specific scales.

A Reassessment of Early Stone Vessel Imports

In the *Emergence*, Renfrew came to the sober conclusion that 'neither economically nor in terms of the flow of ideas does the trade with the east Mediterranean appear very significant in the third millennium B.C. To say this is not to underestimate the effect of stimulus diffusion, or to deny that various specific innovations were suggested by these contacts.' (1972: 474). In fact, this argument remains highly persuasive, at least for the period up until the very late third millennium. The evidence from Crete (see Warren 1995: 1–2, 12) for early contacts is almost always problematic, in terms of establishing either correct identifications or secure stratigraphic contexts, and the actual volume of objects involved is minute. In addition, there is also as yet no evidence for any return trade in Cretan material culture to the third millennium Levant or Egypt. Egyptian and Egyptianizing material on Crete can be divided into three categories (excluding looser stylistic, technological or ideological influences): i) a few portable finished products (e.g. stone vessels and scarabs), ii) local imitations of finished imports (e.g. stone vessels and scarabs), and iii) raw materials (e.g. gold, hippopotamus ivory, carnelian or amethyst) for which an Egyptian origin is possible but not certain. By MMIA our evidence for all of these categories becomes more secure, and extensive (e.g. Watrous 1994: 712, 735–36; Phillips 1996; Pini 2000), but for the preceding periods, both a relatively minimalist assessment (very few contacts of limited overall significance) and Sherratt and Sherratt's 'low-bulk, higher impact' model remain valid interpretations.

Turning to the stone vessels in particular, there is very little evidence for imports from beyond the Aegean before EMIIB-MMI or MMII. Three fragments were found in apparent Late Neolithic (LN) contexts under the Central Court at Knossos (Evans 1928: 16–17, fig. 7a–b; also Warren 1969: 109, n.1; Warren and Hankey 1989: 125–27, pl. 1; Phillips 1991). However, two of these (Evans 1928: fig. 7b) come from the upper Central Court levels which were subject to extensive later Minoan levelling operations and may therefore also include later Bronze Age material. Indeed only one of these, a body fragment in a maroon and grey marble/limestone, can now be traced (AM 1938.653)[2] and it could well be from a (relatively elaborate) Neopalatial vessel. The third piece (also no longer traceable), a limestone base fragment (Evans 1928: fig. 7a), comes from an ostensibly more secure lower LN stratum, but is certainly not well enough preserved to support Evans' reconstruction of it as an Egyptian cylindrical jar. Rather it is likely to be a rare local product at this time or testament to the occasional trade in these items in the pre-BA Aegean (Bevan 2001: 153–54).

More convincing in terms of its stratigraphic context is a small fragment of a possible obsidian vessel from a secure EMIIA level on the Royal Road (Warren 1981: 633–34, fig. 5; 1989). However, apart from a slightly bevelled edge, this piece has no diagnostic features that identify it unequivocally as a vessel, let alone as Egyptian. It could be from the rim of a 1st Dynasty flaring cup (e.g. UC 36621) and hence already an heirloom by EMIIA, but it is sufficiently small that its identification must remain uncertain. If it is an Egyptian import, it is likely to reflect down-the-line exchange, rather than direct and bilateral trading links.

Late Prepalatial Trade and Influence

So we have three fragments from LN levels and one piece from an EMIIA level at Knossos whose contexts and/or identification as Egyptian stone vessel imports are extremely doubtful (only the EMIIA obsidian fragment is really a possibility). In the subsequent late Prepalatial period, our evidence for contact between Egypt and Crete becomes less equivocal, but it nonetheless remains difficult to gauge when within four or five centuries of the late Prepalatial period these pieces were arriving and what sort of trade they represent. Warren records a handful of definite and possible Egyptian products all from EMII(B)-MMI/II contexts at Knossos (1969: 112, D327 P604; 1981: 632–33, fig.3, pl.205b; 1989: 1, n.1). Unfortunately, none of them can be dated any more closely than this broad date range, nor are they shapes with a short period of use in Egypt. In fact, these pieces are not the most common types of material found in contemporary Egypt (late Old Kingdom–12th Dynasty). For example, there are no collared pots, splayed cylindrical jars, lamps, large jars or tables such as those found in large numbers in Egypt and in contemporary contexts in the Levant (see below). In other words, for EMIIB-MMII, we have the tantalizing testimony of one definite and several probable imports, but these artifacts do not offer much insight into the socio-political implications of early contact or to the forms of trade involved.

While this uncertainty about the date and character of the assemblage urges interpretive caution, we should also consider the possible wider influence of Egyptian contact on the local Cretan stone vessel industry. Unlike the Cyclades, with a long, low-intensity ancestry of stone vessel use, it is only in EMIIA that the first substantial *indigenous* stone vessel industry appears in Crete (Warren 1965; Bevan 2001: 168–71). These new vessels were carved in chlorite and heavily decorated, and are unlike most Egyptian stone vessels of any period.[3] After EMIIA, and in stages during EMIIB-MMI that are difficult to pin down with chronological precision, stone vessel production changes. Not only is there a greater diversity of shape and material, but vessels are now often hollowed out by drilling with either a tubular bit (organic or copper) or an abrading stone (Warren 1969: 161; Bevan 2001: 117–19). Both these drilling methods might conceivably have been borrowed from Egyptian stone vessel-making techniques, but more likely, local priorities and demands encouraged the adaptation and refinement of known local drilling technologies (e.g. of beads) to the task of hollowing out vessels from harder stones.

So Egyptian material culture may have provided some limited inspiration for new technological choices and perhaps also for shape preferences. Certainly, amongst the range of stone forms placed in tombs, there is a greater interest in small containers possibly for oils or unguents, reflecting a cosmetic and at least partly funerary role, similar to contemporary Egypt (Aston 1994: shapes 137–141). Indeed, more informative than the actual EMIIB-MMII Egyptian imports is a range of exact and partial Cretan imitations (Warren 1969; Phillips 1996: 461, fig.3; Karetsou 2000: 42–45; Bevan 2003: figs.4:1–2). Three features stand out with regard to these local imitations: i) they concentrate at Mochlos and in the Mesara tombs, but have so far not been found at Knossos; ii) in contrast to the actual imports, they form a coherent group, copying a limited number of highly recognizable, oil container shapes; and iii) they are miniature versions of shapes produced in Egypt in a wider variety of sizes.

The Cretan vessels imitate prototypes made in Egypt during the late Old Kingdom (OK) to 12th Dynasty (Ward 1971: fig. 17), which roughly matches the EMIIB-MMII date range of their find contexts. However, specific vessel shapes allow us to suggest finer chronological (and regional) distinctions. Two imitative shapes – the splayed cylindrical jar and the collared pot (Bevan 2003: fig. 4:1) – are copies of late OK to First Intermediate Period (FIP) products, but especially characteristic of the 6th Dynasty (Aston 1994: types 35, 123–126; Petrie 1937: nos. 584–593, 650–652). Specific local Cretan stones appear to have been chosen that imitate the appearance of the two most important materials in use in contemporary Egypt, travertine and anorthosite gneiss (Aston 1994: 42–47, 63–64).

One of the two splayed cylindrical jars from Mochlos comes from an EMIIB-III context (Soles 1992: 84, fig. 33, pl. 30) and this early date, along with the 6th Dynasty style of the Mochlos jars, might suggest that this area was an important point of contact for early trading ventures. More generally, the splayed cylindrical jar and the collared jar can be distinguished from some slightly later imitations from the Mesara tombs (Bevan 2003: fig. 4:2). The cylindrical jar imitations from the latter region all have sloping sides and a short, roughly squared-off projecting rim and base which is characteristic of FIP-early 12th Dynasty prototypes. Examples in MMI-II contexts from Kamilari (Levi 1961–2: fig. 120 c6) and Kommos (Schwab 1996: 279–80) offer some confirmation that the Mesara imitations are indeed of later date. Likewise, a series of closed jars with short, everted rims are also imitating a FIP-early MK form, and a third form, the squat alabastron, might with much less confidence be linked to rare 12th Dynasty versions. The Mesara's involvement is probably both due to the emergence of Phaistos as a major island centre at this time and to the increased range of maritime exchange made possible by the regular use of sailing ships, which would have broadened the impact of Egyptian objects and ideas (Carinci 2000).

Unfortunately, we have very little contextual information with which to understand how and why these objects were being deployed. The Agia Triada Large Tholos is perhaps the most illuminating case (Banti 1930–1), boasting not only the clearest example of an early Egyptian stone vessel import (an anorthosite gneiss jar, Karetsou 2000: no.5), but also the largest number of imitations known from any single context. Unfortunately, the find spot of the actual import is not recorded, but four of the imitations were found clustered by the south wall of the tomb (Figure 6.2), amongst a group of skulls and long bones, presumably removed from an original, articulated position elsewhere. They appear to be in pairs, two cylindrical jars and two everted rim jars, one slightly smaller than the other. This disturbed context in a communal tomb should be treated with caution, but it is worth noting that the use of combinations of oils and oil jars, from sets of seven or eight to as few as two, is an important Egyptian practice. For example, we could take probable FIP tomb 5009 at Badari as a roughly contemporary example in which two cylindrical and two everted rim jars are also found together (in association with an adult female, Brunton 1927: 41, pl. xlix). It is impossible to say whether such practices were passed on from Egypt alongside the trade in actual vessels, although we can be fairly confident that they often were as far as Byblos. In Crete, the Agia Triada examples at least make us bear in mind that what was imitated may have been not only a vessel shape, but perhaps also its contents and/or a more complex consumption routine.

Predynastic and Old Kingdom-Style Imports: Antiques or Antiquities?

Apart from the probable imports and imitations from secure early contexts, there

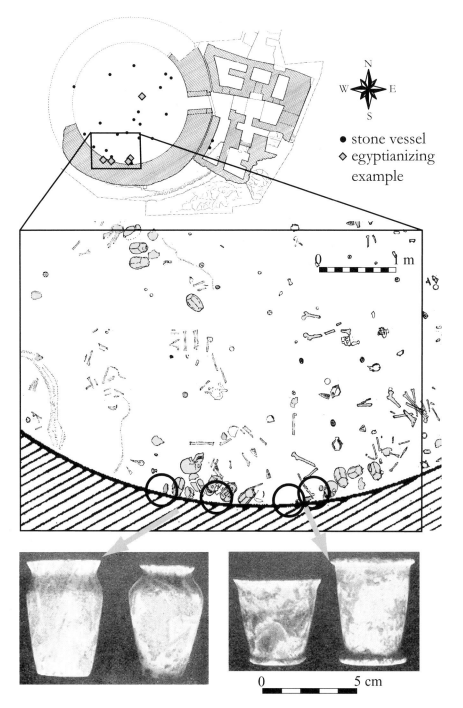

Figure 6.2. Egyptianizing stone vessels from Agia Triada Tholos A (after Banti 1930–1: figs. 2, 4–5, 50c–f)

is also a large number of Predynastic to Old Kingdom (PD-OK) vessels from unstratified or much later, *second* millennium Aegean deposits (Renfrew's 'rather unsatisfactory contexts', 1972: 214), especially at Knossos. There are by now two established and conflicting interpretations of these objects: either i) they were curated or preserved locally since their original exchange in the third millennium (e.g. Warren 1969: 106; 1981: 632); or ii) they arrived in the later Bronze Age probably as the result of tomb-robbing in Second Intermediate Period (SIP) and 18th Dynasty Egypt (Pomerance 1973; 1980; Phillips 1992: 170, 175–76).

In favour of the latter view, we can trace the appearance of such 'out-of-time' PD-OK antiques not just in the Aegean, but also at a large number of MB-LB Nubian, Egyptian and Levantine sites, suggesting a process of recirculation occurring across the whole of the eastern Mediterranean.[4] Some of these antique shapes are also imitated by Cretan artisans in this later period (Warren 1969: types 30A–C), which might point to the impact of peculiarly contemporary events. On the other hand, if any of the PD-OK-style material is to be ascribed to *earlier* trade, then it is much more likely to have occurred in the EMIIB-MMI window for which we have both direct evidence for some Egyptian imports (and imitations) in Crete and the emergence of sail-driven maritime links. Unless we assume a scale of canoe-borne exchange, as yet unwarranted by other evidence, then this discounts the possibility that some of the Predynastic and Early Dynastic-style material ever could have reached Crete at a time contemporary with its production in Egypt.

Again this issue benefits from being approached comparatively. As an example, this section focuses on a particular thin-walled, carinated bowl shape (Aston 1994: shapes 112, 117), of which at least four unstratified and one MMIII fragment are known from Knossos (Figure 6.3a–b). In Egypt, this shape forms a relatively tight 4th–6th Dynasty typological group, a fact which contrasts markedly with most of the other PD-OK types from unstratified-LBA Aegean contexts that are much earlier (Early Dynastic) in style. All the Knossos fragments are made of anorthosite gneiss. This stone (sometimes called 'Cephren diorite')[5] comes from near the Wadi Toshka in the Western Desert (Shaw *et al.* 2001) and was quarried in significant quantities during the late 2nd to 6th Dynasties for statuary, vessels and other objects (Aston 1994: 63–64; Reisner 1931: 140, 180). The late OK vessel shapes for which it was principally deployed were bowls, jars and lamps, essentially as a means of marking out the household equipment and tableware of the royal family and upper elite. Late OK examples of thin-walled carinated bowls and lamps, often in anorthosite gneiss, are known in Egypt from the tomb of Pepi II's wife, Neit (Figure 6.3e; Jécquier 1933; 1934; 1935), and private elite tombs on the Giza plateau (Reisner and Smith 1955: 100–01, figs. 145, 147, pls. 45a–c). Indeed, the use of this material and these sorts of thin-walled shapes seems to correlate strongly with high social status (except in cases of clear re-use).

We can also look to the Levant for valuable comparative evidence. Egyptian

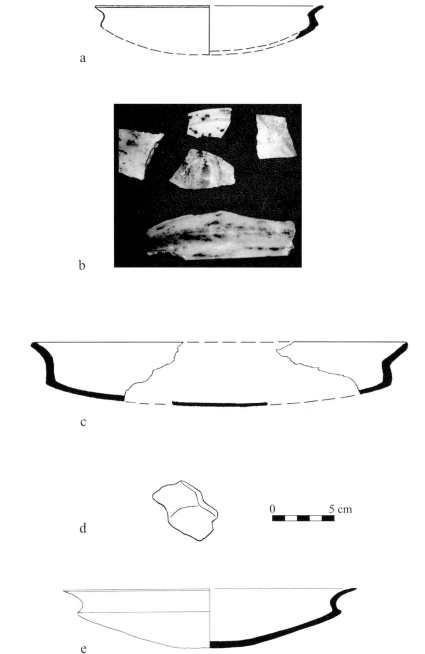

Figure 6.3. Carinated anorthosite gneiss bowls from: a) Knossos, Room of the False-spouted Vessels, MMIII (HM 590, after Warren 1969: D322), b) Knossos (AM AE 2301; 1910.283; 1938.409a, 583), c) Ebla (after Scandone-Matthiae 1981: fig.C.aa1), d) Byblos (after Montet 1928: fig. 26.114) and e) Tomb of Neit, Memphis (after Jécquier 1934: fig.15).

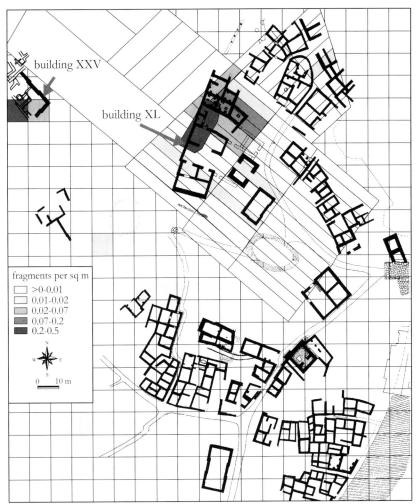

Figure 6.4. Plan of Byblos showing the distribution of Egyptian stone vessel finds (most of which are of Old Kingdom date). Note that three different excavation grids have been approximately combined – the irregular rectangular area around building XL is the rough location of Montet's 'Temple Syrien' sounding; the long rectangular zones are Dunand's earlier excavation zones and the squares are his later excavation grid. The overlying structures are those attributed to Saghieh's phase KIV (after Montet 1928: pl.xxii, Dunand 1939: pls.ccvi–ix, Saghieh 1983: plan 1).

stone vessels (including anorthosite gneiss bowls, Figures 6.3d–e) have been found at late third millennium Byblos and Ebla. At Byblos, stone vessel imports come from two main areas (Figure 6.4): buildings XL (Montet 1928; Dunand 1939: 288–308; Saghieh 1983: 40–45, fig.13) and XXV (Dunand 1958: 899–900; Saghieh 1983: 36–37, fig. 12a). A larger deposit comes from building XL which has been

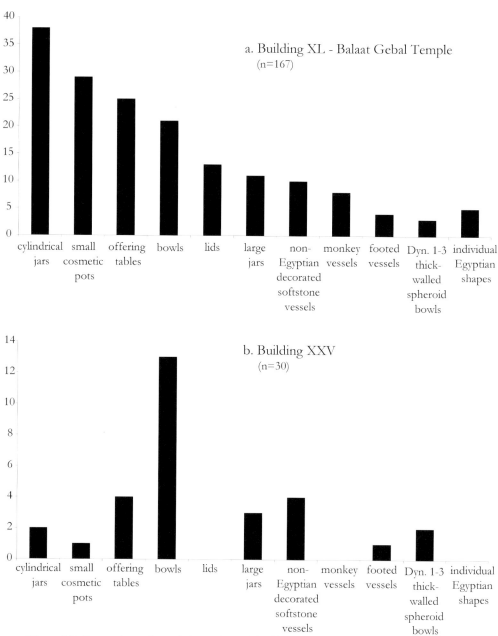

Figure 6.5. Comparison of vessel shapes from a) building XL and b) building XXV at Byblos.

convincingly identified as a temple of the Byblite divinity, Balaat Gebal. Here, there is a predominance of oil jars, offering tables and small collared pots (Figure 6.5a). The stone vessels are one of a series of indicators that link Balaat Gebal with the Egyptian deity Hathor and it is possible that the stone vessels were originally used as ritual equipment in the temple's cult activities (Espinal 2002). Although there are examples of earlier shapes, the vast majority of the assemblage can be ascribed to the 5th–6th Dynasties based on style, material and inscriptions.

The other smaller group of stone vessels was found in building XXV within what seems to have been a large royal or elite residence (Dunand 1958: 899; Saghieh 1983: 37). Here, there is a far greater proportion of bowls and tables (Figure 6.5b) than in the Balaat Gebal deposit, suggesting these items related more to consumption. This greater emphasis, within an apparently secular context, on tableware rather than the storage or ritual dedication of oils and cosmetics, matches quite well the role of ostentatious stone bowl forms within the royal family (as in the tomb of Neit above) and among the upper elite of late OK Egypt.

Further inland at Ebla, the only other third millennium northern Levantine site to produce imported Egyptian stone vessels, 200+ travertine and anorthosite gneiss fragments were found in Palace G (Scandone Matthiae 1979; 1981; 1988). Bowls and lamps predominate (85% of the identifiable pieces) and, as at Byblos building XXV, the link with consumption in an upper elite domestic or administrative context is striking. It is significant that more than a third of the Ebla fragments are of anorthosite gneiss (also present at Byblos, but unquantifiable; Figures 6.3c–d show anorthosite gneiss bowls from both Levantine sites): in Egypt, such proportions would be typical only of the royal family or a very few powerful individuals around it (e.g. Firth and Quibell 1935: 132). In fact, in view of their find spots, shapes and materials, the assemblages from Byblos building XXV and Ebla Palace G both make good candidates for high-level transfers between royal households.

Returning to Crete, the Knossos carinated bowls could conceivably have arrived in a very similar way to the household equipment and tableware found at Byblos and Ebla, as possible official transfers (e.g. greeting gifts, marriage exchanges) cementing the types of long-range, maritime connections now possible using sailing ships. If they were early trade objects, then the Knossos bowls would probably have been stored together in an elite residential or administrative context, as at Byblos and Ebla. Such a deposit would be particularly prone to subsequent disturbance or complete destruction and, given the piecemeal preservation of EMIIB-MMI contexts at Knossos (especially under the later palace), we should not therefore be surprised that our anorthosite gneiss bowls come from secondary contexts.

The case of the carinated bowls highlights the utility of a comparative perspective and other shapes from the 'floating' Aegean group benefit from similar treatment. For example, certain PD-OK thick walled bowls and jars (Warren 1969: types 43A–B; Aston 1994: shapes 79–81, 108) amongst this group could not have arrived at the time of their *floruit* (late 4th millennium–early third millennium BC), unless we assume levels of LN-EMIIA trade unsupported by other evidence. Such objects do occur rarely in later OK contexts in Egypt (e.g. Brunton 1927: 29–30, no. 3143, pls. xxiv.5, xlix) as well as at Byblos (Montet 1928: pls. xliii–xlv) and possibly Ebla (Scandone Matthiae 1988: pl. xii.2), and therefore a few may have made it to Crete in the EMIIB-MMI period. However, there are certainly not sufficient quantities to explain the sheer numbers (20+ examples) found in unstratified or much later Aegean contexts.

Indeed as we have seen, tomb-robbing and re-circulation of these objects later on in the Bronze Age does seem to have been occurring, to judge by their distribution over a wide range of MBA-LBA eastern Mediterranean sites and their imitation on Neopalatial Crete. So we have some evidence (both solid and circumstantial) for both the 'early contacts' and 'later tomb-robbing' scenarios, but fortunately, these two models are not as mutually irreconcilable as they might at first seem. Late Prepalatial exotica (evidence for contact with distant lands) were probably deployed and imitated as important markers of prestige and/or political legitimacy (as they clearly were at Byblos). As a result, later Neopalatial efforts at imitating and acquiring Egyptian antiquities may have been fuelled by: i) the curation of a few of these late Prepalatial trade items (though the intervening period is 500–800 years); or more likely, ii) the memory of these early links, during a period when Egypt-Crete interaction was again an important issue.

Conclusion

This paper has reassessed the evidence for imported Egyptian stone vessels and their imitations from early contexts in Crete and has adopted a wider east Mediterranean perspective on these products. While a great deal of uncertainty remains, some issues are relatively clear. Renfrew was correct to downplay the role of these objects as prime movers in the emergence of palatial society on Crete, let alone in the emergence of 'civilization' in the wider Aegean. Signs of potential Egyptian contact with LN-EMIIA Crete are extremely limited and highly equivocal. More to the point, given the transport technologies involved, any imports that did arrive at this time would necessarily have done so through down-the-line trading, deracinated of any original Egyptian social meanings. In contrast, in EMIIB-MMI some material was definitely arriving and being imitated locally, probably facilitated by the increased range and cargo capacity of sailing ships. Three regions – Knossos, Mochlos and the Mesara were involved in different ways and at different times. Comparative evidence also suggests that some material from mixed or later second millennium contexts at Knossos, such as the anorthosite gneiss carinated bowls, could plausibly have arrived as the result of late third millennium high-level exchanges. The tempo of change during EMIIB-MMI is hard to assess, but by MMIA, familiarity with Egyptian material culture was sufficiently widespread to be influencing the funerary consumption of several Mesara communities. It would not be surprising if early contacts were initiated and directed by Egyptian or Levantine travellers with Cretan shipping not becoming involved until later, perhaps with the start of the palatial period. A likely intermediary in all such trade is Byblos, which was both the main focus for Egyptian activity in the third and early second millennium Levant and a coastal centre closely associated with ships and sailing within the wider eastern Mediterranean.

Acknowledgements

This analysis was begun as part of doctoral research (University College London) into value regimes and stone vessels in the eastern Mediterranean Bronze Age. It is also an expanded version of a section from a broader discussion of the Egyptian stone vessel imports to Bronze Age Crete published elsewhere (Bevan 2003). A Leverhulme Trust Post-doctoral Research Fellowship, while dedicated to other research goals, allowed time for me to attend the Sheffield Round Table and to develop my ideas further. I am particularly grateful to my former supervisors, Cyprian Broodbank and Todd Whitelaw, for help and advice at every stage, and also to Jacke Phillips, Rachael Sparks, Sue Sherratt and Peter Warren for their discussion of and shared enthusiasm for the issues considered in this paper. Permission to reproduce relevant photographs was kindly supplied by the Heraklion Museum, Joseph Shaw, Jeffrey Soles and Peter Warren. Finally, I would like to thank the organizers of this Sheffield Aegean Round Table, John Barrett and Paul Halstead, and Colin Renfrew whose regional synthesis and theoretical perspective in the *Emergence of Civilisation* has inspired and underpinned so much subsequent Aegean research.

Endnotes

1   There are winds that occasionally blow from the south towards Crete, but their frequency is low (mostly in winter) and strength unpredictable (Lambrou-Phillipson 1991: 13). Likewise, while there are plenty of examples of Classical, Roman or Medieval ships sailing from Egypt or the north African coast to Crete, these vessels were equipped with brailed sails (and sometimes also keeled hulls) and hence were much better equipped to deal with the winds changing than most Bronze Age craft.

2   The following abbreviations are used for museum accession details in this paper: AM (Ashmolean Museum; HM (Herakleion Museum); KSM (Knossos Stratigraphical Museum), and UC (Petrie Museum, University College London).

3   Comparisons have been made between the EMIIA chlorite vessels and chlorite/steatite vessels carved with decoration from Byblos (Money Coutts 1936). However, the similarities are vague and, in fact, typical of softstone vessels which can be worked with chisel and/ or punch and hence, cross-culturally, encourage similar (carved, incised) decorative schemes (Bevan 2001: chapters 4-5).

4   In Nubia and Egypt, examples have been found at Badari, Deir el Ballas, Kerma, Qau, Tel el-Amarna, and Thebes (Lacovara 1991; Phillips 1992: 169-71), but this list is far from

exhaustive. In the Levant, these are known from Amman (Hankey 1974: fig. 1.1-2, pl. xxxii.a), Beth Shan (Rowe 1940: pl. 24.3, fig. 16 no.398), Ains Shems (Grant 1932: pls. xlvii.3-4), Kamid el-Loz (Lilyquist 1996: pls. 28-29), Lachish (Tufnell 1958: pl. 26.10), Tel Atchana (Wooley 1955: pl. lxxxi.9), Tel Beit Mirsim (Albright 1938: pl. 31.5) and Ugarit (Caubet 1991: pls. i.1-2, viii.12). In the Aegean, they have been found at Archanes, Agia Triada, Asine, Kythera, Knossos (with by far the most examples), Kato Syme, Katsamba, Mycenae, Myrtos Pyrgos, Palaikastro, Pylos and Zakros (Warren 1969: types 43A-E; Hankey 1972: 213, pl.78-9; Karetsou 2000).

5   Actually, there are two varieties, a lighter one which might be called anorthosite gneiss and a darker one, better termed gabbro gneiss. The lighter version is more frequently used for stone vessels.

Bibliography

Albright, W.S.
    1938   The Excavation of Tell Beit Mirsim II: the Bronze Age. *Annual of the American Institute of Oriental Research* 17.
Aston, B.G.
    1994   *Ancient Egyptian Stone Vessels: Material and Forms.* Heidelberg: Heidelberg Orient-verlag.
Banti, L.
    1931   La grande tomba a tholos di Haghia Triada. *ASA* 13–14: 155–251.
Basch, L.
    1991   Carènes égénnes à l'âge du Bronze. In R. Laffineur (ed.), *Thalassa: l'égée préhistorique et la mer* (Aegaeum 7): 43–50. Liège : Université de Liège.
Bevan, A.H.
    2001   *Value Regimes in the Eastern Mediterranean Bronze Age: a Study through Stone Vessels.* PhD dissertation, University of London.
    2003   Reconstructing the role of Egyptian culture in the value regimes of the Bronze Age Aegean: stone vessels and their social contexts. In R. Matthews and C. Roemer (eds.), *Ancient Perspectives on Egypt.* London: UCL Press.
Bowen, R. LeBaron
    1960   Egypt's earliest sailing ships. *Antiquity* 34: 117–31.
Breasted, J.H.
    1906   *Ancient Records of Egypt.* Chicago: Chicago University Press.
Broodbank, C.
    2000   *An Island Archaeology of the Early Cyclades.* Cambridge: Cambridge University Press.
Brunton, G.
    1927   *Qau and Badari I.* London: Bernard Quaritch.
Carinci, F.M.
    2000   Western Messara and Egypt during the Protopalatial period: a minimalist view. In A. Karetsou (ed.), *Kriti-Egyptos. Politismikoi Desmoi Trion Khilietion*: 31–37. Athens: Kapon.
Casson, L.
    1995   *Ships and Seamanship in the Ancient World.* Baltimore: Johns Hopkins.
Caubet, A.
    1991   Répertoire de la vaisselle de pierre. In A. Caubet, J. Connan, E. Coqueugniot, O. Deschesne, C. Elliott and H. Frost (eds.), *Arts et industries de la pierre* (Ras-Shamra-Ougarit VI): 205–55. Paris: Éditions Recherche sur les Civilisations.

Childe, V.G.
   1957   *The Dawn of European Civilization* (6th edn). London: Routledge and Kegan Paul.
Dunand, M.
   1939   *Fouilles de Byblos I.* Paris: Geuthner.
   1958   *Fouilles de Byblos II.* Paris: Geuthner.
Espinel, A.D.
   2002   The role of the Temple of Ba'alat Gebal as intermediary between Egypt and Byblos during the Old Kingdom. *Studien zur Altägyptischen Kultur* 30: 103–19.
Evans, A.J.
   1921   *Palace of Minos at Knossos, I.* London: Macmillan.
   1928   *Palace of Minos at Knossos, II.* London: Macmillan.
   1930   *Palace of Minos at Knossos, III.* London: Macmillan.
   1935   *Palace of Minos at Knossos, IV.* London: Macmillan.
Faulkner, R.O.
   1940   Egyptian seagoing ships. *Journal of Egyptian Archaeology* 26: 3–9.
Firth, C.M., and J.E. Quibell
   1935   *Excavations at Saqqara: the Step Pyramid.* Cairo: L'Institut Français d'Archéologie Orientale.
Grant, E.
   1932   *Ain Shems Excavations II.* Haverford: Haverford College.
Hankey, V.
   1972   Stone vessels at Myrtos Pyrgos. *Pepragmena tou Tritou Diethnous Kritologikou Synedriou* 1: 210–5.
   1974   A Late Bronze Age temple at Amman: I the Aegean pottery; II vases and objects made of stone. *Levant* 6: 131–78.
Helms, M.
   1988   *Ulysses' Sail: an Ethnographic Odyssey of Power, Knowledge and Geographical Distance.* Princeton: Princeton University.
Jécquier, M.G.
   1933   *Les Pyramides des Reines Neit et Apouit.* Cairo: L'Institut Français d'Archéologie Orientale.
   1934   Vases de pierre de la VIe dynastie. *Annales du Service des Antiquités de l'Égypte* 34: 97–113.
   1935   Vases de pierre de la VIe dynastie. Note additionelle. *Annales du Service des Antiquités de l'Égypte* 35: 160.
Karetsou, A (ed.)
   2000   *Kriti-Egyptos. Politismikoi Desmoi Trion Khilietion. Katalogos*: 31–37. Athens: Kapon.
Lacovara, P.
   1991   The stone vase deposit at Kerma. In W.V. Davies (ed.), *Egypt and Africa. Nubia from Prehistory to Islam*: 118–28. London: British Museum Press.
Lambrou-Phillipson, C.
   1991   Seafaring in the Bronze Age Mediterranean: the parameters involved in maritime travel. In R. Laffineur (ed.), *Thalassa: l'égée préhistorique et la mer* (Aegaeum 7): 11–21. Liège: Université de Liège.
Levi, D.
   1962   La tomba a tholos di Kamilari presso a Festòs. *ASA* 23–24: 7–148.
Lilyquist, C.
   1996   Stone vessels at Kamid el-Loz: Egyptian, Egyptianizing, or non-Egyptian? A question at sites from the Sudan to Iraq to the Greek Mainland. In R. Hachmann (ed.), *Kamid*

    el-Loz 16. Schatzhaus Studien: 133–73. Bonn: Saarbrücker Beiträge zur Altertumskunde 59.

Marcus, E.
    1998   *Maritime Trade in the Southern Levant from Earliest Times through the Middle Bronze IIA Period*. DPhil thesis, University of Oxford.

McGeehan-Liritzis, V.
    1996   *The Role and Development of Metallurgy in the Late Neolithic and Early Bronze Age of Greece*. Jonsered: Paul Åström.

Money-Coutts, M.
    1936   A stone bowl and lid from Byblos. *Berytus* 3: 129–36.

Montet, P.
    1928   *Byblos et L'Egypte*. Paris: Paul Geuthner.

O'Connor, D.
    1991   Boat graves and pyramid origins. *Expedition* 33.3: 5–17.

Petrie, W.M.F.
    1937   *Funeral Furniture and Stone and Metal Vases*. London: Bernard Quaritch.

Phillips, J.
    1991   *The Impact and Implications of the Egyptian and Egyptianizing Material found in Bronze Age Crete ca.3000–ca.1100 B.C.*. PhD dissertation, University of Toronto.
    1992   Tomb-robbers and their booty in ancient Egypt. In S.E. Orel (ed.), *Death and Taxes in the Ancient Near East*: 157–92. New York: Edwin Mellen Press.
    1996   Aegypto-Aegean relations up to the 2nd millennium B.C.. In L. Krzyzaniak, K. Kroeper and M. Kobusiewic (eds.), *Interregional Contacts in the Later Prehistory of Northeastern Africa*: 459–70. Posnan: Studies in African Archaeology 5.

Pini, I.
    2000   Eleven early Cretan scarabs. In A. Karetsou (ed.), *Kriti-Egyptos. Politismikoi Desmoi Trion Khilietion. Meletes*, 107–13. Athens: Kapon.

Pomerance, L.
    1973   The possible role of tomb robbers and viziers of the 18th dynasty in confusing Minoan chronology. In Antichità Cretesi: Studi in onore di Doro Levi 1. *Chronache di Archeologia* 12: 21–30.
    1980   The possible role of the tomb robbers and viziers of the 18th dynasty in confusing Minoan chronology. In *Acts of the Fourth International Cretological Congress, Iraklion, 29 August–3 September, 1976*: 447–53.

Reisner, G.A.
    1931   *Mycerinus: the Temple of the Third Pyramid at Giza*. Cambridge: Harvard University Press.

Reisner, G.A. and W.S. Smith
    1955   *A History of the Giza Necropolis II*. Cambridge: Harvard University Press.

Renfrew, C.
    1972   *The Emergence of Civilisation: the Cyclades and the Aegean in the Third Millennium BC*. London: Methuen.

Roberts, O.T.
    1991   The development of the brail into a viable sail control for Aegean boats of the Bronze Age. In R. Laffineur (ed.), *Thalassa:. l'égée préhistorique et la mer* (Aegaeum 7) : 55–60. Liège: Université de Liège.
    1995   An explanation of ancient windward sailing. Some other considerations. *The International Journal of Nautical Archaeology* 24(4): 307–15.

Rowe, A.
  1940   *Four Canaanite Temples of Beth Shan*. Philadelphia: University of Pennsylvania Press.
Rutter, J.B.
  1993   Review of Aegean prehistory II: prepalatial Bronze Age of the southern and central Greek mainland. *AJA* 97: 745–97.
Saghieh, M.
  1983   *Byblos in the Third Millennium BC. A Reconstruction of the Stratigraphy and a Study of the Cultural Connections*. Warminster: Aris and Phillips.
Scandone-Matthiae, G.
  1979   Vasi iscritti di Cefren e Pepi I nel Palazzo Reale G di Ebla. *Studi Eblaiti* 1: 33–43.
  1981   I vasi egiziani in pietra dal Palazzo Reale G. *Studi Eblaiti* 4: 99–127.
  1988   Les relations entre Ebla et l'Egypte au IIIème et au IIème millénaire av. J.Chr. In H. Waetzoldt and H. Hauptmann (eds.), *Wirtschaft und Gesellschaft von Ebla*: 67–73. Heidelberg: Heidelberger Orientverlag.
Schwab, K.
  1996   Stone vessels. In J.W. Shaw and M.C. Shaw (eds.), *Kommos I. The Kommos Region and Houses of the Minoan Town*: 271–82. Princeton: Princeton University Press.
Shaw, I., E. Bloxham, J. Bunbury, R. Lee, A. Graham and D. Darnell
  2001   Survey and excavation at Gebel el-Asr gneiss and quartz quarries in Lower Nubia (1997–2000). *Antiquity* 75: 33–4.
Sherratt, A.G.
  1993   What would a Bronze Age world-system look like? Relations between temperate Europe and the Mediterranean in later prehistory. *Journal of European Archaeology* 1,2: 1–57.
Sherratt, A.G. and E.S. Sherratt
  1991   From luxuries to commodities: the nature of Bronze Age trading systems. In N.H. Gale (ed.), *Bronze Age Trade in the Mediterranean*: 351–81. Stockholm: Paul Åström.
Simpson, W.K.
  1960   Papyrus Lithgoe: a fragment of a literary text of the Middle Kingdom from El-Lisht. *Journal of Egyptian Archaeology* 46: 65–70.
Soles, J.S.
  1992   *The Prepalatial Cemeteries at Mochlos and Gournia*. Princeton: American School of Classical Studies at Athens.
Tufnell, O.
  1958   *Lachish IV*. London: Oxford University Press.
Wachsmann, S.
  1997   Were the Sea Peoples Myceneans? The evidence of the ship iconography. In S. Swiny, R.L. Hohlfelder and H. Wylde Swiny (eds.), *Res Maritimae: Cyprus and the Eastern Mediterranean from Prehistory to Late Antiquity*: 339–56. Nicosia: Cyprus American Archaeological Research Institute.
Ward, W.A.
  1971   *Egypt and the East Mediterranean World 2200–1900 B.C.* Beirut: American University of Beirut.
Warren, P.
  1965   The First Minoan stone vases and Early Minoan chronology. *Kretika Khronika*: 7–43.
  1969   *Minoan Stone Vases*. Cambridge: Cambridge University Press.
  1981   Knossos and its foreign relations in the Bronze Age. *Pepragmena tou Diethnous Kritologikou Sinedriou* 4:628–37.

1989   Egyptian stone vessels from the city of Knossos: contributions towards Minoan economic and social structure. *Ariadne* 5: 1–9.

1995   Minoan Crete and Pharaonic Egypt. In W.V. Davies and L. Schofield (eds.), *Egypt, the Aegean and the Levant: Interconnections in the Second Millennium BC*: 1–18. London: British Museum.

Warren, P. and V. Hankey

1989   *Aegean Bronze Chronology*. Bristol: Bristol Classical Press.

Watrous, L.V.

1994   Crete from earliest prehistory through the Protopalatial period. *AJA* 98: 695–753.

Woolley, L.

1955   *Alalakh: an Account of the Excavations at Tell Atchana*. Oxford: Oxford University Press.

Yule, P.

1980   *Early Cretan Seals: A Study of Chronology*. Mainz: Philip von Zabern.

7

Getting Past Consumption and Competition: Legitimacy and Consensus in the Shaft Graves

Aaron D. Wolpert

Uncovering structural meaning in crates of pottery sherds is a daunting and often frustrating task. For the prehistorian wading through a swamp of pottery profiles and site plans, shifting to the recovery of complex social structures is a hard transition to make. When the dust has settled on the definitive stratigraphic record, then, cultural reconstruction is often stubbornly materialist in its failure to stray far from the safety of objective physical evidence. Caught in a tangle of artifacts, prehistorians often misplace the societies that constructed and lived the material record. The disarticulation of artifact from social context is inherent in prehistory – inanimate objects are targeted for interpretation as if they existed apart from a living community (Appadurai 1986: 5). Yet it is imperative that we do not retroject that condition into the past, into living societies. When an artifact is reinstalled into its intact social matrix, it loses any stand-alone import and dissolves into a variegated social background. No matter how much some prehistorians argue it, no matter how convenient it is in theory, objects cannot stand for social relations.

For the shaft grave period on the Greek mainland, current interpretations rely on this flawed explanatory shorthand. It is hard to ignore the stunning deposition of material 'wealth' in the shaft graves. And Aegean prehistorians locate structural change *within* the consumption of 'prestige items,' as if the destruction of property is enough to explain a reconfigured social order. The torrent of artifacts interred with the dead has swept away any sense of negotiated ritual, leaving an undifferentiated construct of competitive consumption as the preferred social dynamic. Shaft grave gold has blinded prehistorians – did its lustre captivate a Helladic audience in the same manner? What follows is an attempt to recover the cultural sensibilities that enabled mortuary deposits to accelerate so quickly. I do not assume that competition and consumption are latent forces that leaders can deploy at will to batter tradition and engineer social change. I am more interested in the ideological consensus that legitimated flashy funerary rites, practices that flaunted tradition and that in many societies would look downright garish. Standing in the way of this kind of contextual reading of the past is the indiscriminate application of competition and consumption as general explanation. Such ethnographic shorthand assumes cross-cultural relevance and effectively flattens out real variation from one cultural landscape to the next. How has it happened that after two decades of post-processual thought, world prehistory is still inhabited by blurred societies that look vaguely similar despite marked differences in material culture and historical circumstance?

Processual archaeology developed in part as an attempt to reconstruct a living context for the fragmentary material record. External explanatory frameworks were introduced to bridge gaps in the evidence – systems theory, predictive modelling, and ethnographic analogy stitched artifacts and patterns together with generalizing inference. Lost in the abstraction were individuals, as the structures that moved objects *from person to person* were judged more significant than real people. In the three decades since the publication of *The Emergence of Civilisation*, emphasis has shifted from pattern and abstraction toward specific behaviours that wrote the record of past society. Archaeology no longer considers artifacts as unintended and coincidental debris, shadows of broad social structures and systems – Preserved remains are seen as the result of specific and momentary action, not as a passive record of general conditions and long-term processes. Agency is now an integral part of interpretation, returning people to the societies where they were sometimes missing in systemic approaches. Yet these emergent, no-longer-invisible agents still tend to behave *in general*, as caricatures of 'how people act' in a given situation (cf. Douglas and Isherwood 1979: 63). Archaeology is repeating the mistakes of ethnography, reifying structure and underestimating the multifaceted complexity of practice.

Agents look flat and generic because the behaviours they represent are still drawn from ethnographic analogy. Employed as shorthand for culture-specific practice, categories like shamanism and the chiefdom overwrite the specific historical circumstances that preface every real-life social event. And for the limited record of prehistory, standardized material correlates come to stand for 'typical' social phenomena. Functional assumptions about the purpose of certain expressions shove actors off the stage and strip social action of its cultural matrix. For example, an almost reflexive translation of monumental mortuary architecture as territorial markers effectively blurs historical difference by making disparate practices *look* uniform and 'keeps the potentially active prehistoric individual silent, invisible, and passive since his or her actions would have no creative impact on a symbolic mechanism whose successful operation is already assumed by an interpreter' (Dunham 1999: 117). As far removed as it is from de-peopled interpretation, prehistory still depicts agents as vague summaries of social action.

And as far as much current research is concerned, these faceless agents were primarily engaged in consumption. Consumption deserves the attention it now commands, as an array of affiliated behaviours (display, status competition, gift exchange, mortuary deposition, artifact destruction) determined what traces of prehistory were preserved. For prehistorians a functional emphasis on production has given way to an awareness of the deployment and disposal of material culture (Berthoud and Sabelli 1979). Yet consumption as it is currently conceived represents the convergence of summarized behaviours and artifacts deployed as shorthand for past social conditions. Consumption resonates with the consumer society most prehistorians inhabit, so that acquisition and discard are in many instances rather casual, and barriers to the circulation of commodities in particular are largely imperceptible. That resonance predisposes us to neglect circumstances that manufacture *meaning* for consumption – displaced and floating constructs like conspicuous consumption (for example, van Wijngaarden 1999) presume universal implications for certain practices. Recovering the sensibilities behind consumption is a place to start in challenging the substitution of general behavioural themes for more situation-specific explanation.

Legitimate Consumption

Prehistorians assume that the deployment of prestige capital was obligatory for and inseparable from assertions of status and inequality. Discussions on the mechanics of competition and hierarchy often stop with the identification of prestige capital and modes of consumption/display. Such arguments presuppose that positions in a hierarchy were open for competition – authority figures fought for legitimacy, and contenders attempted to assert it in challenging the political *status quo*. Yet legitimacy was a difficult thing to manipulate, rooted as it was in codes of conduct inextricable from social replication (Giddens 1979; Appadurai 1981; Conrad 1992: 165). Such cultural intransigence is often overlooked; from a modern vantage that takes in several centuries at a time, change looks constant and legitimacy fluid – but this is never the impression from inside a society. Ideology does nothing so well as it projects an image of sanctioned stability.

So when prehistorians fall back on consumption as legitimating strategy, often left out of the explanation is this: consumption had to reference accepted and established *sources for legitimacy*. Acquiring 'wealth' could not strengthen personal prestige nor attract supporters *unless* it was grounded in collective narratives and an accepted cosmology (Weiner 1992: 4; Pauketat 1994: 13–14). For example, depositing some unheard-of foreign item in a grave did not by itself accomplish a prestige conversion (Helms 1993: 50) – for an intrusive object to function as a prestige item, someone had to position it within existing conceptual frameworks, associating it with an origin myth or some forgotten ancestral lineage. Undirected display and indiscriminate consumption were ineffective (and nonexistent) – assertive action had to look credible to whatever audience witnessed it, especially when the practice in question was first introduced. Revising accepted rules of social conduct demanded some justification – sudden ungrounded change just did not work; action without some precedent (fictive or not) was inconceivable. As Richard Lesure (1999: 23–4) puts it, 'with a grateful nod to those prehistoric elites who used durable objects to dramatize their authority and power, archaeologists have become quite adept at identifying the paraphernalia of ranking and stratification in the archaeological record. We often argue – with good reason – that the manipulation of the exotic objects we recover from high-status residences and ceremonial precincts was crucial to the legitimization of inequality. We have made much less progress in understanding how items that legitimated status and authority came over time to acquire such characteristics. The scarcity, hardness, and other material qualities of jade or greenstone obviously made it suitable as a symbol of status and authority in ancient Mesoamerica. But why jade? How did it acquire its central importance in Mesoamerican civilization? How does an elite good become that?' Consumption in the real world has already answered these questions – its existence depends on social authentication.

A Social Rupture

Prestige did not accrue with haphazardly accumulated wealth; for this reason reconstructions of prehistory cannot stop with the recognition of marked shifts in consumption patterns. The challenge is to rebuild the legitimating context for those shifts where it is not always apparent, to make change look *less* sudden and dramatic. Mortuary practice at the Middle Helladic-Late Helladic transition in the Argolid is a classic case, where an explosion in deposition and elaboration apparently signalled fundamental change in the structuring principles that governed Helladic society. Expanded grave facilities and richly appointed corpses are typically taken as symptomatic of a watershed event in mainland social development – the transition from chiefdom to state, the emergence of sanctioned inequality.

Sophia Voutsaki (1998: 41) has steered the discussion away from a processual concern with reading social complexity through effort expenditure models and status indices. She argues that a broad transition from chiefdom to state is not *reflected* in Argolid mortuary practice; although we discern shadows of change in reconfigured funerary ritual, no one context can serve as a passive gauge for increasing complexity and inequality. Death constituted an arena in which a rupture of traditional kinship principles was engineered, with 'mortuary ritual . . . *creating* rather than mirroring social reality . . . shaping people's perception of the world and their position in it' (Voutsaki 1998: 44).

In specific terms, she targets the intensified deposition of material 'wealth,' a sudden and *permanent* dislocation that disrupted circulation patterns and in turn severed long-standing reciprocal relationships. Prestige accrued to those who transcended kinship-based status negotiation, replacing ephemeral prestige with permanent inequality, inequality achieved through the distortion of networks in which prestige markers travelled. Removing artifacts from circulation, *destroying* them in mortuary deposition, created imbalances in formerly stable exchange networks. Vortexes in the social fabric opened up around chiefly lineages, funnelling commodities toward these nodes in unprecedented quantity and permitting accumulation. Resource centralization, sanctioned inequality, and rigid hierarchy followed upon this capacity to stockpile prestige markers (Voutsaki 1997: 38–9).

This reconstruction works as a rough superstructure but stumbles past the reality of practice, that social change never occurs in general – it instead careens along several converging courses (Kirch 1991) with sudden turns marked by actual events and personal decisions. When considered in retrospect, this dynamic chaos looks orderly and orchestrated; agency melts away into inexorable progress (McGuire 1995; Robb 1999: 7). Looking back on the social rupture from its conclusion privileges selected events – those that led directly to sanctioned inequality – and obscures the fact that not all decisions pointed directly at the eventual outcome(s). Reckoning time in the right order – that is, from the past toward the present – introduces an element of uncertainty that makes *every* decision important and contingent. Walking *forward* through prehistory, retracing real trajectories, forces an encounter with the side of unresolved issues that faced decision-making actors. Why did communities suddenly accept the large-scale destruction of non-perishable wealth; what made interring valuables permissible, even conceivable, following centuries in which this was not the case? How did chiefs reconfigure belief structures such that accompanying claims for permanent inequality were credible and legitimate (Pauketat and Emerson 1999)?

Voutsaki stops short of an adequate response to a core question that she *does* ask – why did this sudden shift in consumption rationality happen exactly when it did? Minoan cultural interference is conventionally credited for upsetting the bucolic MH world. A not-so-faintly diffusionist pressure from the islands has always meandered through explanations for mainland social change. This vague force comes into sharper focus for Voutsaki in the form of a perceived aesthetic elaboration in Minoan prestige goods (Voutsaki 1998: 47), aesthetics that introduced an expressive capacity that had to that point escaped mainland artisans. Yet we cannot possibly know what complex meanings were attached to the supposedly 'mundane' artifacts circulating on the mainland in the MH period, nor what social forms did not find material expression (Nordquist 1997: 16). Ethnography has demonstrated just how resourceful people are at conveying complicated narratives with simple objects (Weiner 1992). Minoan symbolic expression was surely an attractive quantity on the mainland, but it was not so potent that it disrupted Helladic social networks through some innate and irrepressible power (cf. Appadurai 1986: 29; Thomas 1991: 83–98). An unfamiliar symbolic code assumed meaning only when assigned a site within the cosmographic landscape (Baudrillard 1981; Pydyn 1998: 98); the fictive mechanisms that positioned Minoan artifacts (and the Minoan and Cycladic traders that delivered them [cf. Gell 1992]) in a reconfigured Aegean cosmos were rather more deeply implicated in profound social changes. Voutsaki (1997: 46) recognizes in passing for Minoan prestige items that 'once deposited in graves they [were] appropriated, refined, incorporated within the mainland norms.' She fails to follow up on this critical point, refusing to speculate on how exactly Minoan prestige capital was reconfigured for mainland deployment.

Consumption *still* stands alone then as explanation for radical change at the MH-LH transition. In order to recover the structural meaning that enabled it, we have to dismantle the concept itself. An uncritical consolidation of ethnographies has made consumption a disembodied abstraction that defies efforts to uncover legitimating context. Abstraction weakens a social rupture resident in objects because several underlying assumptions are flawed. It is commonly supposed that:

1) reciprocity and destructive consumption are opposed;
2) consumptive practice derails gift exchange networks (or 'enclaves' them; Appadurai 1986: 22–26);
3) competitive struggles fought with prestige markers impact status hierarchies; and
4) status predicated on wealth can *replace* kinship as a fundamental structuring principle (Voutsaki 1998: 44, 47).

Reciprocity and Status Competition Revisited

Voutsaki is not alone in marshalling classic ethnography in support of the arguments that reciprocity and consumption are incompatible and that status and political control were quantities acquired through antagonistic competition. Conventional anthropology considers *kula* the paradigm for reciprocity and *potlatch* the embodiment of status competition. Yet the shifting sands of sociology have made these positions untenable. Recent reappraisals have uncovered troubling inferences colouring the ethnographic record and some unexpected misreadings in later synthetic work. Challenges to suspect positions have the potential to upset venerable edifices built on the shoulders of Boas and Bataille, Malinowski and Mauss, for if the basic constructs did not work as advertised in the Trobriands and on the northwest American coast, they will not work as norms for prehistoric worlds.

In tackling reciprocal exchange, we can start with what Annette Weiner (1992) calls keeping-while-giving. Weiner (1992: 28–36, 48) argues that reciprocity in the supposedly 'pure' Trobriand form was a trope manufactured for western economic theory, a mythical antithesis for the commodity market (cf. Malinowski 1922: 58–62; Appadurai 1986: 11–12; Thomas 1991: 12–13, 33–34; Gell 1992). *Some* objects circulated more or less continuously along certain paths through the islands, but there was no such thing as a necklace or armshell that was not convertible and alienable from the network; shells were 'purchased' and used as payments for non-*kula* obligations (Thomas 1991: 51; Weiner 1992: 135; Fotiadis 1999; Godelier 1999: 88). Famous shells were taken out of circulation and 'held' for decades at a time (Weiner 1992: 133) – regardless of whether anybody considered them in-transit while stationary, non-circulation must have looked rather permanent from the perspective of a human life span. What Mauss interpreted as mandatory and perpetual movement was largely the result of historical accident, that Malinowski happened to spend most of his time on Kiriwina, where outlets for shell conversion were more restricted than they were elsewhere (Godelier 1999: 85). More important to the argument, though, is that the shells that made up the bulk of the circulating population *did not really matter* for status negotiation and prestige claims. Ron Brunton (1975: 553) noted that only on Kiriwina were there 'barriers to the convertibility of *kula* items' that afforded effective insulation against the removal of shells from circulation – for this reason Kiriwina was the only island where big men parlayed exclusive access to *kula* competition into chiefly status. For the most part, then, armshells and necklaces were implicated in a kind of secondary competition that had no real impact on general social standing. *Kula* was a game – meaning-laden and tightly regulated, but still a game that did not determine political history (Goldman 1975: 53, 77–78, 138; Weiner 1992: 134). Real power resided in *inalienable possessions*, objects that did not circulate and were kept *out* of exchange networks at all costs (Weiner 1992: 6–11, 40, 99–100; Godelier 1999: 8; Gillespie 1999: 247). Secondary prestige items moved so that these valuables were not removed from the lineage they represented; hence *keeping-while-giving*. Building on this structure, Maurice Godelier (1999: 110–24) discusses the *kwaimatnie* kept out of circulation by the New Guinea Baruya – shredded leaves, flints, and various dried body parts that did not circulate *and* were kept hidden and buried in wooden boxes. *Kwaimatnie* for the Baruya, hair strings wrapped around *tjurunga* for Aborigines, broken and re-assembled coppers for the Kwakiutl, *taonga* cloaks for the Maori . . . all these represented lineage, ancestry, qualities that were inherently non-transferable and that demanded defence against outside appropriation (Godelier 1999: 8, 100).

Reciprocity was often tangled up in consumption, so that there really was no untainted perpetual circulation for contaminating consumption to destroy. Consumption was inextricable from circulation. Moreover, a class of inalienable (not the same as immobile) possessions was where identity and status actually reside. In the case of the *kula*, at least, competitive exchange was not really an arena where political status was negotiated. Yet archaeologists still cling to the materialist view that the consumption and destruction of material wealth heralded and/or caused social inequality. Kwakiutl *potlatch* is cited as an analog for prehistoric consumption, with impressive quantities of valuables accumulated and sometimes destroyed during assemblies convened to commemorate the death of an important person. Most accounts of *potlatch* read open status competition in the language of violence and personal rivalry that natives used in accounts of the gatherings.[1] The destruction of 'excess' blankets and furs testified to the affluent man's disregard for material possessions, a strategy for taking valuables out of circulation and demonstrating separation from the obligations of reciprocity. A closer and subtler study published a quarter of a century ago has not fully dislodged such assumptions. Irving Goldman (1975: 122–23) charges that *potlatch* as typically drawn reflects a Eurocentric model of antagonistic status relations as well as a belief in an innate human propensity for materialistic values.

Status competition was not an open field in precontact Kwakiutl society with its *fixed* status order and strict aristocrat-commoner partition (Goldman 1975: 48, 55, 169). Convention restricted access to a rank-ordered and permanent pool of 658 formal names – any actual status competition was entangled in this hierarchy (Goldman 1975: 142). Names were not up for sale through the destruction of blankets; only large coppers held lineage titles and broadcast lineage identity. These were inalienable possessions for the Kwakiutl; pieces of coppers were sometimes distributed in *potlatch*, fragments broken off from the reserved original. The donor expected to retrieve such token pieces for later re-attachment – they never really left the lineage to which they belonged, and breakage certainly did not signal a destructive impulse. From this refigured Kwakiutl world we can draw this lesson: fierce competition did not guarantee status mobility,[2] as it took more than conspicuous destruction to redraw a status hierarchy that was itself much more than an extension of material wealth (Goldman 1975: 123; cf. Berthoud and Sabelli 1979: 747). Prehistorians often see winners and losers in a struggle for inequality, assuming in retrospect that competition underlay social change. Conflict as the motor for social change runs uncomfortably close to sociobiology – the reduction of complex human behaviour to repetitive survival tactics – and colours interpretation a livid shade of the modern West (Robb 1999: 5). Constructing status was not always an antagonistic process, and political relations were not always perceived as consisting of imposition and subordination, a struggle pitting an elite against commoners. Rather more common was 'hegemony-without-hierarchy,' the misrepresentation of inequality without willful deceit (Pauketat and Emerson 1999: 304–10). Consensus established hegemony much more effectively than does violence and subjugation. As Mihalis Fotiadis (1999: 394) puts it, 'legitimacy is achieved when there is nothing to contest; when the rule of the paramount does not appear as rule but instead fuses seamlessly with the cosmos; when power has no surface and presents us with no object to focus upon and contemplate' (cf. Broodbank 1992: 46; Barker 1992: 68; Conrad 1992: 162–65; Kolata 1992; Pauketat 1994: 14–17; Helms 2000: 4, 11).

Status was *negotiated* in the extended array of kinship obligation, marriage transactions, and lineage affiliation – material symbols marked this array, but the social totality was never completely confined to artifacts. It was never enough to brandish a sword to assume the title attached to it. Chiefs did not acquire titles and ancestral sanction just by stockpiling prestige markers, and indiscriminate destruction accomplished nothing (Bushnell and Bushnell 1977). Voutsaki contends that *diversity* in the mortuary assemblage – not just quantity – marked affluence (cf. Quesada 1998). This departure from convention trips over the arbitrary scoring of diversity as a status index (Voutsaki 1995: 55–56). Quantifying diversity requires sorting the mortuary assemblage into modern categories based on form and function; it is hardly likely that the people equipping the grave selected *kterismata* from mental categories like 'bronze sword' and 'amber beads.' What looks like five swords, two helmets, and eight pots to the modern observer was very possibly three swords-helmet-three pots evoking lineage *x*, two swords-helmet-pot recalling lineage *y*, and four pots exemplifying lineage *z*. Moreover, Voutsaki (1995: 56) rejects any assessment of *quality* as futile: 'judging the quality of the offerings is a dangerous and ultimately subjective exercise: we know neither their symbolic significance nor their relative exchange value.' Again the complex social array is reduced to material shorthand, and prestige is presented as a static condition rather than as networks 'established and reestablished, tactically negotiated at every point, even when they appear archaeologically as orderly patterns, conventions, or finely tuned, lasting institutions. They are perpetually in the making and unmaking . . . of intentions and contestations over (again) definitions of value' (Fotiadis 1999: 391–2; Thomas 1991: 144). In many accounts, the vague construct 'wealth' emerges as a structuring principle that somehow *supplanted* kinship as a more permanent and convertible status marker in societies on the threshold of state-level complexity. That regional polities on the LH mainland were states is an unwarranted assertion (Galaty and Parkinson 1999; Small 1999), and this widely accepted characterization has initiated a series of circular arguments regarding the shaft grave period. Entrenched social inequality is thought prerequisite for the emergence of complex polities. Aegean pre-historians committed to the LH state had to find that permanent inequality in the preceding transitional period . . . and where better to look than in graves? Intensified artifact deposition was a conspicuous candidate for the materialization of this inequality, and the social rupture was sited in the material realm of what were assumed to be prestige valuables. That many of the artifacts interred were Minoan and/or Minoanizing in some form enhanced the model with a symbolic dimension. Such proposals work well enough *except* for the over-reliance on artifacts as nodes for status negotiation and substitutes for living kinship narratives. Consumption of prestige valuables did not erase generations of constructed identities; it *relocated* and/or *extended* kinship negotiation to the mortuary arena.

Realigned Lineages

Revising and fabricating ancestral lineages was what LH funerary ritual achieved with its most striking feature – reused grave facilities. Bounded cemeteries perhaps representing clan burial grounds were common in the MH, and the tumulus persisted into the MH-LH transition, most notably at Argos and Asine. What was distinctive about the mortuary architecture of the transition was the consistent provision for tomb re-opening and subsequent reuse, often across generations. Shaft graves were broad enough and deep enough to accommodate multiple burials and were equipped with removable slabs, tholos tombs had doors and lots of floor space, and chamber tombs accommodated renovation and expansion. Tumuli and reused tombs both refer to lineage, but re-opening a tomb acknowledged a repetitive and specified temporal aspect in a way that a tumulus did not (Brown 1981; Dunham 1999: 125–127); direct contact with the bones of a particular ancestor placed the transformation of 'inert dead into viable ancestral beings' (Helms 1999: 62; Helms 1993: 142) in the proximity of an already established ancestral identity. That generational reuse made reference to vertical relations *with ancestors* is important in itself (cf. Weiner 1992: 42; Dunham 1999: 122; Helms 2000), but for the purpose of this discussion it also *specified consumption*. Accumulation and removal from circulation were attached to specific ancestral personae – it was not random destruction unmoored from social relations (Voutsaki 1997: 38), and in fact the ancestral dimension probably facilitated the removal of artifacts from circulation (cf. Gregory 1980). This removal was *not* permanent destruction – generational reuse guaranteed that interred artifacts were rediscovered and possibly retrieved. Burial itself irrevocably transformed artifacts, perhaps into a class of inalienable possessions *if* retrieval and re-display were common occurrences. This is all speculative, of course, but several characteristics of inalienable possessions are there – a direct association with lineage, dampened circulation, periodic retrieval, and ritual handling (cf. Lesure 1999: 24–5).

While we cannot press the inalienable possessions idea too far, generational reuse does give some direction on what narratives perhaps extended from artifacts interred in transitional graves. Claiming legitimacy through ancestral rehabilitation and vertical kinship fits in with what we know about Argolid chiefdoms. In terms of the schematics Helms (1993) has developed, Helladic cosmographies pictured a 'centre-*out*-there' rather than a 'centre-*up*-there' (Helms 1993: 176–7; cf. Blanton *et al.* 1996), 'prior house origins' with emphasis on relational ties with a definite population resident elsewhere on earth as opposed to 'first principles' stressing direct descent from creator deities and autochthonous populations (Helms 2000: 79). Distant yet known origins for the paramount lineage were expressed in a labyrinthine palace form that cloistered the megaron, not the wide-open public spaces that recreated a cosmographic centre elsewhere. Prestige was affixed to manufactured imports *acquired* from the centre-out-there, not raw materials from the untamed outside *automatically funneled* into the civilized centre (cf. Goldman 1975: 72, 197–98; Emerson and Hughes 2000: 91–95). Chiefs accessed divinity *through* ancestral intermediaries and far-flung affines (cf. Wright 1984; Spencer 1994: 34–35; Scarry 1999), in contrast to the personal deification suggested for Mesoamerican and Cahokian platform-dwelling rulers.

Accessing Practice

The challenge lies in reconstructing authentic narratives that flesh out theoretical structures and ground them in practice. Minoan sanction in the form of imported prestige goods and emulated crafting traditions was clearly important, but how exactly did Crete fit into mainland cosmographies? And what was the position of other regions of the mainland also represented in mortuary assemblages? Answers to these questions are *not* out of reach. There is much to gain from a closer examination of funerary ritual in the transitional Argolid, a record that is unparalleled in the Aegean in terms of event resolution. In contrast to the jumbled bodies and artifacts in Mycenaean chamber tombs and looting-distorted tholos assemblages, it is usually possible to reconstruct specific interment events even in reused shaft and cist graves. What follows is a proposal for where to search for meaning in the shaft graves – no definitive answers, just thoughts on where focussed research can lead.

Discrete interment events are in some ways the most transparent record of ritual activity; the closest approximation to snapshots that archaeologists can expect to recover. For this reason averaging deposition across contemporary interments just does not make sense. Burial practices were not static and were constantly redesigned in response to previous events (cf. Cannon 1989); averages and patterns deaden that variability and blur the boundaries separating the social personae represented. Looking at interment events as separate and distinct yet consecutive and contingent ritual actions (Appadurai 1981) just might reveal the interplay in which rival lineages worked out a consensus on legitimate practice. In the same vein, there is no defensible reason to exclude any part of the mortuary assemblage, regardless of preconceptions about prestige value – with graves unintentional deposition is not likely, so the details of every artifact[3] and every trace of ritual activity carry some significance (Baudrillard 1981: 32; Lesure 1999: 24). Pottery is often left out of the discussion as a low-status artifact; for the shaft graves this is unfortunate not just because pottery was interred with just about every grave. A detailed and prolific ethnographic and archaeological literature comments on all aspects of ceramic production and consumption and demonstrates the range and depth of meaning pottery can express irrespective of the relative prestige it signifies (Balfet 1965; Arnold 1971; Nicklin 1979; Arnold 1984; Kaplan *et al.* 1984; Lacovara 1985; London 1991; Arnold *et al.* 1991; Pauketat and Emerson 1991; Nordquist 1995; Nordquist 1997; Day and Wilson 1998; van de Moortel 1998; Toll 2001). Ceramic traditions are well known for the mainland transition, such that we can reconstruct with some certainty what region and crafting tradition a given fabric would have recalled for those selecting pottery for interment (cf. Lesure 1999: 27). Implied distance is just one aspect of material expression (Helms 1993), of course, but it is an important one that transitional pottery can handle quite well (cf. Arnold 1998) – we are on much more secure ground with provenance (or *perceived* provenance) for pottery than we are for most other classes of artifacts. There is then at least a chance that we can come up with contextual meaning less superficial than Minoan prestige items as floating signifiers ready for elites to plug into plays for power (cf. Gillespie 1999). Ceramic assemblages in transitional mortuary contexts consist of several regional traditions – in fact, the shaft graves at Mycenae are just as notable for quantities of pottery in central Greek traditions like polychrome mainland as they are for decorated Minoan pottery. In order to situate the charged meaning associated with Minoan artifacts, we must consider at the same time what the central Greek axis meant. Reconstructing the selection of ceramic traditions for mortuary deposition sheds light on the structures that *allowed* 'imported' objects – artifacts manufactured elsewhere *and* those manufactured locally in a foreign tradition (Helms 1993) – to confer prestige on ancestors and on the lineage. What matters here is *specified* distance. Overuse has dulled the force of the ethnographies Helms (1988) has assembled, and archaeologists spent the 1990s falling back on the concept of *distance* as a very general crutch in revised perspectives on exchange. Precocious deployment of Minoan(izing) symbolic capital likely signalled the kind of external legitimation that emergent paramountcies pursue (cf. Thomas 1991: 74; Clark and Blake 1994: 25; Pauketat 1994: 12), and the remarkable range of central Greek traditions represented at Mycenae perhaps marks resource-rich Attica and Euboea as a kind of sacred landscape, an inner sphere that furnished raw materials for emergent chief-sponsored industry (cf. Emerson and Hughes 2000).

Regional Consensus

Examining discrete interments uncovers event-specific decisions; it remains to reposition those interments in a *regional* sequence of ritual activity. No mortuary program was an isolated local event - exogamy and regional sodalities are highly probable for the closely packed communities of the Argolid and surely meant that outsiders attended the funerals of prominent individuals. Comprehending legitimacy then demands the assessment of contemporary events from several Argolid sites for the purpose of rebuilding *regional* negotiation. It is not enough to start from Mycenae and presume that other communities were just emulating practice at the emergent centre – burial practices at Argos, Lerna, Asine, and perhaps even Eleusis were all implicated in broader contests over perceived legitimacy (Voutsaki 1995: 57–58). Aggressive chiefs carried out marriage transactions throughout the Argolid and perhaps farther afield, juxtaposing at a distance divergent traditions and hampering efforts for Mycenae to define legitimacy without input from other communities. For this reason I have trouble with the common idea that central authorities in a chiefdom *suppressed* practices that asserted alternative ideologies (Voutsaki 1995: 62); for example, it has been suggested for Messenia that hinterland tholos tombs fell into disuse while those at Ano Englianos did not and that this traces a trajectory of regional political competition – losing lineages were no longer *permitted* to maintain tholos tombs

(Bennet 1995: 598). Following this logic, the nine tholos tombs at Mycenae, in contrast to the one or two at other sites in the Argolid, signalled competitive success and effective enforcement of supremacy (Wright 1987: 175–84; Dabney and Wright 1990: 52; Voutsaki 1997: 45). However, it is very hard to imagine building code inspectors riding out from the palace and forbidding the construction of hinterland tholos tombs – what checked blatant challenges to authority was the force of consensus on legitimacy. It was probably just not conceivable for non-paramount lineages to construct multiple grave monuments; and if they did build more than one tholos tomb, it is just possible that they built it *at* Mycenae alongside those belonging to the paramount lineage.

The *deployment* of prestige capital is at issue here – stipulate the nominal existence of prestige capital, but do not forget that 'display' and 'consumption' as vague references to practice do not reveal exactly how artifacts materialized social relationships. Instead of looking for the *form* for status competition, it is possible to move on to the *content* expressed in every interment, the social relationships reinforced and redefined through mortuary ceremony, and the negotiation of regional consensus on legitimacy. The staggering consumption in the shaft graves was not the mechanism for social change; rather it points out that narratives were being renegotiated and retold and contested, and this is where social change resided. Competition was not enacted in deposition itself but rather in the redefinition of the social networks and lineage claims *through* the connotations attached to and negotiated for discrete assemblages.

Endnotes

1 'The misunderstanding of Kwakiutl ideas about matters we label as "exchange," "property," "wealth," and "rank" arises from the uncritical application of a European model of status relations to a totally different system of meaning. Thus the Kwakiutl expression "fighting with property," struck Boas and later scholars as a native version of conspicuous display in the game of status rivalry. Since their "potlatches" were imagined as extraordinarily extravagant, the Kwakiutl came to be a prime example of mankind's unfortunate obsession with materialistic values' (Goldman 1975: 122–3). '…Boas and later scholars thought they saw in Kwakiutl life a restless contention for ranks and powers. They inferred from the angry language among chiefs during certain property distributions that "potlatches" were the instruments for obtaining higher rank at the expense of less prosperous participants' (Goldman 1975: 48).

2 'Strange that in a society world-renowned for its excesses in the service of status rivalry there should not be a single *bona fide* example of one particular chief reducing the rank of another in a contest over who has more wealth' (Goldman 1975: 173). 'Among the Kwakiutl it is rank that is stable and *nawalak* that is variable. What observers have usually taken to be rivalry over rank are, in fact, invidious demonstrations of supernatural powers – of *nawalak*. The demonstrations do not, however, affect the possession of powers; they are intended only to portray actual states of being. They manifest aggressive hostility against rivals to demonstrate that the capability of destroying is one of the attributes of *nawalak*' (Goldman 1975: 181).

3   Kwakiutl coppers supply an example of just how much *meaning* artifact characteristics can express. Goldman (1975: 84) lists the anthropomorphic characteristics assigned to the copper, which is red (*tlaq*, the word for copper) like blood, the same colour as salmon, the 'reflection of the setting sun on the sea and thus a bridge or a ladder that spirits climb to reach the sky or descend to reach the earth,' a healer and death-dealer, a fire-starter and fire-quencher, carried like a person and named like a chief and killed and resurrected through repair. Such powerful qualities 'in Western eyes the protean dimensions of copper have been reduced to one term, wealth. If we are to retain this term for traditional Kwakiutl, we must ignore all gross national product connotations and recognize it only for its vitalistic and animistic meanings.'

Bibliography

Appadurai, A.
   1981   The past is a scarce resource. *Man* 16: 201–19.
   1986   Introduction: commodities and the politics of value. In A. Appadurai (ed.), *The Social Life of Things*: 3–63. Cambridge: Cambridge University Press.
Arnold, B.
   1998   'Ministers of mead and wine': the Mediterranean wine trade and the institution-alization of Iron Age elites. 100th Annual Meeting of the Archaeological Institute of America.
Arnold, D.E.
   1971   Ethnomineralogy of Ticul, Yucatan potters: etics and emics. *American Antiquity* 36: 20–40.
   1984   Social interaction and ceramic design: community-wide correlations in Quinua, Peru. In P.M. Rice (ed.), *Pots and Potters: Current Approaches in Ceramic Archaeology* (UCLA Institute of Archaeology Monograph 24): 133–61. Los Angeles: Institute of Archaeology, University of California, Los Angeles.
Arnold, D.E., H. Neff and R.L. Bishop
   1991   Compositional analysis and 'sources' of pottery: an ethnoarchaeological approach. *American Anthropologist* 93: 70–90.
Balfet, H.
   1965   Ethnographical observations in North Africa and archaeological interpretation: the pottery of the Mahgreb. In F.R. Matson (ed.), *Ceramics and Man*: 161–77. Chicago: Aldine.
Barker, A.W.
   1992   Powhatan's pursestrings: on the meaning of surplus in a seventeenth century Algonkian chiefdom. In A.W. Barker and T.R. Pauketat (eds.), *Lords of the Southeast: Social Inequality and the Native Elites of Southeastern North America* (Archaeological Papers of the American Anthropological Association 3): 61–80. Washington, D.C.: American Anthropological Association.
Baudrillard, J.
   1981   *For a Critique of the Political Economy of the Sign*. St. Louis: Telos Press.
Bennet, J.
   1995   Space through time: diachronic perspectives on the spatial organization of the Pylian state. In R. Laffineur and W.-D. Niemeier (eds.), *POLITEIA: Society and State in the Aegean Bronze Age* (Aegaeum 12): 587–602. Liège: Université de Liège.

Berthoud, G. and F. Sabelli
  1979   Our obsolete production mentality: the heresy of the communal formation. *Current Anthropology* 20: 745–60.
Blanton, R.E., G.M. Feinman, S. Kowalewski and P. Peregrine
  1996   A dual-processual theory for the evolution of Mesoamerican civilization. *Current Anthropology* 37: 1–14.
Broodbank, C.
  1992   The Neolithic labyrinth: social change at Knossos before the Bronze Age. *JMA* 5: 39–75.
Brown, J.A.
  1981   The search for rank. In R. Chapman, I. Kinnes and K. Randsborg (eds.), *The Archaeology of Death*: 25–37. Cambridge: Cambridge University Press.
Brunton, R.
  1975   Why do the Trobriands have chiefs? *Man* 10: 554–58.
Bushnell, J. and D. Bushnell
  1977   Wealth, work, and world view in native northwest California: sacred significance and psychoanalytic symbolism. In T. Blackburn (ed.), *Flowers of the Wind*: 120–82. Socorro: Ballena Press.
Cannon, A.
  1989   The historical dimensions in mortuary expressions of status and sentiment. *Current Anthropology* 30: 437–58.
Clark, J.E. and M. Blake
  1994   The power of prestige: competitive generosity and the emergence of rank societies in lowland Mesoamerica. In E.M. Brumfiel and J.W. Fox (eds.), *Factional Competition and Political Development in the New World*: 17–30. Cambridge: Cambridge University Press.
Conrad, G.W.
  1992   Inca imperialism: the great simplification and the accident of empire. In A.A. Demarest and G.W. Conrad (eds.), *Ideology and Pre-Columbian Civilizations*: 159–74. Santa Fe: School of American Research Press.
Dabney, M.K. and J.C. Wright
  1990   Mortuary customs, palatial society and state formation in the Aegean area: a comparative study. In R. Hägg and G.C. Nordquist (eds.), *Celebrations of Death and Divinity in the Bronze Age Argolid*: 45–53. Stockholm: Svenska Institutet i Athen.
Day, P.M. and D.E. Wilson
  1998   Consuming power: Kamares ware in protopalatial Knossos. *Antiquity* 72: 350–58.
Douglas, M.T. and B.C. Isherwood
  1979   *The World of Goods: towards an Anthropology of Consumption*. New York: Basic Books.
Dunham, G.H.
  1999   Marking territory, making territory: burial mounds in interior Virginia. In J.E. Robb (ed.), *Material Symbols: Culture and Economy in Prehistory*: 112–34. Carbondale: Center for Archaeological Investigations, Southern Illinois University.
Emerson, T.E. and R.E. Hughes
  2000   Figurines, flint clay sourcing, the Ozark highlands, and Cahokian acquisition. *American Antiquity* 65: 79–101.
Fotiadis, M.
  1999   Comparability, equivalency, and contestation. In J.E. Robb (ed.), *Material Symbols: Culture and Economy in Prehistory*: 385–98. Carbondale: Center for Archaeological Investigations, Southern Illinois University.

Galaty, M.L. and W.A. Parkinson
   1999   Putting Mycenaean palaces in their place: an introduction. In M.L. Galaty and W.A.
           Parkinson (eds.), *Rethinking Mycenaean Palaces: New Interpretations of an Old Idea* (UCLA
           Institute of Archaeology Monograph 41): 1–8. Los Angeles: Cotsen Institute of
           Archaeology, University of California, Los Angeles.
Gell, A.
   1992   Inter-tribal commodity barter and reproductive gift-exchange in old Melanesia. In C.
           Humphrey and S. Hugh-Jones (eds.), *Barter, Exchange and Value: an Anthropological
           Approach*: 142–68. Cambridge: Cambridge University Press.
Giddens, A.
   1979   *Central Problems in Social Theory: Action, Structure, and Contradiction in Social Analysis.*
           Berkeley: University of California Press.
Gillespie, S.D.
   1999   Olmec thrones as ancestral altars: the two sides of power. In J.E. Robb (ed.), *Material
           Symbols: Culture and Economy in Prehistory*: 224–53. Carbondale: Center for Archaeo-
           logical Investigations, Southern Illinois University.
Godelier, M.
   1999   *The Enigma of the Gift.* Chicago: University of Chicago Press.
Goldman, I.
   1975   *The Mouth of Heaven.* New York: John Wiley.
Gregory, C.A.
   1980   Gifts to men and gifts to God: gift exchange and capital accumulation in contemporary
           Papua. *Man* 15: 626–52.
Helms, M.W.
   1988   *Ulysses' Sail: an Ethnographic Odyssey of Power, Knowledge and Geographical Distance.*
           Princeton: Princeton University Press.
   1993   *Craft and the Kingly Ideal: Art, Trade, and Power.* Austin: University of Texas Press.
   1999   Why Maya lords sat on jaguar thrones. In J.E. Robb (ed.), *Material Symbols: Culture
           and Economy in Prehistory*: 56–69. Carbondale: Center for Archaeological Investigations,
           Southern Illinois University.
   2000   *Access to Origins: Affines, Ancestors, and Aristocrats.* Austin: University of Texas Press.
Kaplan, M.F., G. Harbottle and E.V. Sayre
   1984   Tell el Yahudiyeh ware: a reevaluation. In P.M. Rice (ed.), *Pots and Potters: Current
           Approaches in Ceramic Archaeology* (UCLA Institute of Archaeology Monograph 24):
           227–41. Los Angeles: Institute of Archaeology, University of California, Los Angeles.
Kirch, P.V.
   1991   Chiefship and competitive involution: the Marquesas Islands of eastern Polynesia. In
           T.K. Earle (ed.), *Chiefdoms: Power, Economy, and Ideology*: 119–45. Cambridge:
           Cambridge University Press.
Kolata, A.L.
   1992   Economy, ideology, and imperialism in the south-central Andes. In A.A. Demarest
           and G.W. Conrad (eds.), *Ideology and Pre-Columbian Civilizations*: 65–85. Santa Fe:
           School of American Research Press.
Lacovara, P.
   1985   The ethnoarchaeology of pottery production in an upper Egyptian village. In W.C.
           Kingery (ed.), *Ancient Technology to Modern Science*: 51–60. Columbus: The American
           Ceramic Society.
Lesure, R.
   1999   On the genesis of value in early hierarchical societies. In J.E. Robb (ed.), *Material*

Symbols: Culture and Economy in Prehistory: 23–55. Carbondale: Center for Archaeological Investigations, Southern Illinois University.

London, G.A.
  1991   Ethnoarchaeological evidence of variation in Cypriot ceramics and its implications for the taxonomy of ancient pottery. In J.A. Barlow, D.L. Bolger and B. Kling (eds.), *Cypriot Ceramics: Reading the Prehistoric Record*: 221–33. Philadelphia: University Museum Publications, University of Pennsylvania.

McGuire, R.H.
  1995   Review of P.K. Wason (1994), Archaeology of Rank. *Antiquity* 69: 204–06.

Malinowski, B.
  1922   *Argonauts of the Western Pacific.* London: G. Routledge.

Nicklin, K.
  1979   The location of pottery manufacture. *Man* 14: 436–58.

Nordquist, G.C.
  1995   Who made the pots? Production in the Middle Helladic society. In R. Laffineur and W.-D. Niemeier (eds.), *POLITEIA: Society and State in the Aegean Bronze Age* (Aegaeum 12): 201–07. Liège: Université de Liège.
  1997   What about production? Production in the Middle Helladic frame. In C. Gillis, C. Risberg and B. Sjöberg (eds.), *Trade and Production in Premonetary Greece: Production and the Craftsman* (SIMA Pocket-Book 143): 15–27. Jonsered: Paul Åström.

Pauketat, T.R.
  1994   *The Ascent of Chiefs: Cahokia and Mississippian Politics in Native North America.* Tuscaloosa: University of Alabama Press.

Pauketat, T.R. and T.E. Emerson
  1991   The ideology of authority and the power of the pot. *American Anthropologist* 93: 919–41.
  1999   Representations of hegemony as community at Cahokia. In J.E. Robb (ed.), *Material Symbols: Culture and Economy in Prehistory*: 56–69. Carbondale: Center for Archaeological Investigations, Southern Illinois University.

Pydyn, A.
  1998   Universal or relative? Social, economic and symbolic values in central Europe in the transition from the Bronze Age to the Iron Age. In D.W. Bailey (ed.), *The Archaeology of Value: Essays on Prestige and the Processes of Valuation* (BAR International Series 730): 97–105. Oxford: Archaeopress.

Quesada, F.
  1998   From quality to quantity: wealth, status and prestige in the Iberian Iron Age. In D.W. Bailey (ed.), *The Archaeology of Value: Essays on Prestige and the Processes of Valuation* (BAR International Series 730): 70–96. Oxford: Archaeopress.

Robb, J.E.
  1999   Secret agents: culture, economy, and social reproduction. In J.E. Robb (ed.), *Material Symbols: Culture and Economy in Prehistory*: 3–15. Carbondale: Center for Archaeological Investigations, Southern Illinois University.

Scarry, J.F.
  1999   Elite identities in Apalachee province: the construction of identity and cultural change in a Mississippian polity. In J.E. Robb (ed.), *Material Symbols: Culture and Economy in Prehistory*: 342–61. Carbondale: Center for Archaeological Investigations, Southern Illinois University.

Small, D.B.
  1999   Mycenaean polities: states or estates? In M.L. Galaty and W.A. Parkinson (eds.),

Rethinking Mycenaean Palaces: New Interpretations of an Old Idea (UCLA Institute of Archaeology Monograph 41): 43–47. Los Angeles: Cotsen Institute of Archaeology, University of California, Los Angeles.

Spencer, C.S.
  1994   Factional ascendance, dimensions of leadership, and the development of centralized authority. In E.M. Brumfiel and J.W. Fox (eds.), *Factional Competition and Political Development in the New World*: 31–43. Cambridge: Cambridge University Press.

Thomas, N.
  1991   *Entangled Objects: Exchange, Material Culture and Colonialism in the Pacific*. Cambridge, Mass.: Harvard University Press.

Toll, H.W.
  2001   Making and breaking pots in the Chaco world. *American Antiquity* 66: 56–78.

van der Moortel, A.
  1998   Pottery as a barometer of economic change in Neopalatial central Crete. 100th Annual Meeting of the Archaeological Institute of America.

van Wijngaarden, G.-J.
  1999   An archaeological approach to the concept of value: Mycenaean pottery at Ugarit (Syria). *Archaeological Dialogues* 6: 2–23.

Voutsaki, S.
  1995   Social and political processes in the Mycenaean Argolid: the evidence from the mortuary practices. In R. Laffineur and W.-D. Niemeier (eds.), *POLITEIA: Society and State in the Aegean Bronze Age* (Aegaeum 12): 55–66. Liège: Université de Liège.
  1997   The creation of value and prestige in the Aegean Late Bronze Age. *Journal of European Archaeology* 5: 34–52.
  1998   Mortuary evidence, symbolic meanings and social change: a comparison between Messenia and the Argolid in the Mycenaean period. In K. Branigan (ed.), *Cemetery and Society in the Aegean Bronze Age* (SSAA 1): 41–58. Sheffield: Sheffield Academic Press.

Weiner, A.
  1992   *Inalienable Possessions: the Paradox of Keeping-while-Giving*. Berkeley: University of California Press.

Wright, H.T.
  1984   Prestate political formations. In T.K. Earle (ed.), *On the Evolution of Complex Societies*: 41–77. Malibu: Undena.

Wright, J.C.
  1987   Death and power at Mycenae: changing symbols and mortuary practice. In R. Laffineur (ed.), *Thanatos: les coutumes funéraires en Egée à l'âge du Bronze* (Aegaeum 2): 171–84. Liège: Université de Liège.

8

'Some Light on the Early Origins of Them All': Generalization and the Explanation of Civilization Revisited

John C. Barrett and Krystalli Damilati

A commonly voiced criticism of processual archaeology is that the explanations it offers for historical change are too 'deterministic' in their treatment of human creativity and intentionality (Hodder 1982). We expect explanations to be causal; they should satisfy our curiosity as to why certain events occurred by isolating the conditions that gave rise to those events. Processual archaeology rose to the challenge of explaining events linked to social and economic change. It did so on the presumption that explanations should have a general relevance, reasoning that if we can identify certain types of event then we might reasonably expect each type to have resulted from a common set of processes. Why then might processualist explanations appear problematic? The answer seems to lie in the position assigned to human agency in those explanations. If certain general conditions have always given rise to the same type of historical event, then the human agents involved would have had no other role than to act as the medium through which those general historical forces operated.

At a very simple level, the argument between processual and post-processualist positions has turned upon the extent to which particular groups of human beings may have made a difference in history. As conscious beings and as strategic actors, human agents would seem to be inadequately characterized when they are treated merely as dupes whose actions were determined by forces of which they were largely unaware. It is noticeable, however, that both sides of the debate share a common assumption, namely that the motivation of human agency must be distinguished from the material workings of other historical processes. If processual archaeology believed that material conditions drove human agency, then post-processual archaeology has countered that not only did the agents' subjectivity help craft the material conditions of history but that it did so from perspectives that were culturally and historically particular.

It is instructive to return to Renfrew's *Emergence of Civilisation* (1972) with these brief comments in mind. Given that the book remains among the most robust processualist studies of a major period of culture change in European prehistory, we might expect it to carry all the hallmarks of the supposed failures of the processualist approach. By using systems analysis to trace the transformations that accompanied the beginnings of metallurgy in the southern Aegean, Renfrew claims that historical change can be treated as the organizational change in a system that is generated by feedback between the different components of that system. However, whilst internal processes supposedly facilitated systemic change (the 'multiplier effect'), the processes of transformation are regarded by Renfrew as being driven by profoundly human concerns. In other words, behind the growth in subsistence economies, craft production, and the development of trade networks, all of which necessitated an ultimate transformation in systemic organization, there lay a common human motivation that Renfrew suggests was driven by the need to acquire status and prestige (Renfrew 1972: 42).

Without this human motivation Renfrew does not believe that the transformations in the historical processes could have occurred. For Renfrew, at the time he was writing *The Emergence*, human agency was indeed involved in the making of history in its own terms, if not in circumstances of its own choosing. Such a case might go some way towards challenging the accuracy of the post-processualist critique, but it also brings us to a more general, and in many ways more interesting, problem. At the heart of the historical analysis offered in the *Emergence* sits a general assertion about human nature and its operation as a historical force. The validity of this assertion, that history is driven by human motivations of competition and social differentiation, cannot be assessed by any analytical procedure offered by Renfrew. How then are we to treat this seemingly fundamental causal condition of historical change?

We will explore this question in the following way. First, we must clarify how historical conditions are being characterized, for it is upon this characterization that the processes of historical transformation come to be identified. We will then proceed to consider the ways we might treat the conditions of human motivation as contributing to historical change, leading us to reconsider the historical conditions of civilization.

A Perspective on the Past

Renfrew's 1972 study concerned the development of the Bronze Age civilizations of the southern Aegean. The qualitative term may seem problematic in so far as it assigns a particular cultural development (the southern Aegean in the early second millennium) to a general category (civilization). However, if we accept that the world changes, and that the conditions of humanity in the second millennium BC were different from the conditions of the third millennium, then to write of civilization as Renfrew does is simply to employ a marker as to the general nature of those differences. We do not wish to debate the loaded nature of the term but to seek, as Renfrew did, to understand what has changed, to explore the means by which those changes may be understood, and to assess the extent to which a common state of 'civilization' may have existed at the time.

Our enquiry will necessarily involve a brief review of some fundamental issues concerning the way we structure historical knowledge and the role of historical generalization. All branches of the social sciences, be they sociological, anthropological, or historical, require comparative analysis. Indeed, the histories of the social sciences can be written as the exploration of procedures that render particular observations generally available to cross-cultural analysis. Without such analysis we would be unable to trace patterns of continuity and transformation, and we would have no means of expressing the insights we believe we gain from our historical enquiries. We would not be able to say why certain things matter or are of particular importance to us.

The understandings gained by the social scientist are different from those of the participants whom they study. Whilst the latter tend to treat their own lives as particular, the former will treat them as paradigmatic for a certain general condition. This is not to deny that participants cannot become social scientists of a kind; they do so whenever they make explicit the general principles to which their own lives bear testimony. The difference however remains. The participant will see his or her own existence as embedded in a general order (how their world works), which the social scientist will regard as culturally particular (how 'they' see 'their' world as working). We doubt the existence of their gods, spirits and ancestors, and we find their claims to the values of honour, spirituality and purity as not being essential to humanity in general but as a culturally mediated particularity.

The social scientist therefore steps away from the participant's frame of reference to seek the conditions that are believed to give rise to those various forms of cultural mediation. This is a course of action that has routinely treated the material contexts within which the human subject operates, and the subjective experiences and motivations of the subject, as distinct objects of analysis. It is this move that has prompted us to uncover the material forces or conditions that operated behind the backs of the people we study. We should therefore be enormously interested in the means by which our detached and generalizing views of others comes to be constructed. At the risk of repetition we must stress that the move currently requires the analytical distinction between subjective motivation ('their' view of the world) and material context, a distinction often rendered as that dividing the imagined from the real (Godelier 1986).

Historical Conditions

An admittedly simple contrast can be drawn between processual and post-processual archaeology in the ways each attempts to explain human actions. Processualism has privileged the material context as being determinate, while post-processualism has inverted the argument by privileging subjective motivations. In so doing post-processualism has laid stress upon the particularity of each subjective context. As we have already noted, both are committed to the analytical distinction between an external objective world and an inner subjective experience, one or other of which is taken to explain human action. The participants, whose lives we hope to understand, would have been unlikely to find the distinction meaningful. For them the actions of their own lives, with all the emotional commitments and motivations those lives involved, would have stood as testimony to the order of the world of which they were a part. Neither did the world make them, nor they the world, for both were surely the product of a single divine, spiritual, natural, or cataclysmic providence. And that unity was material, real and present.

The generalizations all of us use about the human condition, and which are expressed in the ways we characterize the stabilities and transformations of history and explain the processes that brought those conditions into being, make it possible for us to identify and to interrogate what we take to be certain fundamental and determinate conditions. The dualism that informs contemporary thinking is drawn between internal subjectivities and external material realities. The history of this dualism and some of its implications have been examined in detail by Koerner (forthcoming); suffice it to note that we are currently offered the choice of explaining history as either how material reality determined the development of subjectivity, or how human subjectivity gained access to, and acted upon, a material reality. The general similarities that we seek between our different case studies, and the forces that archaeologists believe drive the historical narrative, are moulded by the choices we currently make concerning these issues.

Civilization is a category used to describe a particular set of material conditions, a type of structural organization, a level of technological achievement, and a set of subjective values. The usual assumption is that civilizations are holistic; they are constituted by the coherent operation of all these various components, and this coherency can be expressed in functional terms by describing how the system of a particular civilization works as a whole. Civilizations have consequently been thought of as coming into being as a high-level of organization, and to have 'collapsed' with the break-up of that organization.

Systems Analysis as a Basis for Generalization

Systems analysis is not only central to Renfrew's work but is also central to the problems we aim to investigate. The strength of systems analysis is the encouragement it gives to the analysis of relationships that operated between different kinds of condition. These relationships are 'structural'. Any temptation to trace the history of say 'religion' or 'settlement organization' is resisted by the realization that the form each takes depended upon the ways the *relationships* between each of them actually structured the system. However, systems analysis also carries with it a great deal of intellectual baggage. The participating elements of the system, whatever we may regard them to have been, are synthesised as an image of systemic stability maintained as a single organizational structure. This structure describes the architecture of the system and therefore describes what guaranteed its coherency. Because any system may then be typified by its principle mode of organization, historical enquiry is drawn inevitably towards the general explanation of how such types of organization arose. In comparative analyses, we are familiar with archaeological accounts of particular kinds of organizational structures (chiefdoms for example), and with accounts of how their stability was achieved through the structural principles that held the various component parts of each system together (redistribution for example). In such accounts historical change seems to occur either by the growth of the system into a higher level of organizational complexity (from chiefdom to state) or by instability and collapse (a dark age), and to be explained in terms of either increasing organizational efficiency or maladaptation.

We owe the concept of the social system to this intellectual tradition. Social systems map relationships between statuses and roles; they distinguish the holders of these positions by establishing their function in maintaining the order of the system and, necessarily, they trace the history of social systems either as a trajectory of increasingly complex categories and grades of distinction, or as the 'collapse' of those distinctions. Social systems thus gain the status of an objective reality and are consequently assumed to contribute to the subjective understandings of their participants. If we accept that human motivation plays a part in the history of social systems, and if we describe the history of social systems in terms of increasing differentiation and complexity, then the claim that human motivation is driven by the desire for differentiation between individuals and groups is perhaps an unsurprising, if circular, argument. This appears to be the position developed in *The Emergence*.

It is easy to overlook that all models are abstractions. They simplify and thus enhance our handling of the enormous complexity of past conditions. However, the causes that gave rise to those conditions actually operated in the context of that complexity and not at the level of the abstraction. Consequently, while the abstraction offers us the sweeping view of history it does so by taking us 'further and further away from the diversity in the data; its intrinsic complexity is homogenized, reduced to manageable classificatory entities, all in the service of convincing narrative construction' (Van der Leeuw and McGlade 1997: 5). In the Aegean case the Neolithic and Bronze Age sequences are very diverse across the Cyclades, southern mainland Greece and Crete. However, by combining all as if they were the components of a single system (and how the boundaries of the system are established remains unclear), it is possible to treat particular examples as representative of the general category. Thus does the evidence for settlement expansion in the Argolid and Thessaly characterize a general history of settlement colonization, exchange patterns in the Cyclades characterize trade in general, and the emergence of the Cretan palaces characterizes the organizational principle of the entire system. The dubious nature of such a synthesis is masked when the organizational logic of the developing system (the emergence of the Cretan palaces) becomes both the historical problem central to the period, and also the proposed solution (in the interminable debate concerning the function of the palaces). Because systems are understood in terms of their organizational coherency and structural logic, it is little wonder that many attempts to explain the emergence of 'complexity' are tempted by the image of a development that was driven by elites who themselves act as all-knowing administrators of the systems that supposedly produced them (Earle 1991).

We must now return to these issues with reference to the Bronze Age itself. In Renfrew's argument, the objective realities that prefigured the rise of Aegean civilization, and which he describes in terms of the systemic conditions of social and economic order, were necessary but not sufficient to explain the rise of that civilization. What he offers additionally is the presence of human motivations that were competitive and acquisitive and so worked to increase the distinctions between categories and ranks of people. It appears from his argument that this subjectivity is timeless; it speaks of humanity in general whose characteristics are self-evident. In exploring these issues further we will question this basic assumption and we will argue for a human agency that emerges through the variable, public, and material affirmation of its different existences. By this means we aim to avoid the idealism that is so often taken to characterize current approaches to the archaeology of human agency (Muller 1991) and regain something of that agency's pragmatic and material existence. Our argument is that historical understanding requires us to engage with the specific conditions in which that agency operated.

The Bronze Age

Although few archaeologists still use the three-age system as a useful typology for prehistory, the idea that a qualitative difference separates Stone Age social and economic systems from those of the Bronze Age is still widely accepted (Earle 2002). Childe first made explicit the organizational differences that he believed distinguished the two economies by claiming that metallurgy required specialist producers in a way that stone working did not, and consequently a level of organization that depended upon the production and management of a food surplus to support such specialists (Childe 1957). Childe emphasized that the development of an agricultural surplus to support specialist craft production, and the political control of that surplus, were the fundamental conditions required to sustain complex levels of technology, specialist knowledge, and the long-term trade links necessary to supply raw materials. The contrast between Neolithic economies that were local and relatively self sufficient, and Bronze Age economies that were task-differentiated and employed widespread trade links, is basic to all subsequent arguments. Earle's recent discussion of the issues is instructive. He contrasts Marshall Sahlins's well-known model of *Stone Age Economics* with his own vision of a *Bronze Age Economics*. He treats the two as demarcating a contrast between the domestic mode of production characteristic of the former, with its household organization and with a balanced reciprocity operating between producers, and the development of a political economy in the latter case that institutionalized differences of status by the accumulation of wealth (Sahlins 1974; Earle 2002). The transformation appears profound. Neolithic social formations are structured as economic collectives, distinguishable from hunter-gatherers by the ways the available resources were managed. Bronze Age social formations were politically structured to maintain and enhance rank and status differences.

At base, the distinction being drawn is between two clusters of social and economic institutions, each with their particular scales of operation and particular material outcomes. By mapping these two sets of conditions in systemic terms we can chart the contrasts in the various components of the two systems – we can see what changes. For example, we may be able to depict changes in the organization and scale of agricultural production, technologies of storage, organization of craft production, patterns of trade, and so forth. In following the sequential relationship in which Bronze Age political structures are taken to have evolved from their Stone Age economic predecessors, we are however confronted with a puzzle: how did Stone Age economic systems that are assumed to have been relatively stable, kinship based, and in which production supposedly satisfied need, give rise to Bronze Age economies that were expansionist, politically competitive, that organized labour beyond the level of kinship, and were exploitative by nature?

Any move to historicize the relationship between these two kinds of condition starts from the relatively un-contentious position that Neolithic societies preceded Bronze Age societies. However, this does not mean that the historical process that created a Neolithic type of order was *necessarily* orientated towards creating a Bronze Age type of order as well. This would bind us to a teleology operating at a systemic scale; it would mean that historical explanations must be lodged at a structural and an organizational level. Furthermore, because these historical processes are assumed to have operated in a linear relationship, moving towards a single outcome, and because that outcome can be characterized as a certain type of organization (Bronze Age polities), we appear to be promised a general explanation for the emergence of the Bronze Age in all its different cases.

Now, we can certainly accept that Neolithic and Bronze Age societies can be characterized by a family of material resemblances, and that on a world scale Neolithic societies are succeeded by Bronze Age societies in many (but by no means all) cases. Nonetheless, it does not follow that an explanation for the transformation from the Neolithic to the Bronze Age must be generally applicable to all cases. We may certainly group the different physical attributes of two kinds of economic system (Stone Age and Bronze Age) in ways that seem applicable to most cases, but it does not follow that we should provide an explanation for change that is based upon these generalized and unified abstractions. Obviously, if such expectations were realistic, then the New Archaeology's aspiration to establish laws or law-like generalizations of social evolution would have been achievable. That we are still waiting for these laws to be established might give the hint that such expectations were misplaced. Bronze Age type societies may indeed arise out of Stone Age type societies, but it does not follow that the causes of that transformation are coherently the same in all cases. History works in the diversity that each case represents, rather than in the family resemblances that are shared by all cases. The latter presents images of relatively stable conditions (the functioning of Stone Age and Bronze Age systems) while the former will expose the specific aspects of disunity and instability as the more productive foci for future research:

> 'We argue that it is precisely the aberrant, the discontinuous and the 'different' categories of data which form the rudiments of an alternative theory of change – one predicated on the importance of *instability* rather than stability as the basis from which a more insightful understanding of historical process can emerge.' (Van der Leeuw and McGlade 1997: 6, emphasis in the original)

This is all well and good, systems may be regarded as inherently unstable because their components at the micro (local) level may fail to behave coherently at different locations within the system, and we might abandon the expectation that any single example of preconditions can possibly provide a prediction for the state of conditions that will follow. Nonetheless we have got no further than expressing these claims in abstraction, whereas we contend that archaeological research must attempt to understand the nature of historical diversity and the reasons for change with reference to specific material conditions. It is surely incumbent upon us to specify how this diversity and unpredictability operated historically, what the actual mechanisms were that produced it, and how we might investigate these mechanisms as material conditions.

Renfrew took the southern Aegean as a single case, clearly expecting that his own study would reveal principles that are applicable beyond that case. He argued that if civilization represents 'a major advance for man', then the inescapable implication was that:

> 'the early civilisations in different parts of the world had certain things in common, that their development was in each case a particular instance of some more general process, the transformation from 'primitive' to 'civilised'. Any understanding of the emergence of one of the world's early civilisations which we may reach would therefore throw some light on the early origins of them all.' (Renfrew 1972: 3)

We would counter that, although complex Bronze Age societies had certain things in common, this still allows that they could have arisen along quite different historical trajectories; different causes can have similar effects and similar causes can have different and unpredictable effects. For example, the contrast between 'Stone Age' and 'Bronze Age' social and economic organizations is taken by some to include the emergence of Bronze Age political institutions that controlled labour, as a source of political power, on a scale larger than the immediate relations of kinship:

> 'In my view rules regarding kin-based rights to labor remained the primary structural constraint to the expansion of tribal or big-man power everywhere. It appears that the fundamental structure of kin-based labor had to rupture for person(s) with chiefly powers to emerge.' (Arnold 2000: 26)

We question why the level of labour mobilization should be taken as the *fundamental* organizational feature to define 'chiefly' Bronze Age societies, and doubt that the means by which traditional labour obligations were 'ruptured' to extend labour obligations could ever have been the same in each and every case.

The Processes of Systemic Change

Since the publication of *The Emergence* a number of studies have sought to extend our understanding of the processes Renfrew identified as facilitating social and economic change. In all cases, the role played by exchange is treated as being fundamental. The emergence of agricultural diversity (with specialist production exploiting ecologically restricted resources), long-distance trade primarily involving metallurgy, and the development of storage facilities (witnessed in the early palaces) are presumed to have worked as a single network of self-reinforcing relationships. These relationships transmitted specialist products around the system. If the Neolithic system can be characterized as largely non-differentiated, comprising similar productive units, such as village households, inhabiting a common range of ecological resources, then the Bronze Age system was one of expansion and diversity. If Neolithic exchanges were structured by reciprocity between co-operating producers, then Bronze Age exchanges were the expressions of political authority, obligations and status. The contrast recalls Durkheim's distinction between mechanical and organic solidarities. The former are built by the mechanical addition of standard components, whilst the latter emerge in the form of a body whose organs fulfil the specialist functions required to maintain the whole.

Exchange is therefore taken as the means by which the relatively autonomous components of a system, such as particular households of producers, changed in terms of their various roles and statuses relative to one another. If increasing levels of functional differentiation occurred between the Neolithic and the Bronze

Age then this marks a systemic change, and exchange mechanisms supposedly offered the structural means by which such change became possible. Thus the move from a uniform pattern of household producers distributed over a region, to the occurrence of specialist producers who were exploiting restricted resources, is presumed to have become possible by virtue of an emergent exchange mechanism for redistribution. However, identifying why a change may have been possible is not the same thing as offering a causal explanation. The latter requires a degree of necessity, allowing us to identify why a relatively egalitarian Neolithic system was driven towards that of the ranked non-egalitarian system of the Bronze Age. Renfrew is quite clear on this matter, the simple availability of different agricultural resources and the existence of long-distance trade presented the possibility of change, but the path had to be traversed by a human agency that, in Renfrew's terms, was motivated by the acquisition of social status through the accumulation of material wealth. It was these motivations that made use of the available conditions, and so resulted in the cycles of positive feedback between the processes of production and acquisition that drove systemic change.

Two models for status acquisition by means of exchange have been employed in archaeology. The differences between them define the principles underpinning two different kinds of political economies: one proposes that social status was acquired through the accumulation of material wealth; the other situates status in the acquisition of debt obligations (cf. Gregory 1982). The former therefore treats material objects as storing a form of social value whose subsequent release offers the means of exercising some control over other resources or over people, perhaps through the purchase of those resources and the payment of those people. The latter, drawing directly upon Mauss's original study of gift exchange (1970), places social value in the 'generosity' of giving and the obligations that arise from receiving the gift. Gift giving and sacrifice become a source of social power and status.

Given that these forms of exchange are presented as general principles upon which models of social evolution are based, it is our contention that there must come a point at which the models fail to deliver the explanations that are expected of them. We will suggest that this failure must occur because the social value of either material things or gift obligations is treated as a general and therefore abstract quality, rather than as something that had to be established in each and every historical context. How that value was established, maintained, and renegotiated was fundamental to the historical transformations that gave rise to Aegean civilization.

Models of exchange

We will illustrate our case with reference to two studies, Halstead and O'Shea's model of social storage (Halstead and O'Shea 1982) and the 'epigenetic' model for the evolution of civilization developed by Friedman and Rowlands (1977). Both have had considerable influence on European Bronze Age studies although, despite its quite extensive use elsewhere, the Friedman and Rowlands model has been strangely absent from the citations of Aegean researchers.

Halstead and O'Shea trace the transformation of Neolithic local economies into Bronze Age polities as a move from the management of subsistence requirements (food) to the management of accumulated material wealth, ultimately in the form of prestige objects. They explain this transformation by reference to the concept of social storage (see also O'Shea 1981 and Halstead 1981). The origins of social storage lay in the need to cope with the year on year uncertainties faced by sedentary agrarian populations whose own direct storage of food could have carried them across seasonal shortages but could not counter the catastrophic failure of an annual harvest. Insurance against such a failure required a way of transferring the security of a local, short-term, and perishable food storage into a larger network of long-term support. Sedentary communities may have achieved this by maintaining the reciprocal exchange of foods between neighbouring groups who were exploiting different ecological zones, but these regional systems remained vulnerable to widespread famine. To extend the network of support further required overcoming the limitations imposed by distance in the transportation of food, and establishing long-term storage that was necessarily constrained by the perishable nature of the material. These problems were solved by 'indirect storage' where food was given an equivalent social value in the form of a non-perishable token:

> 'the transformations characteristic of indirect storage are *cultural* and involve the equivalencing of foodstuffs and non-food items through exchange transactions .... In such transactions food is exchanged for non-food tokens with at least *the implicit understanding* that such tokens can later be re-exchanged for food. This type of exchange transaction will be termed social storage.' (Halstead and O'Shea 1982: 93, our emphasis)

Initially the tokens represented an equivalent value in food, for which they could be cashed in at a later date. However, successful producers began to accumulate tokens as they supported less successful neighbours who, on a year-on-year basis, had to offer tokens for the food they needed. The successful producer, on the other hand, did not require to cash-in the tokens for food:

> 'wherever some social groups regularly produce a surplus and others regularly consume it, an even distribution of food can only be achieved at the expense of an uneven distribution of tokens. The stability of tokens then permits the sustained, unequal *accumulation of wealth* and its transmission across generations within a corporate group. This in turn makes possible the symbolic and active manipulation of wealth by such groups and so provides the critical preconditions for the emergence of institutionalised *social differentiation*.' (Halstead and O'Shea 1982: 93 our emphasis)

The final step, according to this model, was for the elite to exchange local tokens, not for unnecessary food, but for items from distant exchange partners. These exotic items apparently gained an enhanced local value, and this enhanced value accrued even greater social standing for those who used them in acts of display and votive deposition.

This model covers all the elements we associate with Bronze Age political economies. Neolithic patterns of reciprocal exchange within household and village based economies are transformed into larger-scale exchange networks that maintain political structures of differential wealth and authority. They result finally in the subsequent investment of wealth in acts of ideological display that accompany the beginnings of civilization.

The suggestion that political status emerges at the intersections of different exchange networks, where items that have been accumulated in one exchange cycle can be re-invested in another, is central to the model developed by Friedman and Rowlands (1977). However they give a more emphatic role to the logic of gift exchange, wherein the ties between exchange partners are manifest in the gift with its obligation for return. Their model also makes explicit the determinate position taken by the social relations of production that, whilst necessarily operating within the undoubted constraints imposed by technology and environment, structure the system:

> 'relations of production, as we have defined them …, organise and dominate the entire process of social reproduction and determine its course of development within the limits of functional compatibility' [within different categories of material condition] (Friedman and Rowlands 1977: 203–04)

If we want to identify where human agency operates in the making of history, then from this perspective we should seek out the role of agency in maintaining the relations of production.

The basic unit of production and exchange in Sahlins's (1974) domestic mode of production is the household. However, whilst households may be self-sufficient in the short term, their biological reproduction demands that they were linked to a larger community through the exchange of marriage partners. If Halstead and O'Shea's households gained long-term security through reciprocal networks of food exchange, Friedman and Rowlands's households required marriage alliances for their biological reproduction. The important point about the latter case is that it introduces an immediate, albeit presumed, asymmetry between wife givers and wife takers, an asymmetry marked by the upward and reciprocal flow of food renders and labour dues. The larger alliance system therefore tended to be distinguished as a lineage ranked from junior to senior households, along which material products and labour services moved. But here Friedman and Rowlands introduce a further, perhaps surprising, component to the economic structure:

> 'Economic activity in this system *can only be understood* as a relation between producers and the supernatural. This is because wealth and prosperity are seen as

controlled directly by supernatural spirits. The latter, however, are not separated from the world of the living in any absolute way. On the contrary, the supernatural is no more than an extension of the lineage structure so that the ancestors are spirits whose function it is to communicate with higher spirits in order to bring wealth to the group. In fact, the entire universe is usually envisaged as a single segmentary structure in which the most powerful deities are no more than the more distant ancestor-founders of larger groups.' (Friedman and Rowlands 1977: 207, our emphasis)

The subjective hold that a household's members had of their situation in material relations, and of the prosperity they gained (or indeed failed to gain) as a result of those relations, is thus expressed in terms of their relationships with the spiritual. And these relations were practised through the making of alliances by marriage, where some material wealth was given in return for marriage partners and for the establishment of an indebted alliance with a more senior household. This relationship was desirable because it secured a place for a supplicant in a higher-ranking lineage.

If systems such as these characterize, at least in the terms of the model, Stone Age economies, then Bronze Age political economies emerged at the point where the relative and fluctuating ranking of lineage relations was converted into absolute rank. This process involved the appropriation, by a senior lineage, of the right (and indeed, obligation) to mediate with local deities on behalf of the larger community whose well-being that senior lineage now oversaw. Where previously such deities may have been held in common and may have been the focus to which the local community looked as a source for their common security, now:

'a living lineage comes to occupy the position of mediator in this activity [and] is entitled to tribute and corvée as the cost for performing the necessary function of seeing to the welfare of the community.' (Friedman and Rowlands 1977: 211)

This system was also expansionist; alliances and exchange relations drew increasingly stable and politically dominant groups into a 'supralocal' domain through which exotic materials are secured. The outward expansion of these groups by marriage and alliance thus pulled in materials that were loaded with cultural value by virtue of their distant origins (cf. Helms 1988); their use in ritual and display only further secured the dominant position of the local elites.

Structure, Agency and History

Models are simplifications of complex situations, they enable us to sort the information into manageable forms and provide an over-view of the situation under investigation. Models also allow us to think through the implications of changes in their particular components. If we model historical conditions we may trace the changes that occurred through time and may glimpse the factors that contributed to those changes. Shifting patterns of wealth, new technologies, the rise of new social formations: all these represent structural changes and all may have facilitated the possibility of further change in the histories of social formations. We may thus grasp common features in history, be they the possible consequences of local patterns of household production, the demands of chiefly authority, or the territorial organization of early states.

Models are necessarily our abstractions; they are general to the case and not specific to its circumstances. And yet history works in the specifics, and its workings are distributed through the detail of particular conditions. This does not mean that models become redundant in our search for explanation, rather it is at the point where a model fails (as it must) to deliver the historical explanations we require that we finally grasp the point at which empirical research should be applied and the direction that such research might follow. Instead of explaining historical conditions, models direct our understanding as to how we might investigate those conditions.

Throughout this paper we have been concerned with models of social transformation. Each example attempts to explain how the organization of a general kind of social structure may have been transformed. They share a number of common features; the kind of transformation that each describes is, at a very general level, the move from Stone Age subsistence economies to the political economies of the Bronze Age. Our point is not that such models are wrong (some may be stronger than others in terms of their theoretical development), but that the contrasting conditions described by each draws our attention to features held in common by a number of early civilizations. Our concern is with the empirical mechanisms of transformation, and this is where these models do not deliver the kinds of understanding that is often claimed for them. The move required is from the general and the abstractly modelled conditions to the point at which the historical conditions were made concrete; it is at this point that we confront the historical agency that made our ideal case the particular material reality that it once was.

In our view this is precisely the issue that Renfrew recognized. As we have seen, he called upon a human agency that was motivated by competition and the desires of the original 'acquisitive society' to vitalise the general conditions that he used to describe the prehistory of the Aegean. Does such an agency achieve the task of making history in its own terms? In our view it does not.

Exchange and Value

The value of material goods is a quality that is fundamental to the operation of all the models that we have so far considered. This is true for the early bronze daggers whose circulation Renfrew argued helped drive the relationship between local production and long-distance exchange, for the tokens of social storage that transformed a food surplus into the value of ritual display, and for the asymmetrical exchanges of kinship and alliance. If human agents competed for status, then according to these models they seem to have done so by competing for the strategic control of these values. It is therefore surprising that value remains a quality ill-defined in all these studies, only emerging historically when it becomes attached to certain things. Consider for example the ways tokens appear to work in the social storage model. These had an initial value based upon food equivalences, a convention that had to be established and secured over time. We are rarely told what form these tokens took (Halstead 1981: 198), and we are not told how the necessary conventions to under-write their values were secured. Nor indeed are we told how the accumulation of these tokens by successful producers then secured the 'accumulation of wealth' that could be transmitted across generations of a group to whom the basis of that wealth (food) was entirely surplus to their requirements. The further transformation of these tokens into a higher value currency by means of long-distance exchange seems to be explained by the taken-for-granted proposition that the exotic nature of imports automatically secured their value among the local community. It might be countered that all these are 'merely' questions concerning cultural specifics, but this is exactly our point.

Value is an expression of human motivation; it is manifest in the desire that is directed to some particular thing, it is lived and acted upon. And while we can accept that certain values express the desire for life and as such arise in the biological needs of the species, values cannot be explained simply in these terms. The values that concern the development of political structures are maintained communally and in terms that identify qualities in things and in people. Values are therefore conventional in as much as they are shared. It is in the making of values that a commonality of understandings is created between people. And it is in the specific cultural creation of these qualities that history is made. Periods of historical transformation can be characterized as shifts in the ways such values were defined and objectified.

Friedman and Rowlands urge us to understand economic activity as a relationship between producers and the supernatural. Presumably they take the meaning, or value, of exchange items to arise out of that relationship, but if this were the case it would present us with a problem. If we continue to treat the relationship between producers and the supernatural as one operating between objective material relationships (relations of production) and subjective under-standings (spiritual beings) then, while value is supposed to be determined by the former, it actually emerges as a cultural and subjective fetish in terms of the latter. The dichotomy between objective conditions and subjective understanding is employed by Friedman and Rowlands to distinguish between real economic relations and the 'imaginary economy'. On the face of it, subjective understanding is therefore a delusional state that misunderstands the real conditions of life, and as a consequence values are grounded in subjective desires that can only arise as an ideal quality that people project upon things. At best artefacts whose values are founded upon such ideological principles are nothing more than the symbolic representations of these delusions, and yet it is precisely in the redefinition of such values that real historical change occurs.

We are forced to conclude that conventionally accepted values must have been more securely grounded upon some form of reality than is allowed for by Friedman and Rowlands. However, we have already rejected the claim that value is inherent in the things themselves, and we can also discard the suggestion that the relative value of things is merely the deluded projection of a type of social organization by its members. Social organizations do not exist before their members manage to recognize that the world has values for the simple reason that the social is actually constituted by its participants as a system of values in the first place. In other words these values must be grasped as being part of the reality that people live rather than the false representation of some other kind of reality.

In all the accounts with which we have been concerned, society has been modelled as if it were a lattice of social statuses. Each status category functions as a placement to fix people, communities, or sites in terms of value and function, and the placements are wired together by networks of exchange. Change in these arrangements can be observed from the outside as the variations in the distinctions separating both the statuses (increased ranking for example) and the functions (increased specialization for example) that define each placement. New exchange relations then appear to rewire these changes. But changes in these structures cannot be explained in these terms. The reality of any historical situation and the mechanisms of change both involved the ways people made possible that reality in terms of their own identities and the identities of others.

If identities were founded on values that could be rendered discursively when expressed as ideals, they were nonetheless lived as an implicit reality – they simply existed and they worked. And the fundamental demonstration of that reality was the life experience and relative security of those people:

> 'Our judgements concerning the worth of things, big or little, depend on the *feelings* the things arouse in us. Where we judge a thing to be precious in consequence of the *idea* we frame of it, this is only because the idea is itself associated already with a feeling. If we were radically feelingless, and if ideas were the only things our mind could entertain, we should lose all our likes and dislikes at a stroke, and be unable to point to any one situation or experience in life more valuable or significant than any other.' (James 1996: 51, original emphasis)

We now come to the realization that humans accept themselves to be part of the world itself. That is to say we are analytically at fault to treat others' authenticity as either a subjective delusion projected onto the world or as empirically recoverable in something that was external to their own existence. Humans do not see themselves as the source of values, for those values are already in the world of which they are a part. All humans can do is recognize the existence of the value in their own lives, the lives of others, and in the material conditions of life. They live as if they are part of the world whose values they share with others, rather than as uncomprehending strangers. This is a practical recognition, it is expressed in actions that do not so much represent either concepts or social constraints but express a commitment to the way the world is. The values of life are performed and there are times and places where these values may be most obviously expressed in the ways things appear and the ways people act, a reality demonstrated in the confidence to act and the expectation of being recognized by others. It is a state of being that is as unremarkable as it is necessary; this is simply how the world is. From it, all actions must necessarily claim the authenticity of what it is to be human or, more accurately, a particular kind of human, or what it is to fail in that quest. The given nature of the human community is the bedrock upon which conventional values are established; it is the point at which explanation can extend no further than 'this is what we do'. These are the feelings that James refers to, the emotional security of knowing the world and of being known among others.

Exchange occurs between people who constitute themselves in the conditions of confidence and trust, the emotional grounding necessary for any effective intervention upon the world. These conditions are materially constituted because they are literally where one finds one's place in the habitus of routine activity, in the absolute and indeed sacred materials that those activities may confront, and they are the conditions in which one's humanity (or lack of it) is recognized. It is here that the values of humanity are grounded in a material existence. People exist, as does the rest of the world, and on this basis it is reasonable that both should be expected to share a common creation. Consequently the identity of a community may find direct expression in the form of the landscape and the sequences of activities through which that landscape is revealed to its inhabitants (Ingold 2000). The material world therefore shares human qualities, these are the physical manifestations of identity where objects do not represent that quality but are iconic, by which we mean their physical characteristics, the form they take, the mode of their production, their origins and use, all embody values that contribute to a humanly recognizable form. Technology is not the intellect-ualization of problem solving but is the practical realization of the truth of things.

When archaeologists treat material culture as a communicative system they seem to imply that artefacts carried meaning in the way that a material symbol may represent something else. In these terms the meaning of things becomes a question of representation or equivalence. From a similar perspective the question of value becomes one of equivalence, where value is defined by the equivalence struck in the exchange of objects in barter, or by the prestige accrued between partners in gift exchange, or by the sacred authority achieved by the sacrifice of an object. But in all these cases the actions of the practitioners were performed upon the basis of values that were nothing more nor less than their own certainties in the validity of their own existence, and therefore in the certainties of the world of which they were a part. These are the values and meanings that had to exist in the reality of life itself; they were inalienable, being carried in the practices of competent and recognized human beings. Here we encounter the human use of material whose meaning lies entirely in the recognition that its use is correct, adequate, and proper to the moment and whose values lie in a usage that simply expresses that which is correct, unchallenged, necessary and therefore expected. This is the making of an empirical reality that guarantees the existence and continuity of a portion of humanity. This humanity's certainty of its own existence, and its commitment to others and the values that made such a commitment realistic, is the basis upon which exchanges could take place and alliances could be established (Gudeman 2001).

Value arises from commitment, the commitment of humans towards things. Value is neither inherent in the thing itself, nor is it created by an equivalence of exchange values. Human actions are expressions of commitment, towards things, towards an understanding of the world, and towards the place that they claim for themselves, all of which is either confirmed by the successful execution of the action or questioned by its failure. Exchanges are actions directed at other people, and all exchanges whether highly ritualized, embedded in reciprocal obligations, or the product of competitive bartering, contain moral statements of how others might be treated, and express the extent to which an agent might wish to align herself with other communities. We therefore reject the view that gift exchange and barter are mutually exclusive economic procedures (cf. Moreland 2000). Each kind of exchange expresses a different kind of human commitment and a different kind of moral obligation.

Value systems are lived; they are performed. Performance situates people in relation to the material and the populated world and the routines of biographical experiences are narratives that can identify shared or divergent origins. People may occupy different spatial and temporal locations in such performances and thus appear to enact values differentially. The power of enactment embodies a certain value; it makes sense in the scheme of things. Such power does not necessarily facilitate a control over a wider range of resources and people and we wish to distinguish the enabling power to perform from that which controls. This will allow us to question the assumption that the values people live and may thus appropriate to their own identities are necessarily ordered into a single hierarchy of authority. Given that almost all social modelling in archaeology characterizes different social formations against the single axis of hierarchical authority we seek instead an appreciation of the multi-dimensional nature of value systems. The king may be in the castle and the prophet in the wilderness: who has the greater power; whose life expresses the greater value?

Civilization

The dominant image of civilization is one of cultural enrichment; to be civilized is to have culture in abundance. The form taken by this enrichment seems overtly representational, from the images of rulers, through the idols and votives accumulating in temple complexes, to the textual archives of bureaucracy. Indeed the levels of productivity required to create items for display and for building public monuments appear to necessitate the systems of administration and exploitation that we traditionally associate with the civilized world. It is little wonder that the development of civilization has been treated as a question of organizational complexity, that is structured hierarchically, and that the products of civilization are understood as intricate layers of symbolic representations. The symbolic quality of material culture appears to be deployed under these conditions to broadcast civic pride, ritualized display and sacred authority, as well as for the bureaucratic administration of resources and of people.

Does civilization remain useful as a category in the analysis of history? We propose that it does so simply because it allows us to consider the ways complex systems of representation are woven into the embodied certainties of life, with the result that life can appear dominated by discursive practices. We have argued that the values of human security are not primarily anchored by means that are representational, intellectual, and discursive, but are set in the securities of routine practice and emotional certainties. From here we have argued that places and things can carry an iconic status because they embody the values that give security to the human presence. These are the places and things that are protected, inalienable, held in common trust, or are entrusted with those whose responsibility it has become to act as their guardians (Weiner 1992, Godelier 1999). Discursive practices on the other hand operate alongside such certainties and are indeed predicated upon them. Discursive practices provide practitioners with positions of self-reflexivity from which to give testimony, by use of metaphor and simile, to extend the order of the world by making its discovered orders explicit. It is in discursive practices that representations are deployed as place markers for values. Discursive practices therefore state what is already known and extend that knowledge into areas previously disregarded. It is as if the practitioner has stepped to one side to enable reflection upon a world that is now brought into view through representation, and by means of representation to then communicate that understanding to others.

The uses of representations depend upon the claim that a valid relationship exists between a given value and the form of its representation. Such validity can be demonstrated in conventional usage, where the representation may now play the role of the value (as in the case of money for example). At this point we encounter schemes that are neither the silent contemplation of truth nor its practical evocation, but are the discursive negotiation that takes place between value systems. Acts of representation also accept the significant risk that the validity of the convention that links symbol to value will no longer be accepted (as in the case of monetary inflation).

The representation therefore acts as a proxy for its value, in the way that a currency operates. The meaning of a representation appears to be given by that which it represents, but only in so far as the participants of a discursive engagement accept that as a binding convention. Because representations may adopt the value for which they stand by their conventional use, they risk the appropriation of that value by the control of its representational form. This is the accumulation of value that is wealth. It should come as no surprise therefore that there are values that must be defended against such appropriation; these are the gods whose names may not be spoken, and the divine creations that cannot be depicted. Nor should the iconoclasts surprise us, who tear down the representations that debase the truths that they should have restricted themselves to depicting but have since come to embody. Representations can appear to claim too much as if they were reality itself, or alternatively appear inadequate and demonstrably false when the conventions of their discursive use are challenged. The relationship between the form and the value of the representation is ambiguous and thus always open to renegotiation.

Humans draw the metaphysical certainties of life into the discursive practices of representation. Both involve a commitment to conventionally accepted values. The certainties of the former that may be underpinned by the absolute value of the sacred, act as the context of what it is possible to do and to say. Discursive practices are carried by actions that make those securities explicit. The ability to mediate in securing a form of representation is to effect some control over discursive practices. To trade in the forms of those representations is to trade in the currency of political discourse and economic exchange.

Where do civilizations stand as historical projects in general, and where does the emergence of southern Aegean civilization stand in particular? One general characteristic of civilizations is that representational forms are used to extend dominant moral and political values over considerable regions of time and space and, as a consequence, spiritual and economic values are accumulated by a number of elite groups. Instead of treating civilizations as a particular level of social organization we would rather understand them as fields through which operated particular strategies that were intended to secure the validity of dominant values and to extend that validity through specific forms of representation. Such strategies may have attempted political or economic expansion by the appropriation or replacement of the core values of a number of other communities, perhaps directly through their destruction by military conquest or more subtly through the subversion of their moral authority. The latter may have involved demonstrations of empirical failure (that it was no longer possible to live according to tradition) and discursive vulnerability (the larger world could no longer be explained according to a traditional logic). Civilizations engendered empires by the aggressive pursuit of these processes and perhaps the vulnerability of empires has always lain in part with the vulnerability faced by all forms of representation in maintaining the values and meanings that are claimed for them in contexts of divergent experiences.

If the above model sketches an understanding of the strategic purposes of a civilizing agency, then we would argue that such an agency is difficult to identify, and certainly not dominant, in the Early and Middle Bronze Age of the southern Aegean, and may be as difficult to locate in the Late Bronze Age.

The Palace

If one image dominates our perception of the Aegean Bronze Age it is that of the palace. Despite their limited distribution to Crete and the southern mainland, and the changes that occurred in their architectural development and possible function during the second millennium, the palace continues to be treated as if it synthesised the processes of an emergent civilization. We will approach the issue from the perspective of the landscape. This is not because we adhere to the view that landscapes map the archaeological residues of an evolving political unity. Rather it is because the landscape contains the numerous and diverse places wherein humans found their own securities, and the places from which they moved to represent those secure values in contested forms of discursive order. Landscapes mediate between personal histories and the discursive narratives of origins and of global history. And landscapes are vistas from which humans are empowered to act and over which attempts to administer are cast.

Various attempts have been made to move archaeological analysis away from the treatment of sites and monuments as isolated components set upon the landscape's surface. Despite these efforts little progress has been made in inhabiting the landscape with an effective historical agency. We place emphasis upon performance because it evokes the authenticity of the human presence that is enacted with reference to space and time. These were the qualities that underpinned the security of an emergent selfhood located in a network of pathways and historical narratives whose validity was recognized by others. These were not private worlds, subjective and internalized, but the public realization of the values of a certain kind of humanity. It was a security that depended on others, for it was they who recognized the correctness (or otherwise) of the performance. The discursive claims made by such performance drew upon references to materials that set the scene geographically and historically. This may have involved the reworking of materials imported to that place that mapped geographical relationships, or the historical references that could have been made explicit before a mausoleum or the representations of historical events. The ways these discursive qualities may have been made to reach beyond the immediate context of performance offered models of order and the representations of values that others might have adopted, or have been forced to adopt, in the making of their own identities.

In their recent discussion of the Pre- and Protopalatial landscapes of Knossos, Day and Wilson (2002) contrast two different arenas that were inhabited by two different kinds of performative strategies. One focused upon the hill of Kephala that lay in a natural amphitheatre in the valley of the Kairatos river, the other was at the coastal inlet and the mouth of the river at Poros-Katsambas. Both locations were united then as now by the path of the river and by the visual dominance of Mount Juktas. Day and Wilson offer three accounts of these places, one of colonization, the second of activity, and the third of political integration. They link these accounts by means of a historical narrative that explains the ultimate rise of a Bronze Age political structure from an origin in the Neolithic colonization of the island. The account shares some features with the models that we have discussed earlier: an emphasis upon votive display as legitimating political authority, and the political emphasis upon the control of production and asymmetries of gift exchange.

All performance is a kind of colonization in as much as it finds a place for itself in the contexts that are available. The references drawn into the activities on the hill of Kephala were the backdrop of the wider landscape overlooked by Mount Juktas, and the fore-grounded activities of serving and sharing food and drink indicated by the early ceramic assemblages. Both implied a sense of trust, in the security of the place, in the people and the order of the occasion. Certainly such activities may have been exclusive and ordered internally, perhaps by the portions served and the obligations of service. The performances thus made explicit a moral order embodied by the community and situated within a definite geographical setting. It would seem that the wider landscape mattered here, whereas elsewhere the focus was more tightly defined and closed, as when food and drink were shared in front of a tomb. These were not mere variants of ideological illusions; the options for discursive representation varied enormously and were consequential upon them. When the earliest paved courtyards appeared in association with the beginning of palace construction, wider communities appear to have been addressed, the larger landscape was initially referenced, and the options for formalized activity were extended. It is the theatrical quality that distinguishes this architecture, and forces us to confront the sheer diversity of the built environment that began to be inhabited from the Early Bronze Age onwards.

Poros-Katsambas provided both a north coast harbour and access to the mouth of the Kairatos river. The Prepalatial activity here 'presents the image of a major harbour community which acted as a reception point for a substantial amount of raw materials and prepared commodities from the Cycladic islands' (Day and Wilson 2002: 153). The contrast with the material from Kephala is striking; a range of imported pottery from the Cyclades includes a series of transport amphorae, there is evidence for metallurgy, and in addition extensive obsidian working. The port would appear to have acted as a trading and commercial quarter distinct from the inland site, not only in terms of location but also what was done there. Indeed we would have little difficulty in accepting this as an area of commercial activity; our concern is to grasp how those activities established the values upon which they traded. For if the service and consumption of food brought to the fore expressions of commitment and value whilst explicating the basis of those values, then technology achieved the same but at a different scale. The working of material was geographically and temporally situated. The context was no longer the immediately apprehended landscape but instead absent sources and the cumulative traditions of learning. The immediacy of its performance contrasted with the references to distant sources, and the performance objectified the skill of working in the product itself. It was as if the artisans gave absent places and the lengthy acquisition of technical mastery their physical presence in the things that they made. It was thus the processes of making that gave these things their value, and not the things themselves (Helms 1993).

These are different value systems. The former evoked the authenticity of place with reference to the performances there, while the latter's performances drew reference to absent origins. We might speculate that the voyaging communities of the Cyclades that are discussed by Broodbank (2000) sought some kind of integration of these systems, but if so that integration does not appear to have demanded the architectural elaboration that was represented by the palaces. And herein lies a problem. The assertion that the palaces emerged as the centres of political authority, indicative of early state systems and of an emergent 'administered economy' is nothing more than that: an assertion. Politics cannot be read from distribution maps, they require instead that we understand how value systems were negotiated and the extent to which dominant communities appropriated the values expressed in the lives of others. We have already commented on the role of representation in such appropriation. The emergence of civilization in the Aegean is certainly indicated by an elaboration of representational forms and thus the increasing elaboration of discursive practices. It is in this context, for example, that we must place the use of early script (Schoep 1999).

Representation makes something present, be it a person, value or quality. Representations may be made, given, exchanged or appropriated, and those who have access to them may model the order of the world and align or equate things previously distant and unconnected. Representations allow the values of already known and divergent experiences to be made available to others. How these characteristics allow an elite to represent a community, or a performance to represent an ideal, and how these values may be synthesised perhaps in the presence of a sacred ruler, requires a detailed explanation. Such an explanation must draw upon the motivations of the agencies that operated though specific material and historical conditions, rather than upon some abstract notion of social evolution. By accepting the observation originally made by Renfrew, we have sought to develop the belief that the emergence of civilization must have been forged by a human agency. As a result the issue for us has not been to explain the emergence of civilization systemically, but to understand how values concern the things that humans find authentic, how that authenticity is lived, and the ways those values may be renegotiated. Our conclusion is that the rise of different value systems and the forms of political authority that seek their appropriation demands detailed empirical enquiry, and that the task of explaining the emergence of Aegean civilization has barely begun.

This paper is dedicated to the memory of David Turner

Bibliography

Arnold, J.E.
  2000   Revisiting power, labour rights, and kinship: archaeology and social theory. In M.B. Schiffer (ed.), *Social Theory in Archaeology*: 14–30. Salt Lake City: University of Utah Press.
Broodbank, C.
  2000   *An Island Archaeology of the Early Cyclades*. Cambridge: Cambridge University Press.
Childe, V.G.
  1957   The Bronze Age. *Past and Present* 12: 2–15.
Day, P.M. and D.E. Wilson
  2002   Landscapes of memory, craft and power in pre-palatial and proto-palatial Knossos. In Y. Hamilakis (ed.), *Labyrinth Revisited: Rethinking 'Minoan' Archaeology*: 143–66. Oxford: Oxbow Books.
Earle, T.
  1991   (ed.) *Chiefdoms: Power, economy and ideology*. Cambridge: Cambridge University Press.
  2002   *Bronze Age Economics: the Beginnings of Political Economies*. Cambridge MA: Westview Press.
Friedman, J. and M.J. Rowlands
  1977   Notes towards an epigenetic model of the evolution of 'civilisation'. In J. Friedman and M. J. Rowlands (eds.), *The Evolution of Social Systems*: 201–76. London: Duckworth.
Godelier, M.
  1986   *The Mental and the Material*. London: Verso.
  1999   *The Enigma of the Gift*. Cambridge: Polity.
Gregory, C.A.
  1982   *Gifts and Commodities*. London: Academic Press.
Gudeman, S.
  2001   *The Anthropology of Economy*. Oxford: Blackwell.
Halstead, P.
  1981   From determinism to uncertainty: social storage and the rise of the Minoan palace. In A. Sheridan and G. Bailey (eds.), *Economic Archaeology: Towards an Integration of Ecological and Social Approaches* (BAR International Series 96): 187–213. Oxford: British Archaeological Reports.
Halstead, P. and J. O'Shea
  1982   A friend in need is a friend indeed: social storage and the origins of social ranking. In C. Renfrew and S. Shennan (eds.), *Ranking, Resource and Exchange: Aspects of the Archaeology of Early European Society*: 92–99. Cambridge: Cambridge University Press.
Helms, M.
  1988   *Ulysses' Sail: an Ethnographic Odyssey of Power, Knowledge and Geographical Distance*. Princeton: Princeton University Press.

1993   *Craft and the Kingly Ideal: Art, Trade and Power.* Austin: University of Texas Press.
Hodder, I.
   1982   Theoretical archaeology: a reactionary view. In I. Hodder (ed.), *Symbolic and Structural Archaeology.*: 1–16. Cambridge: Cambridge University Press.
Ingold, T.
   2000   *The Perception of the Environment: Essays in Livelihood, Dwelling and Skill.* London: Routledge.
James, W.
   1996   On a certain blindness in human beings. In S.C. Rowe, *The Vision of James*: 51–76. Shaftesbury: Element Books.
Mauss, M.
   1970   *The Gift: Forms and Function of Exchange in Archaic Societies.* London: Cohen and West Ltd.
Moreland, J.
   2000   Concepts of the early medieval economy. In I.L. Hansen and C. Wickham (eds.), *The Long Eighth Century*: 1–34. Leiden: Brill.
Muller, J.
   1991   The New Holy Family: a polemic on bourgeois idealism in archaeology. In R.W. Preucel (ed.), *Processual and Postprocessual Archaeologies: Multiple Ways of Knowing the Past*: 251–61. Illinois: Southern University of Illinois at Carbondale.
O'Shea, J.
   1981   Coping with scarcity: exchange and social storage. In A. Sheridan and G. Bailey (eds.), *Economic Archaeology: Towards an Integration of Ecological and Social Approaches* (BAR International Series 96): 167–83. Oxford: British Archaeological Reports.
Renfrew, C.
   1972   *The Emergence of Civilisation: The Cyclades and the Aegean in the Third Millennium BC.* London: Methuen.
Sahlins, M.
   1974   *Stone Age Economics.* London: Tavistock Publications.
Schoep, I.
   1999   The origins of writing and administration on Crete. *OJA* 18: 265–74.
Van der Leeuw, S. and J. McGlade
   1997   (eds.), *Time, Process and Structured Transformation in Archaeology.* London: Routledge.
Weiner, A.B.
   1992   *Inalienable Possessions: the Paradox of Keeping While Giving.* Oxford: University of California Press.

9

Constructing a *Region*: the Contested Landscapes of Prepalatial Mesara

Maria Relaki

Introduction

This paper, dealing with just one area of Crete during a single period, may at first sight seem out of place in a volume dedicated to the *Emergence of Civilisation* (Renfrew 1972), a work whose legacy should surely be its broad scope. However, one of the cornerstones of the *Emergence* is Renfrew's fruitful comparison of the contrasting nature and pace of cultural change in north and south Greece, and within the latter, in regions such as Messenia, Crete and the Cyclades. In this respect, the 'Emergence' combines an emphasis on the recognition and interpretation of general trends in the archaeological record, and a focus on the region as a basic unit of analysis.

Indeed, the region has been considered the analytic unit *par excellence* in archaeological investigations, offering a great potential for the reconstruction of past societies (Cherry 1983; Kardulias 1994). However, current definitions of region very often rely on criteria which overlook the historical context within which regional pattern develops. In consequence, there is confusion concerning the ways in which local trajectories can be seen to bear upon wider scales of interaction. This inadequate integration is detrimental to the interpretative potential of regional approaches and downplays the importance of small-scale, local patterns. It is a main argument of this paper that the way *regions* are defined within archaeological studies has great repercussions for the understanding and explanation of *social change*, in that local cultural trajectories play an integral part in the creation and the maintenance of wider processes. Therefore, our interpretations would benefit from highlighting the dialectic relationship that exists between local and broader patterns.

In the context of the EBA Aegean, the Mesara in south-central Crete has been considered one of the most clearly defined regions that archaeological analysis has at its disposal by virtue of the restricted occurrence of characteristic types of archaeological artefacts (e.g., tholos tombs) within a distinct topography. Such localized distribution has been interpreted as a sign of pronounced cultural homogeneity and also as a reflection of common social structures and processes (Branigan 1970; 1991; Manning 1994; Sbonias 1999a). This discussion will concentrate first on the criteria by which the Mesara has been defined as the 'ultimate' region, before proceeding to evaluate whether such a picture of homogeneity and regional integration during the prepalatial period is accurate. It is argued that the patterns and motives of regionalism were more diverse and dynamic than the seemingly uniform spread of archaeological artefacts in the landscape might suggest. By re-addressing the regional character of the Prepalatial Mesara, it will be demonstrated that *region* would be a more illuminating unit of analysis if defined in ways that allow us a successful integration of small and large scales. The careful consideration of short-term processes and the importance of historical context in defining and understanding regional pattern are instrumental to such an attempt.

Regional Analysis

Most commonly the criteria for defining analytic regions depend upon modern geographical divisions which have not always been pertinent to the range of historical periods that we study. Natural features may appear to demarcate space, but they do not have inherent delimiting properties. Boundaries and borders, even though making use of natural features, are explicitly culturally constructed (Donnan and Wilson 2001). Their function as delimiting devices can differ not only *diachronically*, from one historical period to another, but also *synchronically*, according to different circumstances. By selecting analytic regions merely on geographical grounds, we risk studying a specific natural topography as though it represents a distinct socio-political unit. Undoubtedly the physical landscape has an impact on the relations that people develop by allowing certain kinds of action and interaction and inhibiting others, but explicitly historical behaviour like regionalism cannot be dismissed as merely the product of geographical propinquity.

Within such rather uncritically accepted frameworks of analysis, the time- and place-specific historical conditions that affect the creation and expression of regionalism are underestimated. We are faced with timeless natural environments, the limits and capacities of which remain static while the human communities that inhabit them develop continuously varying cultures (Ingold 2000: 172–88). Through such approaches, change is rendered rather problematic. If human communities always encounter unchanged possibilities and limitations afforded by their local environments, how do we explain the very diverse forms that responses to these problems have taken through time?

Geography, however, constitutes only one parameter in the definition of archaeological regions. The distribution of similar types of cultural material is to some extent more important in underlining the validity of a distinct topographic area as a unit of archaeological analysis. The existence of material of broadly similar date in a clearly bounded environment is generally considered a sufficient indication of discrete social interactions within the demarcated area. This practice is particularly problematic in the case of material derived from surface surveys. Although the data used to assign sites to particular periods are crude and do not allow great chronological precision, sites plotted on a distribution map for a given period tend to be treated as if they were occupied contemporaneously. If it is not possible to determine whether such sites were inhabited simultaneously, however, then assuming that they were engaging in common processes of social interaction is an unjustified conclusion. Moreover, such distributions rely heavily on long temporal scales, whereas the patterns observed may be the result of an aggregate of short-term strategies (Foxhall 2000: 488). In this sense, the meaning of similar types of material spread over a bounded region may be dependent upon entirely different social practices.

In this sense, definitions of *region* with respect to territories or political centres that are better known for specific historical periods, the hypothetical Palatial territories being the most obvious example, may often be misleading. On the one hand, the location of 'central places' may change through time and, in consequence, the territories defined with respect to such 'centres' will alter. On the other hand, such shifts of power cannot be taken to represent simply the moving of territorial boundaries in a static region. More importantly, they reflect changes in the historical circumstances that impinge on political structure. If people's perceptions of what constitutes the *region* change, then the conceptions and expressions of regionalism are also transformed. In consequence, the social practices that affect the extent and the intensity of regional patterns will be altered.

Alternative *Regions*: Networks of Relevance

If *region* is to be a valid analytic unit, its historical dimension must be restored. Regions are not bounded areas within which cultural pattern unfolds, but structures of belonging. Regions *come about* through the establishment of relations between people and places and the ways that such relations are expressed on the landscape. They are created and reproduced through people's consistent engagement in specific social practices. They are not static geographies, but active *networks of relevance* in which some places are better connected than others. In this way dense and sparse areas can be recognized, not so much on the basis of absolute location, i.e. geographical proximity, as on the basis of relative location, i.e. how closely connected are particular places within a *network of relevance*. It is the *nature* and *intensity* of interactions between places (not their topographical position) that define the extent of a region and also distinguish between different regions.

Such networks of relevance emerge out of people's engagement in common social practices and they change as people's beliefs and validating systems are transformed. They represent shared opinions about the practices through which communal identity may be created, evoked, reproduced and remodelled. Different practices generate or convey different kinds of relevance, giving rise to different networks with diverse reach and potential. Thus different networks bring about different *regions*, within which the participating nodes are more relevant to each other than to positions outside the network (irrespectively of their geographical position). Such *regions* depend entirely on the context according to which relevance is defined and, hence, different kinds of *region* become evident only with respect to specific practices. As places are physically connected through corporeal movement, so they are metaphorically connected by participation in a *network of relevance*, which makes their positions meaningful, allows them to interact. The density of the network creates the boundary beyond which the *region* ceases to be meaningful.

More importantly, networks of relevance underline the dialectic relationship between the local and the extra-local in two ways. On the one hand, the local cannot be meaningful unless there exists a network that defines and validates the characteristics of locality as a structure of belonging (Appadurai 1995; Lovell 1998). In other words, the practices that generate locality can be understood as such only when compared and contrasted to practices which are non-local. On the other hand, the network, as a wider value system bringing together people, places and events, does not become available unless people connect to it locally (Urry 2000), unless people reproduce in their daily routines the practices that make up the network. A *region* then is created when similar practices of belonging are taken up by a number of different communities, thus generating a wider network of relevance.

To study regions in this way, different defining questions need to be set. What kinds of *networks of relevance* pertain to a specific topography? What are the social practices that define what is relevant and what not? In what ways is relevance to a specific region materially expressed and performed?

Defining a Region: the Mesara in the Prepalatial Period

The Mesara is one of the most geographically distinct areas of Crete. The area of study usually comprises the western end of the largest plain in the island, the Asterousia range to the south and the slopes of mount Ida to the north (Figure 9.1). The picture of homogeneity of the Mesara is a product of both its geographical distinctiveness and its characteristic material culture. For the Prepalatial period, the unique mortuary practices set around the tholos tombs constitute the main differentiating element from the rest of the island. Thus a common extrapolation is that the natural topography of the Mesara has favoured

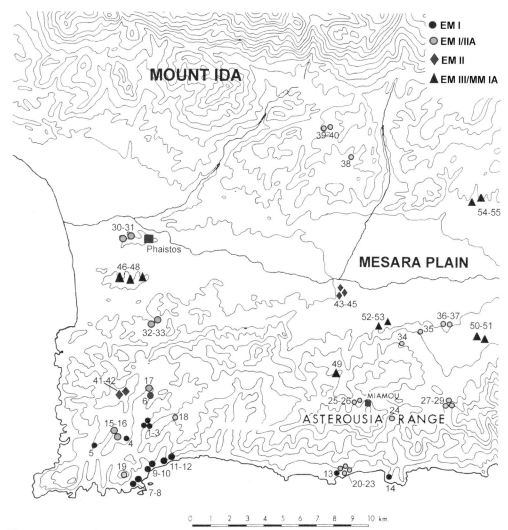

Figure 9.1. *Map of Mesara (adapted from Shaw and Shaw 1995) showing the distribution of tholos tombs:*
1–3. Megaloi Skinoi A-C; 4. Ay. Kyriaki A; 5. Kephali A (Tou Skaniari o Lakkos); 6. Skotomenou Charakas
A; 7–8. Kaloi Limenes A-B; 9–10. Crysostomos A-B; 11–12. Lasaia A-B; 13. Lebena Yerokampos II; 14.
Trypiti; 15. Ay. Kyriaki B-C; 17. Skotomenou Charakas B; 18. Kaminospelio; 19. Ayios Andonis; 20–23.
Lebena Yerokampos IIa, Lebena Papoura 1–1b, Lebena Zervou; 24. Krotos; 25–26. Korakies A-B; 27–29.
Koumasa A, B, E; 30–31. Ay. Triada A-B; 32–33. Sivas N-S; 34. Porti; 35. Salame/Koutsokera; 36–37. Ay.
Eirene E-e; 38. Kalathiana K; 39–40. Marathokephalo A-B; 41–42. Moni Odigitrias A-B (Hatzinas Liofyto);
43–45. Platanos A-C; 46–48. Kamilari A-C (MMIB); 49. Ay. Kyrillos; 50–51. Drakones D-Z; 52–53.
Apesokari I–II; 54–55. Vorou A-B.

the development of rather isolated cultural practices exemplified primarily in the
restricted distribution of the tholos tombs (Branigan 1970: 5–6; 1991: 190). Such a
distribution has also been seen to reflect common social practices promoting a

picture of a largely integrated regional landscape. Ultimately these burial monuments have been approached as the most remarkable signs of a common regional identity during the Early Minoan period.

In light of the alternative perspective on *region* put forward in this paper, the following discussion aims to evaluate: first, whether the presence of the tholoi in the landscape is sufficient to mark the extent of the *region* as a practice of shared values; secondly, whether the widespread distribution of such monuments reflects the adoption of common social practices during the Prepalatial period; and finally, whether the tholoi can be seen as the conveyors of common identity at a regional scale throughout the period of their use.

Methodological restrictions

This analysis focuses on the tholos tombs, but their prominence in the Mesaran landscape may be as much a result of bias in recovery techniques, as of conscious strategies of investment in the preservation and visibility of these sites over time. The widespread looting of the tholoi has enhanced efforts to excavate as many as possible of these monuments, sometimes at the expense of other kinds of sites. On the other hand, there are clear archaeological indications that the ancient inhabitants of the Mesara deliberately enhanced the preservation and durability of these monuments by repeated use and repair.

Partly as a result of the above preoccupation with burial sites, EM settlements in the Mesara are not at present known in much detail. A great number of EM settlements has been identified by surface surveys which, while providing invaluable information on a regional scale, suffer from inherent methodological difficulties (Cherry 1983; Dewar and McBride 1992; Dunnell 1992). Neither the accurate size, nor the duration and internal organization of settlements thus recognized is known, while excavated settlements such as Trypiti and Ay. Triada are only published in preliminary form (Vasilakis 1988; 1995; Laviosa 1969–70; 1972–73; La Rosa and D' Agata 1985; La Rosa 1992a). Moreover, extensive building activity in subsequent periods obscures the extent and nature of the EM occupation at Phaistos, Ay. Triada and Kommos.

In addition, the tholoi have poor stratigraphy due to the repeated burials that took place in them, while extensive looting has in many cases destroyed original contexts of deposition and blurred chronological horizons. As a result, their dating is largely based on typological classification of pottery and other material recovered from the burials, and more often than not is a matter of debate.[1] This situation is further aggravated by regional variations in pottery styles that make the establishment of chronological parallels between sites a very difficult task.[2]

Although previous approaches have taken note of these problems, they have largely underestimated the small-scale and short-term processes that might have contributed to the creation of regional pattern. Bearing in mind the stated weaknesses of currently available evidence, we can make some provisional suggestions about the nature and intensity of regionalism in the EM Mesara.

Divergent Regional Trajectories

For the sake of the clarity of argument, this discussion will be structured chronologically, even though such conventional understanding of time may not be entirely representative of the pattern and pace of change. The proposed view of social change in Prepalatial Mesara envisages very gradual processes that must be understood in relation to what they drew upon. Therefore, to assess the degree of regional integration and the significance of burial monuments as symbols of regional identity during the Prepalatial period, we need first to explore the evidence of the Final Neolithic.

Final Neolithic

The Final Neolithic period in the Mesara is generally known from surveys (Blackman and Branigan 1975; 1977; Watrous *et al.* 1993; Hope Simpson *et al.* 1995). Besides Phaistos (Vagnetti 1972–73), there are only four other excavated sites: Gortyna-Acropolis (Levi 1959; Vagnetti 1973), Miamou (Taramelli 1897), Ay. Kyriaki (Blackman and Branigan 1982) and Kala Selia/Kaloi Limenes (Vasilakis 1987). The pattern of settlement appears homogenous for both the plain and the mountains, with sites of very small size being consistently located on low or higher hills. Most of these consist of only small scatters of material, while those excavated, as Kala Selia and Ay. Kyriaki, seem to represent single deposition phases. On the contrary, the stratigraphy at Phaistos presents a different picture: despite frequent interruptions in the occupation sequence, deposition resumed after each short abandonment and occupation always took place on the same parts of the hill.[3]

Phaistos is also distinguished from the other FN sites of the area by its ceramic assemblage. Certain vessel types, particularly high-necked jars, bottles and miniature cups, seem to be restricted exclusively to Phaistos. In contrast, all other sites, although showing clear typological parallels with the pottery of Phaistos, produced only coarse wares (in contrast to the equal percentage of fine and coarse wares at Phaistos) and the standard bowl typologies typical of FN sites throughout Crete (Manteli 1993). The possibility of sample bias, given that Phaistos produced a much larger assemblage than the other sites, is countered by two factors: first, the vessel shapes associated with liquids occur in both coarse and fine wares within the Phaistos assemblage (Vagnetti 1972–73: 55–88; Manteli 1993, vol. I: 82–83, vol. II: 67–77). Therefore, the absence of fine wares in the other FN sites cannot explain the rarity of the particular vessel types. Secondly, the FN ceramic assemblage of Gortyna-Acropolis, although considerably smaller, showed strong typological affinities to Phaistos with even distribution of fine and coarse wares (Vagnetti 1973: 7–9; Manteli 1993, vol. I: 110–12). Necked jars and bottles, however, were again strikingly lacking.

Phaistos thus seems to be differentiated from the rest of the FN sites in the Mesara by virtue of the longer duration of occupation on the site (itself the product of repeated depositions rather than an uninterrupted sequence) and by the nature of its ceramic assemblage, which shows a specialization in vessel types associated with liquids. Although these types are rare even within the Phaistos assemblage, their absence from all other sites in the Mesara, and also the exaggerated decoration that such shapes receive, very often combining a range of surface treatment techniques on the same vessel (Vagnetti 1972–73; Manteli 1993, vol. II: 67–77), underlines the importance of the activities of which they formed part. It seems possible that such activities involved the ceremonial consumption of drink, on regular or repeated occasions, at a scale encompassing the majority of the FN communities of the area.

It could be suggested thus that during the FN, Phaistos, by being the exclusive setting for ceremonial activity involving the consumption of drink, constituted a regional focus for the entire area, integrating the communities of the plain, the coast and the mountains. The recurrent nature of deposition at Phaistos, in contrast to the rather short-lived character of the other FN sites,[4] may highlight the significance of the activities taking place there as integrative mechanisms in which all the Mesaran communities participated.

Early Minoan I

If the Mesara constituted a fully integrated regional environment already in the FN period, then how can the introduction of tholos burials in subsequent phases be interpreted? Let us first consider the evidence from the *plain*.

Although the evidence is fragmentary, it seems that EMI settlements continued the habitation patterns of the FN as indicated by the preliminary results of the Western Mesara Survey. EMI settlements continued to be placed in high locations, while their very small size has been linked with seasonal occupation (Watrous *et al.* 1993: 224). Similar types of sites have been recognized in the coastal area around Kommos, where EM habitation seems even sparser (Hope Simpson *et al.* 1995: 394–95). Although it is not possible at present to determine whether these sites were occupied on a seasonal basis, their possibly short-term character parallels the short duration of preceding FN sites in the area.

At Phaistos the nature of the EMI habitation is far from clear. Building remains of this phase are strikingly lacking, while EMI pottery has generally been recovered from deposits mixed with FN material (Warren and Hankey 1989: 13; Vagnetti 1972–73: 12, 16–17, 26, 27, 30, 33–34, 38–40; Karantzali 1996: 72–73), pointing perhaps to a continuation of the habitation patterns of the FN period. The rarity of architectural remains has often been attributed to the extensive levelling that took place on the site in preparation for the building of the palace, but the later EMIIA remains in the same areas seem to have survived such disturbance. As regards the evidence for events involving the consumption of drink, fragments of EMI chalices and jugs have been found at the site, most significantly from a possibly open, paved area above the 'Neolithic hut' (Levi 1976: 414–16), indicating that drinking practices may have remained important in the life of the settlement. The range and scale of such activities have been obscured by later disturbance, but the rather sporadic presence of relevant material may imply that they did not retain the central character or large scale they exhibited in the previous period.

This suggestion is corroborated by the evidence from neighbouring Ay. Triada, where a single, extensive EMI deposit has been discovered south of the Piazzale dei Sacelli (La Rosa 1988: 329–30; 1992a: 70; Catling 1988: 66), and consisting mainly of organic remains and a range of fine tableware. It was dated to a phase earlier than the first use of Tholos A (La Rosa 1988: 330) and has been considered an extensive rubbish dump, but may prove to be the result of a particular deposition event rather than of long-term habitation. Wilson and Day (2000: 60) have suggested that this deposit might have been the result of communal, ceremonial consumption of food and drink. If their suggestion proves right, then this deposit would constitute the only example of such activities outside Phaistos and not related to a funerary context. Moreover, its large scale, contrasting with the more fragmented nature of the Phaistos material, may also indicate that such ceremonial activities gradually lost their exclusive association with Phaistos noted in the FN period.

Turning to the mortuary evidence, supposedly the main domain of innovation and integration during the EM period, the picture from the plain is rather controversial. Despite the debate concerning the date of some of the tholos tombs on the plain (see note 1), it seems that tholos burials do not become common in this area until the beginning of the EMII period (Branigan 1993: 15; Branigan forthcoming). On the other hand, the Ay. Onoufrios burial assemblage, discovered in the vicinity of Phaistos (Evans 1895: 105–36; Watrous *et al.* 1993: 224, note 64), indicates that mortuary behaviour was a concern among the communities of the plain. Although this assemblage was the first to be discovered in south-central Crete and, in a way, defined the 'typical tholos assemblage', it seems unlikely that it was deposited in a tholos. As yet, no such monument has been located in the area and, although complete destruction by looters is a possibility, the recent discovery by the Western Mesara Survey of a 'flat' (non-tholos) cemetery on the Ieroditis ridge to the north of Phaistos (Vallianou and Watrous 1991: 121; Watrous *et al.* 1993: 224) may imply that different mortuary traditions were followed in this part of the plain.

The picture is very different in the mountainous area of the *Asterousia*. Acknowledging the problems in dating the tombs, it may still be suggested that the earliest tholoi were established in this area, with concentrations in the Ayiofarango/Moni Odigitria area and the coastal area between Kaloi Limenes and Lebena (Figure 9.1). For some of these monuments (Megaloi Skinoi C, Ay. Kyriaki A, Lebena Yerokambos II, Kaloi Limenes II, Trypiti), a FN foundation date has been suggested (Vasilakis 1989–90: 23, 33, 38–39, 70–71; Vagnetti and Belli 1978: 135; Blackman and Branigan 1975: 20–21; 1977: 67; 1982: 43–44). As the FN material from most of these sites comes from surface and not excavated contexts, however, it may be more plausible to suggest that tholoi were built during the EMI period at or near all the pre-existing FN sites in this area. This preference seems to represent a conscious choice to emphasize the location of FN sites, as even the cave at Miamou received burials of EM date (Taramelli 1897: 294; Manteli 1993: Appendix IX).

In contrast, EMI settlements are striking by their low visibility. Such sites, identified in the form of very thin scatters in which EMI material generally constituted only a small percentage,[5] appeared clearly clustered in the areas around the tholos tombs, and, in the Ayiofarango where such observation was possible, evenly distributed between the different tholoi. Although these sites may represent contemporaneous settlements using the same tholos tomb, their small size and their clustering at very short-distances from each other may favour their interpretation as short-lived installations succeeding each other in the same area, demarcated by the presence of the tholoi. In both cases, there seems to be no pronounced association of particular settlements with specific tombs. The suggestion by Blackman and Branigan (1977: 70), that certain settlements without tombs would have shared the burial grounds of neighbouring sites, would strengthen such an interpretation. It seems then that in the Asterousia, during EMI, the burial grounds constituted the focal points in the landscape, whereas settlements were established with respect to a discrete area delimited by tombs, but in no particular association with any of them.

The tholoi thus represented a focus of ceremonial activity for the communities of the Asterousia during the EMI period, in sharp contrast with the communities of the plain, where mortuary behaviour did not constitute a primary interest. It has been suggested that the tholoi in the Ayiofarango may have been used as territorial markers associated with arable land, a scarce resource in this area (Bintliff 1977a; 1977b). The consistent location of tholoi at or near FN sites (often coinciding with such patches of arable land) may also signify a conscious attempt to lay claim to specific resources, natural and symbolic, thus making the tholos tombs the primary means of social negotiation. Moreover, the burial assemblages of the tholoi, consisting almost entirely of serving/pouring vessels, suggest that drinking ceremonies might have been part of the funerary rites (Branigan 1970; 1993). During EMI in the Asterousia, therefore, it seems that the tholos tombs emerged as the new focal points for community integration, relying on different social strategies, but appropriating at the same time practices of social integration that previously characterized the entire Mesara.

This change in the setting of ceremonial activity, from the exclusivity of FN Phaistos to the context of the tholos tombs, transformed the mechanisms and the scale of regional integration. Moreover, in the plain, the consumption of drink may still have been the primary means of social negotiation, even with the eclipse of Phaistos and the emergence of new 'centres' (e.g. Ay. Triada). In the Asterousia, by contrast, the inclusion of such ceremonies in the funerary ritual was only of peripheral importance, while the funeral itself became the defining element of integrative processes.

The EMI Mesara thus appears to have been characterized by two distinct *networks of relevance* that were both gradually breaking away from the FN pattern of regional integration. In the Asterousia, community/relevance was expressed by burial in tholos tombs. Drinking ceremonies were probably embedded in these new practices to legitimate their status and enhance their effectiveness as integrative devices, but their role remained peripheral in a context where burial was the primary focus. By contrast, in the plain, tholos burials did not represent a relevant medium of negotiation, because pre-existing practices involving the ceremonial consumption of drink prevailed, even if the pre-eminence of Phaistos as the exclusive setting for ceremonial behaviour was now challenged. In the EMI period, therefore, regional integration was achieved rather at the level of two discrete 'sub-regions', the mountains and the plain.

Early Minoan II and Late Prepalatial

In EMII, the expansion of tholoi to all parts of the Mesara has been interpreted as an even stronger sign of regional homogeneity than in previous periods, but how accurate is such a picture?

From EMIIA onwards the proliferation of tholos tombs across the Mesara (Figure 9.1) was also accompanied by greater longevity of settlements. In both the Asterousia and the plain, a larger number of EMII sites has been identified, while the only excavated settlements, Trypiti and Ay. Triada, belong to this period (Vasilakis 1988; 1995; Laviosa 1969–70; 1972–73; La Rosa and D'Agata 1985). For Phaistos in particular, an increase in population has been proposed, on the basis of the better preservation and greater frequency of architectural remains on the hill and it has been suggested that this site may have exceeded the threshold of 'egalitarian' organization in EMIIA (Branigan 1988: 42; 1993: 114–15; 1995: 35; Whitelaw 1983: 339; Watrous *et al.* 1993). It cannot be ascertained whether these very fragmented and scattered remains were in simultaneous use, however, and so any estimates of the population they sheltered must be accepted with caution. Although some allowances must be made for disturbance by later building activity, Levi's (1960) description of EM Phaistos as 'only a transitional stage between the Neolithic and the Palatial', albeit exaggerated and countered by other studies (Zois 1965; Andreou 1978; La Rosa 1992b), hints at a picture of the site far removed from its grandiose status in later periods. The building of the Palace on the Phaistos hill has greatly biased our perceptions of its political position with respect to other Mesaran communities in preceding periods.

By contrast, it can be argued that the settlement at Ay. Triada, in conjunction with the building of one of the largest tholoi there, would have provided significant competition for status against Phaistos at a time when the increase in tholos tombs in the area could reflect the wider adoption of new social practices. The precise nature of the habitation at Ay. Triada cannot be determined, but it seems that the two excavated houses exhibit enough signs of rebuilding to suggest occupation of considerable duration (Laviosa 1969–70; 1972–73). Together with the tholos, therefore, they denote a much more powerful appropriation of the new trends than any remains at Phaistos.

Similarly, in the Asterousia, settlements became more visible; larger quantities of EMII and later material have been identified from surface sites, and it seems that both cemeteries and settlements may have received increased demarcation. At a number of sites in the Ayiofarango valley, remains of 'enclosure walls' have been identified running round the periphery of the hill on which the settlements were located (Blackman and Branigan 1977: 39–47). It is not certain that these remains did indeed 'enclose' the settlements, but the more frequent occurrence of such demarcating elements, in combination with the evidently more permanent (or at least more visible) nature of the dwellings, as the remains at Trypiti show (Vasilakis 1995), point to settlement practices considerably different from the EMI period.

On the other hand, the burial grounds, in both the mountains and the plain, now comprised at least two, and in some cases, three tombs, while the single rooms outside the tombs gradually became complexes of antechambers (Branigan 1970; Blackman and Branigan 1982) and free-standing structures serving as ossuaries (e.g. Platanos) were also added. This architectural formalization proliferated in the later Prepalatial period, with the addition of paved areas (e.g. Koumasa E), enclosure walls (Ay. Kyriaki, Moni Odigitria A-B), altars (Apesokari I, Kamilari A) and platforms on the exterior of many tholos tombs. Moreover, some cemeteries – most located in the Asterousia and in areas with great concentrations of tholoi – ceased to be used after EMII (e.g. Ay. Kyriaki B-C, Kaloi Limenes A, Lasaia B, Ay. Eirene E, Salame, Koutsokera).

This pronounced demarcation of the tholos cemeteries, the increased visibility and longevity of settlements and also the more frequent association of particular cemeteries with specific settlements, as in the case of Ay. Triada and Trypiti, in combination with the demise of certain cemeteries in areas with a high density of tholoi, may indicate a new emphasis on particular *locations*. The introduction in EMII of new funerary goods such as sealstones, stone vases and Cycladic figurines, the greater abundance of materials already in use, such as metal, and their heavy concentration at specific cemeteries (Branigan 1993; 1984) seem equally to highlight an increased importance of particular localities. Although we must be cautious in interpreting the presence of these items in the tombs as expressing differentiation in social status (Papadatos 1999: 89–93), in combination with the other observed trends, these 'innovations' may signify an escalation of competitive strategies. Similar practices may be indicated by the larger number of ceramic imports from the Mesara to Knossos during EMII (Wilson and Day 1994), which perhaps reflects social strategies increasingly reliant on the enhancement of status by 'external' contacts.

Thus it appears that the widespread presence of tholos cemeteries in all parts of the Mesara from EMII onwards may have reflected a marked increase in competition rather than an unprecedented period of regional congruity. In EMII the spread of tholoi in the plain and their proliferation in the Asterousia did not represent the adoption of the same social practices at a larger scale, but rather the appropriation of a pre-existing medium in order to serve different social strategies. As the period unfolded, the increase of tholoi in all areas, the architectural formalization and standardization of cemeteries, as well as the enhanced visibility of settlements and their more explicit association with specific cemeteries, suggest that integration now happened at the level of the individual cemetery/community. Similarly, the drinking ceremonies that had constituted the core of communal practices at a regional level during the FN, were assimilated by different contexts of interaction, the significance of which was transformed in EMI. From EMII onwards, the regular association of the consumption of drink with burials and also the increased scale of such practices and their partial dissociation from strictly funerary rites (Branigan 1993), allowed such strategies to emerge again as the primary ceremonial form, but within much more localized contexts.

Thus the picture emerging for EMII Mesara is far removed from the prevailing image of strong cultural and political homogeneity. The spread of the tholos tombs, far from expressing social and political congruity, seems to be embedded in a web of fierce competition (Sbonias 1999b). In the previous period, each of the two 'sub-regions', the western part of the plain and the Asterousia, was characterized by internal unity and, although different from each other, still shared a common framework of reference, drawing upon the common patterns of the past. By contrast, the emphasis on the particular locations of the tholos cemeteries in EMII suggests a gradual deterioration of wider communal ties, and their replacement by the expression of collective identity at the level of the individual cemetery.

Conclusion

It seems that the Mesara almost never constituted a homogenous cultural environment, but was rather characterized by many diverse and contested social landscapes. Geographical proximity does not suffice to illuminate the social dynamics of regional development in the Prepalatial Mesara. The significance of the *region* as a symbol of identity was not self-evident in geography, but rather became visible to members and non-members through specific social practices that defined what was relevant, local and familiar.

Therefore the shared presence of tholos tombs in a bounded area proves neither sufficient to elucidate the patterns of social interaction that defined the Mesara as a *region* nor indicative of the motives or the scales of such practices. Far from advancing a picture of the Mesara as a largely unified social environment, the divergent patterns of use of the tholos tombs imply that, during the Prepalatial period, different networks of relevance were active, which made use of the same medium for different purposes and with respect to different local conditions. If integration at the scale of the 'sub-region' constituted the EMI network of relevance, in EMII the association with individual cemeteries and single communities emerged as the new currency of negotiation. The extent of the *region* changed and, by implication, the ways in which the *region* was made visible were transformed. New means of expression brought about new 'centres', new focal points for the performance of identity.

In this framework, the supremacy of FN Phaistos as a unifying symbol for the area came under dispute during EMI. Its rather subdued nature throughout the Prepalatial strongly contrasts with the more thriving status of Ay. Triada. The lack of clear EMIII deposits and the rarity of MMIA material at Phaistos (La Rosa 1992b: 232), at the time when some of the richest burials continued to take place in the tholoi of the plain, again make a powerful statement. That the hill of Phaistos still constituted a powerful point of reference, however, is suggested by the rich MMIA assemblage of drinking vessels at nearby Paterikies (Bonacasa 1967–68). The building of the Palace in MMIB, coinciding with the foundation of the tholos at Kamilari (the only tholos cemetery to receive burials till MMIII), would have made this point even more explicit.

It is apparent then that the distribution of funerary monuments is not a sufficient criterion by which to infer homogeneity for the Mesara or distinguish it from other areas of Crete and the Aegean. How different were the practices of the Prepalatial Mesara, where social negotiation was carried out through funerary behaviour, from the rest of Crete and the Southern Aegean, where mortuary practices also constituted the primary arena of social competition? Does the use of different types of tombs suffice to determine differences in regional pattern? On the contrary, as was demonstrated in the case of the Mesara, it is the contexts in which these features acquired meaning that generated and reproduced such differentiation. Such contexts appear to be equally dependent upon general trends and local scales of interaction.

The region thus represented a topography of communication in which places were connected by participating in common networks of relevance. Moreover, social change is better understood along these lines. When new principles of what was relevant to regional identity were introduced in the Mesara during the Prepalatial period, new places became part of the *region* and others abandoned. New resources became available or desirable, new conditions for economic and symbolic interaction arose within which communities engaged in different social practices. New arenas emerged that used different currencies for social negotiation. Through this process, the physical configuration of the regions of the

Mesara – their extent and their boundaries – was also transformed. Such transformation was not so much represented by the differential distribution of sites across the same landscape, but by the emergence of new, contested landscapes. The standardization and formalization of mortuary behaviour did not so much reflect an integrated social landscape, as perhaps promote fragmentation by making strong claims to particular locations which became *regions* of their own.

The patterns of regionalism in the Prepalatial Mesara were not uniform in their development, but rather exemplified several setbacks, breaks with previous traditions and the 're-inventing' of pre-existing communal practices. Such regionalism did not always have the same focus, but rather the emergence of different focal points for ceremonial activity through time created different understandings and practices of regional identity. By implication, the scales at which integration was effected differed, not only from one period to the other, but also with respect to different social strategies.

Acknowledgements

I would like to thank the organizers of the Round Table for inviting me to participate. A great intellectual debt is owed to my thesis supervisors at Sheffield University, Prof. J. C. Barrett and Dr. P. M. Day. I am grateful to Prof. K. Branigan for providing me with his unpublished paper on the Mesara, Prof. L.V. Watrous for his comments on an earlier draft, and Dr. P. Halstead for his contribution to the 're-writing' of this paper. This work would have not been what it is without my 'painful' discussions with Despoina Catapoti and Olia Peperaki, the critical eye of Yiannis Papadatos, and the endurance of James Hollingsworth under the Mesara sun. As always, responsibility for these views remains with the author.

Endnotes

1   Note for example the difference of opinion concerning the date of the foundation and first use of Tholos A at Ag. Triada: Branigan (1993) and Karantzali (1996) date it to EMI, Banti (1930–31) to EMII, Zois (1998) to EMIIA; Wilson and Day (1994: 13 and n.41) note that 'the first use of tholos A (the large tholos) at Ag. Triada need not be earlier than EMIIA'; and La Rosa (2001: 222), in a reconsideration of the stratigraphy of Tholos A, also states that the earliest deposition dates to the end of EMI and to EMIIA. Similar contrasting remarks concern the dates of other Mesara tholoi. In the present study the arguments and observations of all the specialists have been taken into account and, where possible, any information on stratigraphy and excavation context was integrated. Thus the dates for the tholoi followed here are generally based on the agreement of the majority of researchers.

2   For the Mesara in particular, the EMIIB and EMIII periods are a matter of controversy. EMIIB can only be identified by rare imports from other areas (e.g. *Vasiliki Ware*), whereas

apart from one of the levels of the Lebena Yerokambos II Tholos, there seem to be no other stratified contexts of this period in the area (Alexiou 1961–62: 227). Moreover, Watrous *et al.* (1993: 224 and n. 65; also Warren and Hankey 1989: 20) note that no deposit of EMIII has been identified in the Mesara, even though Branigan (1970; Blackman and Branigan 1977: 68) sees no significant break in the occupation of the area during EMIII/MMIA. However, such 'gaps' could equally be the products of our inability to determine the nature of EMIIB and EMIII pottery in the area, and not so much the result of cultural disruption. As most of the material comes from tombs, this may reflect a change in deposition practices rather than abandonment of sites and the beginnings of nucleation (as has been suggested in many cases, Manning 1994; Branigan 1995; Watrous *et al.* 1993; Watrous 2001).

3   As part of my Ph.D. thesis (Relaki 2003), a detailed study of the stratigraphy and structural remains at FN Phaistos indicates that occupation on the hill was not continuous, but rather punctuated by frequent intervals of settlement, abandonment and re-occupation.

4   Miamou is a possible exception, as the deposit shows perhaps repeated deposition sequences. In addition, Manteli (1993: Appendix IX) has identified typological traits in the pottery that could link it to the Late Neolithic tradition as this has been defined at Knossos. However, the characteristic high-necked jars and bottles of the Phaistos typology are again lacking from this assemblage.

5   The settlement at Megaloi Skinoi was the only one to give a greater amount of EMI material (Blackman and Branigan 1977: 41).

Bibliography

Alexiou, S.
    1962   New light on Minoan dating: Early Minoan tombs at Lebena. *Illustrated London News* 237 (*August 1960*): 225–27.

Andreou, S.
    1978   *Pottery Groups of the Old Palace Period in Crete*. PhD thesis, University of Cincinnati.

Appadurai, A.
    1995   The construction of locality. In R. Fardon (ed.), *Counterworks: Managing the Diversity of Knowledge*: 204–25. London and New York: Routledge.

Banti, L.
    1931   La grande tomba a tholos di Haghia Triada. *ASA* 13–14: 155–251.

Bintliff, J.
    1977a   *Natural Environment and Human Settlement in Prehistoric Greece* (BAR Supplementary Series 28). Oxford: British Archaeological Reports.
    1977b   Pedology and land use. In D. Blackman and K. Branigan, An archaeological survey of the lower catchment of the Ayiofarango Valley, S. Crete. *BSA* 72: 24–30.

Blackman, D. and K. Branigan
    1975   An archaeological survey on the south coast of Crete. *BSA* 70: 17–36.
    1977   An archaeological survey of the lower catchment of the Ayiofarango Valley, S. Crete. *BSA* 72: 13–84.
    1982   The excavation of an Early Minoan tholos tomb at Ay. Kyriaki, Ayiofarango, Southern Crete. *BSA* 77: 1–57.

Bonacasa, N.
    1968   Patrikies. Una stazione medio-minoica fra Haghia Triada e Festos. *ASA* 29–30: 7–54.

Branigan, K.
  1970   *The Tombs of Mesara. A Study of Funerary Architecture and Ritual in Southern Crete, 2800–1700 BC.* London: Duckworth.
  1984   Early Minoan society: the evidence from the Mesara tholoi reviewed. In C. Nicolet (ed.), *Aux origines de l'Hellenisme, la Crète et la Grèce*: 29–37. Paris: Centre Gustav Glotz.
  1988   *Prepalatial: the Foundations of Palatial Crete.* Amsterdam: Hakkert.
  1991   Funerary ritual and social cohesion in Early Bronze Age Crete. *Journal of Mediterranean Studies* 1: 183–92.
  1993   *Dancing with Death: Life and Death in Southern Crete, c. 3000–2000 BC.* Amsterdam: Hakkert.
  1995   Social transformations and the rise of the state in Crete. In R. Laffineur and W.-D. Niemeier (eds.), *POLITEIA: Society and State in the Aegean Bronze Age* (Aegaeum 12): 33–42. Liège: Université de Liège.
forthcoming *Diversity and development in the Prepalatial Mesara and Asterousia.* Paper to conference on the Mesara, Iraklion, Crete, November 2001.
Catling, H.W.
  1988   Archaeology in Greece. *AR* 1987–88.
Cherry J.F.
  1983   Frogs round the pond: perspectives on current archaeological survey in the Mediterranean region. In D. Keller and D. Rupp (eds.), *Archaeological Survey in the Mediterranean Area* (BAR International Series 155): 375–417. Oxford: British Archaeological Reports.
Dewar, R.E. and K.A. McBride
  1992   Remnant settlement patterns. In J. Rossignol and L-A. Wandsnider (eds.), *Space, Time, and Archaeological Landscapes*: 227–55. New York and London: Plenum Press.
Donnan, H. and T.M. Wilson
  2001   *Borders. Frontiers of Identity, Nation and State.* Oxford and New York: Berg.
Dunnell, R.C.
  1992   The Notion Site. In J. Rossignol and L-A. Wandsnider (eds.), *Space Time, and Archaeological Landscapes*: 21–41. New York and London: Plenum Press.
Evans, A.J.
  1895   The sepulchral deposit of Haghios Onoufrios near Phaistos and its relation to primitive Aegean culture. In A.J. Evans, *Cretan Pictographs and Prae-Phoenician Script*: 105–36. London.
Foxhall, L.
  2000   The running sands of time: archaeology and the short-term. *World Archaeology* 31: 484–98.
Hope Simpson, R. with P.P. Betancourt, P.J. Callaghan, D.K. Harlan, J.W. Hayes, J.W. Shaw, M.C. Shaw and L.V. Watrous
  1995   The archaeological survey of the Kommos area. In J.W. Shaw and M.C. Shaw (eds.), *Kommos I: the Kommos Region and Houses of the Minoan town, 1, the Kommos Region, Ecology and Minoan Industries*: 325–80. Princeton: Princeton University Press.
Ingold, T.
  2000   *The Perception of the Environment. Essays in Livelihood, Dwelling and Skill.* London and New York: Routledge.
Karantzali, E.
  1996   *Le bronze ancien dans les Cyclades et en Crète* (BAR International Series 631). Oxford: British Archaeological Reports.

Kardulias, N.P. (ed.)
  1994   *Beyond the Site. Regional Studies in the Aegean Area.* Lanham: University Press of America.
La Rosa, V.
  1988   Archaeologikes idisis 1987 Ayia Triada. *Kritiki Estia* 2: 329–30.
  1992a Ayia Triada. In J.W. Myers, E.E. Myers and G. Cadogan (eds.), *The Aerial Atlas of Ancient Crete*: 70–77. London: Thames and Hudson.
  1992b Phaistos. In J.W. Myers, E.E. Myers and G. Cadogan (eds.), *The Aerial Atlas of Ancient Crete*: 232–43. London: Thames and Hudson.
  2001   Minoan baetyls: between funerary rituals and epiphanies. In R. Laffineur and R. Hägg (eds.), *Potnia. Deities and Religion in the Aegean Bronze Age* (Aegaeum 22): 221–27. Liège: Université de Liège.
La Rosa, V. and A.L. D'Agata
  1985   Haghia Triada. In *Ancient Crete: A Hundred Years of Italian Archaeology, 1884–1984*: 108–36. Rome. Italian Archaeological School of Athens.
Laviosa, C.
  1970   Saggi di scavo ad Haghia Triada. *ASA* 47–48: 408–15.
  1973   L'abitato prepalaziale di Haghia Triada. *ASA* 50–51: 503–13.
Levi, D.
  1959   La villa rurale minoica di Gortina. *Bolletino d' Arte* 44: 237–68.
  1960   Per una nuova classificazione della civiltà minoica. *La Parola del Passato* 71: 81–124.
  1976   *Festos e la civiltà minoica*, 1a. Roma: Edizioni dell'Ateneo.
Lovell, N. (ed.)
  1998   *Locality and Belonging.* London and New York: Routledge.
Manning, S.W.
  1994   The emergence of divergence: development and decline on Bronze Age Crete and the Cyclades. In C. Mathers and S. Stoddart (eds.) *Development and Decline in the Mediterranean Bronze Age:* 221–70. Sheffield: J.R. Collis.
Manteli, K.
  1993   *The Transition from the Neolithic to the Early Bronze Age in Crete, Greece, with Special Reference to Pottery.* PhD thesis, University College London.
Papadatos, Y.
  1999   *Mortuary Practices and their Importance for the Reconstruction of Society and Life in Prepalatial Crete: the Evidence from Tholos Tomb G in Archanes-Phourni.* PhD thesis. University of Sheffield.
Relaki, M.
  2003   *Social Arenas in Minoan Crete: a Regional History of the Mesara in South-Central Crete from the Final Neolithic to the End of the Protopalatial Period.* PhD thesis, University of Sheffield.
Renfrew, C.
  1972   *The Emergence of Civilisation: the Cyclades and the Aegean in the Third Millennium B.C.* London: Methuen.
Sbonias, K.
  1999a Diakoinotikes skhesis kai symvoliki ekfrasi stin proanaktoriki Kriti. In *Eliten in der Bronzezeit. Ergebnisse Zweier Kolloquien in Mainz und Athen*, 1 (RGZM Monograph 43): 1–18. Mainz: Römisch-Germanisch Zentralmuseum.
  1999b Social development, management of production, and symbolic representation in Prepalatial Crete. In A. Chaniotis (ed.), *From Minoan Farmers to Roman Traders. Sidelights on the Economy of Ancient Crete*: 25–51. Stuttgart: Franz Steiner.

Shaw, W. and M.C. Shaw (eds.)

1995   *Kommos I: the Kommos Region and Houses of the Minoan town, 1, the Kommos Region, Ecology and Minoan Industries.* Princeton: Princeton University Press.

Taramelli, A.

1897   The prehistoric grotto at Miamou. *AJA* 1: 287–312.

Urry, J.

2000   *Sociology Beyond Societies. Mobilities for the Twenty-First Century.* London and New York: Routledge.

Vagnetti, L.

1973   L' insediamento neolitico di Festos. *ASA* 34–35: 7–138.

1973   Tracce di due insediamenti neolitici nel territorio dell' antica Gortina. In *Antichità Cretesi. Studi in onore di Doro Levi, 1. Chronache di Archeologia* 12: 1–9.

Vagnetti, L. and P. Belli

1978   Characters and problems of the Final Neolithic in Crete. *SMEA* 68: 125–65.

Vallianou, D. and L.V. Watrous

1991   Epifaniaki ereuna dytikis Mesaras. In *Proceedings of the 5th International Cretological Conference*: 113–23. Khania.

Vasilakis, A.

1987   Anaskafi neolithikou spitiou stous Kalous Limenes. In *Eilapini. Studies in Honour of Professor N. Platon*: 45–53. Iraklion.

1988   Archaeologikes idisis 1987 Trypiti. *Kritiki Estia 2*: 331–32.

1990   Proistorikes thesis sti Moni Odigitria/Kalous Limenes. *Kritiki Estia 3*: 11–80.

1995   Trypiti 1986–1991 Zitimata tou proanaktorikou minoikou politismou sti notia kentriki Kriti kai i anaskafi tis Trypitis. In *Proceedings of the 7th International Cretological Congress (A1)*: 69–73. Rethymnon.

Warren, P.M. and V. Hankey

1989   *Aegean Bronze Age Chronology.* Bristol: Bristol Classical Press.

Watrous, L.V.

2001   Crete from earliest prehistory through the Protopalatial period, and addendum 1994–1999. In T. Cullen (ed.), *Aegean Prehistory: a Review*: 157–215 and 216–223. Boston: Archaeological Institute of America.

Watrous, L.V., D. Hatzi-Vallianou, K. Pope, N. Mourtzas, J. Shay, C.T. Shay, J. Bennett, D. Tsoungarakis, C. Vallianos and H. Blitzer

1993   A survey of the western Mesara plain in Crete: preliminary report of the 1984, 1986, and 1987 field seasons. *Hesperia* 62: 191–248.

Whitelaw, T.M.

1983   The settlement at Fournou Koryfi Myrtos and aspects of Early Minoan social organisation. In O. Krzyszkowska and L. Nixon (eds.), *Minoan Society*: 323–45. Bristol: Bristol Classical Press.

Wilson, D.E. and P.M. Day

1994   Ceramic regionalism in Prepalatial central Crete: the Mesara imports at EMI to EMIIA Knossos. *BSA* 89: 1–87.

2000   EMI chronology and social practice: pottery from the early palace tests at Knossos. *BSA* 95: 21–63.

Zois, A.

1965   Faistiaka. *AE*: 27–109.

1998   *Kriti: i Proimi Epokhi tou Khalkou, 5: Mesara.* Athens: Apodexis.

10

Life after Mediterranean Polyculture: the Subsistence Subsystem and the Emergence of Civilisation Revisited

Paul Halstead

Chapter 15 of the *Emergence of Civilisation* is devoted to 'Natural environment and the subsistence subsystem' (Renfrew 1972: 265–307). Although widely and unjustly criticized for disarticulating human culture, the systems approach of the *Emergence* is above all multivariate and its author stresses that 'Nothing could be more misleading than to attribute the emergence of Aegean civilization simply to subsistence changes' (Renfrew 1972: 304). Nonetheless, Renfrew's 'subsistence/ redistribution model' was a major strand in his account of socio-cultural change in the Bronze Age Aegean (1972: 480–82). This emphasis reflected growing archaeological interest in bioarchaeology and subsistence, both within the Renfrew household (e.g., J. Renfrew 1973) and further afield (e.g., Higgs 1972), but may also partly be understood in terms of the autonomist agenda of the *Emergence*.

Understanding of early Mesopotamian civilization had highlighted the importance of irrigation agriculture in both creating the need for a managerial elite and making possible surplus production. This surplus supported elites, urban centres and craft specialists and so, indirectly, financed the long-distance trading ventures which carried civilization to Europe. In seeking to counter the prevailing diffusionist account of the origins of Aegean civilization, therefore, Renfrew looked to the cultural landscape of Mediterranean Europe for a local alternative to irrigation agriculture. He argued that 'Mediterranean polyculture' – the cultivation of wheat, vines and olives – could be traced back to the third millennium BC in the southern Aegean, with two importance consequences. First, the adoption of deep-rooted tree crops, in addition to annual grain crops, allowed more of the landscape to be cultivated and enabled production of a surplus. Secondly, the heterogeneous terrain of the southern Aegean favoured local specialization in cereals, vines or olives and so led to pooling of these products within village communities under the aegis of a managerial elite (Renfrew 1972: 304–07). Mediterranean polyculture thus neatly matched irrigation agriculture in providing indigenous opportunity and motive for the emergence of an elite, and an indigenous rationale for the proliferation of exchange. Renfrew's argument that the antecedents of polyculture could be found in the Aegean, in the form of increasing crop diversity and purity during the later Neolithic, further strengthened the case for autonomous emergence of complex society in Europe.

Thirty years after publication of the *Emergence*, this chapter looks critically at the 'subsistence subsystem' in Aegean later prehistory, addressing in turn the following three questions. How has our knowledge of this field changed in the last three decades? How well has the subsistence/redistribution model stood up to subsequent research, empirical, methodological and theoretical? And, most critically, what part might bioarchaeology and the study of 'subsistence' play in future research into early Aegean 'civilization'?

The 'Subsistence Subsystem' Updated

In the 30 years which have elapsed since publication of the *Emergence*, the number and size of bone and seed assemblages from Aegean sites of Neolithic and Bronze Age date has increased steadily (Hansen 1988; Halstead 1994: 204–05 table 7.1; Payne 1985a; Reese 1994; Halstead 1996). The quality of information has also improved: partly because more or less systematic sampling is now practised at some sites; and especially because of radical advances in published criteria for laboratory analysis. Improvements in taxonomic identification of particular importance to Aegean prehistory include increasing ability to distinguish between sheep and goats (Payne 1985b; Prummel and Frisch 1986; Helmer 2000; Halstead *et al.* 2002), greater awareness of the wide diversity of cereal and legume crops grown in the past (Sarpaki and Jones 1990; Jones 1992a; Jones, Valamoti and Charles 2000), and revised morphological and metrical criteria for separating cultivated and wild grape pips (Smith and Jones 1990; Mangafa and Kotsakis 1996). Approaches to quantification have moved a long way since, and partly in response to, acknowledgement of this issue in the *Emergence* (Renfrew 1972: 274–75; Dennell 1976; Hubbard 1975; Jones 1991; Payne 1985a). Specialists with Aegean interests have been prominent in the investigation of some of the key taphonomic processes affecting the survival and retrieval of bone (e.g., Payne and Munson 1985; Payne 1972) and seed remains (e.g., Boardman and Jones 1990). No less important has been the development of explicit actualistic models: for the recognition of crop processing stages (Hillman 1984; Jones 1984; 1987a; 1988) and crop husbandry regimes (e.g., Bogaard *et al.* 1999; Charles *et al.* 1997; 2002; Jones *et al.* 1999; Jones, Bogaard, Charles and Hodgson 2000) from the physical and ecological characteristics, respectively, of weeds; and for the exploration of strategies of animal management from mortality data (Payne 1973; Halstead 1998). Again, ethnoarchaeological work in the Aegean has played a major role in these developments.

Increasingly, conventional macroscopic bioarchaeology is being complemented by a battery of microscopic and biomolecular techniques, ranging from the investigation of dental microwear as evidence for animal diet (Mainland 2003), through the analysis of isotopic bone chemistry as evidence for the diet of both animals and humans (e.g., Triantaphyllou 2001: 135–40), to the detection of organic residues in ceramic vessels (e.g., Urem-Kotsou *et al.* 2002). Applications in Aegean prehistory are beginning to provide complementary insights to conventional bioarchaeology: bone chemistry sheds light (albeit in a complex fashion) on diet, while macroscopic study of seeds and bones may reveal how individual dietary components are produced and consumed; organic residues for the first time make possible the integrated analysis of bioarchaeological food remains and of the vessels in which these were stored, cooked, served and consumed.

Two fundamental points of departure for the *Emergence* were Renfrew's conviction that 'the growth of the palaces has to be seen in the first instance as the development of redistributive centres for subsistence commodities' (Renfrew 1972: 297) and his assumption that the palatial redistributive system was characterized by central pooling of local ecological specializations (Renfrew 1972: 364). Subsequent work by Linear B scholars (e.g., Killen 1985), however, has necessitated a radical reappraisal of Mycenaean palatial redistribution (see below). At the same time, there has been growing awareness that the textual record is not only incompletely preserved but also highly selective in its administrative involvement (e.g., Chadwick 1987; Whitelaw 2001); comparison of the bio-archaeological and Linear B evidence for crops and livestock has contributed to this reappraisal (Halstead 1995; 1998–99).

The subsistence/redistribution model was equally shaped by Renfrew's perceptions of the nature and dynamics of Mediterranean rural economy and, particularly, of the role of polyculture. Since the mid-1970s, a plethora of Aegean-based ethnoarchaeological or rural historical studies has led to radical reappraisal of many aspects of Mediterranean land use and to growing appreciation that many 'traditional' practices have developed recently in the context of an international market economy (e.g., Forbes 1993; Psikhogios 1987; Psikhogios and Papapetrou 1984; Halstead 1987). Three outcomes of such studies, the relevance of which to the subsistence/redistribution model is made clear below, may be noted. First, recent farmers with limited involvement in the market tend to grow a mixture of crops to reduce the risk of total crop failure (Forbes 1976; 1989). Secondly, risk-averse farmers normally aim for overproduction in order to secure a sufficient harvest in most years (Forbes 1982; 1989; Halstead 1990). Thirdly, in historical perspective, the cultivation of olives and vines has often been very small-scale and the consumption of wine and oil more or less restricted to prestige or ritual contexts (Forbes 1993; Foxhall 1993; Hamilakis 1996).

Finally, it should be noted that the *Emergence* just predates the eruption of a heated debate on the nature and legitimacy of 'economic archaeology' (e.g., Higgs and Jarman 1975; Shanks and Tilley 1987; Barker and Gamble 1985; Charles and Halstead 2001), one outcome of which is that the term 'subsistence' is now regarded as far more loaded than was the case in 1972. In terms of the important distinction drawn by Barker and Gamble (1985: 5) between 'subsistence' (what people live on) and 'economy' (the management and mobilization of resources), Renfrew's subsistence/redistribution model, with its emphasis on the production and control of surplus, was very clearly concerned with the broader issue of economy.

Today, therefore, far more and better information is available on prehistoric economy in the Aegean than was the case in 1972 and the methods of investigation at our disposal are both more diverse and more powerful. At the same time, our understanding has advanced greatly both of the nature and workings of redistribution in the developed Mycenaean palaces and of the dynamics and historical context of 'traditional' Mediterranean land use. It would be disappointing if the field had not changed in this way. What is more surprising (and may be attributed in part to the stimulus of the *Emergence*) is the extent to which so many advances, equally applicable elsewhere in the Mediterranean or further afield, have been achieved in the Aegean.

The Subsistence/Redistribution Model in Hindsight

At a detailed level, research since 1972 has not been kind to the subsistence/redistribution model. Comparison of archaeological and textual data casts doubt on the dominant position of redistribution within the palatial economy (e.g., Halstead 1999a; Whitelaw 2001; and, more radically, Sherratt 2001). Closer attention to the textual record suggests that palatial redistribution more closely resembled upwards mobilization of resources (Cherry 1978: 425; Killen 1985; also Renfrew 1972: 464) than the reciprocal pooling envisaged by Renfrew; that mobilization from widely scattered, dependent communities (as opposed to the hinterland of major centres) was largely in the form of non-staple raw materials and craft goods (de Fidio 1982; Killen 1985) rather than subsistence staples; and that such 'taxation' was remarkably insensitive to local ecological differences (Shelmerdine 1973).

The textual evidence contradicting Renfrew's model is in the deciphered Linear B script of the Mycenaean palaces and so might reasonably be considered irrelevant to the origins, several centuries earlier, of the Minoan palaces. Critical appreciation of 'traditional' Mediterranean land use also casts doubt, however, on the assumption that olives or vines were major subsistence crops in the distant past (Forbes 1993; Foxhall 1993; Halstead 1987), while the sparse archaeobotanical record and somewhat ambiguous evidence of presses and cups is at least compatible with restricted consumption of these tree crops as oil and wine in largely elite contexts (Runnels and Hansen 1986; Hamilakis 1996). Anyway, consideration of the risk-averse tendencies of recent Mediterranean farmers suggests that specialization in vines or olives is most unlikely to have been a domestic initiative (Forbes 1989; Halstead 1987), unless enforced by an already established elite (Gamble 1982), and that prehistoric farmers will routinely have produced a 'normal surplus' long before the emergence of an elite or cultivation of the olive and vine (Forbes 1989; Halstead 1989). In short, it no longer seems plausible that polyculture, and redistribution of the products of polyculture, played a significant part in the emergence of palatial society.

Some of these critical observations are in fact presaged in the *Emergence* or in later work by its author (notably Renfrew 1982). Moreover, the comprehensive way in which the subsistence/redistribution model can now be dismissed is in many ways an eloquent testimony to the success of the *Emergence* in stimulating such a breadth and depth of counter-research. Even if the subsistence/re-distribution model has limited currency, however, several related elements of the approach adopted in the *Emergence* have more enduring value.

One basic heuristic device employed in the *Emergence* was the comparison of developmental trajectories in north and south Greece, stressing the long-term ecological contrast between a wheat-growing north and polyculture-prone south. A historical dimension was introduced by the attempt to examine contrasting regional trajectories of settlement and human demography. This approach, drawing on the *relatively* immutable nature of the Aegean landscape, has been further explored in discussions of the relationship between topography/climate, agricultural risk and exchange (Halstead and O' Shea 1982) and of the extent to which the size and spacing of islands has conditioned the history of human occupation (Cherry 1981; Broodbank 1999; Broodbank and Strasser 1991) and the subsequent expansion of maritime spheres of interaction (Broodbank 1989; 2000). In recent work, this approach has been used to explore both sides of the interaction between autonomous local processes and enveloping world systems (Broodbank 2000) and so offers a common methodology for developing an integrated, indigenous/exogenous approach to our subject.

A second major element in the *Emergence* is the focus on redistribution in the southern Aegean Bronze Age. Here too a wealth of recent work has sought to clarify the content, volume, spatial scale, social context and economic mechanisms involved in the distribution of labour, staple foods and raw materials, and finished artefacts: studies of Linear B texts (e.g., de Fidio 1977; 1982; 1987; 1992; Killen 1983; 1984; 1985; 1993a; 1996; 1998; 2001; Bennet 1999; 2001; Palmer 1989; 1994) and their precursors (e.g., Olivier 1986; Palmer 1995; Schoep 1999), of sealings (e.g., Schoep 1998), of ceramics (e.g., Knappett 1999; Whitelaw 2001), of grave goods (e.g., Voutsaki 2001) and of recent rural economy (e.g., Halstead 1999b; 2001) have shed valuable light on many aspects of Bronze Age society and political economy.

A third important element in the *Emergence* was the attempt to mobilize the then sparse bioarchaeological record in the service of Aegean social archaeology. The remainder of this chapter focusses on the future of this element for two reasons. First, successful exploitation of the potential of bioarchaeology depends on the actions not just of specialist practitioners but also of the whole community of Aegean prehistorians. Secondly, the tendency of the theoretically literate to equate bioarchaeology with such unfashionable buzzwords as 'subsistence', 'functionalism' or 'determinism' threatens to render the field passé before most Aegean excavators have been persuaded to pay more than lip-service to systematic bioarchaeological study. It must be acknowledged that the failure of some bioarchaeologists to address archaeological, rather than narrowly biological, questions has contributed to this state of affairs.

Bioarchaeology, 'Subsistence' and 'Civilization' in Prospect

During the six millennia of the Aegean Neolithic and Bronze Age, the human population exercised a clear and significant influence on the landscape (clearance, probably erosion), especially of the lowlands (e.g., Bottema 1994; van Andel *et al.* 1990; Krahtopoulou 2000); new domestic plants (especially tree crops) and animals (horse, donkey) appeared (e.g., Runnels and Hansen 1986; von den Driesch and Boessneck 1990); at some sites, there are striking increases in the representation of wild animals (e.g., von den Driesch 1987); and there is some evidence for changes in the way plants and animals were managed (notably, adoption of extensive agriculture and ox-traction [Halstead 1992a]; references to a broader 'secondary products revolution' [van Andel and Runnels 1988] are as yet unfounded). Even allowing for the desperate shortage of published bioarchaeological work on Crete, however, it is difficult to argue that the bioarchaeological record matches the radical changes in human society that took place during the Neolithic and Bronze Age. One conclusion might be that bioarchaeology, or the study of animal and plant exploitation and of human diet and health, can shed little light on these processes of social change. A more optimistic inference might be that social change was mirrored not so much by shifts in the species of animals and plants exploited or in their relative contribution to human nutrition or even in the techniques of management adopted, as by transformations of the social context of animal and plant use: that is, by changes in rights of consumption and obligations of production.

For the Late Bronze Age in southern Greece, at least, such optimism seems justified: comparison of textual (Linear B) and bioarchaeological evidence suggests that the palaces exercised very selective control over crop and livestock management (focussing primarily on cereals and sheep) and enjoyed rights of consumption (e.g., to a range of livestock species) by no means coterminous with their restricted committment to production (Halstead 1992a; 1998–99). The potential for integration of bioarchaeological and Linear B evidence has as yet barely been exploited and so one clear priority for future work in Aegean 'economic archaeology' is more systematic retrieval of faunal and archaeo-botanical data from more sites and from a wider range of site types in southern

Greece. That differences in status (or, rather, mortuary elaboration) may have been mirrored by significant differences in nutritional well-being is also suggested by palaeopathological analysis of cemetery populations (e.g., Angel 1971; 1973; Smith 2000). Isotopic analysis of human bone is beginning to yield finer-grained evidence of dietary inequality between gender and other social groups, in access to terrestrial and marine animal protein (Tzedakis and Martlew 1999: 226, 230, 246), but would benefit from fuller integration with macroscopic evidence for the demographic structure, diet and health status of the populations studied (cf. Triantaphyllou 2001: 133–41).

For earlier periods of Aegean prehistory, in the absence of written evidence, the elucidation of scales of production and consumption is more difficult. The social context of production and consumption would be more amenable to investigation, if archaeobotanical and archaeozoological evidence from individual sites was routinely analysed in terms of its spatial as well as broad chronological provenance. As with artefactual evidence (e.g., Whitelaw 1983; 2001), however, examples of such practice are still the exception rather than the rule (e.g., Jones 1987b; Halstead 1992b; Becker 1998). A second clear priority for the future, therefore, is closer attention to the intra-site spatial context of bioarchaeological residues. It should also be noted that such attention is far more likely to be informative in the context of areally extensive excavation than of small-scale sondages, even though systematic sampling strategies are more frequently encountered in the latter case.

One outcome of initial comparative analysis of bioarchaeological and Linear B evidence has been the argument that the palaces were in large part financed by extensive cereal-agriculture, geared to large-scale surplus production through the use of palatial oxen rather than human labour for tillage (de Fidio 1992; Killen 1993b; 1998; Halstead 1999b). On the other hand, as argued above, studies of 'traditional' Greek rural economy have stressed the importance of overproduction as a normal domestic precaution against the risk of crop failure, implying that the origins of surplus production in the Aegean must be sought long before the Bronze Age or the emergence of palatial elites. Archaeobotanical evidence for crop weeds in the Late Bronze Age grain storage complex at Assiros Toumba in northern Greece suggests centralized storage of cereals grown under a relatively intensive regime, arguably more consistent with small-scale horticulture than extensive agriculture (Jones 1987b; 1992b). A third priority for future work, therefore, is the ecological analysis of prehistoric crop weed assemblages to explore elite strategies for mobilizing surplus. When and under what circumstances did elite-sponsored, *extensive surplus production* (as in the Mycenaean palaces) perhaps come to supplement or replace elite *extraction of 'normal surplus'* from subordinate households? Archaeobotanical models have now been developed, based on studies of weed ecology (Bogaard *et al.* 1999; Jones, Bogaard, Charles and Hodgson 2000; Charles *et al.* 2002), which are capable of resolving this issue. Archaeobotanical evidence of sufficient quantity and quality is a scarce resource, however, and it is worth emphasizing that, without the presence on-site of an experienced archaeobotanist, any opportunities which do arise to collect such data will almost certainly be squandered – just as they were, more forgiveably, by our predecessors in the early 20th century.

While palatial grain surpluses may largely have been needed as rations for the numerous dependent craft-workers and servants (Godart 1968; Hiller 1988), the palaces also mobilized and disbursed large quantities of wine, meat and other comestibles intended for feasting (Killen 1994; Palmer 1994). The social and ceremonial significance of wine was underlined in the *Emergence* (Renfrew 1972: 490, 498) and several scholars have subsequently discussed the role of feasting, and more particularly of wine drinking, in creating, cementing or legitimizing relationships of alliance or dependence in palatial society (Moody 1987; Killen 1994; Hamilakis 1996; Wright 1996; Bennet and Davis 1999; Shelmerdine 1999). On the other hand, one of the distinctive features of the material culture of Neolithic and Bronze Age Greece is an almost continuous tradition of fine tableware (Renfrew 1972: 284; Vitelli 1989; Sherratt 1991), suggesting that, throughout later Aegean prehistory, some acts of consumption were significant social events conducted with ceremony (also Hamilakis 2000). Bioarchaeological evidence is also now emerging of consumption on a massive scale at Late Neolithic Makriyalos, northern Greece, raising the possibility that competitive feasting may have been a significant force for social change long before the appearance of the palaces (Pappa *et al.* 2004).

Whether feasting is regarded as cause or consequence of overproduction and social inequality, a fourth major priority for research must be investigation of the scale and social context of consumption. To what extent can domestic or daily consumption be distinguished from that involving a larger social group or taking place at rarer intervals? And to what extent are rare or large-scale or socially restricted consumption events also marked out by the types of resources consumed, by the manner of their preparation, or by the elaboration of material culture or attendant ritual (cf. Goody 1982; Dietler 2001)? The absolute quantity of refuse in a single context may be large enough to suggest collective consumption, as in the case of Makriyalos noted above. At Early Helladic Nemea, a lower incidence of cut marks on bones of cattle than of pigs or sheep/goats may result from less intensive butchery of big carcasses, suggesting consumption of the latter by a larger social group (Halstead in press). At Knossos, more intensive butchery in palatial than pre-palatial contexts suggests changes in both the cooking and serving of meat (Isaakidou 2004). Again in a palatial context, Linear B texts offer hints of high-status foods preferentially consumed at elite banquets (Killen 1994; Bennet 2001: 35), while iconography and architecture (Wright 1996; Shelmerdine 1999; Bennet and Davis 1999), ceramic and metal vessels (Bendall 2004), and animal bones (Isaakidou *et al.* 2002) from Pylos variously reveal the use of material culture and etiquette or ritual to differentiate between groups of consumers or occasions of consumption. Moreover, the analysis of cooking vessel morphology (e.g., Borgna 1997) and of charred food remains (Sarpaki 2001; Jones and Halstead 1993; Valamoti 2002) is beginning to shed light on culinary methods, while organic residues in ceramics may reveal macroscopically undetectable ingredients (cf., with circumspection, Tzedakis and Martlew 1999). Fuller exploration of these topics will require *integrated* analysis of conventional bioarchaeological remains (bones and seeds) with associated cooking, eating and serving vessels and with food residues. Again, a basic prerequisite of such integration is context-based analysis, in order to identify coherent groups of material representing discrete episodes of deposition from single or short-lived consumption events.

While the traditional focus of 'economic archaeology' has been the production and consumption of staple resources, the temporal and spatial dimensions of these activities are important related concerns. These dimensions, which are also crucial to attempts to appreciate how cultural landscapes and built environments were inhabited by, and helped to shape the lives of, individuals in the past (e.g., Barrett 1994), are eminently amenable to bioarchaeological investigation. For example, on an intra-site level, the 'granary' complex devoted to long-term storage of partially cleaned crops at Assiros and the 'larder' containing fully-cleaned grain in the Knossos Unexplored Mansion (Jones 1987b) will have involved very different patterns of accessibility and movement. On an inter-site level, year-round occupation is often assumed rather than demonstrated on Neolithic open-air settlements (Whittle 1997), but models of seasonal abandonment (van Andel and Runnels 1995) are not supported by available bioarchaeological evidence (Becker 1999; Halstead 1999c). Whether mobility and pastoralism are favoured (e.g., Johnson 1996; Cavanagh 1999), however, or sedentism and mixed farming (e.g., Cherry 1988; Halstead 1996), people will certainly have pursued animals, both domestic and wild, across the landscape of the Aegean (Halstead 2000). Such mundane patterns of mobility will have shaped perceptions of both space and time and have influenced patterns of social interaction. As isotopic analyses of bone chemistry are applied to animals as well as humans, speculation on the scale of these movements may be translated into reliable inferences. Thus a final priority is to harness both conventional macroscopic and more recent bio-molecular methods to explore more intensively the ways in which humans, and the animals and plants that they exploited, moved through the built environment and the cultural landscape.

Conclusions

The emphasis of the *Emergence* on 'subsistence' and redistribution has served our field well, stimulating much invaluable research and pointing the way to further and more diverse work in the future. It should be stressed that recent bio-archaeological work, and the avenues of future investigation sketched out above, are by no means restricted to the investigation of 'subsistence' in the narrow sense of 'what people live on', though this too remains opaque in many respects. In closing, it seems appropriate to note some preconditions that must be met if the potential of broad-minded bioarchaeology is to be realized.

- First, to shed light on social change in Bronze Age southern Greece, bioarchaeology must be embraced by the often classically-trained excavators working in Crete and the islands with at least the enthusiasm of their colleagues in northern Greece.
- Secondly, in both north and south Greece, bioarchaeology must be practised systematically, rather than in a token fashion designed to satisfy the commendable conditions of INSTAP funding. And rather than being regarded as an impediment or alternative to extensive excavation, systematic bio-archaeology should be recognized as more worthwhile in the context of large-scale excavation.
- Thirdly, there is a clear need for 'joined up' bioarchaeology, in which the study of ecofacts is integrated with the analysis of artefacts and excavation context; in which 'high-tech' and 'low-tech' methods are combined in a fashion which plays to their contrasting strengths; in which bioarchaeological data are contrasted with textual evidence; in which insights from recent rural economy are embedded in an awareness of the historically contingent nature of the latter; and in which bioarchaeologists address significant archaeological questions.

Bibliography

Andel, T. van and C. Runnels
   1988   An essay on the 'emergence of civilization' in the Aegean world. *Antiquity* 62: 234–47.
   1995   The earliest farmers in Europe. *Antiquity* 69: 481–500.
Andel, T. van, E. Zangger and A. Demitrack
   1990   Land use and soil erosion in prehistoric and historical Greece. *Journal of Field Archaeology* 17: 379–96.
Angel, J.
   1971   *Lerna 2: the People*. Princeton: American School of Classical Studies at Athens.
   1973   Human skeletons from Grave Circles at Mycenae. In G.E. Mylonas, *O Tafikos Kiklos B ton Mikinon*: 379–97. Athens: Arkhaiologiki Etairia.
Barker, G. and C. Gamble
   1985   Beyond domestication: a strategy for investigating the process and consequence of social complexity. In G. Barker and C. Gamble (eds.), *Beyond Domestication in Prehistoric Europe*: 1–31. London: Academic Press.
Barrett, J.C.
   1994   *Fragments from Antiquity: an Archaeology of Social Life in Britain, 2900–1200 BC*. Oxford: Blackwell.
Becker, C.
   1998   Can animal bones reflect household activities? A case study from a prehistoric site in

Greece. In P. Anreiter, L. Bartosiewicz, E. Jerem and W. Meid (eds.), *Man and the Animal World: Studies in Archaeozoology, Archaeology, Anthropology and Palaeolinguistics in Memoriam Sándor Bökönyi*: 79–86. Budapest: Archaeolingua Press.

1999   The Middle Neolithic and the Platia Magoula Zarkou – a review of current archaeozoological research in Thessaly (Greece). *Anthropozoologica* 30: 3–22.

Bendall, L.M.
2004   Fit for a king? Hierarchy, exclusion, aspiration and desire in the social structure of Mycenaean banqueting. In P. Halstead and J. Barrett (eds.), *Food, Cuisine and Society in Prehistoric Greece* (SSAA 5). Oxford: Oxbow.

Bennet, J.
1999   The Mycenaean conceptualization of space or Pylian geography . . . yet again. In S. Deger-Jalkotzy, S. Hiller, O. Panagl and G. Nightingale (eds.), *Floreant Studia Mycenaea*: 131–57. Salzburg: Österreichische Akademie der Wissenschaften.

2001   Agency and bureaucracy: thoughts on the nature and extent of administration in Bronze Age Pylos. In S. Voutsaki and J. Killen (eds.), *Economy and Politics in the Mycenaean Palace States* (Cambridge Philological Society Supplementary Volume 27): 25–37.

Bennet, J. and J. Davis
1999   Making Mycenaeans: warfare, territorial expansion, and representations of the other in the Pylian kingdom. In R. Laffineur (ed.), *Polemos: le contexte guerrier en Égée à l'âge du bronze* (Aegaeum 19): 105–20. Liège: Université de Liège.

Boardman, S. and G. Jones
1990   Experiments on the effects of charring on cereal plant components. *JAS* 17: 1–11.

Bogaard, A., C. Palmer, G. Jones, M. Charles and J.G. Hodgson
1999   A FIBS approach to the use of weed ecology for the archaeobotanical recognition of crop rotation regimes. *JAS* 26: 1211–24.

Borgna, E.
1997   Kitchen-ware from LM IIIC Phaistos: cooking traditions and ritual activities in LBA Cretan societies. *SMEA* 39(2): 189–217.

Bottema, S.
1994   The prehistoric environment of Greece: a review of the palynological record. In P.N. Kardulias (ed.), *Beyond the Site: Regional Studies in the Aegean Area*: 45–68. Lanham: University Press of America.

Broodbank, C.
1989   The longboat and society in the Cyclades in the Keros-Syros culture. *AJA* 93: 319–37.
1999   Colonization and configuration in the insular Neolithic of the Aegean. In P. Halstead (ed.), *Neolithic Society in Greece* (SSAA 2): 15–41. Sheffield: Sheffield Academic Press.
2000   *An Island Archaeology of the Early Cyclades*. Cambridge: Cambridge University Press.

Broodbank, C. and T.F. Strasser
1991   Migrant farmers and the Neolithic colonization of Crete. *Antiquity* 65: 233–45.

Cavanagh, W.
1999   Revenons à nos moutons: surface survey and the Peloponnese in the Late and Final Neolithic. In J. Renard (ed.), *Le Péloponnèse: archéologie et histoire*: 31–65. Rennes: Presses Universitaires Rennes.

Chadwick, J.
1987   L' économie palatiale dans la Grèce mycénienne. In E. Lévy (ed.), *Le système palatial en Orient, en Grèce et à Rome*: 283–90. Leiden: Brill.

Charles, M., A. Bogaard, G. Jones, J. Hodgson and P. Halstead

2002   Towards the archaeobotanical identification of intensive cereal cultivation: present-day ecological investigation in the mountains of Asturias, northwest Spain. *Vegetation History and Archaeobotany* 11: 133–42.

Charles, M. and P. Halstead
2001   Biological resource exploitation: problems of theory and method. In D.R. Brothwell and A.M. Pollard (eds.), *Handbook of Archaeological Sciences*: 365–78. Chichester: Wiley.

Charles, M., G. Jones and J.G. Hodgson
1997   FIBS in archaeobotany: functional interpretation of weed floras in relation to husbandry practices. *JAS* 24: 1151–61.

Cherry, J.F.
1978   Generalization and the archaeology of the state. In D. Green, C. Haselgrove and M. Spriggs (eds.), *Social Organisation and Settlement: Contributions from Anthropology, Archaeology and Geography* (BAR International Series 47): 411–37. Oxford: British Archaeological Reports.
1981   Pattern and process in the earliest colonization of the Mediterranean islands. *Proceedings of the Prehistoric Society* 47: 41–68.
1988   Pastoralism and the role of animals in the pre- and proto-historic economies of the Aegean. In C. R. Whittaker (ed.), *Pastoral Economies in Classical Antiquity* (Cambridge Philological Society Supplementary Volume 14): 6–34.

Dennell, R.W.
1976   The economic importance of plant resources represented on archaeological sites. *JAS* 3: 229–47.

Dietler, M.
2001   Theorizing the feast: rituals of consumption, commensal politics, and power in African contexts. In M. Dietler and B. Hayden (eds.), *Feasts: Archaeological and Ethnographic Perspectives on Food, Politics and Power*: 65–114. Washington: Smithsonian Institution Press.

Driesch, A. von den
1987   Haus- und Jagdtiere im vorgeschichtlichen Thessalien. *Prähistorische Zeitschrift* 62: 1–21.

Driesch, A. von den and J. Boessneck
1990   Die Tierreste von der mykenischen Burg Tiryns bei Nafplion/Peloponnes. In H.-J. Weisshaar, I. Weber-Hiden, A. von den Driesch, J. Boessneck, A. Rieger and W. Böser (eds.), *Tiryns Forschungen und Berichte* 11: 87–164. Mainz am Rhein: von Zabern.

Fidio, P. de
1977   *I Dosmoi Pilii a Poseidon*. Rome: Edizioni dell' Ateneo.
1982   Fiscalità, redistribuzione, equivalenze: per una discussione sull economia micenea. *SMEA* 23: 83–136.
1987   Palais et communautés de village dans le royaume mycénien de Pylos. In P.H. Ilievski and L. Crepajac (eds.), *Tractata Mycenaea*: 129–49. Skopje: Macedonian Academy of Sciences and Art.
1992   Mycènes et Proche-Orient, ou le théorème des modèles. In J.-P. Olivier (ed.), *Mykenaïka* (BCH Supplementary Volume 25): 173–96.

Forbes, H.
1976   'We have a little of everything': the ecological basis of some agricultural practices in Methana, Trizinia. *Annals of the New York Academy of Sciences* 268: 236–50.
1982   *Strategies and Soils: Technology, Production and Environment in the Peninsula of Methana, Greece*. PhD dissertaton, University of Pennsylvania.

1989   Of grandfathers and grand theories: the hierarchised ordering of responses to hazard in a Greek rural community. In P. Halstead and J. O. 'Shea (eds.), *Bad Year Economics*: 87–97. Cambridge: Cambridge University Press.

1993   Ethnoarchaeology and the place of the olive in the economy of the southern Argolid, Greece. In M.-C. Amouretti and J.-P. Brun (eds.), *La production du vin et de l'huile en Méditerranée* (BCH Supplementary Volume 26): 213–26.

Foxhall, L.
1993   Oil extraction and processing equipment in classical Greece. In M.-C. Amouretti and J.-P. Brun (eds.), *La production du vin et de l'huile en Méditerranée* (BCH Supplementary Volume 26): 183–200.

Gamble, C.
1982   Leadership and 'surplus' production. In C. Renfrew and S. Shennan (eds.), *Ranking, Resource and Exchange*: 100–05. Cambridge: Cambridge University Press.

Godart, L.
1968   Le grain à Cnossos. *SMEA* 5: 56–63.

Goody, J.
1982   *Cooking, Cuisine and Class*. Cambridge: Cambridge University Press.

Halstead, P.
1987   Traditional and ancient rural economy in Mediterranean Europe: plus ça change? *JHS* 107: 77–87.

1989   The economy has a normal surplus: economic stability and social change among early farming communities of Thessaly, Greece. In P. Halstead and J. O. 'Shea (eds.), *Bad Year Economics*: 68–80. Cambridge: Cambridge University Press.

1990   Waste not, want not: traditional responses to crop failure in Greece. *Rural History* 1: 147–64.

1992a   Agriculture in the Bronze Age Aegean: towards a model of palatial economy. In B. Wells (ed.), *Agriculture in Ancient Greece*: 105–16. Stockholm: Swedish Institute at Athens.

1992b   Dimini and the 'DMP': faunal remains and animal exploitation in Late Neolithic Thessaly. *BSA* 87: 29–59.

1994   The North-South divide: regional paths to complexity in prehistoric Greece. In C. Mathers and S. Stoddart (eds.), *Development and Decline in the Mediterranean Bronze Age*: 195–219. Sheffield: J.R. Collis.

1995   Late Bronze Age grain crops and Linear B ideograms *65, *120 and *121. *BSA* 90: 229–34.

1996   Pastoralism or household herding? Problems of scale and specialisation in early Greek animal husbandry. *World Archaeology* 28: 20–42.

1998   Mortality models and milking: problems of uniformitarianism, optimality and equifinality reconsidered. *Anthropozoologica* 27: 3–20.

1999   Texts, bones and herders: approaches to animal husbandry in Late Bronze Age Greece. *Minos* 33–34: 149–89.

1999a   Towards a model of Mycenaean palatial mobilization. In M.L. Galaty and W.A. Parkinson (eds.), *Rethinking Mycenaean Palaces*: 35–41. Los Angeles: Cotsen Institute of Archaeology, UCLA.

1999b   Surplus and share-croppers: the grain production strategies of Mycenaean palaces. In P. Betancourt, V. Karageorghis, R. Laffineur and W.-D. Niemeier (eds.), *MELE-THMATA. Studies Presented to Malcolm H. Wiener as he Enters his 65th Year* (Aegaeum 20): 319–26. Liège: Université de Liège.

1999c   Neighbours from hell: the household in Neolithic Greece. In P. Halstead (ed.), *Neolithic Society in Greece* (SSAA 2): 77–95. Sheffield: Sheffield Academic Press.

2000   Land use in postglacial Greece: cultural causes and environmental effects. In P. Halstead and C. Frederick (eds.), *Landscape and Land Use in Postglacial Greece* (SSAA 3): 110–28. Sheffield: Sheffield Academic Press.

2001   Mycenaean wheat, flax and sheep: palatial intervention in farming and its implications for rural society. In S. Voutsaki and J. Killen (eds.), *Economy and Politics in the Mycenaean Palace States* (Cambridge Philological Society Supplementary Volume 27): 38–50.

in press Faunal remains from FN-EH Nemea Tsoungiza: husbandry, butchery, consumption and discard of animals. In D. Pullen, *Nemea Valley Archaeological Project I: The Early Bronze Age Village on Tsoungiza Hill.* American School of Classical Studies at Athens.

Halstead, P., P. Collins and V. Isaakidou

2002   Sorting the sheep from the goats: morphological distinction between mandibles and mandibular teeth of adult *Ovis* and *Capra. JAS* 29: 545–53.

Halstead, P. and J. O'Shea

1982   A friend in need is a friend indeed: social storage and the origins of social ranking. In C. Renfrew and S. Shennan (eds.), *Ranking, Resource and Exchange*: 92–99. Cambridge: Cambridge University Press.

Hamilakis, Y.

1996   Wine, oil and the dialectics of power in bronze age Crete: a review of the evidence. *OJA* 15: 1–32.

2000   The anthropology of food and drink consumption and Aegean archaeology. In S.J. Vaughan and W.D.E. Coulson (eds.), *Palaeodiet in the Aegean*: 55–63. Oxford: Oxbow.

Hansen, J.M.

1988   Agriculture in the prehistoric Aegean: data versus speculation. *AJA* 92: 39–52.

Helmer, D.

2000   Discrimination des genres Ovis et Capra à l' aide des prémolaires inférieures 3 et 4 et interpretation des ages d' abattage; l' exemple de Dikili Tash (Grèce). *Anthropozoologica* 31: 29–38.

Higgs, E.S. (ed.)

1972   *Papers in Economic Prehistory.* London: Cambridge University Press.

Higgs, E.S. and M.R. Jarman

1975   Palaeoeconomy. In E.S. Higgs (ed.), *Palaeoeconomy*: 1–8. London: Cambridge University Press.

Hiller, S.

1988   Dependent personnel in Mycenaean texts. In M. Heltzer and E. Lipinski (eds.), *Society and Economy in the Eastern Mediterranean* (Orientalia Lovaniensia Analecta) 23: 53–68. Louvain.

Hillman, G.

1984   Interpretation of archaeological plant remains: ethnographic models from Turkey. In W. van Zeist and W.A. Casparie (eds.), *Plants and Ancient Man*: 1–41. Rotterdam: Balkema.

Hubbard, R.

1975   Assessing the botanical component of human palaeoeconomies. *Bulletin of the Institute of Archaeology* 12: 197–205.

Isaakidou, V.

2004   *Bones from the Labyrinth: Faunal Evidence for the Management and Consumption of Animals at Neolithic and Bronze Age Knossos, Crete.* PhD dissertation, University College London.

Isaakidou, V., P. Halstead, J. Davis and S. Stocker

2002   Burnt animal sacrifice at the Mycenaean 'Palace of Nestor', Pylos. *Antiquity* 76: 86–92.

Johnson, M.
  1996 Water, animals and animal technology: a study of settlement patterns and economic change in Neolithic southern Greece. *OJA* 15: 267–95.
Jones, G.
  1984 Interpretation of archaeological plant remains: ethnographic models from Greece. In W. van Zeist and W.A. Casparie (eds.), *Plants and Ancient Man*: 43–61. Rotterdam: Balkema.
  1987a A statistical approach to the archaeological identification of crop processing. *JAS* 14: 311–23.
  1987b Agricultural practice in Greek prehistory. *BSA* 82: 115–23.
  1988 The application of present-day cereal processing studies to charred archaeobotanical remains. *Circaea* 6: 91–96.
  1991 Numerical analysis in archaeobotany. In W. van Zeist, K. Wasylikowa and K. Behre (eds.), *Progress in Old World Palaeoethnobotany*: 63–80. Rotterdam: Balkema.
  1992a Ancient and modern cultivation of Lathyrus ochrus (L.) DC. in the Greek islands. *BSA* 87: 211–17.
  1992b Weed phytosociology and crop husbandry: identifying a contrast between ancient and modern practice. *Review of Palaeobotany and Palynology* 73: 133–43.
Jones, G., A. Bogaard, M. Charles and J. Hodgson
  2000 Distinguishing the effects of agricultural practices relating to fertility and disturbance: a functional ecological approach in archaeobotany. *JAS* 27: 1073–84.
Jones, G., A. Bogaard, M. Charles and H. Smith
  1999 Identifying the intensity of crop husbandry practices on the basis of weed floras. *BSA* 94: 167–89.
Jones, G. and P. Halstead
  1993 An early find of 'fava' from Thebes. *BSA* 88: 103–04.
Jones, G., S. Valamoti and M. Charles
  2000 A 'new' glume wheat from archaeological sites in northern Greece. *Vegetation History and Archaeobotany* 9: 133–46.
Killen, J. T.
  1983 PY An 1. *Minos* 18: 71–79.
  1984 The textile industries at Pylos and Knossos. In T.G. Palaima and C.W. Shelmerdine (eds.), *Pylos Comes Alive*: 49–63. New York: Lincoln Center, Fordham University.
  1985 The Linear B tablets and the Mycenaean economy. In A.M. Davies and Y. Duhoux (eds.), *Linear B: a 1984 Survey*: 241–305. Louvain: Louvain University Press.
  1993a Records of sheep and goats at Mycenaean Knossos and Pylos. *Bulletin on Sumerian Agriculture* 7: 209–18.
  1993b The oxen's names on the Knossos Ch tablets. *Minos* 27–28: 101–07.
  1994 Thebes sealings, Knossos tablets and Mycenaean state banquets. *BICS* 67–84.
  1996 Administering a Mycenaean kingdom: some taxing problems. *BICS* 41: 147–48.
  1998 The role of the state in wheat and olive production in Mycenaean Crete. *Aevum: Rassegna di Scienze Storiche Linguistiche e Filologiche* 72: 19–23.
  2001 Some thoughts on ta-ra-si-ja. In S. Voutsaki and J. Killen (eds.), *Economy and Politics in the Mycenaean Palace States* (Cambridge Philological Society Supplementary Volume 27): 69–115.
Knappett, C.
  1999 Assessing a polity in Protopalatial Crete: the Malia-Lasithi state. *AJA* 103: 615–39.
Krahtopoulou, A.

2000   Holocene alluvial history of northern Pieria, Macedonia, Greece. In P. Halstead and C. Frederick (eds.), *Landscape and Land Use in Postglacial Greece* (SSAA 3): 15–27. Sheffield: Sheffield Academic Press.

Mainland, I.
2003   Dental microwear in modern Greek ovicaprids: identifying microwear signatures associated with a diet of leafy hay. In E. Kotjabopoulou, Y. Hamilakis, P. Halstead, C. Gamble and P. Elefanti (eds.), *Zooarchaeology in Greece: Recent Advances*: 45–50. London: British School at Athens.

Mangafa, M. and K. Kotsakis
1996   A new method for the identification of wild and cultivated charred grape seeds. *JAS* 23: 409–18.

Moody, J.
1987   The Minoan palace as a prestige artifact. In R. Hägg and N. Marinatos (eds.), *The Function of the Minoan Palaces*: 235–41. Stockholm: Swedish Institute at Athens.

Olivier, J.-P.
1986   Cretan writing in the second millennium BC. *World Archaeology* 17: 377–89.

Palmer, R.
1989   Subsistence rations at Pylos and Knossos. *Minos* 24: 89–124.
1994   *Wine in the Mycenaean Palace Economy* (Aegaeum 10). Liège: Université de Liège.
1995   Linear A commodities: a comparison of resources. In R. Laffineur and W.-D. Niemeier (eds.), *Politeia: Society and State in the Aegean Bronze Age* (Aegaeum 12): 133–55. Liège: Université de Liège.

Pappa, M., P. Halstead, K. Kotsakis and D. Urem-Kotsou
2004   Evidence for large-scale feasting at Late Neolithic Makriyalos, N Greece. In P. Halstead and J. Barrett (eds.), *Food, Cuisine and Society* (SSAA 5). Oxford: Oxbow.

Payne, S.
1972   Partial recovery and sample bias: the results of some sieving experiments. In E.S. Higgs (ed.), *Papers in Economic Prehistory*: 49–64. London: Cambridge University Press.
1973   Kill-off patterns in sheep and goats: the mandibles from Asvan Kale. *Anatolian Studies* 23: 281–303.
1985a   Zoo-archaeology in Greece: a reader's guide. In N.C. Wilkie and W.D.E. Coulson (eds.), *Studies in Honor of William A. McDonald*: 211–44. Minneapolis: University of Minnesota Press.
1985b   Morphological distinctions between the mandibular teeth of young sheep, *Ovis*, and goats, *Capra*. *JAS* 12: 139–47.

Payne, S. and P.J. Munson
1985   Ruby and how many squirrels? The destruction of bones by dogs. In N.R.J. Fieller, D.D. Gilbertson and N.G.A. Ralph (eds.), *Palaeobiological Investigations – Research Design, Methods and Data Analysis* (BAR International Series 266): 31–40. Oxford: British Archaeological Reports.

Prummel, W. and H.-J. Frisch
1986   A guide for the distinction of species, sex and body side in bones of sheep and goat. *JAS* 13: 567–77.

Psikhogios, D.
1987   *Proikes, Foroi, Stafida kai Psomi: Oikonomia kai Oikogenia stin Agrotiki Ellada tou 19 Aiona.* Athens: Ethniko Kentro Koinonikon Erevnon.

Psikhogios, D. and G. Papapetrou
1984   Oi metakinisis ton nomadon ktinotrofon. *Epitheorisi Koinonikon Erevnon* 53: 3–23.

Reese, D.
  1994   Recent work in Greek zooarchaeology. In P.N. Kardulias (ed.), *Beyond the Site: Regional Studies in the Aegean Area*: 191–221. Lanham: University Press of America.
Renfrew, C.
  1972   *The Emergence of Civilisation: the Cyclades and the Aegean in the Third Millennium BC.* London: Methuen.
  1982   Polity and power. In C. Renfrew and M. Wagstaff (eds.), *An Island Polity. The Archaeology of Exploitation in Melos*: 264–90. Cambridge: Cambridge University Press.
Renfrew, J.
  1973   *Palaeoethnobotany.* London: Methuen.
Runnels, C. and J. Hansen
  1986   The olive in the prehistoric Aegean: the evidence for domestication in the Early Bronze Age. *OJA* 5: 299–308.
Sarpaki, A.
  2001   Processed cereals and pulses from the Late Bronze Age site of Akrotiri, Thera; preparations prior to consumption: a preliminary approach to their study. *BSA* 96: 27–40.
Sarpaki, A. and G. Jones
  1990   Ancient and modern cultivation of Lathyrus clymenum L. in the Greek islands. *BSA* 85: 363–68.
Schoep, I.
  1998   Sealed documents and data processing in Minoan administration: a review article. *Minos* 31–32 (for 1996–97): 401–15.
  1999   Tablets and territories? Reconstructing Late Minoan IB political geography through undeciphered documents. *AJA* 103: 201–21.
Shanks, M. and C. Tilley
  1987   *Reconstructing Archaeology: Theory and Practice.* Cambridge: Cambridge University Press.
Shelmerdine, C.W.
  1973   The Pylos Ma tablets reconsidered. *AJA* 77: 261–75.
  1999   Administration in the Mycenaean palaces: where's the chief? In M.L. Galaty and W.A. Parkinson (eds.), *Rethinking Mycenaean Palaces*: 19–24. Los Angeles: Cotsen Institute of Archaeology, UCLA.
Sherratt, A.
  1991   Palaeoethnobotany: from crops to cuisine. In F. Queiroga and A.P. Dinis (eds.), *Paleoecologia e Arqueologia* 2: 221–36. Vila Nova de Famalicao.
Sherratt, S.
  2001   Potemkin palaces and route-based economies. In S. Voutsaki and J. Killen (eds.), *Economy and Politics in the Mycenaean Palace States* (Cambridge Philological Society Supplementary Volume 27): 214–38.
Smith, H. and G. Jones
  1990   Experiments on the effects of charring on cultivated grape seeds. *JAS* 17: 317–27.
Smith, S.K.
  2000   Skeletal and dental evidence for social status in Late Bronze Age Athens. In S.J. Vaughan and W.D.E. Coulson (eds.), *Palaeodiet in the Aegean*: 105–13. Oxford: Oxbow.
Triantaphyllou, S.
  2001   *A Bioarchaeological Approach to Prehistoric Cemetery Populations from Central and Western Greek Macedonia* (BAR International Series 976). Oxford: British Archaeological Reports.

Tzedakis, Y. and H. Martlew (eds.)
  1999   *Minoans and Mycenaeans: Flavours of their Time*. Athens: Greek Ministry of Culture, National Archaeological Museum.
Urem-Kotsou, D., B. Stern, C. Heron and K. Kotsakis
  2002   Birch-bark tar at Neolithic Makriyalos, Greece. *Antiquity* 76: 962–67.
Valamoti, S.M.
  2002   Food remains from Bronze Age Archondiko and Mesimeriani Toumba in northern Greece? *Vegetation History and Archaeobotany* 11: 17–22.
Vitelli, K.D.
  1989   Were pots first made for food? Doubts from Franchthi. *World Archaeology* 21: 17–29.
Voutsaki, S.
  2001   Economic control, power and prestige in the Mycenaean world: the archaeological evidence. In S. Voutsaki and J. Killen (eds.), *Economy and Politics in the Mycenaean Palace States* (Cambridge Philological Society Supplementary Volume 27): 195–213.
Whitelaw, T.
  1983   The settlement at Fournou Korifi, Myrtos and aspects of Early Minoan social organization. In O. Krzyszkowska and L. Nixon (eds.), *Minoan Society*: 323–45. Bristol: Bristol Classical Press.
  2001   Reading between the tablets: assessing Mycenaean palatial involvement in ceramic production and consumption. In S. Voutsaki and J. Killen (eds.), *Economy and Politics in the Mycenaean Palace States* (Cambridge Philological Society Supplementary Volume 27): 51–79.
Whittle, A.
  1997   Moving on and moving around: neolithic settlement mobility. In P. Topping (ed.), *Neolithic Landscapes*: 15–22. Oxford: Oxbow.
Wright, J.C.
  1996   Empty cups and empty jugs: the social role of wine in Minoan and Mycenaean societies. In P.E. McGovern, S.J. Fleming and S.H. Katz (eds.), *The Origins and History of Wine*: 287–309. Philadelphia: Gordon and Breach.

11

Simplicity vs Complexity: Social Relationships and the MHI Community of Asine

Theodora Georgousopoulou

The *Emergence of Civilisation*, as is evident from its title, deals with the origins of the paradigm *par excellence* of social complexity – civilization. It espouses an evolutionary view of prehistory, according to which human societies are allocated to specific levels of advancement on the basis of the presence or absence of certain criteria (writing, monumental architecture, craft specialization). The Minoan palace, embodying an expansion of the physical and social environment, is seen to epitomize civilization, while a range of new material artifacts enriched symbolic expression (Renfrew 1972: 11–12). Craft specialization and population increase led to changed conceptions of human society and introduced radically new relationships between people. Pre-palatial societies (predating the emergence of civilization) are described as *simple* village economies; they displayed little or no evidence for social stratification and limited diversity in subsistence or craft production, while their social structure and the symbolic expression of their cosmology were undeveloped (Renfrew 1972: 52–53, 416–17). The aim of this chapter is to present a critique of this opposition between 'simple' and 'complex' societies, as expressed in the *Emergence of Civilisation*, and to argue that a different theoretical perspective may contribute to a richer understanding of society and social change in the Aegean Bronze Age.

'Simple' and 'Complex' Societies in the *Emergence of Civilisation*

It must be acknowledged that, in contrast with many previous and subsequent works, the *Emergence* offers explicit definitions of precisely what the writer means by various sociological terms. Civilization, however, as defined above, is equated with urban life (Renfrew 1972: 5), and value-judgements are made concerning the complexity of 'non-civilized' human societies. On the evolutionary ladder of social organization, 'savage' bands are characterized as assemblages of nuclear families, integrated by individual kinship alliances, while 'barbarian' tribes are regarded as simple, small-scale, independent, self-contained and homogenous, with a weak organization not solely based on kinship (Renfrew 1972: 363). Both bands and tribes are condemned to 'simplicity' by the absence of *hierarchy*, organized authority and political control such as is found in a 'chiefdom' or 'state' and is embodied by a chief (or prince or king) and noble elite.

In Renfrew's model, hierarchy and wealth go hand in hand, wealth bringing power and power bringing wealth. Power can thus be traced archaeologically, since wealth can be identified directly in the archaeological record (Renfrew 1972: 370). In this sense, Renfrew's criteria for the archaeological recognition of complexity, and thus for the evolutionary evaluation of human communities, are based on *depositional patterns*. Such patterns, however, are not passive reflections of social relationships. The absence of 'rich' grave-goods (funerary assemblages constitute Renfrew's main evidence) does not necessarily indicate that such objects were not in circulation. Funerary performances embody potent strategies for negotiating the identities of individuals, collectivities and whole communities and cannot be viewed in isolation from other such strategies in the everyday lives of people. Thus, treatment in death may not reflect reality, and sometimes deliberately so. To assume that all funerary practices, other than the most ostentatious, were an 'uncomplicated business' (Renfrew 1972: 427, 434), is unjustified.

On the Complexity of 'Simple' Societies

The point of contention here is not Renfrew's use of the term 'complex' for urban, hierarchical societies with clear-cut forms of political authority. What is contested is his uncritical attribution of the term 'simple' to closely-knit communities with few inhabitants and no clearly discernible 'pecking order' (as Renfrew puts it). Organizational roles for the management of everyday relationships and the obviation of tensions have always existed. How simple, then, is the management of roles within a 'simple' community, in a society seemingly lacking hierarchical traits?

At a local level, people with different and complementary identities may share not only common interests and a similar conception of appropriate behaviour, but also day-to-day use of the same space. Communication is intense and takes place in a wide range of activities (Cohen 1985; Emmett 1982). Life is further complicated by the fact that so much is public knowledge: people in a community are known to each other as family members, friends, ex-lovers, workers in a specific occupation, drinkers or non-drinkers, people who have quarrelled or kissed; and as people encounter each other in different situations, the picture continues to be enriched. More often than not, these various dimensions of social life are communicated and compared through gossip, so that there is little room for manoeuvres of self-presentation. Everything is known or discussed, and this lack of privacy can often be oppressive and constraining. How then is tension avoided, and how does the community retain its cohesion? Through the everyday interaction of community members and with the intervention of symbolic markers, institutions and ritual, a powerful sense of belonging and shared identity is created; through eating, gossiping, story-telling, joking, people bring each other up to date and participate in a continuous fashioning of themselves and their community.

Moreover, the absence of hierarchical structures does not mean the levelling of any vertical differentiation. Such a view would perceive power in terms only of control and subordination, arguably an oversimplification of social strategies, and would assume that power operates only on one level and resides in fixed places. Competing groups, self-defined as different, need not be absolutely equal: differences co-exist with similarities, and differentiation is always present. Strategies of identity negotiation are implemented by different but *equally* exclusive narrower identities. Differentiation and stratification are two different terms, but not necessarily mutually exclusive; rather, they are co-existing, intersecting strands of interaction integral to social relationships. In this sense, the seeds of inequality and of claims to superiority are always inherent, but voiced only on certain occasions.

This point may be clarified by considering a case study. Chronologically, the Middle Bronze Age of southern Greece postdates the emergence of civilization, as defined by Renfrew. Thanks, however, to the absence of rich finds and monumental buildings and thus to a lack of obvious evidence for social stratification, the Middle Helladic period in southern mainland Greece has earned many a derogatory adjective (e.g. 'the "Third World" of the Aegean' – Dickinson 1989: 133). The prehistoric community of MHI Asine, in the Argolid, may thus serve as a suitable case for illustrating the complexity of social identities, and of strategies for negotiating identity, within a seemingly 'simple' community.

MHI Asine

The settlement of Asine lies on the NW slope of the rocky promontory of Kastraki (Figure 11.1). For the MHI period (2050/2000–1950/1900 BC), the remains of two houses provide evidence for the usual household activities. More striking, however, is the existence of a plethora of graves (of men, women and children), built on top of, under and around houses (for details, see Frödin and Persson 1938; Nordquist 1987; 1996; Georgousopoulou 2003); the dead 'dwell' *among* the living. Grave types display a wide variety, from simple pits to cists and stone enclosures, with or without pebble floors and cover-stones. Offerings range from simple obsidian chips and clay whorls to the combination of bronze earrings and a jug (grave MH98 – Nordquist 1987: 93), while many graves were empty. Regardless of the simple and mundane character of most of the offerings, the mere fact that they were taken out of their everyday context, withdrawn from

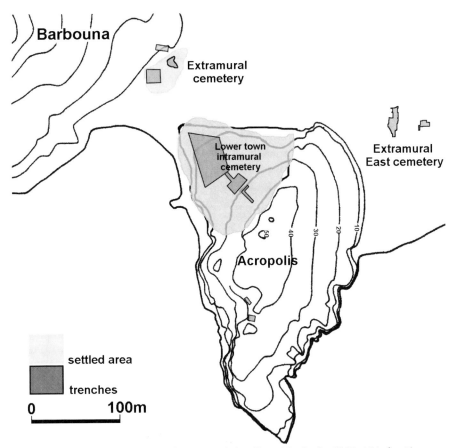

Figure 11.1. The MH settlement at Asine (from Nordquist 1987: 154, fig. 8)

circulation and deposited in graves, associated them forever with a uniquely performative activity, and with the specific identities of the person buried and of those participating in the burial. Therefore, they become 'valuable' in creating a lasting memory, a narrative of identities. Arguably, there was nothing un-complicated about the cosmology underlying the lack of 'rich' grave goods at MHI Asine.

It is striking that everyday life at Asine was so intrinsically associated, both spatially and conceptually, with the dead. The latter were encountered not only at the time of the funeral, or when specific activities occasionally brought the living inhabitants close to the burial place, but on an everyday and day-long basis; graves existed within, below and around houses, with no attempt to demarcate a distinct area even *within* the settlement reserved for burials. This practice cannot be attributed to lack of space, since abundant land existed all around the settlement. What is apparent is a lack of fear of contamination by the dead, since the same space was shared every day. One consequence of this close juxtaposition of the living and the dead is that building work, undeterred either by any extant grave-markers or by the discovery of a burial during the digging of foundations, often disturbed graves. This apparent disrespect or indifference to graves runs counter to the care taken in disposal of the body at the time of the funeral.

To understand this apparent contradiction in the treatment of the dead we must start by reminding ourselves that the choice of burial ground is not fortuitous. The dead, the burial places, the objects associated with them, as well as the performances at the time of the funeral, are vested with symbolic meaning; as such, they are a powerful tool for the negotiation of identities within the community, for the communication of the cosmology of the community and for the legitimation of relationships of power. The location of burials at MHI Asine, therefore, does not merely represent passive adherence to tradition, but rather a deliberate strategy: the living *wanted* the dead around them. Cemeteries and graves often serve as symbolic markers, demarcating the existence and solidarity of a group, the boundaries of identities, and also the boundaries of spaces. In Asine, however, where graves and houses were juxtaposed indiscriminately, what spaces could graves have demarcated? A plausible answer is that they demarcated property. The term property is not used here to denote private ownership of land, where land is the object of a transaction between people, but *traditional* land that is integral to the definition of a group – not as a possession, but as the essence of the group's identity. In this sense, areas of land may belong to groups in the same way as the groups themselves belong to the land. Such groups practise intra-mural burial as a strategy for the legitimation of claims of ownership, placing the dead within their plots as markers of traditional property. The spatial and conceptual boundaries are thus not between the dead and the living, but between traditional groups of *both dead and living.*

The practice of intra-mural burial, as a strategy for the legitimation of property, indicates a cosmology in which people at the time of death, after crossing the liminal threshold during the funeral, lost their individual persona and became collective dead, creating, maintaining and guarding the identity of groups. The dead were, therefore, benevolent and not the subject of fear or superstition, because with their death they became part of the collective identity, a property of the group. Accordingly, it was not the individual grave that should be respected and protected as the essence of their identity, but the land that the grave, as the ancestral spirit of tradition, legitimated. This form of burial brought together the past and the present in a dynamic relationship of interdependence and legitimation, with the living incorporating the distant life-stories and narratives of the dead into their present lives through constant and close interaction in the same spaces.

We may now reconsider the 'uncomplicated' nature of social relationships within the apparently 'simple' society of MHI Asine. From the variability evident in grave types and offerings, we can infer a widespread desire for differentiation, within the boundaries of the community, and to express group solidarity to other, spatially distinct groups. Yet, the differences between these different identities cannot have been great. The strategy for their expression, negotiation and legitimation was common to all groups within the community: the burial of the dead of each group in their specific plot. Burial exhibited a range of differences and a multitude of combinations, bordering on individuality of expression, but within the framework of a *uniform* practice. Competition and the need of groups to demarcate traditional land are evident, but there is no indication that any group was vying for a privileged position or seeking to express a particularly distinct identity. In this context, differentiation does not amount to vertical, stratified structures of authority and control; rather, it takes the form of horizontal and intersecting, but specific identities. This does not, however, imply the levelling of every perception of vertical relationships.

The intersection of vertical and horizontal relationships can be discerned in the distribution of habitation 'plots' within the settlement. The NW slope and the top of Kastraki are by no means uniform, and not only in the obvious sense of the variable suitability of the terrain for the construction of houses. Other factors that may have given meaning to specific locations within the settlement include proximity to the sea, an imposing view, seclusion from or proximity to the hub of interaction, associations with past performances and collective memories, and access to paths to certain everyday or exclusive activities. These specific, meaningful places may have become associated with distinct kin-groups, so that the threads of their different life-stories, identities, thereafter became entwined and inseparable. Nor will different kin-groups have been identical or equal: their distinct identities, their narratives, were formed by the individual life-stories of their members, marked by exceptional achievements in all kinds of activities, from hunting through cooking special recipes to the telling of stories and jokes. Land and kin-groups alike, with different characters and identities, were not stratified, but nor were they equal.

Conclusion

The example of MHI Asine illustrates how societies with no monumental buildings or stratified political structures may have been far from 'simple', in the sense that everyday practices could have been components of strategies for the demarcation, negotiation and maintenance of distinct identities. While tensions were obviated and balance maintained through a prevailing projection of uniformity and equality, threads of differentiation and competition will have run through the lives of people in intersecting vertical and horizontal relationships of interaction.

Complexity is not a matter of the presence or absence of objects, and simplicity is not inherent in the apparent lack of structures of authority. The maintenance of everyday life, with the interaction and negotiation of identities, is not simple for any member of any type of society. The study of all societies, therefore, including prehistoric societies, should not be concerned with simplicity or complexity, nor with the *degree* of complexity, but with the *kind* of complexity discernible in the evidence.

Bibliography

Cohen, A.P.
   1985   *The Symbolic Construction of Community*. London: Ellis Howood and Tavistock.
Dickinson, O.T.P.K.
   1989   'The Origins of Mycenaean Civilisation' revisited. In R. Laffineur (ed.), *Transition: le monde Egéen du Bronze Moyen au Bronze Récent* (Aegaeum 3): 131–6. Liège: Université de Liège.
Emmett, I.
   1982   Place, community and bilingualism at Blanau Ffestiniog. In A.P. Cohen (ed.), *Belonging: Identity and Social Organisation in British Rural Cultures*: 202–21. Manchester: Manchester University Press.
Frödin, O. and A.W. Persson
   1938   *Asine. The Results of the Swedish Excavations, 1922–1930*. Stockholm: A. Westholm.
Georgousopoulou, T.
   2003   *The Negotiation of Identity in MH Asine*. PhD dissertation, University of Sheffield.
Nordquist, G.C.
   1987   *A Middle Helladic Village. Asine in the Argolid* (Boreas 16). Uppsala: Academia Upsaliensis.
   1996   New information on old graves. In R. Hägg, G.C. Nordquist and B. Wells (eds.), *Asine III. Supplementary Studies on the Swedish Excavations 1922–1930*: 19–38. Stockholm: Svenska Institutet i Athens.
Renfrew, C.
   1972   *The Emergence of Civilisation: the Cyclades and the Aegean in the Third Millennium BC*. London: Methuen.

12

The House of the Tiles at Lerna: Dimensions of 'Social Complexity'

Olympia Peperaki

Introduction

Seeking to understand the origins of the palace-centred societies with reference to earlier developments in the wider Aegean region, Renfrew highlighted the Early Bronze Age on the Greek Mainland as a period 'of major change, when the foundations of civilisation were being laid' (1972: 99). More specifically, he was among the first to read an emergent social complexity in a series of developments of the second phase of the period (EHII or 'Korakou Culture' in his terminology).

Probably nowhere did this understanding find fuller support than in the House of the Tiles at Lerna (Figure 12.1). Excavated early in the 1950s, this structure was already famous, not only for its unusual dimensions and complex design, but also for a unique large collection of clay sealings from jars, boxes and baskets, recovered in a small compartment of the building. While a vague comparison to the Minoan-Mycenaean palatial structures was inescapable almost from the beginning (see Caskey 1955), for Renfrew the House of the Tiles foreshadowed the complex societies of the 'Minoan-Mycenaean civilization' in a more straightforward and concrete manner: to the extent that the sealings testified to the centralized management of the production and distribution of goods, this presumably public building represented the inception of institutions that he regarded as key to understanding the emergence of palatial complexity (Halstead 1988).

Over the past 30 years, the evolutionary premises and large-scale perspective of Renfrew's project have been seriously questioned on both factual and theoretical grounds (Pullen 1985; also Cherry 1984 and Manning 1994). Nonetheless, Renfrew's contribution had already set the terms of much subsequent inquiry into Early Helladic social organization. Indeed, the very questions asked of the material and the terminology used to address them echo the lingering effect of the conceptual framework established in the *Emergence*. Within this framework, the House of the Tiles, still the best preserved and documented

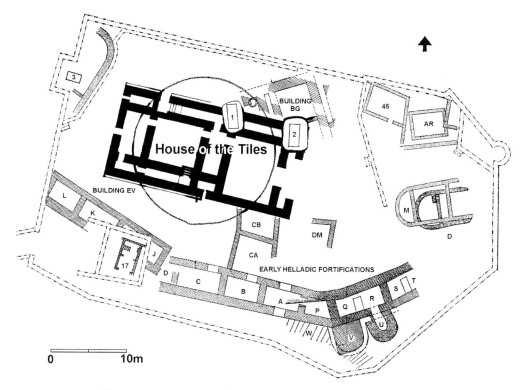

Figure 12.1. Lerna, area plan (adapted from Caskey 1958: 128, fig. 1)

example of the so-called 'corridor-house' type of structure (Shaw 1987), continues to be interrogated not simply as an index of a fundamental alteration in social organization, but as the architectural icon *par excellence* of the highest degree of complexity achieved by Early Helladic societies.

This continuing interest in the building has instigated, since the publication of the *Emergence*, a series of thorough and systematic analyses of its architecture and inventory, affording further important insights into its character and functions. This paper begins with an account of these empirical developments, first setting out those aspects of the evidence that have conventionally been granted analytical and interpretive emphasis and, secondly, spelling out the specific understandings that have thereby been promoted. The second part of the paper evaluates these understandings in the light of a series of observations, first on the architectural features and then on the inventory of the building. In the context of this evaluation, the building itself and the particular range of activities it hosted emerge less as the end result of an irreversible process towards social complexity, and more as a contribution towards its ongoing creation. This perspective provides a framework not only for challenging and refiguring existing

perceptions of 'social complexity', but also for achieving an enhanced understanding of the site of Lerna itself.

Architecture and Sealings: the Functions of the House of the Tiles

The idea that a more rounded understanding of the architecture may allow more
plausible inferences on the building's status and functions has caused recent
studies to expend considerable effort on recording details of construction,
describing formal features, and mapping modes of room interconnectedness.
These exercises eventually offered a corrective to the characterization of the
building as 'public'. In view of its restoration as a two-storey edifice with five
axially laid rooms on the ground-floor, narrow spaces (corridors) containing
staircases on the north and south, and a series of galleries or balconies on the
upper floor (Figure 12.2; see in particular Shaw 1987; 1990), it became possible to
distinguish between two distinct patterns of circulation in the building (Pullen
1986; Shaw 1987: 79). Moderating the initial impression of permeability generated
by the multiple (at least five) entrances to the ground-floor, such a reading drew
a distinction between spaces of *restricted access* (the rooms of the upper floor and
in particular its western half, accessible only from the interior of the House) and
more accessible rooms (the eastern part of the upper floor, accessible only from the
exterior, and especially Room 12, the largest room in the building, which was
carefully plastered and probably equipped with a central hearth – Pullen 1985:
171; Shaw 1987: 62). This understanding afforded an attractive solution, in that it
identified the provision of both 'private' and 'public' spaces, the former obviously
reserved for the privileged residents of the House (introducing thus a tangible
'elite' into the scene), the latter particularly suitable for activities that gathered
larger groups of people (Shaw 1987: 79).

The recently analysed (Wiencke 2000) ceramic deposit found in association
with the sealings provided a clue as to the possible nature of these 'collective'
activities. Vessels related to the preparation and serving of food and drink, along
with an unusually large number of individual saucers, seemed to represent the
(stored) paraphernalia of large-scale feasts – and where better to host them than
in the 'public' spaces of the house (Wiencke 2000: 651). The constituency of these
assemblies remained speculative, but if indeed one could imagine the building as
the abode of a higher order social group or even of a 'chief' (Wiencke 1989: 504–
05; also Pullen 1994), it seemed reasonable to propose that the attested hospitality
would be given to persons of equivalent rank and position with the residents of
the House. Such occasions therefore may well have involved 'the affirmation of
ties with [elite] groups from other similar sites' (Wiencke 2000: 651).

Obviously, this picture would remain frustratingly incomplete unless the
function and significance of the collection of sealings could be clarified. Renfrew's
basic idea that the sealings document 'the developing organisation of the

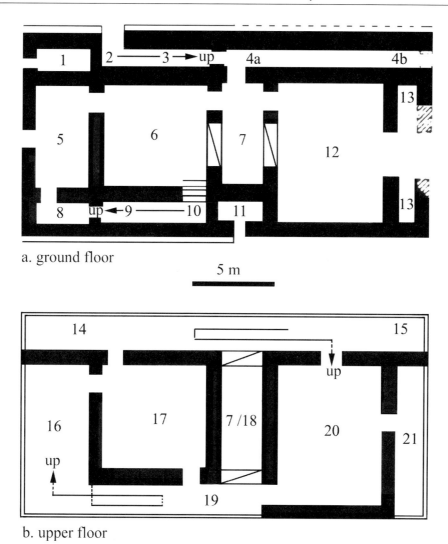

a. ground floor

5 m

b. upper floor

Figure 12.2. The House of the Tiles: plan of the ground floor and the upper storey (adapted from Shaw 1987: 62, Fig. 3a,b)

redistribution system' (Renfrew 1972: 482) has proven pervasive enough to be maintained in its essentials in a number of subsequent studies (Konsola 1984: 53; Pullen 1985; 1994; Renard 1995). While there was a certain measure of consensus over the identification of the sealings as playing 'a role in the community's management of resources' (Weingarten 1997: 149), the task of defining with greater precision the nature, scale, and operational details of the administrative system was a perfectly logical one (see Renard 1995: 292–94). To this end, the question, paraphrasing Weingarten (1997: 150), became 'what was sealed, by whom, when, and why?'

First of all, and as Heath's (1958) analysis had previously made clear, the particular types of containers sealed (chests or box-like containers and baskets, with only a very limited number of jars)[1] indicate that these goods were probably mainly dry (and some possibly manufactured – Renard 1995: 292) – rather than bulk foodstuffs (certainly not wine or oil and probably not grain – Weingarten 1997: 150). On the other hand, the high number of distinct seals identified (70), and the relative incidence of seal types and sealing types (*the same type of seal may occur on different types of container* and, conversely, one type of container may bear different seal impressions – see Heath 1958: 84–85 Table of Incidence) indicate individual seal owners (Heath 1958) rather than a centralized system using the seals to identify different types of goods. Finally, as the great majority of seals were used just once, and only some reused a limited number of times,[2] a non-intensive pattern of seal-use was inferred, better explained by 'non-resident seal owners sending a few sealed objects to the site' as opposed to resident seal-owners repeatedly sealing and unsealing on the spot (Weingarten 1997: 150). Such sealed goods (probably 'prestige' goods, subject by definition to 'elite' control – Wiencke 2000) most plausibly represent, therefore, either tribute to a chief residing at the House (see Pullen 1994 for a re-interpretation of the distributional system in terms of taxation) or, at least, 'property that was to be kept safe and made available to, or received from, persons who would not need (or be allowed?) to enter the house proper' (Wiencke 2000: 302). The problematic position of the sealings within a room accessible only from the exterior was thus also resolved.[3] If the nature of the sealing system itself, combined with the limited storage provision in the building (Halstead 1994), seemed to negate the operation of a sophisticated bureaucratic system for the control of subsistence commodities (Weingarten 1997; also Broodbank 2000: 283), then, as Weingarten argues, the sealings seemed to indicate 'an earlier stage of social and economic development' (1997: 149).

These analyses thus served to reaffirm, albeit with some corrections and additions, the picture originally provided by the *Emergence*. Given a clear architectural distinction between insiders and outsiders, evidence for control over the distribution of valuables, and provision for the hosting of public events that promote solidarity possibly at a regional, or inter-regional, level, the House both reflects well established asymmetries of wealth and power, and fulfils integrative functions at a wider geographical scale. It epitomizes, in other words, all the diagnostic features of 'an organized social system which ought to involve some degree of ranking' (Wiencke 2000: 651).

The identification of such functions not only served to highlight Lerna itself as an 'exceptional settlement that had moved up a notch in the scale of complexity' (Weingarten 1997: 148); it was guided by, and implicitly reproduced, particular expectations about the position that such a site would assume within a broader political geography, the range of activities that it should exhibit, and the types of material traces by which those activities should be archaeologically identifiable (see also Cherry 1984; Hägg and Konsola 1986: 101).

With more recent and detailed analyses now available, this prevailing understanding of complexity can now be subjected to closer scrutiny. A series of simple observations on both the architectural elements of the building and its exceptional inventory allow an interpretation less encumbered by the imposition of pre-conceived categories on the material, and more revealing of the manifold material possibilities and explicit strategies by which different social 'realities' could have been produced and reworked.

The Architectural Setting Reconsidered

Positing two essentially autonomous entities, the private and the public, the current reading of the architecture projects the image of an inherently fragmented space, in which societal organization is inscribed. This understanding may have registered some progress over previous analyses, but there is much more to the private-public distinction than is suggested by the seemingly mutually exclusive nature of these categories (Giddens 1985: 278). Indeed, such a *straightforward* and *static* distinction risks losing sight of one of the building's most important characteristics: the potential use of different architectural features in ways that not only enabled the ordering of *multiple, temporally specific* settings for interaction, but also placed particular emphasis on the *transition* from one setting to another.

The starting point for this contention is the possibility that at least some of the doors could also close. Interestingly, the only secure evidence for wooden jambs relates to the three doors that afford access to the 'public' zones of the building (Pullen 1985: 172; 1986: 79; Caskey 1955: plate 19b): the external northern entrance leading to Corridor 2–4 (and thence to the eastern part of the upper floor); the inner doorway from Anteroom 13 to Room 12; and the doorway in the northwestern corner of Room 12 (Figure 12.3). This possibility of isolating Room 12 also from the interior of the House is reinforced not only by the offset position of the inner doorway (which inhibits long views inside the House), but also by the unique raised threshold testified at this position (Pullen 1985: 172), which functioned as a clear transition point crossed by those leaving (or entering) the room. We may thus envisage the use of doors not only to control access, and to isolate and segregate spaces (Foster 1989; see also Palyvou 1987), but also to facilitate the *temporal* organization of different sections of the building (Giddens 1984: 121); that is, to define circulation or interaction that would be both space- and time-specific.

The potential of the architecture to create a series of graded or intersecting levels of communication becomes even more evident when we consider the dynamic and multifarious modes of articulation of the *interior* of the building to

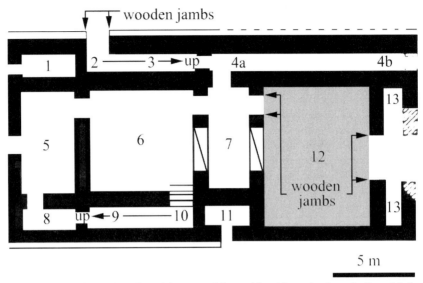

Figure 12.3. The House of the Tiles: plan of the ground floor with evidence for doors indicated (adapted from Shaw 1987:62, fig. 3a; Pullen 1986: fig. 34)

the *exterior*, equipped with benches and designed to receive people (Figure 12.4). These two categories do not reflect hermetically separated domains of activity, since a number of distinctive architectural elements enabled and ensured *transfer* from one category to the other (Lawrence 1990: 76). It is significant, in this sense, that those *within* the building could have monitored, regulated, or participated in what was taking place outside in various ways: by *occasionally* opening the doors of the main entrance to go out or to receive (at least some) people into the front room; by using the stairs of the northern corridor to *come down* to the exterior space; or by using the upstairs balconies, from which they could both see and be seen by those standing in the open space.

It is also important that the architectural elements employed in expanding and, if required, modifying the conditions of interaction (doors, narrow corridors, stairways, thresholds, and balconies) also served to *sharpen* the effect of these modifications. The spatial organization not only enabled a particular zoning and partitioning of activities, but may also have provided formal cueing devices for their framing, serialization, and punctuation (see Goffman 1974: 252; also Giddens 1985: 274). The formal opening and closing of a door, the appearance of a person on a balcony or the crossing of a threshold, both served to bracket off different contexts of interaction ('encounters' or 'regionally bounded episodes'), but also placed particular emphasis on the *transition* from one such context to another.

The first conclusion to draw from the above is the potential to achieve *multiple* levels of differentiation. Where previous approaches established a simple and

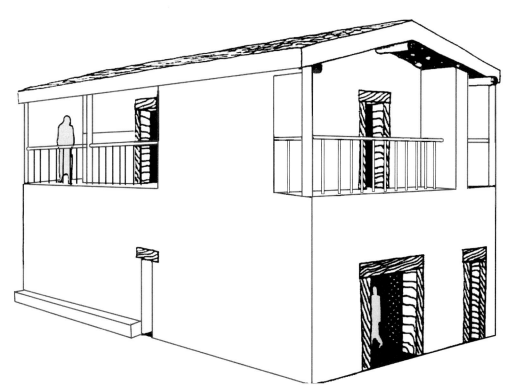

Figure 12.4. Perspective view of the House of the Tiles as seen from the southeast (after Shaw 1987: 64, fig. 5)

static insiders-outsiders distinction, we can envisage principles of inclusion-exclusion ranging from access to the mound, through involvement in what was taking place in the exterior space, to admission to the front room (note also the sequenced, gradual movement through Antechamber 13) or further inside.

Secondly, this was more than a simple distribution of people among the spaces defined architecturally. And indeed, while the architectural elements may have ensured that encounters were sustained in different parts of the building without intruding upon one another, they also enabled their interface and interconnection. Keeping this flexibility, mutability and temporal contingency of boundaries in focus allows us to dispense with a view of 'private' and 'public' as given categories that existed prior to interaction. The definition of these categories, of what *on each occasion* would become visible or accessible (and for whom), and of what would remain or be rendered out of bounds and shielded from view, is most plausibly seen as an ongoing process, constituted *in* interaction and thereby open to redefinition and negotiation.

The third point follows from the foregoing. If the spaces of the building can be regarded as providing the locus of such situated and often conflicting interpretations, then we can begin to look more closely at the relations of power that could have been spun out across these contexts. This is important because each of these contexts of interaction not only indicated (and constrained) the way people could have moved and operated within it, but also imposed a relative spatial positioning of participants which may often have privileged different relations among them. The balconies, for example, would have enabled the direct observation or even supervision of the conduct of those standing below them (see Giddens 1985), a spatial relation quite different from anything allowed for by previous or contemporary architectural configurations. Or, to take this a step further, the mound itself, on which the House was built, enabled activities staged outside to be not only physically separated from their surroundings but also, if the earlier fortification system had indeed been obliterated by this time, conspicuous at a distance. Such asymmetries indeed contrast strongly with the sense of community generated by the open or 'public' spaces of the house. And, as will be argued further below, it is probably from this very potential to create and blur multiple distinctions, and occasionally to separate or unify different groups of practitioners, that the building may have derived part of its significance.

Such observations allow us to think of the architecture less as the fossilized imprint of pre-existing social distinctions or as the product of 'a differentiated ranking of the community' (Wiencke 1989: 505) and more as the referent against which, and by means of which, such distinctions could be effectively reproduced by being practised (Barrett 1990; also 1994: 29–32).

Occupying the House of the Tiles: the Activities

What kind of activities could have been deemed possible and appropriate within this setting? As most of the rooms were found virtually empty,[4] such an understanding has inevitably built almost exclusively on the contents of the small Compartment 11, often to the extent that the activities inferred from this assemblage have been conceived as integral to the identity and function of the building over a considerable span of time. At the very least this necessitates some reflection on both the exact nature of those activities and the time scale over which they were performed.

Curiously enough, and although considerable energy has been directed towards examining the two elements of the assemblage (i.e. sealings and ceramics) as separate sources of information, their relationship has hardly been probed. An association between the collection of sealings and ceramics was of course implied by their deposition together in the small Compartment 11. Given the framework of study, however, this could only lead to the proposition that both the sealed 'prestige' goods and the pottery were *supplies* for the occasional gatherings held in the public rooms of the building (Wiencke 2000). This series of hastily made pots sits somewhat uncomfortably in such exceptional occasions, however, and becomes even more surprising when set against examples from earlier deposits at the site, which exhibit a persistent investment in the presentation and consumption of food and drink. The proposition of a (chronologically significant?) emphasis on undecorated, mass-produced pottery (Wiencke 2000) may describe, but hardly explains how such a remarkably different assemblage fits into such consumption events.

An important issue is the time scale represented by the deposit. Implicit in most accounts is the repetitive nature of these ('administrative', 'central') activities represented by the sealings and the ceramics – a necessary assumption to any attempt to read *institutionalized* inequality into the building. As a result, the deposit of sealings has been understood as the product of a series of discrete episodes of deposition – even if this could not have stretched over more than 'a few years', given that the great majority (53 out of 70) of seals were used just once, or 'perhaps only a few months if foodstuffs or other perishable goods were stored there' (Pullen 1994: 47). This limited temporal depth of the deposit of sealings seems also to accord well with the remarkable homogeneity of the ceramic assemblage, most of which does not seem to be the result of gradual and varied accumulation (Wiencke 2000; for a similar argument, see Day and Wilson 2002: 149).

In reality, however, the evidence may hint at an even shorter span of use. First, even in the case of 'repetitive' contributions (i.e. the cases of repeated use of the same seal), there is no reason to suppose that these were made over successive intervals of time – *contra* Pullen 1994: 47).[5] Secondly, the ceramic deposit seems to consist of pots which, if not *produced,* were at least *selected* and *assembled* for the requirements of a particular occasion. In the case of saucers, the standardization in surface treatment (predominance of plain surfaces) is further underscored by equivalences in size and proportions, which furthermore cross-cut the morphological variations (types 1 and 2) indicated by typological analysis (Wiencke 2000). More specifically, the saucers from this room fall into both of the types distinguished in the ceramic corpus of Lerna on the basis of formal details (differences in the modelling of the base and rim) and height/rim diameter ratio (type 2 saucers being generally shallower). Comparison with Type 1 and 2 saucers from several other deposits from the site, however, reveals that Type 2 saucers in Room 11 of the House of the Tiles exhibit a restricted range of dimensions particularly close to that of Type 1 saucers (Figure 12.5).

If the ceramic deposit represents such an occasion-specific category, a 'category of use' in other words, then the hitherto unnoticed comparability in the number of seals represented among the sealings (70) and the number of individual vessels (62 saucers catalogued, originally probably as many as 77) may be more than an intriguing coincidence. This correspondence, given the common locus of deposition, suggests that the *offering* of goods and the eating event may have involved the same people. It also raises the possibility that just *a single event* is represented in the deposit.

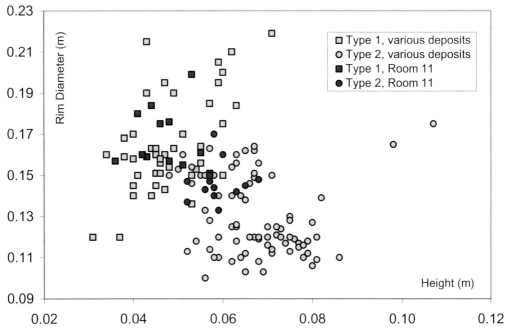

Figure 12.5. Height/rim diameter scatter-plot of Lerna III saucers (data from Wiencke 2000)

Further comparison of the two assemblages reveals a shared emphasis on (conspicuous) *exchange* and *consumption* (i.e transformation – see Gell 1986: 112) rather than on the *accumulation* of goods: not only are storage vessels virtually non-existent, but also there is no secure evidence that the sealed goods themselves were stockpiled in Room 11. As practically nothing survives of these goods, it has been assumed that they were either perishable or looted before the destruction of the house (Pullen 1985: 282; Wiencke 2000: 302). The possibility that only the sealings were kept in this room (Stewart 1988; also Renard 1995: 295) has been less widely accepted, although this receives some support not only from the limited storage capacity of the room, but also from the fact that most of the sealings seem to have been broken *before* the fire that destroyed the building (Heath 1958: 81). In view of this latter observation, the possibility cannot be excluded that some of those objects circulated during the event, by being displayed or used (see Renard 1995: 292, for the possibility that the sealings may represent *direct* exchanges supervised or administered by the House). It may be significant in this respect that 'contributions' could have included provisions for the feast (all sealed jars are of moderate size and hence portable).

The possibility of collapsing the two transactions (i.e. the offering of goods and communal eating and drinking) into a *single* event accommodated *at some point* by the building[6] may open up new interpretive possibilities. Most importantly, it allows us to chart the synchronized convergence of persons and things in the production and structuring of a context of action (Pred 1984: 282; Thomas 1996: 162). Reflecting upon the structure, the performance, and the means of execution of the transactions represented by sealings and pots can therefore be promising, revealing as it is of the meaningful contribution of each aspect of this context's materiality in the structuring of action.

The association of the unfolding of such an event with one particular segment of the architecture must remain speculative (although, given its scale and locus of deposition it does seem more plausibly connected with the exterior space). It is instructive, nonetheless, to think of the event in terms of what Appadurai has called a 'tournament of value' (1986: 21), a context of practice providing the resources not simply for the 'intercalibration of the biographies of people and things' (1986: 22) but for their very production (Strathern 1992). Let us first of all consider the offering of sealed goods. It is difficult not to see in the act of sealing itself a forceful statement, ensuring that attention would be drawn to the background of particular materials, persons, skills and relations involved in the history of the object offered.[7] Moreover, although the vast majority of seals had been used only once, the few instances of repeated occurrence of the same seal do imply differences in the quantities of goods offered, which, whether imposed or motivated by a kind of 'competitive generosity', did emphasize distinctions between contributors.

Such potential for the emergence of, and competition between, distinct identities, as provided by the transfer of materials, is negated by the communal eating and drinking: individual vessels provide no field for differentiation either in terms of appearance (quite similar, unpainted and rapidly made) or in terms of food and/or drink apportionment (similar capacities). Even within the homogenizing effects of this previously unattested uniformity of vessels used for food and drink *consumption*, however, distinct roles may still have been allowed for by a formality in the *service* of food (see Wiessner 2001; also Sørensen 2000; Visser 1991). For this stage of the commensal cycle, vessels were employed which provided focal points both by privileging a specific positioning of participants towards the suppliers of food and drink and by involving a series of formalized gestures in their manipulation. This refers not only to ladling from potentially static basins, but also to the main pouring vessels, the sauceboats. The morphological features of the latter (an unstable shape) imposed a physical manipulation requiring both hands and slow and controlled movements to avoid spilling of contents, that may have discouraged their being passed around, instead favouring their use by specific persons in charge of serving.

What may have taken place at the mound, therefore, not only drew together, connected and juxtaposed people, materials and the places from which these originated; it also afforded the context for evoking, addressing, and contesting these links in double-edged transactions that enabled conflicting claims to authority, and provided a range of material resources with which to ground and reinforce the enactment of these claims.

Concluding Comments

In the context of the foregoing observations, the building itself, as a distinct location, and the particular activities it accommodated – at least at a particular stage in its life – emerge less as the culmination of some irreversible process towards ranking or inequality and more as a locus of ongoing contests and conflicts (and of the efforts to prevent, suppress or repress them). Insofar as 'complexity' retains interpretive prominence, this alternative understanding enables us to explore it in more elaborate – and potentially more fruitful – ways than those allowed for by singular models of hierarchy. A sense of complexity 'in the making' is evoked, that is contingent on expedient and strategic action. Such complexity arises not simply from the drawing of lines between social categories, but more essentially from the provision of ways in which some of those boundaries could at times be crossed or even blurred. It is achieved by establishing a co-operative atmosphere ('outbursts of togetherness' to paraphrase Bauman 1992: xix), while also leaving room for skillful and timely demonstrations of authority, and by allowing competing interpretations and constructions of social reality.

The House of the Tiles now emerges as what it may have been – a 'multiplex interpretive site' (Appadurai 1995: 209), which both provided the frames or settings within which various forms of human action could be initiated and conducted meaningfully, and was itself evaluated and defined by means of this action. In this way, we may also move beyond the static image of Lerna as a 'central place' *dominating* a territory, in favour of a *place* to and from which different people may have moved to fulfill particular needs or *obligations* and to promote and pursue different *aspirations*. The possibility is afforded, in this respect, to follow the *constitution* of a place as a context-contingent process (Pred 1984), which formalizes and foregrounds a particular set of relations (which are of significance to a particular situation) while moving others into the background.

What made the House of the Tiles an appropriate place for the negotiation of such relations may be seen harking back to and building upon earlier patterns of occupation of the mound, and in particular in the previous phase of the period under consideration (Lerna IIIC), stratigraphically defined by the construction of the fortification system and the first 'monumental' building (Building BG). The (collective?) labour requirements for the building and maintenance of a series of substantial constructions, the patterns of sealing activity from deposits of this phase (repeated sealing, opening and resealing of possibly the same storage vessels by as many as eight different seals in Room DM), and the variable fabrics of a large percentage of the 'common tableware' employed at the site (Attas *et al.* 1987; Betancourt and Myer 2000) may indicate not only a pronounced long-term commitment to a particular locale, but also a place that may have attracted different people at different times and for different reasons.

To what extent activities at the House of the Tiles demonstrate an attempt to build upon, appropriate or redefine such perceptions of the mound remains an interesting question. It may also at least partly hold the key to understanding how the brief episode arguably represented by the much discussed contents of Room 11 drew creatively upon practices with a much longer history, as well as being defined in relation and by reference to actions of a wider spatial extent (see Munn 1990; Giddens 1984: 142, 298; Gregory 1994: 97–99; Moore 1987).

This possibility provides a clear riposte to Sherratt's (1993: 126; see also Thomas 1996: 96–97) argument that a recent focus on the transient and the local has caused much archaeological analysis to become far too myopic; for such occurrences, far from being surface disturbances that divert attention away from some underlying 'real' pattern (as Braudel would put it), were active parts of a continuous process of uncertain outcome (Moore 1987); particular moments where things were made possible, reinvented, debated, reinterpreted. It is probably by pursuing such questions that we may go some way to understanding how particular activities at this famous Early Helladic site not only became historically possible, but could ultimately acquire their distinctive character – what makes Lerna 'special'.

Acknowledgements

The paper is based on research undertaken for my PhD dissertation in the University of Sheffield. I would like to thank my supervisors J.C. Barrett and P. Halstead for inviting me to the conference and for their very useful comments on drafts of my paper, though responsibility for all conclusions lies with myself. Many thanks to Michalis Catapotis for his constant support and help with the illustrations and to Despina Catapoti and Maria Relaki for many fruitful discussions.

Endnotes

1   There is some disagreement as to whether all the Type B sealings come from boxes; see the argument that at least some may have come from doors (Weingarten 1997).

2   As Weingarten (1997: 150) puts it, 'the three most active seal-owners together stamped less than 20% of the sealings, whereas the least active seal owners together accounted for over 60% of all sealings'.

3   That both the ceramics and the clay sealings were originally deposited or stored within this room prior to the destruction of the building by fire (and had not fallen from the upper floor as suggested by Pullen 1985), has been recently confirmed by a more careful study of the state of preservation and the find spots of both the ceramic material and the

sealings. Neither the pots nor the sealings were widely scattered, as one would have expected if they had fallen from an upper room. Moreover, some of the vessels either were preserved intact or could be mended from the fragments recovered from the room (Wiencke 2000: 235).

4   The possibility has been raised that the building may have been looted or deliberately cleared before the fire that destroyed it (Wiencke 2000: 301). If so, we may be dealing with a quite selective picture of the inventory of the building, a deliberately created assemblage deposited within a purposefully selected part of the building. Either way, the building seems to have been occupied for some time before its destruction, as suggested by the scanty pottery and small finds from the other rooms.

5   The possibility of successive seal-use is raised by the suggestion (based on a brief inspection of the sealings by Fiandra early in the 1970s, and recently presented in Weingarten 1996, 1997; see also the discussion in Aruz 1994) that all the 'Type B' sealings may come from only three containers or objects. Judging from Weingarten's reports, a basic problem is the homogeneity of the groups of sealings which represent the three distinct containers. This is certainly the case for the first (and by far the largest) group which 'could not be further subdivided', yet '*includes,* but is not necessarily limited to sealings on a conical wooden pommel' (Weingarten 1997: 152, emphasis added). Whether such inconsistencies in the description reflect the preliminary nature of these observations or difficulties inherent in this kind of analysis, they do serve to raise some uncertainty as to the weight of the evidence. Also, one cannot help wondering whether the speculated existence of some fixed containers within the room is in fact more influenced by Near Eastern or other Aegean parallels than based on unambiguous evidence from the assemblage itself. In this sense, the alternative explanation of fairly standardised containers (accounting for the similarities in the impressions left on the sealings) and, by extension, the representation by Type B sealings of a rather larger number of containers, cannot at present be dismissed.

6   For an ethnographically attested example of such 'ceremonial' exchange, involving the transfer of goods in large public gatherings, followed by the presentation of a feast, see Thomas 1991: 59–65.

7   Statements of a particular identity are preserved in the 'exceptional' instances of joint sealing (pairs of seals on the same sealing – Weingarten 1997: 153), with two or more people connected in the offering of one object.

Bibliography

Appadurai, A.
    1986   Introduction: commodities and the politics of value. In A. Appadurai (ed.), *The Social Life of Things: Commodities in Cultural Perspective*: 3–63. Cambridge: Cambridge University Press.
    1995   The production of locality. In R. Fardon (ed.), *Counterworks: Managing the Diversity of Knowledge*: 204–25. London: Routledge.
Aruz, J.
    1994   Seal imagery and sealing practices in the early Aegean world. In P. Ferioli, E. Fiandra, G.G. Fissore and M. Frangipane (eds.), *Archives before Writing, Proceedings of the International Colloquium Oriolo Romano*: 211–35. Rome.
Attas, M., J.M. Fossey and L. Yaffe
    1987   An archaeometric study of Early Bronze Age pottery production and exchange in Argolis and Corinthia, Greece. *Journal of Field Archaeology* 14: 77–90.

Barrett, J.C.
   1990   The monumentality of death: the character of Early Bronze Age mortuary mounds in southern Britain. *World Archaeology* 22: 179–89.
   1994   *Fragments from Antiquity: an Archaeology of Social Life in Britain, 2000–1200 B.C.* Oxford: Blackwell.
Bauman, Z.
   1992   *Intimations of Postmodernity*. London: Routledge.
Betancourt, P. and G. Myer
   2000   Petrographic examination of pottery samples from Lerna III. In M. Wiencke, *Lerna IV: the Architecture, Stratification, and Pottery of Lerna III*: 680–703. Princeton (NJ): American School of Classical Studies at Athens.
Broodbank, C.
   2000   *An Island Archaeology of the Early Cyclades*. Cambridge: Cambridge University Press.
Caskey, J.L.
   1955   The House of the Tiles at Lerna. *Archaeology* 8: 116–20.
   1958   Excavations at Lerna 1957. *Hesperia* 27: 125–44.
Cherry, J.F.
   1984   The emergence of the state in the prehistoric Aegean, *PCPS* 30: 18–48.
Day, P.M. and D.E. Wilson
   2002   Landscapes of memory, craft and power in Prepalatial and Protopalatial Knossos. In Y. Hamilakis (ed.), *Labyrinth Revisited*: *Rethinking Minoan Archaeology*: 142–66. Oxford: Oxbow.
Foster, S.M.
   1989   Analysis of spatial patterns in buildings (access analysis) as an insight into social structure: examples from the Scottish Atlantic Iron Age. *Antiquity* 63: 40–50.
Gell, A.
   1986   Newcomers into the world of goods: consumption among the Muria Gonds. In A. Appadurai (ed.), *The Social Life of Things: Commodities in Cultural Perspective*: 110–38. Cambridge: Cambridge University Press.
Giddens, A.
   1984   *The Constitution of Society: Outline of the Theory of Structuration*. Cambridge and Berkeley: University of California Press.
   1985   Time, Space, Regionalisation. In D. Gregory and J. Urry (eds.), *Social Relations and Spatial Structures*: 265–95. London: Macmillan.
Goffman, E.
   1974   *Frame Analysis: an Essay on the Organisation of Experience*. New York: Harper and Row.
Gregory, D.
   1994   Social theory and human geography. In D. Gregory, R. Martin and G. Smith (eds.), *Human Geography: Society, Space, and Social Science*: 78–109. London: MacMillan.
Hägg, R. and D. Konsola
   1986   Conclusions and prospects. In R. Hägg and D. Konsola (eds.), *Early Helladic Architecture and Urbanization* (*SIMA* 76): 95–101. Göteborg: Paul Åström.
Halstead, P.
   1988   On redistribution and the origin of Minoan-Mycenaean palatial economies. In E.B. French and K.A. Wardle (eds.), *Problems in Greek Prehistory*: 519–30. Bristol: Bristol Classical Press.
   1994   The north-south divide: regional paths to complexity in prehistoric Greece. In C. Mathers and S. Stoddart (eds.), *Development and Decline in the Mediterranean Bronze Age*: 195–219. Sheffield: J.R. Collis.

Heath, M.C.
    1958   Early Helladic clay sealings from the House of the Tiles at Lerna. *Hesperia* 27: 81–120.
Konsola, D.
    1984   *I Proïmi Astikopoïïsi stous Protoelladhikous Oikismous: Sistimatiki Analisi ton Kharaktiristikon tis.* Athens.
Lawrence, R.J.
    1990   Public collective and private space: a study of urban housing in Switzerland. In S. Kent (ed.), *Domestic Architecture and the Use of Space: an Interdisciplinary Cross-Cultural Study*: 73–91. Cambridge: Cambridge University Press.
Manning, S.
    1994   The emergence of divergence: development and decline on Bronze Age Crete and the Cyclades. In C. Mathers and S. Stoddart (eds.), *Development and Decline in the Mediterranean Bronze Age*: 221–70. Sheffield: J.R. Collis.
Moore, S.F.
    1987   Explaining the present: theoretical dilemmas in processual anthropology. *American Ethnologist* 14(4): 727–51.
Munn, N.
    1990   Constructing regional worlds in experience: kula exchange, witchcraft and Gawan local events. *Man* 25: 1–17.
Palyvou, C.
    1987   Circulatory patterns in Minoan architecture. In R. Hägg and N. Marinatos (eds.), *The Function of the Minoan Palaces*: 195–203. Stockholm: Svenska Institutet i Athen.
Pred, A.
    1984   Place as historically contingent process: structuration and the time-geography of becoming places. *Annales of the Association of American Geographers* 74: 279–97.
Pullen, D.J.
    1985   *Social Organization in Early Bronze Age Greece: A Multi-dimensional Approach.* PhD dissertation, Indiana University.
    1986   A 'House of Tiles' at Zygouries? The function of monumental Early Helladic architecture. In R. Hägg and D. Konsola (eds.), *Early Helladic Architecture and Urbanization* (SIMA 76): 79–84. Göteborg: Paul Åström.
    1994   A lead seal from Tsoungiza, ancient Nemea, and Early Bronze Age sealing systems. *AJA* 98: 35–52.
Rénard, J.
    1995   *Le Peloponnese au Bronze Ancien* (Aegaeum 13). Liège: Université de Liège.
Renfrew, C.
    1972   *The Emergence of Civilization: the Cyclades and the Aegean in the Third Millennium B.C.* London: Methuen.
    1974   Beyond a subsistence economy: the evolution of social organisation in prehistoric Europe. In C.B. Moore (ed.), *Reconstructing Complex Societies* (Supplement to the Bulletin of the American Schools of Oriental Research 20): 69–95. Ann Arbor.
Shaw, J.W.
    1987   The Early Helladic II corridor house: development and form. *AJA* 91: 59–79.
    1990   The Early Helladic II corridor house: problems and possibilities. In P. Darcque and R. Treuil (eds.), *L' Habitat Egéen Préhistorique* (BCH Supplementary Volume 19): 183–94. Paris: École Française d' Athènes.
Sherratt, A.
    1993   The relativity of theory. In N. Yoffee and A. Sherratt (eds.), *Archaeological Theory: Who Sets the Agenda?* 119–30. Cambridge: Cambridge University Press.

Sørensen, M-L.S,
   2000   *Gender Archaeology*. London: Polity Press.
Stewart, S.T.
   1987   Bureaucracy and packaging at Lerna: evidence from the clay sealings in the House of
           the Tiles (abstract). *AJA* 92: 253.
Strathern, M.
   1992   Qualified value: the perspective of gift-exchange. In C. Humphrey and S. Hugh-
           Jones (eds.), *Barter, Exchange and Value: An Anthropological Approach*: 169–91.
           Cambridge: Cambridge University Press.
Thomas, J.
   1996   *Time, Culture and Identity: an Interpretive Archaeology*. London and New York:
           Routledge.
Thomas, N.
   1991   *Entangled Objects: Exchange, Material Culture and Colonialism in the Pacific*. London:
           Harvard University Press.
Visser, M.
   1991   *The Rituals of Dinner: the Origins, Evolution, and Eccentricities of Table Manners*. London:
           Viking.
Weingarten, J.
   1997   Another look at Lerna: an EHIIB trading post? *OJA* 16(2): 147–66.
Wiencke, M.H.
   1989   Change in Early Helladic II. *AJA* 93: 495–509.
   2000   *Lerna IV: the Architecture, Stratification, and Pottery of Lerna III*. Princeton (NJ): American
           School of Classical Studies at Athens.
Wiessner, P.
   2001   Of feasting and value: Enga feasts in historical perspective (Papua New Guinea). In
           M. Dietler and B. Hayden (eds.), *Feasts: Archaeological and Ethnographic Perspectives on
           Food, Politics, and Power*: 115–43. Washington and London: Smithsonian Institution
           Press.

13

Alternative Pathways to Complexity in the Southern Aegean

Todd Whitelaw

Introduction

The most radical argument of *The Emergence of Civilisation* was that the development of the state was an endogenous process within the Aegean, and owed little or nothing to antecedents in the Eastern Mediterranean. By providing an alternative to the diffusionist assumptions of previous research, Aegean archaeologists, for the first time, had to engage explicitly with theories of early state formation. Regardless of how one debates the details, this is a fundamental and lasting legacy of the *Emergence*.

In this paper, I want to look critically at a group of assumptions which have generally not received explicit attention, but underlie the approach to the origin of the state as developed in the *Emergence*, and which I believe still dictate the agenda most Aegean archaeologists are working to (implicitly or explicitly), involving on the one hand pattern and on the other process.

In the Aegean in the Early Bronze Age (and indeed throughout the Bronze Age), the archaeological evidence is usually partitioned into a series of regional sub-divisions, specialized to the degree that researchers only rarely cross these intellectual boundaries or, when they do, have equal familiarity with the data from more than one region. However, to put together a multi-dimensional picture of Aegean societies in the third millennium BC, Colin Renfrew drew upon evidence from all over the region: settlement evidence from some areas (e.g., the mainland, northwest Anatolia), burial evidence from other areas (e.g., the Cyclades, Crete), evidence for fine craft-working (e.g., northwest Anatolia, Crete), etc.. This transcended the traditionally recognized specializations, and enabled him to assemble a picture of a pan-Aegean Early Bronze Age, so-called 'proto-urban' stage of development (Renfrew 1972: 49–53).

This process, and the approach to explaining Aegean cultural development which depended on this pan-Aegean reconstruction, embodied four assumptions:

1) that complexity emerged gradually;
2) that broadly comparable developments took place in different sub-regions of the Aegean;
3) that there was a uni-lineal trajectory of development, representing one underlying set of processes; and
4) these processes were essentially presented as natural, which implied that areas which failed to follow this trajectory – to develop greater social complexity – were the exceptions.

Considering problems of pattern, at the time Renfrew was writing, one could not rule out that the differences perceived between regions were largely the result of investigation biases, given that most research in the Aegean had focused on the later palatial phases of the Bronze Age. However, 30 years of further intensive research, largely focused by the challenge of the *Emergence*, have only served to document these differences in ever greater detail. While there are areas of close cultural contact, such as Attica, Euboea, Kythera, and north Crete, the various sub-regions can still be studied as distinct entities, as embodied, for example, in the recent series of geographically-defined 'Reviews of Aegean Prehistory' (Cullen 2001).

These differences in pattern have serious implications for our understanding of process, since they make it difficult to maintain that similar processes of cultural development were at work in the different areas. However, the partitioning of the region still tends to inhibit comparative research, such that it is rarely asked how societies or communities in adjacent regions differed from each other, what this tells us about them, and what it tells us about the processes whereby the earliest states in the Aegean emerged at the end of the Early Bronze Age, and only in Crete.

In arguing for similar processes of developing complexity throughout the region, the fact that states developed early in the second millennium only on Crete, was an anomaly which had to be explained by Renfrew by disruptions of or constraints on the similar trajectories anticipated for the other sub-regions (1972: 116, 255–64, 477). In this view, it was the relative isolation of Crete (and its extensive inland areas) which allowed it to develop, while regions such as the mainland and the Cyclades suffered disruptions of various kinds (Caskey 1960; 1964; Warren 1975; Cadogan 1986; Wiencke 1989; Forsén 1992; Doumas 1988; Manning 1994; 1997).

John Cherry initiated a challenge to one of these assumptions, with his advocacy of a revolutionary, rather than gradualist evolutionary model (1983; 1984; 1986), but at the end of the day, the EB III lacunae throughout the Aegean were a stumbling block – the available data were not sufficient to distinguish between the evolutionist or revolutionist alternatives. This challenge, therefore, was reduced to empirical problems of chronology and timescale (e.g., Cherry 1986: 44–45; Manning 1995: 33–34) – we had too few closed stratified contexts, and so had difficulty ascertaining the nature and pace of change.

What was not challenged was the assumed uni-lineal framework of expectations. This is the model which I think most Aegeanists are still struggling to force the data to fit, as embodied in models which have been developed in criticism or modification of the *Emergence*, and are themselves presented as of Aegean-wide relevance (e.g., Gilman 1981; 1991; Halstead 1981; 1988 (though see 1994); van Andel and Runnels 1988; Sherratt 1993; Sherratt and Sherratt 1991).

Comparisons between the patterns of development in the different areas, which would be instrumental in identifying different patterns of change and highlight the need for different models for the processes of change, are difficult to make. This is, first, because of the degree of regional specialization in Aegean studies, already noted. But this is exacerbated where, because of the character of different regional archaeological records, one is trying to compare inferred characteristics of societies based on different types of material behaviours – for instance, inferences about social organization principally based on a burial record from one area (e.g., the Cyclades) and a settlement record from a neighbouring area (e.g., the southern mainland).

Further complications, however, are both theoretical and methodological, and are caused by the abstractness of the theories we attempt to apply to the data, and significant problems of the middle range – how we interpret specific characteristics of the archaeological record. Here, I want to try to side-step these last difficulties, not to imply that they are not important, but, through a largely empirical exploration, to explore directly the issues of pattern and process. I want to make the basic point that it is time we recognize explicitly the homogenizing assumptions of the *Emergence* model, and begin to explore alternative perspectives which are more oriented to recognizing difference, contingency and agent-centred dynamics in the emergence of complex societies in the Aegean.

Recognizing the problems of comparison noted above, I will focus particularly on evidence from Crete – where we can, by and large, compare similar sorts of evidence from different sites – and see whether it conforms to the uni-lineal model that was implicit in Renfrew's work, and in most of what has been written about Minoan state formation in the succeeding three decades.

Investigating Social Development in Prepalatial Crete

Crete was relatively isolated from the rest of the Aegean during the third millennium, though this picture changed in the second millennium, when Minoan cultural influence spread throughout the southern Aegean. While a certain degree of regionalism has increasingly been recognized in Cretan material culture and patterns of behaviour in the Prepalatial period (Branigan 1974: 127–30; Andreou 1978; Betancourt *et al.* 1979; Walberg 1983; Betancourt 1984; Cadogan 1994; 1995; Wilson and Day 1994; Whitelaw *et al.* 1997; Day *et al.* 1998; Kiriatzi *et al.* 2000; Sbonias 1999; 2000; Schoep 1999b; Bevan 2001), we can legitimately speak of a common culture area, and the evidence for extensive exchange indicates a relatively high degree of communication and shared ideas throughout the island.

Unfortunately, the *Emergence* was slightly premature for assessing the nature of Early Minoan society: Keith Branigan's synthesis of the evidence from the Mesara tombs had just been published (Branigan 1970a; also 1970b), while Peter Warren's publication of his excavations at Myrtos Fournou Korifi (Warren 1972), as well as John Evans' summary of his excavation of the West Court House at Knossos (Evans 1972), came out in the same year as the *Emergence*. The discussion of the Early Minoan evidence in the *Emergence* was also complicated by what has proven to be a non-issue (Renfrew 1972: 84–98): EMIII is a significant period of time, and witnessed important developments on the island (Cadogan 1986; Momigliano 1991; 2000; Haggis 1999; Watrous 2001).

Two decades ago, I tried to pull some of this post-*Emergence* information together, highlighting significant differences among the better understood Prepalatial communities on the island, and suggesting that an understanding of the nature of these differences would be essential to understanding the processes involved in the development of social complexity and the emergence of the state on the island, soon after 2000 BC (Whitelaw 1983). I was, in fact, trying to argue against an even more basic model which saw sites such as Vasiliki and Fournou Korifi as precursors of the later palaces (Hutchinson 1962: 145; Branigan 1970b: 44–49; 1975). Given that small rural communities usually co-exist alongside the most complex urban centres, there was no reason why one should expect a site such as Fournou Korifi to represent a microcosm of the later palaces (e.g., Warren 1972: 260–61; 1983: 266; 1987: 49–50).

To a significant degree, such special pleading was a consequence of advocating an endogenous origin for the Aegean states. Given the relatively poor documentation of the EB III period throughout the Aegean, to see a local origin for the Middle Bronze Age palace-centred societies of Crete, one had to get a running start in the EB II period – so EB II evidence tended to be interpreted with a great deal of hindsight, which itself often encourages teleological assumptions.

But, despite focusing on differences, in 1983 I was still working to a uni-lineal model: my community size estimates situated the farmsteads represented by some of the Mesara tombs, the egalitarian hamlet of Fournou Korifi, the stratified village of Mochlos, and the nascent state of Knossos, along a continuum of social complexity as well as size. While I was documenting diversity among contemporary sites, which might also represent different components of a settlement hierarchy, these could also be imagined to represent a developmental trajectory, in a time-honoured tradition of anthropological and archaeological theorizing.

Inter-site Comparisons in Prepalatial Crete

Another couple of decades on, recent publications of both old and new

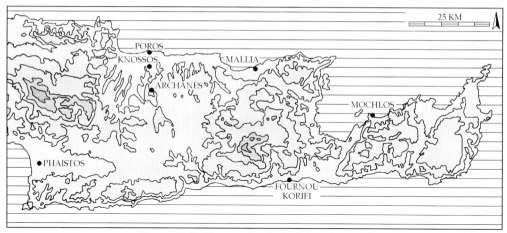

Figure 13.1. Crete with principal sites discussed

investigations at a number of Cretan sites now provide an opportunity to wrestle more effectively with some of this diversity in pattern, in a way which I think allows us both to reflect on and to build on the understanding of processes outlined in the *Emergence* (Figure 13.1).

Turning first to Fournou Korifi, the work I have been doing with various colleagues on the ceramics (e.g., Whitelaw *et al.* 1997) has demonstrated that, while ceramic production at even such small hamlets was specialized, and exchange relations were extensive, there is no evidence that either production or distribution was centrally organized, and there is no evidence for redistribution at that local scale.

Turning next to Mochlos, the study and republication of the tombs excavated early this century (Soles 1992), and renewed excavations both in the cemetery and the town (Soles and Davaras 1992), are providing significant new evidence about the Prepalatial community. Within the cemetery, the largest and most elaborate tombs occupy key locations, defined by the routes of access across the slope, determined by rock outcrops. Tombs IV–VI, at the upper end of the cemetery, are particularly elaborately constructed, and have a unique paved area and system of platforms, which would appear to have been the focal point for the entire cemetery. Differences in tomb size, elaboration and offerings suggest systematic and sustained differences in wealth between burying groups – the earliest evidence for social stratification in Crete (Whitelaw 1983; Soles 1988; 1992). The phases of use of the different tombs indicate a boom in wealth consumption at the site in the later Prepalatial period, with a sharp decline afterwards (Soles 1978; 1992; Soles and Davaras 1992: 417, 420–28), at about the time that the first major palaces were being constructed elsewhere in Crete (Figure 13.2).

Mallia, also situated on the north coast, has recently been receiving over-due attention, because of the wealth of contexts preserved from the Protopalatial

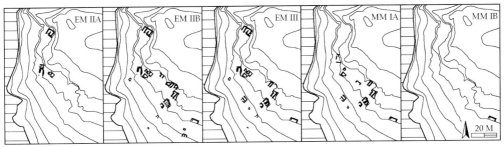

Figure 13.2. Evidence for the use of tombs within the cemetery at Mochlos

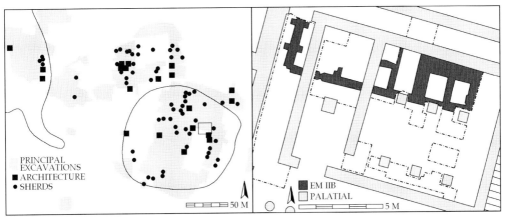

Figure 13.3. Early Minoan Mallia: deposits and detail of structure at core of site

period (van Effenterre 1980a; 1980b; Poursat 1983; 1988; Knappett 1999; Schoep 2002a), though the Prepalatial evidence from that site, one of those which emerged as a major palatial centre early in the second millennium, also has begun to be reassessed (van Effenterre 1980a; Pelon 1987). Soundings beneath the later town indicate the existence of a sizeable community by the middle of the Prepalatial period (Figure 13.3; van Effenterre 1980a: 83–94; Whitelaw 1983: 338–39; Pelon 1989; 1991; 1993; Poursat and Darque 1990; Farnoux 1989; 1990; Baurain and Darque 1993). Directly under the later palace structure, a carefully laid-out building has been partially revealed, leading to suggestions that it might represent an EM IIB fore-runner of the later palace (Pelon 1993; Schoep 1999a).

In the cemetery, the use of individual tombs again allows us to recognize distinctions between social groups, with a restricted number of burials in elaborate built ossuaries, while many others were simply placed in crevices in the rock (Demargne 1945; van Effenterre and van Effenterre 1963; Olivier and McGeorge 1977; van Effenterre 1980a: 229–52; Baurain 1987; de Pierpont 1987; Soles 1988; 1992). In contrast to the situation at Mochlos, burial facilities at Mallia continue to become more elaborate throughout the later Prepalatial period, culminating in the construction of a monumental tomb, the Chrysolakkos, at about the same time as the first monumental palace structure (Figure 13.4). The architecture and the finds that survived earlier looting justify viewing this as the tomb of the palatial elite of the early Mallia state (Demargne 1945; Shaw 1973; van Effenterre 1980a: 241–47; de Pierpont 1987).

The Prepalatial community at Mallia was much more extensive than that at Mochlos, and the community continued to expand through the early second millennium (van Effenterre 1980a: 155–228; Müller 1990; 1991; 1992; 1997; Schoep 2002a). The development of Mallia into a palatial centre, the focal community of a regional state (Cadogan 1995; Knappett 1999; Schoep 2002a), is in direct contrast with the decline of the community at Mochlos, despite the parallels in development at these two north coast communities earlier in the Prepalatial period.

The most apparent difference between the two sites lies in their immediate hinterlands (Figure 13.5). Mallia is situated on a broad coastal plain, one of the finest agricultural areas of northern Crete, where intensive survey has identified numerous sites of the late Prepalatial and Protopalatial periods (Müller 1996; 1998; Müller Celka 2002). Mochlos, on the other hand, appears to have been oriented toward the sea, with much more limited agricultural potential in its immediate hinterland. These two sites reveal dramatic differences in their patterns of development – but what does this empirical difference in patterns suggest about the processes involved?

Trading Sites and the 'International Spirit'

Following relative isolation in the Neolithic period, evidence from several north coast communities documents the development of extensive exchange relations with communities in the Cyclades and the mainland, during the first half of the Prepalatial period (Renfrew 1964; Stucynski 1982; Rutter and Zerner 1983; Warren 1984; Branigan 1991; Karantzali 1996; Dimopoulou 1997; Sakellarakis and Sapouna-Sakellaraki 1997; Day *et al.* 1998; Carter 1998; Papadatos 1999; Wilson *et al.* in press). Extensive contacts are represented by distinctive Cycladic imports, and particularly Cycladic raw materials (Figure 13.6), such as obsidian (Torrence 1986; Carter 1998), copper (Stos-Gale 1993; 1998; 2001; Betancourt *et al.* 1999), and lead and silver (Stos-Gale 1985).

By the middle of the Prepalatial period, when Mochlos really takes off, Cycladic finished artefacts appear to be declining in popularity (Stucynski 1982; Wilson 1994: 39–41; Karantzali 1996; Papadatos 1999), but raw materials such as obsidian and copper continued to be imported. While such materials did find their way to even quite small hamlets, such as Fournou Korifi, there is a significant decline in quantity with distance from the north coast, and coastal sites such as Mochlos are likely to have been acting as points of access for raw materials, and also as local centres for specialized craft production – such as bronze-working,

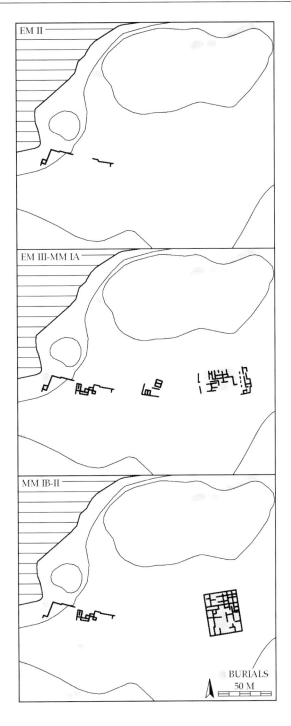

Figure 13.4. Evidence for the use of tombs within the cemetery at Mallia

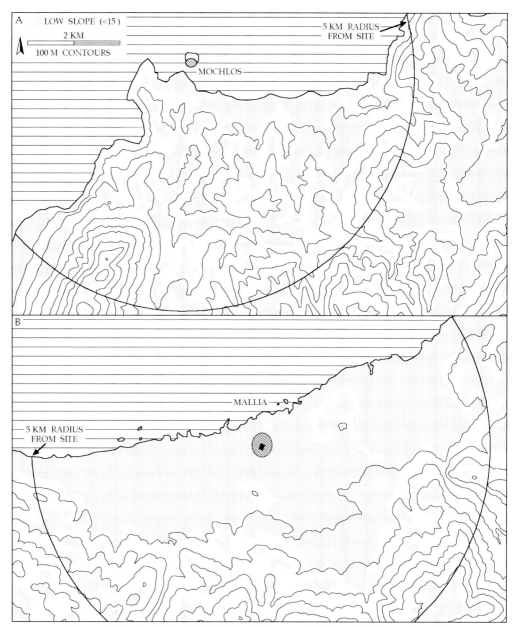

Figure 13.5. Agricultural suitability of the coastal plains at Mallia and Mochlos

gold-working and stone vase production (Warren 1965: 28–36; Branigan 1991; Betancourt *et al.* 1999; Bevan 2001).

This pattern is paralleled, in the middle of the third millennium, by the emergence of a small number of relatively large sites in the Cyclades, at

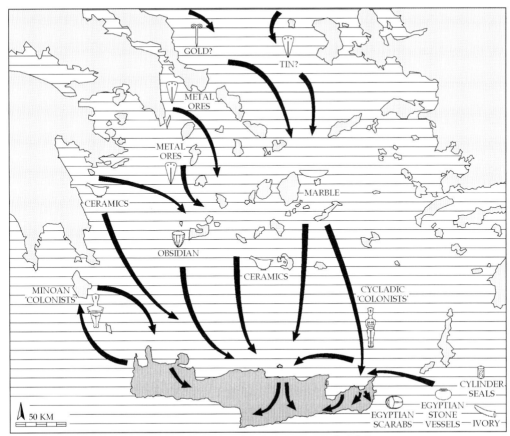

Figure 13.6. Sources of imports into Prepalatial Crete

demographic and communication nodes. It has been argued plausibly by Cyprian Broodbank that the wealth and exotica documented at such sites provide evidence for the operation of a prestige goods system, structured around trading networks (Broodbank 1989; 1993; 2000a; 2000b). The evidence from Mochlos suggests that it, and perhaps other Cretan north coast communities (such as Poros: Dimopoulou 1997; Wilson *et al.* in press), may have developed in a similar way, acting as channels for the movement of raw materials and finished prestige goods south into Crete, initially from the Cyclades (Broodbank 2000a: 306–09), but by the later Prepalatial period (MMIA), also including rare imports from the East Mediterranean such as Egyptian stone vessels (Warren 1969: 105–15; 1995; Bevan 2001), scarabs (Yule 1983; 1988; Pini 1989; 2000; Phillips 1996), Near Eastern cylinder seals (Strom 1980; Møller 1980; Davaras and Soles 1995; Aruz 1995), and ivory (Krzyszkowska 1989).

While quantified evidence is not yet available for Cretan sites, an idea of the potential of such exchange systems to establish and maintain differentials between

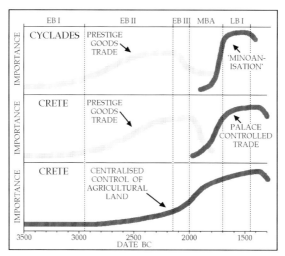

Figure 13.7. Alternative bases for power in Crete and the Cyclades

communities can be seen from Mochlos and Fournou Korifi, only some 30 km apart on the north and south coasts, respectively. Only 181 pieces of obsidian were recovered from the near complete excavation of the settlement at Fournou Korifi (Jarman 1972), while deposits of hundreds of blades and cores have been noted within the cemetery at Mochlos (Soles and Davaras 1992). Similarly, fragments of only three stone vessels were recovered at Fournou Korifi (Warren 1972: 236–37), as against hundreds recovered from the Mochlos tombs (Seager 1912). While the depositional contexts at each site are different (settlement versus tomb), the contrasts are so gross as to merit attention.

While these networks collapsed (or were transformed: Broodbank 2000a: 320–61) in the Cyclades, Mochlos seems to have continued to maintain its position to the end of the millennium, probably sustained by the local Cretan demand for off-island raw materials, particularly metals (Figure 13.7). Remarkably, though perhaps an index of our uni-lineal expectations, the subsequent decline of this site has received little comment (Seager 1909; Soles 1978: 11; Branigan 1991; though see now Soles and Davaras 1992: 417, 426–28).

An Agriculturally-Based Alternative?

An alternative pattern of development, already noted at Mallia, can be more clearly documented at the site of Knossos. While also near the north coast, the site is several kilometres inland, relatively distant from the sea, but central to one of the richest agricultural regions of the island. It was to develop into the largest prehistoric site in the Aegean, reaching nearly three quarters of a square kilometre in the middle of the second millennium BC (Whitelaw 2000; in press). As the

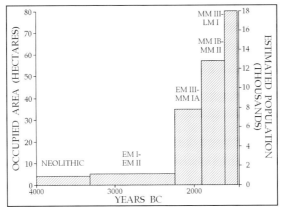

Figure 13.8. Estimated population growth at prehistoric Knossos

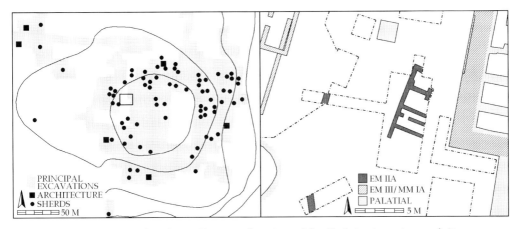

Figure 13.9. Early Minoan Knossos: deposits and detail of structure at core of site

result of a century of intensive investigation, we can chart its growth more precisely than we can for Mallia, and it is now clear that it grew phenomenally in the late Prepalatial period, just prior to the construction of the first palace in MM IB (Figure 13.8).

As with Mallia, at the core of the site, adjacent to and under the later palace, there were significant structures dating to the middle (Evans 1972; Wilson 1985) and late Prepalatial (Peatfield 1988; Wilson 1994: 38; MacGillivray 1994: 49) periods, which were erected and rebuilt in the context of major terracing operations, themselves denoting considerable power by an organizing authority (Figure 13.9). These constructions represent the first manifestation of the elites who, soon after 2000 BC, began construction of a palace which was to be adapted and expanded throughout the next six centuries.

At Mallia and Knossos, in contrast to Mochlos (and the Cycladic sites), we can see a process of accelerating growth and increasing complexity beyond the end of the third millennium, culminating in the formation of palace-centred regional polities. However, to date, these different patterns in settlement development in the middle and late Prepalatial periods have been linked together into a single trajectory, with the prestige goods elite model being seen as ancestral to the emergence of the Minoan state (e.g., Van Andel and Runnels 1988; Branigan 1988; 1995; Manning 1994; 1997; Haggis 1999), as anticipated by the *Emergence*.

Yet, as the written documents from the Later Bronze Age from both Crete and mainland Greece indicate, the large-scale palace systems of the Middle and Late Bronze Age were based on the centralized control of agricultural production and agricultural land. According to the uni-lineal model, a trade-based system such as can be argued for some sites in the Cyclades, and for sites such as Mochlos on Crete, somehow developed (or in the case of the Cyclades, would have developed) into the agriculturally-based palace states centred at sites like Mallia and Knossos. However, when one looks at specific sites, such as Mochlos, it is clear that they did not. The relatively small scale and inherent instability of the prestige-goods, trade-based, coastal communities of the mid-third millennium do not appear to provide adequate antecedents for the later urban-centred palace states. Indeed, the parallel development during the middle Prepalatial of another large centre at the later palatial site of Phaistos (Whitelaw 1983; Watrous *et al.* 1993; Carinci 2000), in an inland location in the southern Mesara plain, seems to separate the two patterns of development entirely. The growth of these agri-culturally-based sites is contemporary with, but independent of, the development of the trade-based communities – they appear to be parallel rather than sequential processes. This distinction may be most clearly embodied in the contrasts in the mid-Prepalatial evidence from Knossos and neighbouring Poros (Dimopoulou 1997; Wilson *et al.* in press).

I would suggest that what we are seeing is the eclipse of the early trading communities, in the face of a new, much larger-scale and much more effectively expansionist type of polity, with power rooted firmly in control over agricultural production and surpluses. At the moment, we cannot actually chart the development of the regional systems associated with the expanding, eventually palatial, centres, though the surveys in the Mallia coastal plain and the West Mesara promise to give us just such information (Müller 1996; 1998; Müller Celka 2000; Watrous *et al.* 1993). However, even existing data (Blackman and Branigan 1975; 1977; Hope Simpson *et al.* 1995; Vasilakis 1989–90) suggest the development of a small-scale regional settlement system around Phaistos in the middle Prepalatial, a picture supported by the preliminary reports on the West Mesara survey.

Consideration of one final site can perhaps nuance this picture of two parallel, or perhaps even competing, processes. Data from the remarkable cemetery complex of Phourni at Archanes indicate that, early in the Prepalatial period, the

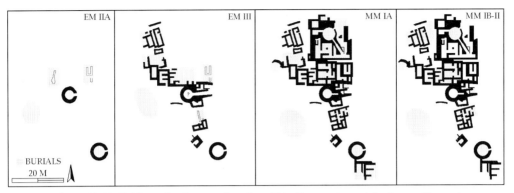

Figure 13.10. Evidence for the use of tombs within the cemetery at Archanes: Phourni

site was well provided with raw materials and material culture from the Cyclades (Sakellarakis 1977; Sakellarakis and Sapouna-Sakellaraki 1997), and may have acted as a point of distribution for such material further south, over the watershed to southern Crete (Carter 1998; Papadatos 1999).

In the middle of the Prepalatial period, strangely, there is no evidence that the cemetery was in use, and this must represent a disruption of some kind in the previous patterns of behaviour. Burials resume in the later Prepalatial period, with rapid expansion in the number of tombs constructed and in use, followed by a cessation of new construction in the Protopalatial period (Figure 13.10). The intensification of use of the cemetery in the late Prepalatial period saw multiple phases of expansion of the main tomb complexes, including the dismantling of one tomb (Building 7) and its complete replacement by another (Tholos B). This otherwise unprecedented behaviour implies intense competition between burying groups within the community, probably as the site was developing as a regional centre (see also Maggidis 1998; Sbonias 1999; Karytinos 2000).

The cessation of expansion at the Phourni cemetery coincides with the end of the Prepalatial period, when calculations of the area necessary to support the rapidly expanding population of Knossos indicate that Archanes would almost certainly have become incorporated into the sphere of influence of the emerging palatial centre to the north.

What I suggest we can see in the episodic development of the Phourni complex, is the instability of the early exchange-based power structures, and the subsequent growth of an agriculturally-based, local centre. This process involved intense competition between land-holding groups within the community, expressed through mortuary aggrandisement. This local competition was eventually curtailed when the community was incorporated within the regional network of the neighbouring site of Knossos, whose inhabitants had embarked on an agriculturally-based trajectory of growth centuries earlier, in the early Prepalatial period.

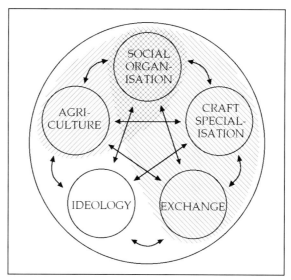

Figure 13.11. Renfrew's cultural sub-systems and principal feedback linkages during the Prepalatial Aegean

Conclusions: Multiple Patterns, Processes, and Perspectives

In defining his systemic perspective for the emergence of the state in the Aegean, Renfrew emphasized the inter-connectedness of various processes, though in illustration he outlined two specific positive feedback loops, on which most subsequent debate has focussed (Figure 13.11; 1972: 479–504). One of these was based in the development of bronze metallurgy, craft specialization, and exchange systems, while the other was based in diversification and specialization in agriculture, linked to the domestication of the olive and the vine – an agricultural intensification model. Research since then has considerably modified our understanding of each set of processes, but what I would like to suggest is that what the data are indicating, whether we compare evidence between regions such as Crete and the Cyclades, or even, as I have done here, compare sites in detail within one of those cultural systems, is that these are, actually, two distinct social dynamics. They may often inter-link, but such articulation itself will be a variable and dynamic process.

In the three decades since the publication of the *Emergence*, various models have been proposed as challenges to, or modifications of the *Emergence* model, but in each case they have aimed to replace one general model, applicable throughout the southern Aegean, with another, equally broadly applicable. This largely empirical comparison between patterns of development at different Cretan Prepalatial sites, suggests that we need explicitly to consider multi-lineal trajectories of social development, and recognize that there were multiple pathways to complexity in the prehistoric southern Aegean. Stepping back from this specific case and looking more widely at communities in the Early Bronze Age around the Aegean, leads me to ask whether there might not be other pathways as well. Unfortunately, in most cases, we as yet lack the detailed data necessary to conduct the sort of controlled comparison which I have pursued here for Crete.

However, we also need to analyse and interpret our data in ways which allow us to recognize differences, and challenge us to try to explain them. What I hope I have been able to do in this paper, is to suggest how such an approach, based in detailed comparison of individual site characteristics and histories, can contribute to the analysis and interpretation of cultural difference and change, and help us to appreciate and encourage us to try to understand differences in both pattern and process. While adopting this approach to advance a fairly simple argument, I would also suggest that the approach has considerable advantages over debates between theories which, on theoretical and methodological grounds, can only weakly be grounded to the existing data.

Three decades ago, in the *Emergence of Civilisation*, Colin Renfrew defined a question and a research agenda which we are still trying to address today. The integrating comparative perspective which he initiated was essential to introduce a processual perspective on the question of the emergence of complex societies in the prehistoric Aegean. Likewise, the systemic framework he espoused is as valid now as it was essential then. Three decades on, building on each of these perspectives, I think both the Aegean data, and models of social change which are being explored elsewhere in archaeology, demand that we think about this issue more pluralistically, as various recently published papers (e.g., Bevan 2001; Broodbank 2000b; Carter 1998; Dabney 1995; Dabney and Wright 1990; Day and Wilson 2002; Day and Relaki 2002; Haggis 2002; Hamilakis 1996; 2002; Karytinos 2000; Knappett 1999; 2002; Knappett and Schoep 2000; Maggidis 1998; Sbonias 1999; 2000; Schoep 1999b; 2001; 2002a; 2002b; Voutsaki 1997; Whitelaw *et al.* 1997), and others at this Round Table indeed illustrate.

One could argue that a multi-lineal perspective, as advocated here, is implicit in much recent work. However, the actual tendency has been to try to replace one monolithic theory (which a systemic approach was originally designed to try to avoid), with another. This assumes that the various complex societies we are trying to understand in the Aegean basin were at least structurally comparable to each other, and that their pattern of development was also similar. This is currently being provocatively and productively questioned for Protopalatial Crete (e.g., Knappett 1999; Schoep 2001; 2002a; Tsipopoulou 2002), though the degree to which the perceived differences between polities represent past behaviour, rather than data biases, still needs consideration.

Looking positively at this often antagonistic situation, structural similarity between contexts has been assumed rather than demonstrated, and many of the models which have been put forward as competing alternatives, may be more or less relevant to different cases – in different times and places within the prehistoric Aegean. Recognizing diversity in the patterns we are trying to explain may help us to identify the specific models which are most relevant to particular cases, while not insisting that they must be relevant to all other cases as well. In such a manner, we can build on the insights of the *Emergence*, without either being bound to its assumptions or its conclusions.

Acknowledgements

I am grateful to the organizers of the Round Table for inviting me to contribute to it, and to the other participants for comments on the presentation (and laughing at some of the jokes). This argument has been developing for some time, and I am also grateful to audiences in Cambridge, Athens, London and Oxford for comments on other presentations over many years. I enjoyed Keith and Nong's hospitality, and thank the Sheffield staff and students, and other contributors, who all contributed to such an invigorating weekend. The intellectual debt of this paper to Colin Renfrew, and his *Emergence of Civilisation*, is obvious, and I am also happy to record my gratitude for his encouragement when I first began research on Early Minoan Crete, and later ventured into the Early Cyclades.

Bibliography

van Andel, T.H. and C.N. Runnels
    1988   An essay on the 'emergence of civilization' in the Aegean world. *Antiquity* 62: 234–47.
Andreou, S.
    1978   *Pottery Groups of the Old Palace Period in Crete.* PhD dissertation, University of Cincinnati.
Aruz, J.
    1995   Syrian seals and the evidence for cultural interaction between the Levant and Crete. In I. Pini and J.-C. Poursat (eds.), *Sceaux Minoens et Mycéniens* (Corpus der Minoischen und Mykenischen Siegel 5): 1–21. Berlin: Mann.
Baurain, C.
    1987   Les nécropoles de Malia. In R. Laffineur (ed.), *Thanatos: les coûtumes funéraires en Égée à l'âge du bronze* (Aegaeum 1): 61–73. Liège: Université de Liège.
Baurain, C. and P. Darque
    1993   Les abords nord-est du palais. *BCH* 117: 671–75.
Betancourt, P.
    1984   *East Cretan White-on-Dark Ware.* Philadelphia: University Museum.
Betancourt, P., T. Gaisser, E. Koss, R. Lyon, F.R. Matson, S. Montgomery, G.H. Meyer and C. Swann
    1979   *Vasiliki Ware: an Early Bronze Age Pottery Style in Crete* (SIMA 56). Göteborg: Paul Åström.
Betancourt, P.P., J.D. Muhly, W.R. Farrand, C. Stearns, L. Onyshkevych, W. Hafford and D. Evely

   1999   Research and excavation at Chrysokamino, Crete 1995–1998. *Hesperia* 68: 344–70.

Bevan, A.
   2001   *Value Regimes in the Eastern Mediterranean Bronze Age: a Study Through Stone Vessels.* PhD dissertation, University College London.

Blackman, D. and K. Branigan
   1975   An archaeological survey on the south coast of Crete, between the Ayiofarango and Chrysostomos. *BSA* 70: 17–36.
   1977   An archaeological survey of the lower catchment of the Ayiofarango valley. *BSA* 72: 13–84.

Branigan, K.
   1970a *The Tombs of Mesara. A Study of Funerary Architecture and Ritual in Southern Crete, 2800–1700 B.C.* London: Gerald Duckworth.
   1970b *The Foundations of Palatial Crete. A Survey of Crete in the Early Bronze Age.* London: Routledge and Kegan Paul.
   1974   *Aegean Metalwork of the Early and Middle Bronze Age.* Oxford: Clarendon Press.
   1975   Review of P. Warren (1972), Myrtos: an Early Bronze Age Site in Crete. *Classical Review* 25: 116–18.
   1988   Some observations on state formation in Crete. In E. French and K. Wardle (eds.), *Problems in Greek Prehistory*: 63–72. Bristol: Bristol Classical Press.
   1991   Mochlos: an early Aegean 'gateway community'? In R. Laffineur and L. Basch (eds.), *Thalassa: l'Égée préhistorique et la mer* (Aegaeum 7): 97–105. Liège: Université de Liège.
   1995   Social transformations and the rise of the state in Crete. In R. Laffineur and W.-D. Niemeier (eds.), *Politeia: Society and State in the Aegean Bronze Age* (Aegaeum 12): 33–42. Liège: Université de Liège.

Broodbank, C.
   1989   The longboat and society in the Cyclades in the Keros-Syros culture. *AJA* 93: 319–37.
   1993   Ulysses without sails. Trade, distance, knowledge and power in the early Cyclades. *World Archaeology* 24: 315–31.
   2000a *An Island Archaeology of the Early Cyclades.* Cambridge: Cambridge University Press.
   2000b Perspectives on an Early Bronze Age island centre: an analysis of pottery from Dhaskaleio-Kavos (Keros) in the Cyclades. *OJA* 19: 323–42.

Cadogan, G.
   1986   Why was Crete different? In G. Cadogan (ed.), *The End of the Early Bronze Age in the Aegean* (Cincinnati Classical Studies 6): 153–71. Leiden: E.J. Brill.
   1994   An Old Palace period Knossos state? In D. Evely, H. Hughes-Brock and N. Momigliano (eds.), *Knossos, a Labyrinth of History. Papers Presented in Honour of Sinclair Hood*: 57–69. Oxford: British School at Athens.
   1995   Malia and Lasithi: a palace-state. *Proceedings of the Seventh International Cretological Congress, A*: 97–104. Rethymnon: Historical Society of Crete.

Carinci, F.
   2000   Western Messara and Egypt during the Protopalatial period: a minimalist view. In A. Karetsou (ed.), *Kriti-Aigyptos. Politismikoi Desmoi Trion Khilietion*: 31–37. Athens: Kapon.

Carter, T.
   1998   Reverberations of the international spirit: thoughts upon 'Cycladica' in the Mesara. In K. Branigan (ed.), *Cemetery and Society in the Aegean Bronze Age* (SSAA 1): 59–77. Sheffield: Sheffield Academic Press.

Caskey, J.L.
   1960   The Early Helladic period in the Argolid. *Hesperia* 29: 285–303.
   1964   Greece, Crete and the Aegean islands in the Early Bronze Age. In I.E.S. Edwards, C.J.

Gadd and N.G.L. Hammond (eds.), *The Cambridge Ancient History, 2nd ed., 1, 2B*: 771–807. Cambridge: Cambridge University Press.

Cherry, J.F.
1983   Evolution, revolution and the origins of complex society in Minoan Crete. In O. Krzyszkowska and L. Nixon (eds.), *Minoan Society*: 33–45. Bristol: Bristol Classical Press.
1984   The emergence of the state in the prehistoric Aegean. *PCPS* 30: 18–48.
1986   Polities and palaces: some problems in Minoan state formation. In C. Renfrew and J.F. Cherry (eds.), *Peer Polity Interaction and Socio-Political Change*: 19–45. Cambridge: Cambridge University Press.

Cullen, T.
2001   *Aegean Prehistory. A Review*. Boston: Archaeological Institute of America.

Dabney, M.
1995   The later stages of state formation in palatial Crete. In R. Laffineur and W.-D. Niemeier (eds.), *Politeia: Society and State in the Aegean Bronze Age* (Aegaeum 12): 43–47. Liège: Université de Liège.

Dabney, M. and J. Wright
1990   Mortuary customs, palatial society and state formation in the Aegean area: a comparative study. In R. Hägg and G. Nordquist (eds.), *Celebrations of Death and Divinity in the Bronze Age Argolid*: 45–53. Stockholm: Swedish School at Athens.

Davaras, C. and J. Soles
1995   A new oriental cylinder seal from Mochlos. Appendix: catalogue of the cylinder seals found in the Aegean. *AE* 134: 29–66.

Day, P.M., D.E. Wilson and E. Kiriatzi
1998   Pots, labels and people: burying ethnicity in the cemetery at Aghia Photia, Siteias. In K. Branigan (ed.), *Cemetery and Society in the Aegean Bronze Age* (SSAA 1): 133–49. Sheffield: Sheffield Academic Press.

Day, P.M. and M. Relaki
2002   Past factions and present fictions: palaces in the study of Minoan Crete. In J. Driessen, I. Schoep and R. Laffineur (eds.), *Monuments of Minos. Rethinking the Minoan Palaces* (Aegaeum 23): 217–34. Liège: Université de Liège.

Day, P.M. and D.E. Wilson
2002   Landscapes of memory, craft and power in Pre-palatial and Proto-palatial Knossos. In Y. Hamilakis (ed.), *Labyrinth Revisited. Rethinking 'Minoan' Archaeology*: 143–66. Oxford: Oxbow.

de Pierpont, G.
1987   Reflexions sur la destination des edifices de Chrysolakkos. In R. Laffineur (ed.), *Thanatos: les coûtumes funéraires en Égée a l'âge du bronze* (Aegaeum 1): 79–93. Liège: Université de Liège.

Demargne, P.
1945   *Fouilles executées à Mallia: explorations des nécropoles (1921–1933), 1*. Paris: Geuthner.

Dimopoulou, N.
1997   Workshops and craftsmen in the harbour-town of Knossos at Poros-Katsambas. In R. Laffineur and P. Betancourt (eds.), *TEKHNH: Craftsmen, Craftswomen and Craftsmanship in the Aegean Bronze Age* (Aegaeum 16): 433–38. Liège: Université de Liège.

Doumas, C.
1988   EBA in the Cyclades: continuity or discontinuity? In E.B. French and K.A. Wardle (eds.), *Problems in Greek Prehistory*: 21–29. Bristol: Bristol Classical Press.

Evans, J.
   1972   The Early Minoan occupation of Knossos: a note on some new evidence. *Anatolian Studies* 22: 115–28.

Farnoux, A.
   1989   La Crypte hypostyle. *BCH* 113: 768–71.
   1990   Sondages autour de la Crypte hypostyle. *BCH* 111: 920–21.

Forsén, J.
   1992   *The Twilight of the Early Helladics. A Study of Disturbances in East-Central and Southern Greece towards the End of the Early Bronze Age* (SIMA Pocket-Book 116.) Jonsered: Paul Åström.

Gilman, A.
   1981   The development of social stratification in Bronze Age Europe. *Current Anthropology* 22: 1–24.
   1991   Trajectories towards social complexity in the later prehistory of the Mediterranean. In T. Earle (ed.), *Chiefdoms: Power, Economy and Ideology:* 146–68. Cambridge: Cambridge University Press.

Haggis, D.
   1999   Staple finance, peak sanctuaries, and economic complexity in late Prepalatial Crete. In A. Chaniotis (ed.), *From Minoan Farmers to Roman Traders: Sidelights on the Economy of Ancient Crete*: 53–85. Stuttgart: Franz Steiner.
   2002   Integration and complexity in the late Pre-palatial period. A view from the countryside in eastern Crete. In Y. Hamilakis (ed.), *Labyrinth Revisited. Rethinking 'Minoan' Archaeology*: 120–42. Oxford: Oxbow.

Halstead, P.
   1981   From determinism to uncertainty: social storage and the rise of the Minoan palace. In A. Sheridan and G. Bailey (eds.), *Economic Archaeology* (BAR International Series 96): 187–213. Oxford: British Archaeological Reports.
   1988   On redistribution and the origins of the Minoan-Mycenaean palatial economies. In E.B. French and K. Wardle (eds.), *Problems in Greek Prehistory*: 519–30. Bristol: Bristol Classical Press.
   1994   The north-south divide: regional paths to complexity in prehistoric Greece. In C. Mathers and S. Stoddart (eds.), *Development and Decline in the Mediterranean Bronze Age*: 195–219. Sheffield: J.R. Collis.

Hamilakis, Y.
   1996   Wine, oil and the dialectics of power in Bronze Age Crete: a review of the evidence. *OJA* 15: 1–32.
   2002   Too many chiefs? Factional competition in Neopalatial Crete. In J. Driessen, I. Schoep and R. Laffineur (eds.), *Monuments of Minos. Rethinking the Minoan Palaces* (Aegaeum 23): 179–99. Liège: Université de Liège.

Hope Simpson, R., P. Betancourt, P. Callaghan, D. Harlan, J. Hayes, J. Shaw, M. Shaw and L.V. Watrous
   1995   The archaeological survey of the Kommos area. In J.W. Shaw and M.C. Shaw (eds.), *Kommos I, I: the Kommos Region, Ecology and Minoan Industries*: 325–402. Princeton: Princeton University Press.

Hutchinson, R.W.
   1962   *Prehistoric Crete*. Harmondsworth: Penguin.

Jarman, M.
   1972   The obsidian. In P. Warren, *Myrtos. An Early Bronze Age Settlement in Crete* (Supplementary Volume 7): 326–28. London: British School at Athens.

Karantzali, E.
   1996   *Le bronze ancien dans les Cyclades et en Crète: les relations entre les deux régions – influence de la Grèce continentale* (BAR International Series 631.) Oxford: Tempus Reparatum.
Karytinos, A.
   2000   The stylistic development of seals from Archanes-Phourni throughout the Prepalatial period – style and social meaning. In I. Pini (ed.), *Minoischen-Mykenisch Glyptik, Stil, Ikonographie, Funktion* (Corpus der Minoischen und Mykenischen Siegel 6): 123–34. Berlin: Mann.
Kiriatzi, E, P.M. Day and D.E. Wilson
   2000   Diakinisi tis keramikis kai koinonikopolitiki organosi: i grapti keramiki tis PM II kai I periodou stin anatoliki Kriti. *Proceedings of the Eighth International Cretological Congress, 1*: 99–115. Iraklion: Historical Society of Crete.
Knappett, C.
   1999   Assessing a polity in Protopalatial Crete the Malia-Lasithi state. *AJA* 103: 615–39.
   2002   Mind the gap: between pots and politics in Minoan studies. In Y. Hamilakis (ed.), *Labyrinth Revisited. Rethinking 'Minoan' Archaeology*: 67–88. Oxford: Oxbow.
Knappett, C. and I. Schoep
   2000   Continuity and change in Minoan palatial power. *Antiquity* 74: 365–71.
Krzyszkowska, O.
   1989   Early Cretan seals. New evidence for the use of bone, ivory and boar's tusk. In I. Pini (ed.), *Fragen und Probleme der Bronzezeitlichen Ägäischen Glyptik* (Corpus der Minoischen und Mykenischen Siegel 5): 111–26. Berlin: Mann.
MacGillivray, J.A.
   1994   The early history of the palace at Knossos (MM I–II). In D. Evely, H. Hughes-Brock and N. Momigliano (eds.), *Knossos, a Labyrinth of History. Papers Presented in Honour of Sinclair Hood*: 45–55. Oxford: British School at Athens.
Maggidis, C.
   1998   From polis to necropolis: social ranking from architectural and mortuary evidence in the Minoan cemetery at Phourni, Archanes. In K. Branigan (ed.), *Cemetery and Society in the Aegean Bronze Age* (SSAA 1): 87–102. Sheffield: Sheffield Academic Press.
Manning, S.
   1994   The emergence of divergence: development and decline on Bronze Age Crete and the Cyclades. In C. Mathers and S. Stoddart (eds.), *Development and Decline in the Mediterranean Bronze Age*: 221–70. Sheffield: J.R. Collis.
   1995   *The Absolute Chronology of the Aegean Early Bronze Age. Archaeology, Radiocarbon and History.* Sheffield: Sheffield Academic Press.
   1997   Cultural change in the Aegean c. 2200 BC. In H. Nuzhet Dalfes, G. Kukla and H. Weiss (eds.), *Third Millennium BC Climate Change and Old World Collapse*: 149–71. Berlin: Springer-Verlag.
Møller, E.
   1980   A revaluation of the Oriental cylinder seals found in Crete. In J. Best and N. de Vries (eds.), *Interaction and Acculturation in the Mediterranean, 1*: 85–104. Amsterdam: B.R. Grüner.
Momigliano, N.
   1991   MMIA Pottery from Evans' excavations at Knossos: a reassessment. *BSA* 86: 149–272.
   2000   On the Early Minoan III–Middle Minoan IA sequence at Knossos. *Proceedings of the Eighth International Cretological Congress, 1*: 335–45. Iraklion: Historical Society of Crete.
Müller, S.
   1990   Malia: prospection de la plaine de Malia. *BCH* 114: 921–30.

1991   Malia: prospection de la plaine de Malia. *BCH* 115: 741–49.

1992   Malia: prospection de la plaine de Malia. *BCH* 116: 742–53.

1996   Malia: prospection archéologique de la plaine de Malia. *BCH* 120: 921–28.

1997   Malia et la Crète de l'âge du bronze: l'organisation d'un territoire minoen. *Dossiers d'Archéologie* 222: 52–53.

1998   Malia: prospection archéologique de la plaine de Malia. *BCH* 122: 548–52.

Müller Celka, S.

2000   Malia: prospection archéologique de la plaine de Malia. *BCH* 124: 501–05.

Olivier, J.-P. and T. McGeorge

1977   Fouille d'urgence de l'entrée du 'charnier no. 4', en C4/f 5–6. *BCH* 101: 701–03.

Panagiotopoulos, D.

2002   *Das Tholosgrab E von Phourni bei Archanes* (BAR International Series 1014). Oxford: British Archaeological Reports.

Papadatos, Y.

1999   *Mortuary Practices and their Importance for the Reconstruction of Prepalatial Society and Life: the Evidence from Tholos Gamma, in Archanes-Phourni.* PhD dissertation, Sheffield University.

Peatfield, A.

1988   Knossos palace excavations. *Kritiki Estia* 2: 322–23.

Pelon, O.

1987   Particularités et développment des palais Minoens. In E. Levy (ed.), *Le Système palatial en Orient, en Grèce et à Rome*: 187–201. Strasbourg: University of Sciences and Humanities.

1989   Le palais. *BCH* 113: 771–86.

1991   Le palais. *BCH* 115: 726–35.

1993   La Salle à piliers du Palais de Malia et ses antécédents: recherches complémentaires. *BCH* 117: 523–46.

Phillips, J.

1996   Egypto-Aegean relations up to the 2nd millennium B.C. In L. Krzyzaniak, K. Kroeper and M. Kobusiewicz (eds.), *Interregional Contacts in the Later Prehistory of Northeastern Africa*: 459–70. Poznan: Poznan Archaeological Museum.

Pini, I.

1989   Zehn frühkretische Skarabäen. In T. Hackens and G. Moucharte (eds*.), Technology and Analysis of Ancient Gemstones*. PACT 23: 99–111.

2000   Eleven early Cretan scarabs. In A. Karetsou (ed.), *Kriti-Aigyptos. Politismikoi Desmoi Trion Khilietion*: 107–13. Athens: Kapon.

Poursat, J.-C.

1983   Ateliers et sanctuaires à Malia: nouvelles données sur l'organisation sociale à l'époque des premiers palais. In O. Kryzszkowska and L. Nixon (eds.), *Minoan Society*: 277–81. Bristol: Bristol Classical Press.

1988   La ville minoenne de Malia: recherches et publications récentes. *Revue Archéologique* 1: 61–82.

Poursat, J.-C. and P. Darque

1990   Sondages autour du quartier Mu. *BCH* 111: 908–12.

Renfrew, C.

1964   Crete and the Cyclades before Rhadamanthus. *Kritika Khronika* 18: 107–41.

1972   *The Emergence of Civilisation. The Cyclades and the Aegean in the Third Millennium B.C.* London: Methuen.

Rutter, J. and C. Zerner

1983   Early Hellado-Minoan contacts. In R. Hägg and N. Marinatos (eds.), *The Minoan Thalassocracy: Myth and Reality*: 75–83. Stockholm: Swedish Institute in Athens.

Sakellarakis, Y.
1977   Ta kikladika stoikhia ton Arhanon. *AAA* 10: 93–113.

Sakellarakis, Y. and E. Sapouna-Sakellaraki
1997   *Archanes. Minoan Crete in a New Light*. Athens: Ammos.

Sbonias, K.
1999   Social development, management of production, and symbolic representation in Prepalatial Crete. In A. Chaniotis (ed.), *From Minoan Farmers to Roman Traders: Sidelights on the Economy of Ancient Crete*: 25–51. Stuttgart: Franz Steiner.
2000   Specialization in the Early Minoan seal manufacture: craftsmen, settlements and the organization of production. In I. Pini (ed.), *Minoischen-Mykenisch Glyptik, Stil, Ikonographie, Funktion* (Corpus der Minoischen und Mykenischen Siegel 6): 277–93. Berlin: Mann.

Schoep, I.
1999a   The origins of writing and administration in Crete. *OJA* 18: 265–76.
1999b   Tablets and territories? Reconstructing Late Minoan IB political geography through undeciphered documents. *AJA* 103: 201–21.
2001   Managing the hinterland: the rural concerns of urban administration. In K. Branigan (ed.), *Urbanism in the Aegean Bronze Age* (SSAA 4): 87–102. Sheffield: Sheffield Academic Press.
2002a   Social and political organization on Crete in the Proto-Palatial period: the case of Middle Minoan Malia. *JMA* 15: 101–32.
2002b   The state of the Minoan palaces or the Minoan palace-state? In J. Driessen, I. Schoep and R. Laffineur (eds.), *Monuments of Minos. Rethinking the Minoan Palaces* (Aegaeum 23): 15–33. Liège: Université de Liège.

Seager, R.B.
1909   Excavations on the island of Mochlos, Crete, in 1908. *AJA* 13: 273–303.
1912   *Explorations in the Island of Mochlos*. Boston: American School of Classical Studies.

Shaw, J.W.
1973   The Chrysollakos facades. *Proceedings of the Third Cretological Congress, 1*: 319–31. Athens.

Sherratt, A.
1993   What would a Bronze-Age world system look like? Relations between temperate Europe and the Mediterranean in later prehistory. *Journal of European Archaeology* 1: 1–58.

Sherratt, A., and S. Sherratt
1991   From luxuries to commodities: the nature of Mediterranean Bronze Age trading systems. In N. Gale (ed.), *Bronze Age Trade in the Mediterranean* (SIMA 90): 351–86. Göteborg: Paul Åström.

Soles, J.
1978   Mochlos. A new look at old excavations: the University Museum's work on Crete. *Expedition* 20, 2: 4–15.
1988   Social ranking in Prepalatial cemeteries. In E.B. French and K.A. Wardle (eds.), *Problems in Greek Prehistory*: 49–61. Bristol: Bristol Classical Press.
1992   *Prepalatial Cemeteries at Mochlos and Gournia and the House Tombs of Bronze Age Crete* (Hesperia Supplement 24). Princeton: American School of Classical Studies.

Soles, J. and C. Davaras
1992   Excavations at Mochlos, 1989. *Hesperia* 61: 413–45.

Stos-Gale, Z.
1985 Lead and silver sources for Bronze Age Crete. *Proceedings of the Fifth Cretological Congress, A*: 365–72. Athens.
1993 The origin of metal used for making weapons in Early and Middle Minoan Crete. In C. Scarre and F. Healy (eds.), *Trade and Exchange in Prehistoric Europe*: 115–29. Oxford: Oxbow.
1998 The role of Kythnos and other Cycladic islands in the origins of Early Minoan metallurgy. In L.G. Mendoni and A. Mazarakis Ainian (eds.), *Kea-Kythnos: History and Archaeology* (Meletimata 27): 717–35. Athens: Research Centre for Greek and Roman Antiquity, National Hellenic Research Foundation.
2001 Minoan foreign relations and copper metallurgy in Protopalatial and Neopalatial Crete. In A. Shortland (ed.), *The Social Context of Technological Change. Egypt and the Near East, 1650–1550 BC*: 195–210. Oxford: Oxbow Books.
Strøm, I.
1980 Middle Minoan Crete: a re-consideration of some of its external relations. In J. Best and N. de Vries (eds.), *Interaction and Acculturation in the Mediterranean, 1*: 105–23. Amsterdam: Grüner.
Stucynski, S.
1982 Cycladic 'imports' in Crete: a brief survey. *Temple University Aegean Symposium* 7: 50–59.
Torrence, R.
1986 *Production and Exchange of Stone Tools*. Cambridge: Cambridge University Press.
Tsipopoulou, M.
2002 Petras, Siteia: the palace, the town, the hinterland and the Protopalatial background. In J. Driessen, I. Schoep and R. Laffineur (eds.), *Monuments of Minos. Rethinking the Minoan Palaces* (Aegaeum 23): 133–44. Liège: Université de Liège.
Van Effenterre, H.
1980a *Le Palais de Malia et la cité Minoenne* (Incunabula Graeca 76). Rome: Ateneo.
1980b Jalons pour une nouvelle histoire des premiers palais. *Proceedings of the Fourth International Cretological Congress. 1*: 137–49. Athens.
Van Effenterre, H. and M. Van Effenterre
1963 *Fouilles exécutées à Mallia: étude du site (1956–1957) et exploration des nécropoles (1915–1928), 2*. Paris: Paul Guenther.
Vasilakis, A.
1990 Proistorikes thesis sti Moni Odigitrias, Kaloi Limenes. *Kritiki Estia* 3: 9–80.
Voutsaki, S.
1997 The creation of value and prestige in the Aegean Late Bronze Age. *Journal of European Archaeology* 5: 34–52.
Walberg, G.
1983 *Provincial Middle Minoan Pottery*. Mainz: Von Zabern.
Warren, P.
1965 The first Minoan stone vases and Early Minoan chronology. *Kritika Khronika* 19: 7–43.
1969 *Minoan Stone Vases*. Cambridge: Cambridge University Press.
1972 *Myrtos: an Early Bronze Age Site in Crete* (Supplementary Volume 7). London: British School at Athens.
1975 *The Aegean Civilizations*. London: Elsevier-Phaidon.
1983 The settlement at Fournou Korifi, Myrtos (Crete) and its place within the evolution of the rural community of Bronze Age Crete. In, Les Communautés Rurales, 2: Antiquité. *Recueils de la Société Jean Bodin pour l'Histoire Comparative des Institutions* 41: 239–71.

1984   Early Minoan-Early Cycladic chronological correlations. In R. Barber and J.A. MacGillivray (eds.), *The Prehistoric Cyclades. Contributions to a Workshop on Cycladic Chronology*: 55–62. Edinburgh: Department of Classical Archaeology.

1987   The genesis of the Minoan Palace. In R. Hägg and N. Marinatos (eds.), *The Function of the Minoan Palaces*: 47–56. Stockholm: Swedish Institute in Athens.

1995   Minoan Crete and Pharaonic Egypt. In W.V. Davies and L. Schofield (eds.), *Egypt, the Aegean and the Levant: Interconnections in the Second Millennium BC*: 1–18. London: British Museum Press.

Watrous, L.V.

2001   Crete from earliest prehistory through the Protopalatial period. Addendum: 1995–1999. In T. Cullen (ed.), *Aegean Prehistory. A Review*: 216–23. Boston: Archaeological Institute of America.

Watrous, L.V., D. Hatzi-Vallianou, K. Pope, N. Mourtzas, J. Shay, C. Shay, J. Bennet, D. Tsoungarakis, E. Angelomati-Tsoungarakis, C. Vallianos and H. Blitzer

1993   A survey of the western Mesara plain in Crete. Preliminary report on the 1984, 1986 and 1987 field seasons. *Hesperia* 62: 191–248.

Whitelaw, T.

1983   The settlement at Fournou Korifi, Myrtos, and aspects of Early Minoan social organisation. In O. Krzyszkowska and L. Nixon (eds.), *Minoan Society*: 323–45. Bristol: Bristol Classical Press.

2000   Beyond the palace: a century of investigation in Europe's oldest city. *BICS* 44: 223–26.

in press Estimating the population of Neopalatial Knossos. In G. Cadogan and E. Hatzaki (eds.), *Knossos: Palace, City, State*. London: British School at Athens.

Whitelaw, T., P.M. Day, E.Kiriatzi, V.Kilikoglou, and D.E. Wilson

1997   Ceramic traditions at EM IIB Myrtos, Fournou Korifi. In R. Laffineur and P. Betancourt (eds.), *TEKHNH: Craftsmen, Craftswomen and Craftsmanship in the Aegean Bronze Age* (Aegaeum 16): 265–74. Liège: Université de Liège.

Wiencke, M.H.

1989   Change in Early Helladic II. *AJA* 93: 495–509.

Wilson, D.

1985   The pottery and architecture of the EM II A West Court house at Knossos. *BSA* 80: 281–364.

1994   Knossos before the palaces: an overview of the Early Bronze Age (EM I–EM III). In D. Evely, H. Hughes-Brock and N. Momigliano (eds.), *Knossos, a Labyrinth of History. Papers Presented in Honour of Sinclair Hood*: 23–44. Oxford: British School at Athens.

Wilson, D. and P.M. Day

1994   Ceramic regionalism in Prepalatial central Crete: the Mesara imports at EM I to EM IIA Knossos. *BSA* 89: 1–87.

Wilson, D., P. Day and N. Dimopoulou

in press The pottery from EM I–IIB Knossos and its relations with the harbour site of Poros-Katsambas. In G. Cadogan and E. Hatzaki (eds.), *Knossos: Palace, City, State*. London: British School at Athens.

Yule, P.

1983   Notes on scarabs and Aegean chronology. *BSA* 78: 359–67.

1988   Early and Middle Minoan foreign relations: the evidence from seals. *SMEA* 26: 161–75.

14

Rethinking *The Emergence*

Colin Renfrew

To subject *The Emergence of Civilisation* to close scrutiny some thirty years after its publication was an interesting experience. So much has changed, in terms of new discoveries and new ideas, over that time period. But other things have not: some of the surrounding debates, for instance the old diffusion (now read 'world system') versus independent invention (now read 'endogenous morphogenesis') debate has a whiff of the *déja vu*, and would have had a hint of the *déja vu* already in 1972.

That the trigesimal celebration in Sheffield in January 2002 was a fruitful and interesting enterprise was due to the various insights offered by the participants in the Round Table, and I am grateful to them for the sympathy which they showed for a work which now belongs to a different century. In the comments which follow I should like to acknowledge the validity of many of the points, corrections and criticisms which were made. They certainly prompt a re-evaluation of the purposes and shortcomings of the entire enterprise. Certainly the most encouraging recognition which the book could receive is the very real interest and value of the papers contained in the present volume.

In what follows I should like to review the nature of the original project itself. Probably the best way of judging the utility of the formulation of such a project and the theoretical constructs and the modelling which it entails, is to examine the extent to which it has encouraged the application of new data to those theories and constructs, and the extent to which that application has permitted the development of new synthetic and theoretical perspectives. The critique of redistribution, led by Paul Halstead and his colleagues, has been one of these, and the application of systematic survey, reviewed here by John Cherry and Todd Whitelaw, has been another: their papers here, and the work over three decades which they encapsulate, are significant and positive examples of this process. The reconsideration of the role of the House of the Tiles at Lerna by Olia Peperaki is another.

Models and theoretical approaches have to be stretched and re-formulated if they are to continue to play an active role, and the identification by Todd Whitelaw of what he calls (this volume) 'the homogenising assumptions of the *Emergence* model' opens the way to useful and positive developments. Some of these are well and constructively exemplified in Cyprian Broodbank's *An Island Archaeology of the Early Cyclades* (Broodbank 2000), the first such synthesis which seeks to identify and examine the consequences of what is characteristic and special to a specific region in the Aegean. Although Broodbank does not have a paper in the present volume, he was a participant at the Round Table. His comment that: '*The Emergence*, though a landmark in some many ways, is simultaneously much more, and decidedly less, than a truly satisfactory study of what lies behind the archaeology of the Cycladic islands' (Broodbank 2000: 56) is well taken and seems today a perceptive one. His book, as well as a critique, shows how one may transcend some of those limitations and 'homogenising assumptions'.

Some component models in the enterprise can perhaps benefit from complete reformulation. No issue, when we are dealing with fairly deep prehistory, is more sensitive and problematic that than of social process and social structure, vulnerable as our insights are to the varying qualities of evidence from settlements and from cemeteries. The problem of the emergence of inequality is central to the entire archaeological endeavour, and has indeed been seen to be so since the time of Hobbes and Rousseau, even before the discipline of archaeology was invented, and from its early days in the work of Marx. So it is refreshing that Jim Wright's paper on 'The emergence of leadership' goes to the heart of some of these issues. They were discussed also at the Round Table in the contribution by Yannis Hamilakis, 'The de(con)struction of "civilisation": consumption, embodiment and power in the Bronze Age Aegean'. It is not included in the present volume, but some of the points he made are set out in a recent paper (Hamilakis 2002) which, like Broodbank's book, can well be regarded as an element of the debate.

As I shall indicate below, I feel myself that the area most overlooked in discussions of Aegean archaeology since the publication of *The Emergence* has been the articulation which links what one would today term the cognitive sphere ('the symbolic and projective subsystem'), including the ritual and religious dimension, with other aspects of the life of the time. Such articulations can come about only through the human individual, a point which I made clearly in the last chapter of the book (Renfrew 1972: 504), indeed in its concluding paragraph. This is an issue central to the thoughtful discussion here by John Barrett and Krysti Damilati. It is very much the subject matter also of recent discussions, which are touched upon in a number of the contributions here on the nature of 'agency'. This was a term which was not widely current in the theoretical archaeology of the 1970s, and it is one about which I have reservations, since it seeks to establish a somewhat detached abstraction (i.e. agency) out of human action, which by its nature is always direct, and embedded in events and rooted within their immediate contexts. But I am not in a position to be over-critical about abstractions, since the articulations in question are, in *The Emergence*, found in the equally abstract interactions between the sub-systems of the culture system in the model which I formulated.

These are important debates, and such issues are indeed difficult to discuss without some degree of abstraction. This can easily lead us to miss or undervalue other realities, such as embodiment or corporeality, which Hamilakis (2002: 20) seeks to emphasize, and with which I am sympathetic (see Renfrew 2003b, 108 – 129). But these are debates which inevitably rest upon the use of language, and of linguistic constructs such as the term 'state' or 'civilization'. And while it is possible to use such terms in the prescriptive, unilineal manner which Hamilakis (2002: 7–15) chooses to term 'neo-evolutionary', to abandon them altogether, as he proposes, risks throwing out the processual baby with the post-processual bathwater. Haggis (2002: 121) partakes of the same critique when he asserts 'The study of Aegean societies uses paradigms that are diachronic in scope and therefore implicitly developmental if not evolutionary in outlook'. But that, I am afraid, is a critique with which we shall have to learn to live, for as archaeologists we are inescapably interested in the diachronic, and so development (and perhaps therefore even 'evolution') is very much our business. I am not sure that this makes us 'evolutionists', or even – perish the thought, 'neo-evolutionists'. But we can write only with words, and words represent concepts, so that concepts are not easily avoided.

The Project

The project of analysing the development of a large and internally-structured socio-political community, such as a state society, is an ambitious one. In the Preface to *The Emergence* what may perhaps be an over-bold claim is made (Renfrew 1972: xxvi): 'This is the first time, I believe, that an attempt has been made to examine, in such detail the emergence of one of the world's early civilisations'. It is of course the case that there have been many more detailed treatments of individual sites, more thorough surveys of specific regions and indeed several splendidly illuminating treatments of individual complex societies (e.g. Kemp 1989; Postgate 1992). But to develop a theoretical framework, whereby the processes of growth and of emergence can be analysed, has rarely been the primary focus of interest. The most notable exception is the splendid treatment of the Zapotec and Mixtec civilizations of Oaxaca by Flannery and Marcus (1983; see also Flannery 1976), which gets to the nub of many of the central problems. These were already, as Cherry (this volume) remarks, adumbrated in a seminal paper (Flannery 1972), published in the same year as *The Emergence*.

In contemplating so ambitious a project it is worth reviewing some of the properties which a satisfactory analysis should be expected to possess. A simple narrative may not be enough. The project must involve a number of elements, many of them discussed in the papers in this volume, which are not often made explicit. It is pertinent to do so here. These elements, I suggest, would be relevant to any such undertaking applied to a society flourishing at whatever time in whichever place. Some of these elements relate not to the first application but to the subsequent uses of the model, and to its ensuing development as further data come to light. That is certainly the position in which the framework presented in *The Emergence* finds itself after thirty years of further archaeological work in the Aegean.

Such a review gives the opportunity of noting the merits of the observations which have been made in relation to *The Emergence* in the papers presented here, and perhaps also of questioning some of their criticisms. I suggest that the project, and the theoretical framework which it employs should possess the properties listed below. It should be:

1.   *Potentially comparative.* That is to say the general framework adopted should, with appropriate modifications, be capable of being applied to other societies (or 'complex societies' or 'state societies', if these terms are not dismissed as 'neo-evolutionary') in other parts of the world. This is not to deny that each of the Aegean societies in question was itself unique, and that each can only adequately be understood in its own specific context. But at the same time, we shall not adequately understand the societies of the Cretan Late Bronze Age or the Cycladic Early Bronze Age, if we are not able to compare them with others which might seem relevant, as for instance in the sense of Broodbank's 'island archaeology'. To reject any such comparative approach would simply be to accede to the demands of the anti-evolutionary thought police and so work in the complete isolation which the logic of their demands would imply.

2.   *Diachronic.* The analysis must look at earlier and later developments – I would say at earlier and later stages of the developmental trajectory, but am not particularly arguing for a division into developmental stages, as such. Stages are just heuristic tools. It is relevant, however, that the diachronic analysis should be based upon a chronology that is accurate. It will need also to partition the world into different sites, different societies, different regions and perhaps different 'cultures'. Such spatial, social or geographical divisions will often be as arbitrary as the chronological divisions (stages) employed. But they are inevitable if the geographical and chronological continua in which humans and human societies exist are to be spoken of.

3.   *Holistic yet aspective.* Human societies cannot rigorously be divided into separate thematic compartments. Yet if we are seeking to examine a settlement (e.g. a city) or a community (e.g. a nation) we need to be able simultaneously to see it functioning as a whole, yet to focus also upon the different kinds of action or of process which are at work. We need to be able to look at the

social structure, or to consider the religious beliefs and rituals of the inhabitants. We need to be able to consider health, or agriculture, or commerce. We need to be able to review fertility and longevity. We are entitled to look at burial customs, or to examine class structure. Yet in each of these undertakings we do not wish to lose track of the human individual, nor of specific actions of that individual. We do not wish to be fobbed off with the faceless token worker of the sociologist or the economist. We want to be able to operate at the micro-level as well as at the macro-level. This I take to be the concern of those who today write about agency and the individual actor. But at the same time we have to look at the unintended consequences of action. This point is considered again in (8) below.

It was to have the opportunity of working both at the level of the society as a whole and at that of the varying processes within it, that a systems framework was chosen for *The Emergence*. The community or group of societies working together in a larger unit, such as a state, could thus be regarded as constituting the system, while different aspects, such as subsistence or external trade, could be considered as sub-systems. Such partitioning is never easy, and the 'systems' terminology, as Carl Knappett and Ilse Schoep note in this volume, has not always found favour. In its articulations it can seem somewhat robotic. But the behaviour of large and complex systems is itself a valid subject of study, as they note. And I agree with Schoep and Knappett that the notions of morphogenesis (see Rosen 1979; 1982) and of self-organization, as developed for instance by Ilya Prigogine (see Allen 1982; Renfrew 1982; van der Leeuw and McGlade 1997), as well as of catastrophe, in the positive as well as the negative sense (Zeeman 1979; Renfrew and Poston 1979; Friedman 1982) have a potential that remains to be further explored. But the trouble with simulation studies, as I came to realize some years ago (Renfrew and Cooke 1979; Renfrew 1981), is that they have hitherto had difficulty in coping with the emergent properties which arise from the unexpected richness of human creativity and from the uniquely human ability to formulate new symbolic constructs in the course of the engagement process between humans and the world (see further below).

That the theoretical framework should be both holistic and aspective continues to seem an appropriate requirement. And it does carry with it the aspiration, well asserted here by Schoep and Knappett, that continuing developments in the analysis of very large systems – including chaos theory and fractal theory – might be involved. In doing so they will not thereby incur the approbation of the particularistic tendency among interpretive archaeologists, who prefer to work exclusively at the level of the human individual, and thus to eschew the allegedly hegemonic aspects of very large systems. But the opportunities are there.

4. *Recursive with respect to data.* As noted earlier, any theoretical approach, if it is to be useful, must lead the worker back to the data. And, when the data make this desirable, the theory must be modified. As I have noted elsewhere, this property of being open to rectification, or indeed where appropriate, rejection (i.e. the criterion of testability) may be summarized in the recursive relationship:

Theory ⟷ Data

This is one of the basic tenets of the scientific method (although paradoxically it has also been claimed by some post-modernists as a property of the 'hermeneutic circle').

As noted above, and further below, the project of documenting and understanding the Aegean Bronze Age, has been substantially modified over the past three decades by the data arising from contemporary survey methods. It has also benefited from reconsiderations by Halstead and his colleagues of the notion of redistribution in the palace economies and earlier, using data deriving not only from the evidence of animal husbandry, but also from the Linear B tablets.

5. *Open to theoretical innovation.* Any useful theoretical approach must be open to extension and innovation, as well as to the modification or correction implied in the last section. Just as the 'symbolic and projective system' (see point 8 below) has been little developed in recent years, so the social system, which likewise received a separate chapter in the initial exposition, today looks in need of further consideration. That need not entail the demolition of the entire approach, as Hamilakis seems to advocate. But it will involve the consideration of the different theoretical issues raised in the paper by Wright, as well as the more constructive issues which Hamilakis (2002) himself makes when encouraging the discussion of gender issues or developing notions of corporeality.

It seems strange, also, that the entire discussion, in all the papers cited above, whether in this volume or beyond, has managed to escape issues of ethnicity (Jones 1997; Renfrew 1995). This may not be the place to raise issues concerning the languages of the prehistoric Aegean (Renfrew 1998), but it may be worth asking what it actually meant to be 'Mycenaean' or 'Minoan' (Renfrew 1996).

6. *Expansive to variability.* In his contribution to this volume, Todd Whitelaw, as observed above, notes what he calls 'the homogenising assumptions of the *Emergence* model', which served among other things to obscure the variability between the different regions of the Aegean. As he points out, ' 30 years of further intensive research… have only served to document [the] differences

in ever greater detail'. That is right, and the approach we use must be able to recognize the validity of that comment, and to accommodate the degree of variety between the regions and between the trajectories of development which are now visible. He recognizes that 30 years ago these differences were less easy to discern, and it may be fair to say that to achieve any coherence at all it was then in some cases necessary to pool the evidence, and so write a single story, where several should now be discerned. He begins to rectify these omissions with the two alternative developmental pathways which he presents.

As noted above, Broodbank's comment (2000: 56), that *The Emergence* was a less than satisfactory study of the Cycladic islands, is in many ways a valid one. Ironically perhaps it applies with equal validity to a later work, *An Island Polity* (Renfrew and Wagstaff 1982). For while that may have been effective in looking at one island as a unit, and in reviewing the changes in its general relations with the Aegean world, it did not concentrate as Broodbank himself has so effectively done, upon the quality of *insularity* of Melos, and indeed of the other Cycladic islands. The project of discussing Aegean developments has to be open to ever-improving analyses of the different regions of the Aegean, and of their differing trajectories of development. That is a task which Maria Relaki herself undertakes in her paper (this volume), where she looks in detail at the Mesara region of Crete.

7. *Endogenous – autonomist.* The project of analysing change in a society must, I would argue, begin by looking in detail at factors within that society, and only at a later stage should external factors be considered. Halstead (this volume) has referred to 'the autonomist agenda of *The Emergence*', and I think that the implications of his point have to be conceded. For on the first page of the book I wrote (Renfrew 1972: xxv):

'I have come to believe that [the] widely held diffusionist view, that Aegean civilisation was something borrowed by Europe from the Orient, is inadequate. It fails to explain what is actually seen in the archaeological record. We can no longer accept that the sole unifying theme of European prehistory was, in the words of Gordon Childe, "the irradiation of European barbarism by Orient civilization."'

Now it may seem strange to propose as a principle for the Project what must ultimately be an empirical matter: whether or not the main thrust towards change has come from outside the region in question. For just as it has been my own critique that the secondary status of Aegean Bronze Age civilization has often been assumed, so it could justly be observed that to assume the converse, its primary nature, is equally inappropriate. In the last analysis I accept that point: indeed I would assert it with vigour.

However, as a heuristic device, it does seem necessary to make the attempt to see the changes which we observe as essentially the result of processes operating within and between the societies in question. For only by making that attempt can we see whether or not the approach is indeed a viable one. The alternative is to fall back into the assumption made by Childe, based ultimately upon a circularity of diffusionist chronological reasoning, quoted in the passage above. What I regard as an entirely homologous argument to that of Childe, although garbed in the new apparel of World Systems Theory, is the centre-periphery approach which Andrew Sherratt (e.g. A. Sherratt 1993) has vigorously advocated in relation to prehistoric Europe, along with other well-qualified scholars such as Kristian Kristiansen. Sometimes, it seems to me, the analytical procedure they employ is little more than one of proclamation. Area X is proclaimed as a centre and region Y as a periphery. It suffices then to find a few imports in region Y which derive from area X and the case is felt to be established. What might in other circumstances be taken as evidence to the contrary, such as the presence in area X of imports from region Y, is instead seen as further proof of the centre-periphery relationship.

This point is further considered below, in relation to the Early Bronze Age Aegean, on the basis of the empirical evidence. The whole general issue does, however, present theoretical problems which have not yet been fully resolved. I concede that this principle will be seen by critics as a shade dogmatic, and also that it could not be maintained as a valid one in all circumstances. I do, however, regard it as appropriate for the Aegean case in the current state of our knowledge.

8.   *Human (agentive)*. The project has to give particular attention to 'the uniquely human ability to find symbolic means' (Renfrew 1972: 304) of relating different aspects of the world, involving social relationships and technological innovation. That ability operates through the human individual, the human agent. I am sympathetic, as noted above, to the intentions of those who today are advocates of 'agency', although I do not personally find the abstraction of that quality from direct human action particularly helpful. In the section on the Cognitive Dimension below this issue will be further addressed, since it touches on the most neglected of the subsystems to which a chapter was assigned in *The Emergence*, dealing with the symbolic and projective, or what one might today call the cognitive.

These, then, are some of the properties which I suggest are appropriate to the task of explaining the emergence of a civilization. It is scarcely necessary to address them all again below. But some further points need to be made.

Some Reconsiderations

Diachronic Aspects

It was Sir Mortimer Wheeler who observed, in a book review, that *The Emergence* was inconveniently long, that it was really two books rather than one. That was a fair criticism, and indeed the work was divided into two parts: 'Culture sequence' and 'Culture process', the former largely dependent on my doctoral dissertation of 1965. The first part is, however, a necessary prelude to the second, and so far as the Early Bronze Age is concerned the culture sequence for each area has not been changed fundamentally or re-structured by later discoveries or syntheses. Certainly the Early Minoan sequence is now rather better understood, and our lack of understanding of the Cretan Neolithic, as noted below, is becoming increasingly apparent. The Cycladic sequence, with additions introduced by the work of Doumas (1977), is still viable. However I agree with the observations of Broodbank (2000: 209) as well as those of Rambach and Sotirakopoulou, that the so-called 'Amorgos group' of the Cycladic Early Bronze Age is not a well-defined entity in space and time, and that it can effectively be abandoned. On the other hand the Kastri group, which has generated so much discussion, still seems a useful concept, situated in the later part of the Keros-Syros culture, without necessarily carrying with it implications of a 'gap'.

The absolute chronology is likewise little changed. The new radiocarbon dates from Markiani on Amorgos (Marangou et al., in press) support a picture differing only by a century or so from that which could be set forth 30 years ago through the calibration of the radiocarbon dates then available (Renfrew 1972: 220–21).

The vast quantities of new data that have become available are well reviewed in the volume edited by Cullen (2001). In the Cyclades the main developments for the Early Bronze Age are the excavation of the extensive Early Bronze 2 site of Skarkos on Ios by Marisa Marthari, of the multi-phase settlement of Markiani on Amorgos and of the deep-soundings at Akrotiri on Thera, together with the investigations at the very rich but looted Early Cycladic site of Dhaskalio Kavos on Keros. The picture for the Neolithic period is however being transformed by new sites of the Late Neolithic period, broadly contemporary with Saliagos, such as Ftelia on Mykonos (Sampson 2002), and by the extraordinary Final Neolithic site of Strophilas on Andros, excavated by Christina Televantou. These and other Cycladic developments are reviewed in a forthcoming volume (Brodie *et al.*, in press). The finds at Strophilas include an extensive fortification wall, which reshapes our understanding of the history of defensive works in the prehistoric Aegean, and rock engravings which feature depictions of longboats, possibly analogous to those long known from the frying pans of Early Cycladic Chalandriani on Syros. These must imply significant revisions of our understanding of Aegean seafaring and its social implications.

Data-based Revisions

Three papers in the present volume deal very effectively with two important areas where the evaluation of new data has substantially modified the picture set out in 1972. The first such area is that of settlement and population, where the perspective has been changed profoundly by the development of systematic survey, as the papers by Cherry and by Whitelaw effectively document. As Cherry has noted elsewhere (Cherry 2003), the development of systematic survey has brought new insights into the nature of landscape archaeology, although many interpretive difficulties remain. If *The Emergence* were to be re-written today, it would start with a formidably transformed database, and one presenting many interpretive problems. It would, moreover, need to operate with drastically revised (and generally reduced) estimates of population and population density. Whitelaw (2001) in particular has shown that the estimates for average site size, and for population per unit area employed in *The Emergence* need to be scaled down rather drastically. If the book were indeed to be re-written, which might be an overwhelming task in view of the quantities of data now available, Chapter 14 (Patterns of Settlement and Population), would be the most radically revised, at least in so far as the absolute figures offered are concerned.

Another area where subsequent research has profoundly altered the earlier picture is that of the role of the Mycenaean palaces (and probably the Minoan ones also) and the whole question of a redistributive economy. In a series of papers Halstead (1992; 1999; 2001; this volume; Halstead and O'Shea 1982) has successfully questioned the status of the palatial economy as a redistributive one in the sense defined by Polanyi and as employed in *The Emergence*. That the palace as an organization was in part a redistributive system need not be in doubt, but it is now clear that this applied to only one part of the rural economy, and that other aspects of the palace economy (for instance wool production) were not necessarily redistributive in that sense. Moreover, while Mediterranean polyculture may well have played a significant role from the Early Bronze Age onwards (of which more below), the importance of the olive and the vine may have been more limited in scale. Nor need they have been produced in significantly different areas in such a way as to make their redistribution beneficial on a large scale. The economic role of the palace as an organization, not least in providing for their elite and for their craft specialists, does not have to be called into doubt – even if Susan Sherratt's idea of Potemkin palaces (S. Sherratt 2001), dismissing their real economic significance, is in some ways an attractive one. David Small's suggestion that the Mycenaean polities be regarded as estates rather than states (Small 1999) carries similar implications. That the whole economy worked on a redistributive basis has been shown to be a misconception.

A fascinating insight into another case where our data have hitherto been severely limited is offered by the paper contributed by Peter Tomkins (this volume). The extraordinary revelation on the basis of ceramic petrology that, during the Early to Middle Neolithic period at Knossos, something like half of the ceramic vessels represented are non-local products comes as a considerable surprise, since until very recently no other sites at all of that period were known in Crete. The observation reminds us, in the first place, how very fragmentary is our knowledge, and what a small proportion it often represents of the original picture. Tomkins goes on to point out that the opposition, which he not unreasonably discerns in *The Emergence* between the relative autonomy and independence of Neolithic communities as depicted there, and the diversity and interdependence of Early Bronze Age societies, may be a misleading one. Of course the elucidation of the sources of Aegean obsidian long ago dispensed with any notion of isolation in the Aegean Neolithic. But Tomkins is right to suggest that the picture is changing, and that new models of Neolithic economy and society are called for.

Endogenous Change

The role of early metallurgy in developing the 'international spirit' of the Early Bronze 2 period in the Aegean has long been acknowledged, as has the precocious development of copper metallurgy in the Balkans. What has only recently become apparent, however, is the extent to which copper metallurgy was indeed practised during the later Neolithic period. The trouble has been that many of the Aegean metal finds that one might wish to describe as 'chalcolithic' were not from well-stratified contexts. The position has shifted significantly, however, with the find of metal objects including a copper dagger from Late Neolithic levels of the Cave of Zas in Naxos (Zachos and Douzougli 1999). Metal finds from Late Neolithic Ftelia on Mykonos (Sampson 2002) as well as from Final Neolithic Strophilas on Andros fall into place alongside the evidence of metallurgy from Final Neolithic Kephala on Kea (Coleman 1977) to give a much more convincing indication of the use of metal in the Late Neolithic Aegean (Zachos 1996) and its subsequent development (Nakou 1995). Metallurgical practice involving the use of crucibles for casting is now well documented for the later fifth millennium BC at Sitagroi in East Macedonia (Renfrew and Slater 2003). So the early development of Aegean metallurgy is well documented. There is always the possibility that finds of the same period from western Anatolia will yet emerge. But for the present the Aegean context of one of the major innovations underlying the later developments of the Aegean Early Bronze Age seems well established.

The finds of clay sealings from the Kastri group levels at the Cave of Zas in Naxos (Zachos, in press) and from the rather modest Early Cycladic settlement at Markiani on Amorgos (Marangou et al., in press) certainly brings to the fore once again the question of the precise kind of organization which they represent, as is well brought out by the paper by Peperaki on the most important such find of the period in the House of the Tiles at Lerna. Acknowledging the point accepted earlier, simply to introduce the notion of 'redistribution' may not offer the most appropriate model. But some form of organization is certainly involved, as the occasional finds of seals from the Mainland (Pullen 1994) as well as from the Cyclades document. Schoep and Knappett in their paper introduce the notion of heterarchy in contrast to hierarchy in their discussion of the rather scanty finds of sealings from Early Minoan Crete, and heterarchy is a term favoured also by Haggis (2002). I predict that we can expect some interesting further developments in this direction.

But just as the find of seals and sealings need not necessarily indicate redistribution in the now-conventional sense, nor need it necessarily be taken as the consequence of external trade (Weingarten 1997), whether with Anatolia or the Near East. While the form of the seals and some of their designs may be influenced from that direction, as Aruz (1999) has recently and plausibly asserted, and as indeed was recognized in *The Emergence*, particularly when ivory seals from Early Minoan Crete were in question, this does not necessarily imply that their use and the organization which these sealings implies can be regarded as exogenous. There is, after all, a very respectable Neolithic ancestry in the Aegean and the Balkans for what may be termed 'stamp seals' (Makkay 1984) and indeed for some of the designs. It is only four decades since the distinguished Sumerologist Falkenstein (1965) was proclaiming the Sumerian nature of the 'writing' on the Tartaria tablets of Romania. Yet the rich Balkan and Aegean context for the 'cylinder seals' of the Late Neolithic (Renfrew 2003a) makes unnecessary any appeal to direct Near Eastern contact at that time. When it comes to the Early Bronze Age some such contacts are well established, and glyptic in the Aegean was no doubt their beneficiary. But we shall need to understand better the nature of the context in which they were used, and the organization which these sealings represent, before their function need be described as other than local. The useful paper by Andrew Bevan (this volume) works in the same sense, documenting the import of Egyptian stone vases into Early Minoan Crete, yet without exaggerating their significance. Such contacts indeed took place, but that does not mean that they had a decisive role in promoting change.

The Cognitive Dimension and the Human Individual

The specifically human ability to use symbols and to define new purposes and intentionalities, today often related to the concept of agency, was the focus of Chapter 19 of *The Emergence*, 'Symbolic and Projective Systems'. In it were reviewed in turn the description of the physical world (including mensuration and number, writing and depiction), society as a projection of itself, technology for the unknown (including religion, ritual and burial), and projections for pleasure: beauty, style and play. The chapter was thus devoted to what might today be termed cognitive archeology. Yet its content has been the most neglected of all the chapters in the book. This was brought home to me when, in the autumn of 2001, I attended a very interesting seminar in Cambridge in which the speaker was reviewing work in Aegean prehistory over the past 30 years, and was taking *The Emergence* as a point of departure. Her review was constructive and interesting in a number of ways. She took in turn each of the principal themes or subsystems of the book, chapter by chapter, but somehow contrived to overlook Chapter 19. She then felt able to suggest that the interests of post-processual or interpretive archaeology had been somewhat lacking in the book. In one sense that may have been a fair comment, since in 1972 the 'post-processual' movement had yet to emerge. But her comment failed to recognize that the subject matter of Chapter 19 is precisely the symbolic and structural archaeology which post-processual archaeology took as its starting point. Indeed I feel that over the past 30 years we have all in Aegean archaeology failed to take up very effectively the themes which were already hinted at in that chapter and to integrate them more effectively with the others that have been more actively researched. These may indeed be issues which should have been addressed more comprehensively there at the time – questions of ideology, of religious belief and ritual, of the construction of identities, and of the creation and exercise of power. Until very recently it would have been possible to assert, at least as far as the Early Bronze Age is concerned, that not very much has happened in these areas, other than the publication of Lucy Goodison's excellent but little-quoted book *Death, Women and the Sun, Symbolism of Regeneration in Early Aegean Religion* (Goodison 1989). That is perhaps reflected in Figure 13.11 of Whitelaw's paper in the present volume, where all the subsystems other than 'ideology' (which is his term for the symbolic and projective) are shaded to show their participation in the major feedback linkages in operation. Indeed if there is a criticism to be made of Broodbank's excellent *Island Archaeology of the Early Cyclades* it might be that issues of religious belief and cult practice are scarcely addressed there, despite the strong evidence which we have for the use of a range of visual symbols at that time.

There are encouraging signs, however, that new lines of enquiry are being followed. John Cherry (1986) perhaps initiated the discussion, so far as Crete is concerned, by his integration of the peak sanctuaries with the political develop-ments that led to the first palaces. That the so-called 'palaces' of Minoan Crete were not simply administrative or redistributive centres in the economic sphere has long been realized, and the point is more clearly taken in the light of the earlier discussion of redistribution. The notion of Knossos as a cosmological centre has been developed by Soles (1995) and utilized by Day and Wilson (2002) in their study of consumption at Knossos in the Early Minoan II period as documented by ceramic finds, interpreted by them as indicative of feasting. Hamilakis (1999) is no doubt right, following the perspective of Dietler (1990) to stress the social context of wine in the later Bronze Age of the Aegean, but he may set too late its emergence as a significant factor. The domestication of the grape is now well documented for the Early Bronze Age of northern Greece on the basis of abundant examples, preceded in the Neolithic by finds which lack the morphological indications of domestication (J. Renfrew 2003). The emphasis in *The Emergence* upon wine already in the Early Bronze Age of the southern Aegean was based partly upon this evidence, but also on the striking development at this time of drinking cups, in metal as well as in pottery, and in pouring vessels. It still seems to me likely that the 'sauceboat' both in Early Helladic II and in the Keros-Syros culture was a drinking vessel used primarily for wine. And Day and Wilson may well be correct in suggesting that the context of the use of drinking vessels at this time was not simply feasting, but feasting in the context of religious rituals, and no doubt funerary rituals as well.

It is tempting at this point to go on to discuss the perspectives introduced by James Wright's very interesting paper (this volume), his productive use of Hayden's analysis of the development of ranking in 'transegalitarian' societies (Hayden 1995) and his concluding focus upon the individual. That is the point where, in a sense *The Emergence* itself concludes (Renfrew 1972: 503): ' Such interactions at the macro-level simply describe in aggregate the interaction at the level of the human individual, the atomic or micro-level. For when social changes, for instance, favour economic growth... individual human beings are making economic decisions for social reason. Human individuals can and do equate social and material values, and this symbolic equivalence, when widely accepted among the population, sets the multiplier effect in operation.' But Wright's remarks hint at a much broader perspective, and it is one too complex and too fruitful (and hence too lengthy) to comment upon in detail here. The further effective development of those ideas will require more extended treatment, indeed another book. When it is written, it will integrate more effectively these cognitive and often subjective elements, and set the individual more securely at the centre of the stage than *The Emergence* was able to do.

Acknowledgements

My first debt is to John Barrett and Paul Halstead who convened the Round Table in January 2002 to mark the thirtieth anniversary of the publication of *The Emergence*. That the occasion should take place at the Centre for Aegean Archaeology in Sheffield was indeed appropriate since the book was itself written in Sheffield, in my office on the seventh floor of the Arts Tower. I should like to thank Paul and John for their invitation, the other participants for their contributions, and Keith and Nong Branigan for a splendid instance of their now-legendary convivial hospitality. I recall also with gratitude that it was the late Professor Robert Hopper who, with Dr. Warwick Bray, invited me to join them in the Department of Ancient History in Sheffield in 1965 where, with Andrew Fleming, Paul Mellars and Jane Renfrew, we set up the degree course in Prehistory and Archaeology, and incidentally established the encouraging working environment which produced *The Emergence*.

Bibliography

Allen, P.M.
  1982   The genesis of structure in social systems: the paradigm of self-organization. In C. Renfrew, M.J. Rowlands and B.A. Segraves (eds.), *Theory and Explanation in Archaeology*: 347–74. New York: Academic Press.
Aruz, J.
  1999   The oriental impact on the forms of early Aegean seals. In P. Betancourt, V. Karageorghis, R. Laffineur and W.-D. Niemeier (eds.), *Meletemata, Studies in Aegean Archaeology Presented to Malcolm H. Wiener* (Aegaeum 20): 7–14. Liège, Université de Liège.
Brodie, N., J. Doole, G. Gavalas, K. Boyle and C. Renfrew (eds.)
  in press *Horizon, a Colloquium on the Prehistory of the Cyclades*. Cambridge: McDonald Institute.
Broodbank, C.
  2000   *An Island Archaeology of the Early Cyclades*. Cambridge: Cambridge University Press.
Cherry, J.
  1986   Polities and palaces: some problems in Minoan state formation. In C. Renfrew and J.F. Cherry (eds.), *Peer Polity Interaction and Socio-political Change*: 19–45. Cambridge: Cambridge University Press.
  2003   Archaeology beyond the site: regional survey and its future. In R. Leventhal and J. Papadopoulos (eds.), *Theory and Practice in Mediterranean Archaeology: Old World and New World Perspectives*: 137–60. Los Angeles: Cotsen Institute of Archaeology, UCLA.
Coleman, J.
  1977   *Keos I: Kephala, A Late Neolithic Settlement and Cemetery*. Princeton: American School of Classical Studies.
Cullen, T. (ed.)
  2001   *Aegean Prehistory, a Review*. Boston: Archaeological Institute of America.
Day, P.M. and D.E. Wilson
  2002   Landscapes of memory, craft and power in Prepalatial and Protopalatial Knossos. In Y. Hamilakis (ed.), *Labyrinth Revisited, Rethinking 'Minoan' Archaeology*: 143–66. Oxford: Oxbow Books.
Dietler, M.
  1990   Driven by drink: the role of drinking in the political economy and the case of Early Iron Age France. *Journal of Anthropological Archaeology* 9: 352–406.
Doumas, C.
  1977   *Early Bronze Age Burial Habits in the Cyclades* (SIMA 48). Göteborg: Paul Åströms Förlag.
Falkenstein, A.
  1965   Zu den Tontafeln aus Tartaria. *Germania* 43: 269–73.
Flannery, K.V.
  1972   The cultural evolution of civilization, *Annual Review of Ecology and Systematics* 3: 399–426.
  1976   (ed.)   *The Early Mesoamerican Village*. New York: Academic Press.
Flannery, K.V. and J. Marcus (eds.)
  1983   *The Cloud People: Divergent Evolution of the Zapotec and Mixtec Civilisations*. New York: Academic Press.
Friedman, J.
  1982   Catastrophe and continuity in social evolution. In C. Renfrew, M.J. Rowlands and

B.A. Segraves (eds.), *Theory and Explanation in Archaeology*: 175–96. New York: Academic Press.

Goodison, L.
1989   *Death, Women and the Sun: Symbolism of Regeneration in Early Cycladic Religion* (ICS Bulletin Supplement 53). London: Institute of Classical Studies.

Haggis, D.C.
2002   Integration and complexity in the Late Prepalatial period: a view from the countryside in eastern Crete. In Y. Hamilakis (ed.), *Labyrinth Revisited, Rethinking 'Minoan' Archaeology*: 120–42. Oxford: Oxbow Books.

Halstead, P.
1992   Agriculture in the Bronze Age Aegean: towards a model of palatial economy. In B. Wells (ed.), *Agriculture in Ancient Greece*: 105–16. Stockholm: Swedish Institute at Athens.
1999   Towards a model of Mycenaean palatial mobilization. In M.L. Galaty and W.A. Parkinson (eds.), *Rethinking Mycenaean Palaces*: 35–41. Los Angeles: Cotsen Institute of Archaeology at UCLA.
2001   Mycenaean wheat, flax and sheep: palatial intervention in farming and its implication for rural society. In S. Voutsaki and J. Killen (eds.), *Economy and Politics in the Mycenaean Palace States*: 38–50. Cambridge: Cambridge Philological Society.

Halstead, P. and J. O'Shea
1982   A friend in need is a friend indeed: social storage and the origins of social ranking. In C. Renfrew and S. Shennan (eds.), *Ranking, Resource and Exchange*: 92–99. Cambridge: Cambridge University Press.

Hamilakis, Y.
1999   Food technologies/technologies of the body: the social context of wine and oil production and consumption in Bronze Age Crete: *World Archaeology* 31: 38–54.
2002   What future for the 'Minoan' past? Re-thinking Minoan archaeology. In Y. Hamilakis (ed.), *Labyrinth Revisited, Rethinking 'Minoan' Archaeology*: 1–28. Oxford: Oxbow Books.

Hayden, B.
1995   Pathways to power. Principles for creating socioeconomic inequalities. In T.D. Price and G.M. Feinman (eds.), *Foundations of Social Inequality*: 15–86. New York: Plenum Press.

Jones, S.
1997   *The Archaeology of Ethnicity*. London: Routledge.

Kemp, B.
1989   *Ancient Egypt, Anatomy of a Civilisation*. London: Routledge.

Makkay, J.
1984   *Early Stamp Seals in South-East Europe*. Budapest: Akademiai Kiado.

Marangou, L., C. Renfrew, C. Doumas and G. Gavalas (eds.)
in press *Markiani, an Early Bronze Age Settlement on Amorgos*. London: British School of Archaeology at Athens.

Nakou, G.
1995   The cutting edge, a new look at Aegean metallurgy. *JMA* 8: 1–32.

Postgate, N.
1992   *Early Mesopotamia, Society and Economy at the Dawn of History*. London: Routledge.

Pullen, D.
1994   A lead seal from Tsoungiza, Ancient Nemea, and Early Bronze Age sealing systems. *AJA* 98: 35–52.

Renfrew, C.
  1972   *The Emergence of Civilisation, the Cyclades and the Aegean in the Third Millennium BC.* London: Methuen.
  1981   The simulator as demiurge. In J.A. Sabloff (ed.), *Simulations in Archaeology*: 283–306. Albuquerque: University of New Mexico Press.
  1982   Comment: the emergence of structure. In C. Renfrew, M.J. Rowlands and B.A. Segraves (eds.), *Theory and Explanation in Archaeology*: 459–64. New York: Academic Press.
  1995   'Ever in process of becoming': the autochthony of the Greeks. In J.A. Koumoulides, *The Good Idea, Democracy in Ancient Greece*: 7–28. New Rochelle, N.Y.: Aristide D. Caratzas.
  1996   Who were the Minoans? Towards a population prehistory of prehistoric Crete. *Cretan Studies* 5: 1–17.
  1998   Word of Minos: the Minoan contribution to Mycenaean Greek and the linguistic geography of the Bronze Age Aegean. *Cambridge Archaeological Journal* 8: 239–64.
  2003a   Special clay objects: cylinders, stamp seals, counters, biconoids, and spheres. In E. Elster and C. Renfrew (eds.), *Prehistoric Sitagroi: Excavations in Northeast Greece 1968–1970, Volume 2: The Final Report* (Monumenta Archaeologica 20): 403–19. Los Angeles: Cotsen Institute of Archaeology at UCLA.
  2003b   *Figuring It Out, the Parallel Visions of Artists and Archaeologists.* London: Thames and Hudson.
Renfrew, C. and K.L. Cooke (eds.)
  1979   *Transformations, Mathematical Approaches to Culture Change.* New York: Academic Press.
Renfrew, C. and T. Poston
  1979   Discontinuities in the endogenous change of settlement pattern. In C. Renfrew and K.L. Cooke (eds.), *Transformations, Mathematical Approaches to Culture Change*: 437–62. New York: Academic Press.
Renfrew, C. and E. Slater
  2003   Metal artifacts and metallurgy. In E. Elster and C. Renfrew (eds.), *Prehistoric Sitagroi: Excavations in Northeast Greece 1968–1970, Volume 2: The Final Report* (Monumenta Archaeologica 20): 301–24. Los Angeles: Cotsen Institute of Archaeology at UCLA.
Renfrew, C. and M. Wagstaff (eds.)
  1982   *An Island Polity, the Archeology of Exploitation in Melos.* Cambridge: Cambridge University Press.
Renfrew, J.M.
  2003   Grains, seeds and fruits from prehistoric Sitagroi. In E. Elster and C. Renfrew (eds.), *Prehistoric Sitagroi: Excavations in Northeast Greece, 1968–70, Volume 2: the Final Report* (Monumenta Archaeologica 20): 3–28. Los Angeles: Cotsen Institute of Archaeology at UCLA.
Rosen, R.
  1979   Morphogenesis in biological and social systems. In C. Renfrew and K.L. Cooke (eds.), *Transformations, Mathematical Approaches to Culture Change*: 91–112. New York: Academic Press.
  1982   On a theory of transformations for cultural systems. In C. Renfrew, M.J. Rowlands and B.A. Segraves (eds.), *Theory and Explanation in Archaeology*: 301–14. New York: Academic Press.
Sampson, A.
  2002   *The Neolithic Settlement at Ftelia, Mykonos.* Rhodes: University of the Aegean: Department of Mediterranean Studies.

Sherratt, A.
   1993   What would a Bronze Age world system look like? Relations between temperate
           Europe and the Mediterranean in later prehistory. *Journal of European Archaeology* 1:
           1–58.
Sherratt, S.
   2001   Potemkin palaces and route-based economies. In S. Voutsaki and J. Killen (eds.),
           Economy and Politics in the Mycenaean Palace States: 214–38. Cambridge: Cambridge
           Philological Society.
Small, D.B.
   1999   Mycenaean polities, states or *estates*? In M.L. Galaty and W.A. Parkinson (eds.),
           Rethinking Mycenaean Palaces, New Interpretations of an Old Idea: 43–47. Los Angeles:
           Cotsen Institute of Archaeology at UCLA.
Soles, J.S.
   1995   The functions of a cosmological centre: Knossos in Palatial Crete. In R. Laffineur and
           W.-D. Niemeier (eds.), *Politeia, Society and State in the Aegean Bronze Age* (Aegeum 12):
           405–14. Liège and Austin: Université de Liège and University of Texas at Austin.
Van der Leeuw, S. and J. McGlade (eds.)
   1997   *Time, Process and Structured Transformation in Archaeology*. London: Routledge.
Weingarten, J.
   1997   Another look at Lerna: an EH IIB trading post? *OJA* 16: 147–66.
Whitelaw, T.
   2001   From sites to communities: defining the human dimensions of Minoan urbanism. In
           K. Branigan (ed.), *Urbanism in the Aegean Bronze Age* (SSAA 4): 15–37. Sheffield:
           Sheffield Academic Press.
Zachos, K.
   1996   Metallurgy. In G.A. Papathanassopoulos (ed.), *Neolithic Culture in Greece*: 140–45.
           Athens: N.P. Goulandris Foundation Museum of Cycladic Art.
 in press Observations on the Early Bronze Age sealings from the Cave of Zas on Naxos. In N.
           Brodie, J. Doole, G. Gavalas, K. Boyle and C. Renfrew (eds.), *Horizon, a Colloquium on
           the Prehistory of the Cyclades*. Cambridge: McDonald Institute.
Zachos, K. and A. Douzougli
   1999   Aegean metallurgy: how early and how independent? In P. Betancourt, V. Kara-
           georghis, R. Laffineur and W.-D. Niemeier (eds.), *Meletemata, Studies in Aegean
           Archaeology Presented to Malcolm H. Wiener* (Aegaeum 20): 959–70. Liège: Université
           de Liège.
Zeeman, E.C.
   1979   A geometrical model of ideologies. In C. Renfrew and K.L. Cooke (eds.), *Mathematical
           Approaches to Culture Change*: 463–80. New York: Academic Press.